THE TERRITORIAL MANAGEMENT
OF ETHNIC CONFLICT

THE CASS SERIES IN REGIONAL AND FEDERAL STUDIES
ISSN 1363-5670
General Editor: John Loughlin

This series brings together some of the foremost academics and theorists to examine the timely subject of regional and federal issues, which have become key questions in political analysis and practice all over the world.

1. *The Political Economy of Regionalism*
   edited by Michael Keating and John Loughlin

2. *The Regional Dimension of the European Union: Towards a Third Level in Europe?*
   edited by Charlie Jeffery

3. *Remaking the Union: Devolution and British Politics in the 1990s*
   edited by Howard Elcock and Michael Keating

4. *Paradiplomacy in Action: The Foreign Relations of Subnational Governments*
   edited by Francisco Aldecoa and Michael Keating

5. *The Federalization of Spain*
   by Luis Mereno

6. *Ethnicity and Territory in the Former Soviet Union: Regions in Conflict*
   edited by James Hughes and Gwendolyn Sasse

7. *Region, State and Identity in Central and Eastern Europe*
   edited by Judy Batt and Kataryna Wolczuk

8. *Local Power, Territory and Institutions in European Metropolitan Regions*
   by Bernard Jouve and Christian Lefèvre

The Territorial Management of Ethnic Conflict

Editor

John Coakley

SECOND REVISED AND EXPANDED EDITION

FRANK CASS
LONDON • PORTLAND, OR

First published in 2003 in Great Britain by
FRANK CASS PUBLISHERS
2 Park Square, Milton Park, Abingdon, Oxon, OX14 4RN

and in the United States of America by
FRANK CASS PUBLISHERS
270 Madison Ave,
New York NY 10016

Transferred to Digital Printing 2005

Website http://www.frankcass.com

Copyright c 2003 Frank Cass & Co. Ltd.

British Library Cataloguing in Publication Data

The territorial management of ethnic conflict. - 2nd rev. and
 expanded ed. - (The Cass series in regional and federal studies ; 9)
 1.Ethnic relations 2.Conflict management 3.Human
 territoriality 4.Jurisdiction, Territorial
 I.Coakley, John
 305.8

ISBN 0714649880

ISBN 0 7146 4988 0 (cloth)
ISBN 0 7146 8051 6 (paper)
ISSN 1363-5670

Library of Congress Cataloging-in-Publication Data:

The territorial management of ethnic conflict / edited by John
Coakley.–2nd rev. and expanded ed.
 p. cm. – (The Cass series in regional and federal studies, ISSN
1363-5670)
Includes bibliographical references and index.
ISBN 0-7146-4988-0 (cloth) – ISBN 0-7146-8051-6 (paper)
1. Ethnic conflict. 2. Conflict management. 3. Human territoriality.
4. Jurisdiction, Territorial. I. Coakley, John. II. Series.
GN496 .T47 2003
305.8–dc21

2002153037

Printed and bound by Antony Rowe Ltd, Eastbourne

Contents

Tables and Figures

Maps

Notes on Contributors

John Coakley is a Senior Lecturer in Politics at University College Dublin and Director of the Institute for British-Irish Studies there, and former Secretary General of the International Political Science Association (1994–2000). He has published extensively on Irish and comparative politics, on nationalism and on ethnic conflict. He has edited *The Social Origins of Nationalist Movements* (Sage, 1992) and *Changing Shades of Orange and Green: Redefining the Union and the Nation in Contemporary Ireland* (UCD Press, 2002) and co-edited *Politics in the Republic of Ireland* (3rd ed., Routledge, 1999).

Daniele Conversi is a Senior Lecturer at the European Policy Research Centre, Department of Policy Studies, University of Lincoln. He has published widely in the area of ethnicity and nationalism. His recent books include *The Basques, the Catalans, and Spain: Alternative Routes to Nationalist Mobilization* (University of Nevada Press, 2000), *La desintegratió de Iugoslàvia* (Editorial Afers-El Contemporani, 2000) and, as editor, *Ethnonationalism in the Contemporary World: Walker Connor and the Study of Nationalism* (Routledge, 2002).

Anthony Egan, SJ, is a Jesuit priest working in the fields of politics, history and applied ethics. He has published articles on South African Catholic intellectual history, postmodern theology, and the ethics of terrorism, as well as a monograph, *The Politics of a South African Catholic Student Movement* (Centre for African Studies Monographs, University of Cape Town, 1991). He is currently coordinator of the Department of Applied Ethics at St Augustine's College, Johannesburg.

Ronald J. Hill is Professor of Comparative Government at Trinity College, Dublin. He has written widely on Soviet and communist politics, with particular emphasis on the Soviet Communist Party and local government in the former Soviet Union. He has edited *Beyond Stalinism: Communist Political Evolution* (Frank Cass, 1992) and (with Michael Marsh) *Modern Irish Democracy* (Irish Academic Press, 1993).

Liesbet Hooghe is Associate Professor of Political Science at the University of North Carolina at Chapel Hill. She is the author of *The European Commission and the Integration of Europe: Images of Governance* (Cambridge University

Press, 2002); *Separatisme* (K.U. Leuven, 1989); *A Leap in the Dark: The Belgian Federal Reform* (Cornell, 1991); co-author with Gary Marks of *Multi-Level Governance and European Integration* (Rowman & Littlefield, 2001); and editor of *Cohesion Policy and European Integration: Building Multi-Level Governance* (Oxford University Press, 1996).

Charles H. Kennedy is Professor of Political Science at Wake Forest University in Winston-Salem, North Carolina. He has written about South Asian comparative political and governmental systems since 1975, and served as Director of the American Institute of Pakistan Studies (1988–2000). He has written or edited numerous books dealing with South Asia, including most recently *Pakistan: 2000* (Oxford University Press, 2001) and *Government and Politics in South Asia* (5th edn., Westview, 2001) and, as editor, *Pakistan at the Millennium* (Oxford University Press, 2002).

Stanislav J. Kirschbaum is Professor of International Studies and Political Science at York University, Glendon College, Toronto. He is a specialist on Central European politics, especially the Slovaks, author of *A History of Slovakia: The Struggle for Survival* (St. Martin's Griffin, 1996), *Historical Dictionary of Slovakia* (Scarecrow Press, 1999) and editor of *East European History* (Slavica Publishers, 1988) and *Historical Reflections on Central Europe* (Macmillan, 1998). He is a Fellow of the Royal Society of Canada.

J.A. Laponce is Professor of Political Science at the University of British Columbia. His publications include *The Protection of Minorities* (California Press, 1961) and *Langue et territoire* (Presses de l'Université Laval, 1984) translated as *Languages and their Territories* (Toronto University Press, 1987). He was co-president, with Jean Gottmann, of the Research Committee on Political Geography of the International Political Science Association. He now chairs that association's Research Committee on Language and Politics.

Joseph Ruane lectures in Sociology at University College Cork. His present research is on the impact of globalization on Ireland. He has published extensively on Irish development, the Northern Irish conflict and the changing European context, including (with Jennifer Todd) *The Dynamics of Conflict in Northern Ireland: Power, Conflict and Emancipation* Cambridge University Press, 1996).

Rupert Taylor is Associate Professor in the Department of Political Studies, University of the Witwatersrand, Johannesburg. His fields of research include 'race', ethnicity and nationalism in South Africa; political violence in South Africa; and the Northern Ireland conflict. He is editor of *Voluntas: International Journal of Voluntary and Nonprofit Organizations*.

Jennifer Todd lectures in Politics at University College Dublin and, in 2001, was Visiting Professor at the Institut d'Etudes Politiques, Toulouse. Her present research is on the differential impact of globalization. Her most recent book is (co-edited with Joseph Ruane) *After the Good Friday Agreement: Analysing Political Change in Northern Ireland* ; CD Press, 1999.

Alex Weingrod is Emeritus Professor of Anthropology in the Department of Behavioral Sciences, Ben Gurion University of the Negev, Beersheba, Israel. His main research interests include ethnicity, political anthropology and the analysis of public events and celebrations. His publications include *The Saint of Beersheba* (State University of New York Press, 1990), and (with M. Romann) *Living Together Separately: Arabs and Jews in Contemporary Jerusalem* (Princeton University Press, 1991). His most recent book (with Andre Levy) is *Homelands and Diasporas: Holy Lands and Other Places* (Stanford University Press, 2003).

A. Jeyaratnam Wilson was Professor of Political Science at the University of New Brunswick, Canada from 1972 to 1994. He died on 31 May 2000. He published numerous books, including *The Break-Up of Sri Lanka: The Sinhala-Tamil Conflict* (Hurst, 1990), *S.J.V. Chelvanayakam and the Crisis of Ceylon Tamil Nationalism: A Political Biography 1947-1977* (Hurst, 1994), *Sri Lankan Tamil Nationalism: Its Origins and Development in the Nineteenth and Twentieth Centuries* (Hurst, 2000) and, as co-editor, *The Post-Colonial States of South Asia: Democracy, Identity, Development and Security* (Curzon, 2000).

Preface to Second Edition

This book began its life at a round table meeting of the Research Committee on Politics and Ethnicity of the International Political Science Association (IPSA), held at the University of Limerick on 4–7 July 1990. Founded in 1976, this committee has been particularly active in promoting research in the area of nationalism and ethnic politics, and has been responsible for the production of a large number of publications. In the case of the Limerick round-table, two strands of publications followed. A set of papers appeared in revised form as a special issue of the *International Political Science Review* entitled 'Resolving Ethnic Conflicts' (Vol.13, No.4, October 1992). Another set appeared, along with some newly commissioned pieces, as a special issue of *Regional Politics and Policy* with the same title as the present book (Vol.3, No.1, Spring 1993). This was subsequently published in book form by Frank Cass.

Close to a decade later, the appearance of a second edition of this book is testimony to the continuing salience of the problem that it addresses. Ethnic protest is still a central political issue in many societies, and territorial considerations remain at the forefront when the menu of options for tackling it is considered. It seems appropriate, therefore, to take stock of the position at this point, by undertaking a cross-national, comparative study of the stage we have now reached.

In addition to updated (and, in some cases, entirely re-written) versions of chapters that appeared in the original book, the present volume also includes assessments of three additional cases that are of great significance: Northern Ireland, South Africa and the dissolution of Yugoslavia. One important chapter that appeared in the first edition (by Philip Mawhood and Malcolm Wallis, on the cases of Kenya and Tanzania) is not included in the present volume, reflecting in part the relative ethnic peace at the moment in that part of Africa. Sadly, one author, A. Jeyaratnam Wilson, died before getting a chance to complete the revision of his chapter on Sri Lanka, but it is to be hoped that the version that appears here will be a fitting tribute to his memory. To facilitate comparison between case studies, a set of maps, drawn to a standard template, has been prepared, and a new introduction and conclusion have been added to the book.

As always in enterprises of this kind, many debts are accumulated by the editor. The first, historically, is to IPSA's Research Committee on Politics and Ethnicity, whose child this project is. The second is to the Irish Peace Institute, University of Limerick, which generously supported the meeting at which the original papers were presented. The third is to Cathy Jennings of Frank Cass Publishers, who was responsible for the idea of a second edition and who patiently piloted the project through to production. But the biggest debt is to the authors who have so diligently worked on their pieces and deferred to editorial bullying, and to four other people who helped in particular aspects of the preparation of the book: Joe Brady, Tom Farrell, Elizabeth Roberts and Jennifer Todd.

John Coakley
July 2002

1

Introduction

The Challenge

JOHN COAKLEY

While ethnic conflict has many dimensions, one of the first to strike the observer is the territorial one. Marching rituals in Northern Ireland, for instance, are designed frequently to express symbolic control over territory, and the very creation of Belfast's 'peace line' represents an effort to give concrete geographical shape to a profound interethnic division. The contours of the ethnic mosaic of Cyprus became increasingly clearly defined in the 1960s, and in 1974 the ethnic map of the country was radically reformed, as the long-established bicommunal patchwork yielded to a partitioned country, a 'green line' extending through Nicosia and the rest of the island separating the Turkish North from the Greek South. In a similar development, intercommunal conflict in Lebanon was eventually transformed into competition over territory, with another 'green line' stretching through Beirut and partitioning it into western (Muslim) and eastern (Christian) sectors. This pattern is commonly to be found elsewhere, with Kashmir and Israel/Palestine offering vivid contemporary examples.

The prominence of territorial demands in the rhetoric of ethnic activists is an extremely common phenomenon – demands for autonomy within a state, for separation from it, or for unification with another state. The link between ethnicity and territoriality is, then, well established, but it is also complex. Ethnic affiliation and territorial location have long been acknowledged as sources of national identification; the distinction between the two may be traced back to that between *jus sanguinis* and *jus soli* in public international law.[1] Just as these two criteria of identification may give conflicting answers regarding the position of an individual, so too may they give rise to conflict at the collective level, at the level of the community.

In this domain, two sources of potential conflict between the state and the community or communities that reside within its borders may in principle be identified. Both arise from the essentially territorial nature of the state. It is hardly necessary to go back to Weber's description of the state as 'a compulsory organisation with a territorial basis' to make the point that state boundaries are frequently clear-cut in physical reality, and that they are almost always clearly defined in graphic representation.[2] Since the boundaries of social groups nearly always lack these characteristics, the potential for conflict is immediate. Corresponding to the legal distinction between *jus sanguinis* and *jus soli*, social psychologists have noted *people* and *land* as the two primary stimuli of patriotism and nationalism, in that they act as powerful foci for group loyalty.[3] From the state's perspective, the problem is that these two sources of identification may give different answers to the question where any boundary should lie, and that both of these answers may conflict with the preferences of the dominant group within the state itself.

The first difficulty arises from the fact that it is obviously the case that persons who feel that they belong to the same ethnic community may occupy a very imprecisely defined territory, and that, even if the territory in which they predominate may be precisely defined, this does not necessarily coincide with the territory of a state. Almost every state includes non-members of the ethnic community with which it is associated, but it also fails to include some members of this community. As the gap between the territory actually occupied by the ethnic community and the territory of its state increases, so too does the probability of ethnic tension, other things being equal.

Second, whatever the spatial distribution of their members, many ethnic communities feel a strong association with a particular relatively clearly defined segment of territory. In the case of indigenous peoples, this may be seen as having a sacred character.[4] Many 'modern' ethnic communities identify a so-called 'national' territory, and use historical, pseudo-historical or even fabricated arguments to press their claims to this. Outlying portions of this territory may be inhabited by other ethnic groups (as in the case of the North East of Ireland), the core of the 'national territory' itself may be inhabited predominantly by an 'alien' community (as in the cases of Vilnius in Lithuania in the past or Pamplona in the Basque Country), or the entire territory may be inhabited by another community (as in the case of Israel at the beginning of the twentieth century), but the claim nevertheless attracts powerful public support. Historical arguments may, indeed, be reinforced by geographical, economic or strategic ones.[5]

The object of this book is to examine the extent to which demographic and political realities, together with other pressures, have permitted or encouraged territorial approaches to ethnic conflict management, and the degree to which these have had to be supplemented or replaced by other conflict-resolving strategies. It should be acknowledged that this perspective is a state-centred one: with a view to maintaining coherence of approach, the central question being addressed is the response of the state to the challenge of ethnic protest. This is not an endorsement of this particular perspective; from the point of view of minority (and perhaps other) ethnic groups, it is typically the state, not the ethnic group, that is the problem, a viewpoint that is at least implicit in several of the contributions in this volume. The case studies in the chapters that follow thus seek to address the issue holistically within particular contexts, but deliberately focus on the state response as the central intellectual issue.

Before going on to look at territorial demands of ethnic groups and the response of the state to these in particular cases in the rest of this volume and on the basis of material in other sources, it is necessary to define the context of these case studies. The first general issue is the character of the challenge faced by the state: the form that ethnic mobilization takes, and the nature of the programmes put forward by ethnic activists. The second is the territorial context within which this mobilization takes place – an issue that has a crucial bearing both on the nature of the demands that ethnic activists may make and on the prospects for a solution that may realistically receive the acquiescence, if not the blessing, of the state. The third issue is an empirical one: it is important to provide some indication of the global pattern in order to indicate the basis of selection of the cases considered here.

ETHNIC MOBILIZATION

Given the great variety of types of ethnic group, it is not to be expected that a simple generalization about the nature of their demands will be possible. Scholars in the area have made several efforts to classify such groups. In one early example, five categories of subordinate ethnic groups were identified: pariahs, the lowest stratum in a caste-based society; indigenous peoples isolated by the process of modernization; groups subordinated to neighbouring groups following a process of annexation; immigrants; and peoples reduced to subordination by the process of colonization.[6] Subsequent classifications, as will be seen below, have tended to rest on two dimensions implicit in this classification: socio-economic and political status, and geopolitical history. But no matter how we try to simplify in the process of classification, the sheer variety of resulting types draws our attention to the enormous complexity of the phenomenon of ethnicity. It should, indeed, be pointed out that in the present volume this misleadingly simple term has been used to cover a range of types of political conflict that are differentiated not merely by the dynamics of competition between rival groups but also by the very significance of ethnicity itself, in whatever language this is described. The reality is that the same label is used here as an umbrella for a great diversity of types of conflict. While this may be useful in drawing parallels between such conflicts to our attention, the fundamentally different meaning of ethnicity in different types of society must also be borne in mind.

Thus, quite apart from the differential impact of language, culture, religion and perceived descent in the process of ethnic group formation, other factors add to the complexity of the issue. In many cases, for instance, a colonial or quasi-colonial relationship forms part of the picture: some local ethnic groups may have been favoured over others by the metropolitan power, as was the case in varying degrees in Ireland, Cyprus, Pakistan, Sri Lanka, Kenya and Tanzania. In such cases, but in greatly varying degrees, former metropolitan or other external powers may play a continuing role in the conflict. In addition, there may be competing settlement myths, with two or more groups claiming to have 'got there first'; this was the case between Swedes and Finns in Finland, Germans and Czechs in the former Czechoslovakia, Tamils and Sinhalese in Sri Lanka, and Sindhis and Muhajirs in Pakistan. At the opposite extreme, although they are not treated in the present volume, there exist many movements made up of recent immigrants who, however influential they may be politically, do not make territorial demands of any kind. In addition, interethnic differences may coincide with strikingly different levels of economic development; elements of a 'cultural division of labour' have been extremely common, and stark interethnic differences in lifestyle persist in the territories of the former Soviet Union. But it should not be assumed that minorities rank lower in all aspects of social status than the numerically and politically dominant group: the Muhajirs in Pakistan and the Tamils in Sri Lanka are examples of high-status minorities, and others may be found in Europe, such as the Swedish speakers in Finland.[7]

As in the case of so many other social processes, then, intergroup relations have been conditioned by historical developments. Economic, social and political change rarely (or never) leaves relationships between dominant and subordinate groups undisturbed, and a fundamental change tends to take place in the context of the modern state based on the notion of equality of citizenship. Over a long time-span, the transition to modern statehood is marked by two phases through which subordinate ethnic groups potentially pass. For certain types of group, the first phase is not necessarily relevant. There may also be other types to whom *only* the first phase is relevant: having made gains in this area, they rest satisfied. It should also be noted that although the discussion below implies a particular attraction of ethnic militants to egalitarian ideologies in the early phase of the ethnic revival, there are also groups which have demonstrated a disposition favourable to ideologies of the right.

The First Phase

Quite commonly, then, the process of ethnic mobilization is kick-started by a sense of economic and social grievance and by allegations of discriminatory treatment by the state authorities. This phase is, thus, characterized by a demand for equality of all citizens: for individual rights, resting on an assumption of a fundamental identity of all humans. This phase often begins in a period in which the subordinate group's identity is other-defined (i.e. it is the dominant group which is most anxious to highlight and maintain the ethnic boundary) and in which it is discriminated against. The history of the Jews and of the Romany populations of Europe provides numerous examples of subordinate groups of this kind, but there are others, as in the European colonial empires and the United States in the slave-owning era. In Ireland, Catholics were at one stage similar outcasts, prohibited by law from owning or bequeathing property, from voting and from occupying a whole range of public sector positions. In some cases, the criterion for exclusion was social in theory, but ethnic in effect; thus, prior to the ending of serfdom, Estonian and Latvian peasants were formally subjected to their German masters. This form of subordination was frequently accompanied by the stigmatization of the subordinate group, whose ethnic name was used as a term of abuse and in which sub-human characteristics were detected.[8]

An essential component of the transition to modern statehood was the removal of formal disabilities, the extension of citizenship and the establishment of the principle of individual equality before the law. This typically had the effect of thrusting certain 'rights' on everyone, whether or not they wanted them, though in some cases this process took place too slowly for the minorities, and the struggle for equality of treatment with the members of the dominant group became the first step in a campaign of ethnic assertiveness. This campaign also depended, of course, on a changed definition of identity: ethnicity now became self-defined, with the subordinate group drawing attention to the boundary separating it from the dominant one and complaining of inequalities in the treatment of the two.

In many cases, though, the institutionalization of formal equality before the law was not sufficient to remove *de facto* patterns of apparent discrimination that survived from the period of formal inequality. These patterns could be maintained by the use of surrogate criteria of ethnic selection (such as literacy tests, wealth thresholds or residency requirements), by leaving large sectors of public administration and private enterprise open to unregulated management by institutions controlled by the dominant ethnic group, or by simply leaving established patterns of social and economic inequality to continue under their own momentum. In such cases the initial, 'individual rights' phase might extend into the contemporary period, as in the case of Blacks in the United States or Catholics in Northern Ireland. Right up to the present, then, subordinate ethnic groups have demanded equality – in effect, full implementation of their basic human and civil rights, the rights first codified in the French 'Declaration of the Rights of Man and of the Citizen' in 1789, subsequently incorporated in most western constitutions and reformulated in the UN-sponsored Universal Declaration of Human Rights in 1948.[9]

The Second Phase

Some groups may be happy with the gains made in the first phase; for others, the agenda may shift to a new set of demands; and for yet others political mobilization may begin at this point. In this phase, the subordinate group's characteristic demand is for *recognition* of its separateness.[10] While its members may be satisfied with the attainment of at least formal equality, ethnic self-consciousness may, depending on concrete circumstances, propel subordinate groups to make an additional set of demands. In important respects, these demands are based on a premise incompatible with that of equality: they now rest on the claim that members of the ethnic minority are *different*, and that this difference should receive institutional recognition. The demand for individual rights has been followed by a demand for ethnic *group rights*.

Unlike individual rights, group rights have never been coherently codified in a package that has attracted general agreement. The rights of religious minorities – though they might be placed in the 'individual' rather than in the 'group' rights category – first found a distinctive place as an issue on the agenda of European politics in the Treaty of Westphalia (1648). Although this is best known for institutionalizing the principle of religious uniformity within the state – popularized in the expression *cuius regio, eius religio* – it also made provision for the rights of religious minorities in certain circumstances. Similar rights were accorded to religious minorities in later treaties.[11] A new phase in the international recognition of such rights is said to have been reached in the Congress of Vienna of 1814–15, which placed an obligation on Austria, Prussia and Russia to respect the rights of their Polish subjects and which, in allocating Belgium to the Kingdom of the United Netherlands, in effect placed an obligation on the state to respect the rights of the Catholic Belgians. The creation of the Kingdom of Greece in 1830 and the concession of near-independence to the principalities of Moldavia and Wallachia in 1856 were the occasion of similar international guarantees to minorities, while the Congress of Berlin in 1878 applied the principle to a number of Balkan states. It was finally extended to the field of linguistic minorities in the postwar settlements of 1919, and given formal expression in the

League of Nations system for the protection of minorities.[12] The failure of the League system, in part a consequence of the alleged willingness of certain minorities in the 1930s to use it to damage the interests of the signatory states, indeed highlights a great difficulty with the defence of group rights: it is difficult to identify precisely which groups are entitled to defence, and it is difficult to specify what the rights are to which they should be entitled.[13]

In the period after the Second World War, there was a reaction to the perception that the group rights principle was open to abuse by unscrupulous minorities, and the emphasis shifted back to the individual. Thus the Universal Declaration of Human Rights (1948) dealt only with individual rights, and the United Nations, unlike the League, concerned itself little with national minorities. Opinion has nevertheless evolved, with the result that the International Covenant of Civil and Political Rights (1966) included specific guarantees of group rights.[14] Similarly, the Conference on Security and Cooperation in Europe in its Charter of Paris (1990) followed guarantees of individual rights by guarantees of group rights:

> We affirm that the ethnic, cultural, linguistic and religious identity of national minorities will be protected and that persons belonging to national minorities have the right freely to express, preserve and develop that identity without any discrimination and in full equality before the law.[15]

The Conference's successor, the Organisation for Security and Cooperation in Europe, developed this line of thinking further, leading to more detailed specifications of the rights of national minorities in the areas of education (1996), language (1998) and effective participation in public life (1999).[16]

This still leaves us with the need to describe what, typically, the demands of subordinate ethnic groups are. In terms of their relationship with the state, they may be seen in terms of four levels. Although the boundaries between the levels are imprecise, we may identify the levels themselves quite clearly in theory. The first, of particular importance to politically and legally marginalized groups (and being the dominant demand in the first phase), refers to individual rights, the other three to group rights (though category 2 is a transitional one).

1. A demand for *equality of citizenship*, ranging from a call for formal equality before the law to a demand for special measures to ensure economic and social equality, possibly extending to positive discrimination.
2. A demand for *cultural rights*, ranging from symbolic use of the minority language in public (for example, in signposting) and in the

educational system to the right to transact business with all public institutions through the medium of the minority language, and the right to receive an education at all levels through its medium (subject to practicalities of scale).

3. A demand for *institutional political recognition*, ranging from symbolic autonomy in local government or symbolic representation in state institutions to fully-fledged confederalism and consociationalism.
4. A demand for *secession*, ranging from frontier adjustment to allow the minority to be incorporated in a neighbouring state to independence as a separate state.

The distinction between the four is in principle categorical. In the first case, the basic civil rights being pursued are universalizable. It could be argued that this is also true of the second case, where what is being sought can be justified as an extension of the individual rights principle. For example, the 'right to education' has now become the 'right to education through one's mother tongue', and interaction with the state is now seen as carrying the requirement that state officials be capable of communicating in the minority language.[17] In the third case, however, members of the minority clearly require to be treated as a group for certain purposes, and desire that the state should relate to them not just as a collection of individuals but also as members of a recognized group. In the fourth case the minority wants no dealings at all with the state (though the distinction between independence and membership in a loose confederation need not be clear-cut).[18]

It should be pointed out, in conclusion, that these demands are not, of course, mutually exclusive. Within any minority group the leadership may include some or all of these four demands in its political programme, but different sections of the leadership and different groups within the minority may attach different priorities to the demands. The minority is not, in other words, monolithic. In terms of their implications for the territorial structure of the state, the demands become more serious as one progresses from the first (which has no territorial implications) to the fourth (which has little else).

THE TERRITORIAL CHALLENGE

The extent to which an ethnic group makes territorial demands on the state is clearly related to a number of general factors: the absolute size of the group (because of considerations relating to critical mass, which will render certain options more administratively realizable than others) and the group's relative size (since this will condition its power relative to that of the dominant group and render certain options more politically feasible than others). But these demands are likely also to depend on the pattern of territorial distribution of the group itself. It is therefore worth reviewing the kinds of relationships that ethnic groups may have to the territories in which their members reside, before considering the options that these patterns generate for the state.

Ethnoterritorial Patterns

It may be stated that, as a general principle, and other things being equal, a group's territorial claims become stronger as (1) the group increases as a proportion of the population of 'its' territory and (2) the proportion of the total membership of the group within this territory increases. The relationship between these two trends is illustrated in Table 1.1, which gives examples of a number of types of relationship between ethnicity and territory. This is based on the assumption that one can make meaningful distinctions (1) between groups which dominate 'their' territory and groups which are in a minority in 'their' own territory and (2) between groups that are concentrated in 'their' territory and groups which live mostly outside it. Clearly, this table oversimplifies by reducing linear patterns to dichotomies; most ethnic groups are not territorially concentrated in a manner that can be described as 'high' or 'low', and a

TABLE 1.1
A TYPOLOGY OF RELATIONSHIPS BETWEEN ETHNIC GROUPS AND
ETHNIC TERRITORIES: FOUR MODELS

| | | Territorial concentration of ethnic group | |
		Low	High
Ethnic Cohesiveness of Territory	Low	Birobidzhan	Bosnia
	High	Åland	Slovenia

group's share of the population of its 'own' territory can similarly vary enormously. Nevertheless, the four resulting ideal types give a useful perspective on the dilemmas of ethnoterritorial relationships. We may consider examples of each type.

1. The locally weak, territorially dispersed group (the *Birobidzhan* model): most of the population of the group's designated territory consists of non-members of the group, and most members of the group live outside this territory. Birobidzhan affords an excellent example: designated an ethnic territory of the Soviet Jews, only 5.4% of the local population was Jewish, and the territory accounted for only 0.6% of the Soviet Jewish population. The Tatar Republic is a second example: only 47.7% of the local population was Tatar, and the

republic accounted for only 26.0% of the total Tatar population.[19] A number of other examples are to be found, especially in the territories of the former Soviet Union.

2. The locally weak, territorially concentrated group (the Bosnia model): most of the population of the group's designated territory consists of non-members of the group, but most members of the group live within this territory. Here Bosnia is the prototype. This was the former Yugoslav republic associated with ethnic Muslims, who, however, accounted for only 39.5% of the population; nevertheless, the republic included 81.5% of Yugoslavia's ethnic Muslims.[20] The former Soviet republic of Kazakhstan, similarly, though populated predominantly by non-Kazakhs (only 36.0% of the population were Kazakhs in 1979), was the territory in which the vast majority (80.7%) of Kazakhs lived. If Karelians are to be distinguished from Finns, Karelia offers a third example: although 58.7% of Karelians lived there, its population was only 11.1% Karelian.

3. The locally strong, territorially dispersed group (the Åland model): most of the population of the group's designated territory consists of members of the group, but most members of the group live outside this territory. The autonomous Åland Islands offer a reasonable example: they are 93.8% Swedish-speaking, but they account for only 8.3% of Finland's Swedish-speaking population.[21] Of course, this interpretation is based on the debatable assumption that the Åland Islanders are part of the Swede-Finn community rather than constituting a separate group of their own (similar questions arise regarding the relationship between Quebecois and French Canadian identity). The new Greek state of the early nineteenth century in its original form is another example: overwhelmingly Greek in composition, it accounted for only a portion of the total Greek population of the Ottoman Empire.

4. The locally strong, territorially concentrated group (the *Slovenia* model): most of the population of the group's designated territory consists of members of the group, and most members of the group live within this territory. Slovenia within the former Yugoslavia offered such an example – it was not only overwhelmingly Slovene (90.5%), but also accounted for the great bulk of the Slovene population of Yugoslavia (97.7%). Slovakia and Flanders are other examples that arise in this volume, but there are numerous others from the histories of independence movements in Europe and elsewhere.

Other things being equal, the power of the subordinate ethnic group increases as we move from the first to the fourth of these types. This is especially the case to the extent that the subordinate group's demands have territorial implications. Territorial solutions imply on the one hand territorial concentration of the group making the demand, and on the other hand ethnic homogeneity of the territory on behalf of which the demand is being made. To the extent that these conditions fail to be satisfied, any concession of a demand for a territorial settlement is likely to run into opposition from members of other groups.

State Options

What, then, is the range of potential strategies that the state may adopt in response to pressure from ethnic minorities, taking account of their territorial status? It should be noted in the first place that the state may take pre-emptive measures to redefine an ethnic group's relationship to the territory in which its members reside. There are in principle two strategies open to the state in doing this: it may alter territorial boundaries, or it may seek to redistribute the ethnic group itself. The strategies are not, of course, mutually exclusive; the state may in practice attempt both.

The process of administrative boundary delimitation may be guided by a number of criteria. First, some states are content to adhere to internal boundaries that have evolved as a consequence of historical accident and that have been given a particular legitimacy by the passage of time. The principal components of the United Kingdom (including England, Scotland and Wales) are defined in this way; so too were the German *Länder* – and, to some extent, they still are – and the Swiss cantons. Second, the criterion of administrative rationality or convenience may be used to justify radical reform, possibly underpinned by economic or geographical considerations. The French *départements* are the prototype of this approach, which has been very widely followed in Europe (for example, the provinces in Belgium, the Netherlands and Italy and the counties in Norway, Sweden and Finland).[22] Third, ethnic criteria may be dominant, as in the former Soviet Union, whose republics and other major territorial subdivisions were based largely on ethnic considerations.

While these distinctions hold up quite well in theory, it may be more difficult to classify boundaries in practice according to this typology. Boundaries devised in terms of administrative or ethnic criteria, for instance, may in time be given added permanence by eventually being seen as sanctified by history. In other cases, more than one criterion may be in operation: in Canada, for example, the provinces have evolved from a mixture of historical accident and administrative considerations, and in post-1945 Yugoslavia a mixture of ethnic and historical criteria was used to justify the boundaries of the new republics.

It is undoubtedly the case that the state can fundamentally redefine the territorial relationships of ethnic groups within its borders by altering internal boundaries. Thus the interwar Republic of

Czechoslovakia recognized the territorial distinctiveness of its two principal Slav minorities, the Slovaks and the Ruthenes (Ukrainians), at least to the extent of acknowledging territories named Slovakia and Ruthenia, but withheld such recognition from the largest minority, the Germans; though territorially concentrated in Bohemia and Moravia, internal administrative district boundaries were drawn in such a way that they could not claim a territory of their own.

An alternative (or additional) approach to the redefinition of ethnic and territorial frontiers is to attempt to alter the spatial distribution of members of an ethnic group. Members of particular ethnic groups may be expelled from the state, as was the experience of Germans in Czechoslovakia, Poland and elsewhere after the Second World War, or the ethnic complexion of their territories may be changed by policies of resettlement or colonization, as happened in a large number of European colonies. Within Europe, resettlement was an instrument of ethnic policy in the twentieth century in the Soviet Union, elsewhere in central and eastern Europe, and in Israel and its occupied territories; it was also used in other parts of Europe in earlier periods (for example, in the British Isles in the seventeenth century, when the roots of the Northern Ireland problem were created, and in Cyprus after 1570).

Not all ethnic resettlement policies are necessarily articulated as such; ethnic resettlement may be a predictable and planned consequence of other policies in the economic and social domains, but it may also be an unintended consequence of these. In the modern state labour markets are typically state-wide, and the labour force tends to disperse itself in the long term in accordance with economic criteria that may cut across lines of ethnic division. This was the case, for instance, in the former Soviet Union, and population movement of this kind has also added to the ethnic complexity of Pakistan. In such cases as the former Soviet Union, Sri Lanka and Israel, settlement by the dominant ethnic group in territories inhabited by subordinate groups had a fundamental impact on patterns of ethnic relations to the advantage of the dominant group, even though the public authorities may never have explicitly stated that such was the intention of the economic planning strategies that gave rise to these settlements in the first place.

The impact of geographical mobility on ethnic relations depends greatly on the relationship between ethnicity and language. If this relationship is close and geographical mobility is low, the salience of territoriality will be high, since migrants will tend to be absorbed in the language and culture of the host community, especially given the natural tendency towards communal unilingualism.[23] If the relationship between language and ethnicity is close but there is a high and sustained level of geographical mobility, the host community may be unable to absorb the immigrants with sufficient speed and unresolved ethnic problems may be the consequence.[24] This outcome is likely to arise also if ethnicity is defined in terms of some non-linguistic criterion, such as religion, race or origin, even if the level of migration is modest.

Intense ethnic mixing of this kind, or more moderate patterns of mixing where the minority is not protected by distinctive linguistic, cultural or other traits, may also result in the long term in the absorption of the subordinate community. When there is no ethnically dominant community, however, and especially if the language of general communication is one external to the state, intense patterns of migration may result in the creation of new, state-wide ethnic communities, as in Kenya and Tanzania, where the process is facilitated by the relatively weak attachment of existing groups to 'their' regions.[25] When several languages are forced to coexist, a solution may be found in di- or polyglossia rather than in bi- or multilingualism. Tanzania is an example of the former, where English is generally accepted as a language in one part of the public domain and Swahili in another, while local languages may be used in the private domain. Canada is an example of the latter, where English and French compete as languages in all domains. In all such cases, the 'melting pot' process is likely to lead to a reduction in the intensity of ethnic minority demands, especially those which might originally have had territorial implications, and to make the ethnic challenge to the state easier to manage.

ETHNICITY AND TERRITORY IN THE CONTEMPORARY WORLD

Having looked at the position from a general if not abstract perspective, it is time to review the extent to which territorially based ethnic conflict is an issue in the contemporary world. As already mentioned, the relationship between ethnicity and territory is commonly characterized by a degree of tension. In seeking to provide a global overview of this relationship, it is important to begin with those cases where it is politically salient: where, in other words, the tension is given some kind of political expression. We may do this in two stages: first, by undertaking an overview of ethnic conflict in general, and, second, by focusing on those cases where ethnic conflict has a significant territorial dimension.

Political Conflict and the Ethnic Dimension

Ethnic conflict in the contemporary world may be set in context by considering the universe of cases. But describing this universe is quite a challenge, as will be seen if we examine four wide-ranging surveys that are rather different in character. The four overlap substantially in terms of the cases they include, but there are significant differences. These may derive in part from variation in information sources, difficulties of measurement and varying criteria of definition and classification; but they arise in particular from the fact that the four do not purport to describe precisely the same phenomena.

The first survey is a French encyclopaedia of *internal conflict*, dealing with civil wars and political violence of varying degrees of intensity.[26] This volume, *Mondes rebelles*, covers more than 90 countries as well as a number of transnational groups or conflicts, and it reports on an indefinite number of actual or potential cases of contemporary political violence. Its essentially qualitative approach – relying on detailed case descriptions of considerable historical depth – highlights the huge challenge of definition and classification, and draws appropriate attention to the international context, identifying four periods that helped to define the shape of domestic political conflict: the transformation of the postwar allies into two powerful blocs (1945–60), a redefinition of these blocs and intensification in interbloc conflict during the height of the Cold War (1960–75), the progressive weakening of Cold War tensions (1975–90), and the new world order after the collapse of the Soviet Union (since 1990).[27] In the first three of these phases, the bipolar nature of world politics drew domestic conflicts within its magnetic field, making it relatively easy to place dissident groups on the 'left' or the 'right'. By the 1990s, though, such conflicts had become increasingly diverse, so much so as to make any kind of meaningful classification that would be valid across continents extremely difficult. However, the central role of ethnicity or nationalism in most – but by no means all – instances emerges clearly from the case studies.

If we try to classify and quantify more systematically, we run into some immediate and obvious difficulties; a price must be paid for the loss of information that is entailed in reducing a large number of cases into a small number of classes. This may be seen in a recent global survey reported in Levinson's encyclopaedia of ethnic relations and linked to a more systematic typology. This is based on one of three principles for the classification of *ethnic conflict* that Levinson sees as underlying this phenomenon (degree of ranking in interethnic power relations, global regional zone, and goals of participants).[28] Using the last of these dimensions, he identifies five types, in terms of group goals: (1) separation, as in the case of the Basques in Spain, (2) internal pursuit of autonomy, political power or territorial control in competition with other groups, as in the case of the major ethnic groups in Nigeria, (3) conquest, of which no pure type is listed, (4) survival, as in the case of the East Timorese in Indonesia up to 1999, and (5) irredentism, as in the case of the Armenians in Azerbaidzhan. This approach poses obvious theoretical challenges. For instance, a conflict whose object may be 'survival' from one perspective may be classified as 'conquest' from another. It also raises the usual difficulties of operationalization. The overall classification is nevertheless of interest: out of a total of 41 cases of ethnic conflict, 24 are seen as falling into a single category, while 17 fall into more than one (13 into two categories and four into three). The most commonly occurring type was 'survival' (13 cases, with a further 13 as part of composite categories), followed by 'separatism' (eight and nine, respectively), 'internal rivalry' (two and seven), 'irredentism' (one and seven), and 'conquest' (no pure case, but part of two composite cases). This account understates the true numbers, since some of the 'cases' are in fact plural ones (for example, Russians in the former Soviet republics are listed as a single case), and the classification is in any case by country, so multiple conflicts are not classified separately.

A third classification, based on systematic and detailed analysis of a large number of cases as part of a major *Ethnic Conflicts Research Project*, in many respects combines the historical and sociological richness of the qualitative approach with the painful compromises of classification. This focuses on *violent conflicts*, and rests on a seven-category typology.[29] Using this typology, 80 conflicts continuing during the period 1995–96 were identified. Few (no more than four) fell into a single category; almost all were composite in character, though a dominant type of conflict could be identified in each case. The most important category was ethnonationalist conflict, typically between the state and a particular nationalist group (dominant in 31 cases, present in 19 others). Other types of ethnically related conflict accounted for most other cases: interethnic conflicts, typically between two ethnic groups within a single state (17 and 21 cases respectively), decolonization wars (four and five cases) and cases of genocide (dominant in two cases and present in one other). The remaining categories were in principle non-ethnic: anti-regime wars, or political and ideological conflicts (dominant in 18 cases and present in 38 others), gang wars (five and ten), and interstate conflicts (three and four). It will be clear from this that the ethnic factor was identified as the primary one in 54 out of the 80 cases.

The three overviews just considered are based on cases where conflict (specifically ethnic conflict in one study, and predominantly this type in the other two) has actually broken out. They thus ignore the large number of cases where conflict lies below the surface, with potential to erupt in the medium or longer term. This wider group is captured in a fourth classification that has a broader reach, that of the large, long-running *Minorities at Risk* project directed by Ted Robert Gurr. This focuses on minorities that have achieved a minimum degree of political mobilization (described as *politicized communal groups*), even if this mobilization falls well short of violent conflict. This typology begins with a distinction between 'national peoples' (regionally concentrated groups that have lost their former autonomy but retain elements of cultural distinctiveness) and 'minority peoples' (groups, frequently but not necessarily made up of immigrants, which do not have this background, but which have a definite status in society that they wish to improve or defend). Each of the two resulting categories is further broken down, to give five broad types:

- Ethnonationalists: 'national peoples' of relatively large size pursuing a struggle to regain autonomy
- Indigenous peoples: 'national peoples' descended from the conquered original population but now economically and politically marginalized
- Ethnoclasses: 'minority peoples', frequently based on immigration, that are ethnically or culturally distinct and that occupy a characteristic economic niche, typically a low-status one
- Militant sects: 'minority peoples' whose primary political goal is defence of their religious beliefs
- Communal contenders: 'minority peoples' in heterogeneous societies who hold or seek to share state power, and who in turn are divided into three sub-types: disadvantaged (subject to political or economic discrimination), advantaged (enjoying relative political advantage) and dominant (enjoying both economic and political advantage).[30]

This classification is based on analysis of a large number of cases; the 1999 version of the database includes 275 current cases, comprising 177 groups spread across 116 countries (many of the groups occur in more than one country).[31] In terms of the typology used by the study, this comprised an equal number of communal contenders and indigenous peoples (68 of each), followed by national minorities (44), ethnoclasses (42), ethnonational groups (40) and religious sects (13). The continued and striking centrality of the ethnic dimension in the contemporary world emerges clearly from this overview; most countries are seen as having some kind of significant minority of an ethnic character. Some of the characteristics of these groups are considered further below.[32]

Ethnic Conflict and the Territorial Dimension

The public policy issues raised by ethnic minorities, and the prospects for solutions based on territorial approaches, will, as noted above, rest in part on such concrete questions as the absolute and relative size of the group and its degree of territorial dispersion. The *Minorities at Risk* dataset provides a useful source of information on these questions. If we look at the issue of absolute size, it becomes clear that the groups included in this dataset are quite large: only 12 have a population of less than 100,000, and 21 have a population in excess of 10 million. In terms of relative size, it is true that 63% account for less than 10% of the population of the state in which they are located, but in many of these cases they constitute a much higher proportion of a politically relevant region, and, even at the level of the state, some of the 'minorities' are very large indeed: no fewer than six of them account for a majority of the population of their state. These groups are classified as 'minorities' for other, non-arithmetical, reasons, that typically include considerations of socio-economic disadvantage and political discrimination.

For purposes of this book, what is even more important is the degree of spatial concentration of the minorities. The *Minorities at Risk* dataset permits us to form an overall impression of the pattern. In Table 1.2 those groups in respect of which adequate data are available are grouped according to degree of territorial concentration and degree of ethnic cohesiveness of their territory. Because of the relatively precise nature of the data, it is possible to be little more refined than in Table 1.1 – we may also distinguish 'medium' (and not just 'low' and 'high') degrees of concentration and cohesiveness.

Thus, it is possible to identify 72 cases where the group is concentrated in a particular region. In 12 of these cases, the group also dominates its region; the Turks in Northern Cyprus are a good example. In a further 34 cases, the group has a majority, typically a clear one, in its region; we may cite the instance of the Quebecois in their own province in Canada. In the remaining 26 cases the group is regionally concentrated, but does not enjoy a local majority (the Abkhazians in Abkhazia, in Georgia, are an example). Second, there are some 14 groups that are concentrated in one area but that are spread out also in adjacent areas

TABLE 1.2
DISTRIBUTION OF POLITICIZED MINORITIES BY DEGREE OF COHESIVENESS
AND DEGREE OF TERRITORIAL CONCENTRATION, 1999

| | | Territorial concentration of group | | | |
		Low	*Medium*	*High*	*Total*
	Low	77	2	26	**105**
Ethnic cohesiveness of territory	*Medium*	10	10	34	**54**
	High	2	2	12	**16**
	Total	**89**	**14**	**72**	**175**

Note: 'Territorial concentration' refers to whether the group was concentrated in a single region (high), was a majority in one region but was also dispersed among neighbouring areas (medium), or was a dispersed group, though it might enjoy local majorities in certain rural areas or in cities (low). 'Ethnic cohesiveness' refers to the proportion of the population that the group accounted for in its 'own' region: 90% or more (high), 50% to 90% (medium), and less than 50% (low). In a further 100 cases, there was insufficient information to classify the groups.

Source: Calculated from *Minorities at Risk* dataset, downloaded from www.cidcm.umd. edu/inscr/mar [2002-07-10].

where they constitute a minority. In two cases, they entirely dominate their 'own' area, according to the *Minorities at Risk* dataset; the Armenians of Azerbaidzhan (in Nagorno-Karabakh) are an example. In ten other cases, they constitute a clear majority in this area, as in the case of the Albanians of western Macedonia. But in other areas they are a minority even in their 'own' area; the Buryats in Russia's Buryat Republic are an example. Finally, we have 89 widely dispersed minorities. In exceptional circumstances, of which 12 are reported in this table, these may constitute a politically significant local majority; in two cases this is an overwhelming one (as in the case of Hispanics in parts of the United States); and in ten others it is strong but not overwhelming (as in the case of the Tatars in Russia). More typically, though, this kind of group does not enjoy any local majority. In rural areas, the many indigenous peoples are examples; in cities we frequently find larger ethnic minorities, often of immigrant origin.

In terms of territorial approaches to ethnic conflict, then, the most manageable cases are those in the bottom right-hand cell of Table 1.2 (high concentration, high cohesiveness). The problem, however, is that this contains only 12 cases. If we include the three cells immediately to the left, above, and diagonally to the left and above this (thus extending to 'medium' and 'medium-high' categories), the number of potential cases increases slightly, but, at 58, it still remains only a fraction of the total number. For most of the minorities included in this dataset, in other words, the notion of any kind of territorial devolution is largely irrelevant, and there are circumstances where they might even see its effects as negative.

CONCLUSION

It is appropriate, then, to turn from this quantitative global overview to undertake a more systematic, qualitative analysis of particular cases. The present volume brings together a collection of studies that consider evidence from a range of countries in which, in varying degrees, territorial solutions to ethnic conflict have been contemplated. Of the ten case studies, seven comprise instances where the question of relations between the state and ethnic groups within it continues to be an issue, and where territorial management has been an option. At one extreme, in Belgium, a degree of institutional stability appears to have been attained, and a mixture of approaches, including territorial ones, seems to have largely resolved the intercommunal issue. At the opposite extreme, in Israel, conflict over territory and its allocation continues to be violent and intense, with little indication that a solution lies around the corner. Canada lies close to the first pole, followed by South Africa and

Northern Ireland, with Pakistan somewhere in the middle and Sri Lanka veering towards the second pole.

Of these seven cases, two each are based in Europe and Asia, and one each in North America, Africa and the Middle East. In this respect they are not perfectly representative of global regions.[33] The cases do, however, illustrate the range of minority types. In two cases, Canada and Northern Ireland, the minorities (Quebecois or French Canadians, and Northern Irish Catholics) are ethnonational according to the *Minorities at Risk* classification. In two further cases, both ethnonational and ethnoclass components are present (Ceylon Tamils and Indian Tamils respectively in Sri Lanka, and Palestinians and Israeli Arabs respectively in Israel). In two further cases, the groups are essentially communal contenders (of which there are two in Belgium, and five have been identified in South Africa). In the last case, Pakistan, some of these types are present, but so also are representatives of two of the remaining types identified in the *Minorities at Risk* typology, national minorities and religious sects.[34] In terms of their relationship to territory, these groups are both concentrated and locally dominant in the cases of Canada, Belgium, Israel and Sri Lanka, but rather more dispersed – though not without a regional base – in the cases of Northern Ireland, South Africa and Pakistan.

If these states show varying degrees of success in coping with ethnic demands, the same cannot be said of the three remaining cases: each of them has entirely failed. The collapse of the Soviet Union, Czechoslovakia and Yugoslavia in the early 1990s provided important lessons about the territorial management of ethnic conflict. Each of these states was multinational, and provided examples of a whole range of types of minority group. It is striking that the outcome of territorial reconstitution in these areas has been to multiply the number of minorities: in the old Czechoslovakia, Yugoslavia and Soviet Union there were, according to the criteria used in the *Minorities at Risk* dataset, respectively two, three and 18 minorities; these numbers have now climbed to four, 13 and 35, respectively, in these three cases.

This book is designed, then, to enquire into the circumstances surrounding the handling of ethnic issues in selected multinational states. Each chapter begins with an overview of the ethnic problem and its historical roots, examines the range of strategies on which the state authorities embarked in response to this, and assesses the importance of the issue of territory. To illustrate the significance of the territorial dimension, each case study has been accompanied by a map; and to facilitate comparison the maps have been prepared to a specific format. Rather than seeking to illustrate gradations that may be of purely local significance, they show the distribution of selected groups in terms of standard bands of intensity: areas where the group is entirely dominant (accounting for 80% or more of the population), where it constitutes a majority (50–80%) but there are significant minorities, where it is a size-able minority (20–50%), and where it is a small minority or is entirely unrepresented (less than 20%). The experience in each case has, of course, in important respects been unique; but there has been a sufficient range of common strands to permit generalization about the broader issue, a topic to which we return in the concluding chapter.

ACKNOWLEDGEMENTS

I would like to thank Ron Hill, Charles Kennedy, Stanislav Kirschbaum, Jean Laponce, Rupert Taylor, Tobias Theiler and Alex Weingrod for comments on an earlier draft.

NOTES

1. These two criteria refer respectively to the definition of citizenship by descent and to the definition of citizenship by place of birth. For very many illustrations of the application of these principles in citizenship law, see Richard W. Flournoy, Jr. and Manley O. Hudson (eds.), *A Collection of Nationality Laws of Various Countries as Contained in Constitutions, Statutes and Treaties* (New York, NY: Oxford University Press, 1929).
2. Max Weber, *Economy and Society: An Outline of Interpretive Sociology*, ed. Guenther Roth and Claus Wittich (Berkeley, CA: University of California Press, 1978), Vol.1, p.56.
3. Leonard W. Doob, *Patriotism and Nationalism: Their Psychological Foundations* (Westport, CT: Greenwood Press, 1976), pp.24–30 [originally published 1964].
4. David M. Smith, 'Introduction: The Sharing and Dividing of Geographical Space', in Michael Chisholm and David M. Smith (eds.), *Shared Space: Divided Space: Essays on Conflict and Territorial Organization* (London: Unwin Hyman, 1990), pp.1–21 (at p.3).
5. John Coakley, 'National Territories and Cultural Frontiers: Conflicts of Principle in the Formation of States in Europe', in Malcolm Anderson (ed.), *Frontier Regions in Western Europe* (London: Frank Cass, 1983), pp.34–49.
6. See R.A. Schermerhorn, *Comparative Ethnic Relations: A Framework for Theory and Research*, 2nd ed. (Chicago, IL: University of Chicago Press, 1978), pp.95–102.
7. See Kennedy (ch.7) and Wilson (ch.8) in this volume, and John Coakley, 'National Minorities and the Government of Divided Societies: A Comparative Analysis of Some European Evidence', *European Journal of Political Research*, Vol.18, No.4 (1990), pp.437–56.
8. See, for example, the tendency for the Irish to be given ape-like characteristics in English magazines in the second half of the nineteenth century; L. Perry Curtis, Jr., *Apes and Angels: The Irishman in Victorian Caricature* (Newton Abbot: David & Charles, 1971).
9. For the French declaration, see Maurice Duverger, *Constitutions et documents politiques*, 8th ed. (Paris: Presses Universitaires de France, 1978), pp.9–10; the Universal Declaration of Human Rights is reproduced in A.H. Robertson, *Human Rights in the World* (Manchester: Manchester University Press, 1972), pp.185–90.
10. See Erik Allardt, *Implications of the Ethnic Revival in Modern, Industrialized Society: A Comparative Study of the Linguistic Minorities in Western Europe* (Helsinki: Societas Scientiarum Fennica, 1979), pp.27–30, 43–7.
11. See Jean Laponce, *The Protection of Minorities* (Berkeley, CA: University of California Press, 1960).
12. See L.P. Mair, *The Protection of Minorities: The Working and Scope of the Minorities Treaties under the League of Nations* (London: Christophers, 1928), pp.30–36, and Inis L. Claude, *National Minorities: An International Problem* (Cambridge, MA: Harvard University Press, 1955), pp.6–16; see also Jószef Galántai, *Trianon and the Protection of Minorities*

(Boulder, CO: Social Science Monographs, 1992).

13. For a summary of the general principles underlying the League of Nations' minorities policy, see 'Documents Relating to the Protection of Minorities', *League of Nations Official Journal Special Supplement* No.73 (1929), esp. pp.47–8.

14. For example, Article 1 declared that 'All peoples have the right of self-determination' (though 'peoples' was not defined), and Article 27 gave certain rights to 'ethnic, religious or linguistic minorities'; for the text of the Covenant, see Robertson, *Human Rights*, pp.202–20.

15. 'The Charter of Paris for a new Europe', Appendix 17B to *SIPRI Yearbook 1991: World Armaments and Disarmament* (Oxford: Oxford University Press, 1991), pp.603–10.

16. See OSCE High Commissioner on National Minorities, *Recommendations*. Available at www.osce.org/hcnm/documents/recommendations/index.php3 [2002-06-21]; see also Stephen D. Krasner and Daniel T. Froats, 'Minority Rights and the Westphalian Model', in David A. Lake and Donald Rothchild (eds.), *The International Spread of Ethnic Conflict: Fear, Diffusion, and Escalation* (Princeton, NJ: Princeton University Press, 1998), pp.227–50.

17. Jean Laponce has described the right to one's language as 'both an individual and a collective right'; see *Languages and Their Territories* (Toronto: University of Toronto Press, 1987), p.150.

18. See Jorgen Elklit and Ole Tonsgaard, 'The Absence of Nationalist Movements: The Case of the Nordic Area', in John Coakley (ed.), *The Social Origins of Nationalist Movements: The Contemporary West European Experience* (London: Sage, 1992), pp.81–98.

19. These data, and the Soviet data referred to in the next paragraph, are from 1979, and are computed from *The Great Soviet Encyclopedia*, Vol.31 (New York: Macmillan, 1982).

20. These data, like those on Slovenia quoted below, are from 1981, and are computed from the *Statesman's Yearbook*, 1992.

21. These data refer to December 2000, and have been computed from Svensk Finlands Folkting, *Svenskt i Finland* (Helsinki: Svensk Finlands Folkting, 2001), pp.19–20; available at www.folktinget.fi/svenskt/svefi.pdf [2002-07-10].

22. For reviews of these patterns, see Samuel Humes and Eileen Martin, *The Structure of Local Government: A Comparative Survey of 81 Countries* (The Hague: International Union of Local Authorities, 1969), and Donald C. Rowat (ed.), *International Handbook on Local Government Reorganisation: Contemporary Developments* (London: Aldwych Press, 1980).

23. Laponce, *Languages*.

24. This is the well-known scenario to which Karl Deutsch drew attention; see *Nationalism and Social Communication: An Inquiry into the Foundations of Nationality*, 2nd ed. (Cambridge, MA: MIT Press, 1966), pp.132–52.

25. See Philip Mawhood and Malcolm Wallis, 'Ethnic Minorities in Eastern Africa: Kenya and Tanzania', in John Coakley (ed.), *The Territorial Management of Ethnic Conflict* [1st ed.] (London: Frank Cass, 1993), pp.170–89.

26. Jean-Marc Balencie and Arnaud de La Grange, *Mondes rebelles: guerres civiles et violences politiques*, Rev. ed. (Paris: Éditions Michalon, 1999).

27. Jean-Christophe Rufin, 'Les temps rebelles', in Balencie and de La Grange, *Mondes rebelles*, pp.13–34.

28. David Levinson, 'Ethnic Conflict', in David Levinvon (ed.), *Ethnic Relations: A Cross-Cultural Encyclopedia* (Santa Barbara, CA: ABC Clio, 1994), pp.62–70.

29. Christian P. Scherrer, 'Towards a Comprehensive Analysis of Ethnicity and Mass Violence: Types, Dynamics, Characteristics and Trends', in Håkon Wiberg and Christian P. Scherrer (eds.), *Ethnicity and Intra-State Conflict* (Aldershot: Ashgate, 1999), pp.52–88.

30. Ted Robert Gurr, with Barbara Harff, Monty G. Marshall and James R. Scarritt, *Minorities at Risk: A Global View of Ethnopolitical Conflicts* (Washington, DC: United States Institute of Peace, 1993), pp.15–23.

31. *Minorities at Risk* dataset, downloaded from www.cidcm.umd.edu/inscr/mar/ [2002-07-10].

32. In a spin-off from this project, a sub-set of 58 cases where violent conflict has been taking place in the recent past shows that in 28 cases this was continuing in 2000; in 19 cases an agreement (not necessarily an uncontested one) had been reached; and in

a further 11 cases hostilities had ceased, for one reason or another; see Deepa Khosla, 'Armed Self-Determination Conflicts in 2000: Mobilization, War, Negotiation, and Settlement', available at www.bsos.umd.edu/cidcm/mar/autonomy.htm [2002-04-09].

33. Following the classification of the *Minorities at Risk* project, 30 minorities were located in the western democracies (represented by three cases here), 59 in Eastern Europe and the former Soviet Union (the three cases of 'dissolution' discussed here), 59 in Asia (two cases here), 28 in North Africa and the Middle East (one case), 67 in Sub-Saharan Africa (one case), and 32 in Latin America and the Caribbean (not represented in this book).

34. In its list of ethnic minorities in Pakistan, the *Minorities at Risk* typology classified Muhajirs, Pashtuns and Sindhis as communal contenders, Baluchis as a national minority and Ahmadis and Hindus as religious sects.

2

Canada

The Case for Ethnolinguistic Federalism in a Multilingual Society

J.A. LAPONCE

The continuing constitutional debate in Canada and the apparent intractability of the issue of provincial–federal relations draws attention to one of the most fundamental challenges facing many contemporary states: devising a system of government for a multilingual society such that different linguistic groups can give it their allegiance. The Canadian dilemma needs thus to be seen in the context of a more general conflict between languages – conflict between individuals and between communities, of course, but also conflict within the individual.

In this chapter, I shall first consider certain general questions that arise from sustained contact among languages, and then describe the specific Canadian situation before making the case for a Swiss type of ethnolinguistic federalism as a means of reducing the tensions between Canada's two official language communities.

LANGUAGES AND LANGUAGE CONFLICT

Languages are born and languages die. Some live long and some do not; some have many descendants while others disappear without successor. To reflect on that history of successes and failures, it helps if we reverse the more common way of studying languages and if we think of languages as having people rather than people having languages. The latter, like religions or other symbolic systems, compete for scarce resources; they compete for speakers, writers, and thinkers; more precisely, they compete for people who have a limited capacity and a limited willingness to think, speak and write. How many languages are now competing for survival? As in the case of animals the count varies according to the criteria used to identify differences. The better estimates range from roughly 4,000 to 7,000.[1]

The War among Languages

Much attention has been given in recent years, in the scientific as in the popular media, to the disappearance of eagles and whales. Languages have attracted less attention. Yet, a momentous event is likely to have occurred in this generation, a true revolution in the history of culture – a steady decline in the number of living languages. The limited information available indicates that, up to the twentieth century, languages had, world wide, a positive birth rate. More were being born than died. A trend dating back, almost certainly, to the origins of mankind appears to have been reversed.

When the world was fragmented into communities that were isolated or at best very loosely tied to one another, spoken tongues tended to diverge. Cailleux estimates that, among major languages such as Latin and Greek, two languages were born for every one that died.[2] His statistics are subject to caution, his ratio is too precise but the trend they indicate is almost certainly correct: languages used to have a positive birth rate. In an era of weak communication density, which was also an era of spoken rather than written communication, and at a time when standardized writing was very much the exception, physical separation meant divergence and contact meant the creation of hybrids evolving their own separate way. When the world was empty there was 'room' for more and more languages. The populations that migrated to New Guinea before colonization brought – it is assumed – only very few languages to the islands; but these languages multiplied as the population spread and became separated by seas, forests, and mountains. Where there were few originally, there are now over 700 distinct tongues.[3]

By contrast, in a world characterized by high communication density – in what Valéry called the *monde fini* (a completed world, a global system) – there is less room for new languages, less likelihood of divergence. Much more often than before, languages come into close and frequent contact and become locked in a fight for life. The political consequences of the intensification of the war among languages are considerable: minority languages, or more precisely the languages of political minorities, are more at risk. Those that are to survive will need stronger protection, which typically means boundaries (social boundaries of course but also territorial boundaries);[4] hence the argument around which this chapter is structured, an argument in favour of a regional federalism based on language for multilingual societies such as Canada.

The Mind as a Battleground for Languages

Languages could theoretically be in contact yet ignore one another. It could be that the speakers of language A, knowing the existence of speakers of a strange language B, would not seek to communicate with them even though they occupied a common territorial niche. This situation, frequent among animals, is unknown among humans: man is incapable of ignoring man. Once contact has been established among people, communication by means of language will follow. The only recorded failures at translation are between living and dead languages. Attempts at reading Indic and Cretan have failed but that is not for lack of trying. Among living languages there are *no* exceptions. Since mutual ignorance is not an option, the relationship between languages (let us say 'between' instead of 'among' in order to simplify) will be either symmetrical or asymmetrical and, like all human relationships, it is more likely to be asymmetrical. Asymmetric language relationships are more likely to lead to conflict when there is bilingualism without diglossia than when bilingualism is accompanied by diglossia. There is likely to be a greater need for boundaries – boundaries that separate competitors – in the first than in the second case.

Diglossia – in the sense given here to a term that has acquired a variety of meanings – implies the segregation of languages by social roles,[5] for example when a religious language such as Latin, Hebrew, or old church Slavonic is associated with social roles markedly distinct from those that call for the use of a secular language, such as French, Yiddish or Russian. Diglossia frequently juxtaposes a local language, typically a mother tongue, with a regional or with an international language: Swiss German with high German in Switzerland, Luxembourgese with French and German in Luxembourg and Guarani with Spanish in Paraguay, for instance. Diglossic situations are not without territorial ethnic underpinnings (the German dialects used in Switzerland vary from canton to canton) but, typically, the boundary separating diglossic languages is social rather than territorial. The native of Luxembourg who switches from Luxembourgese to either French or German does so as the type of interaction varies, and this in the absence of any geographical mobility. A businessman in his office will, typically, within minutes, read a French newspaper, draft a contract in German and speak Luxembourgese to a friend or colleague. To operate effectively throughout Luxembourg, that businessman needs to carry along three languages at all times. Drawing a map of Luxembourg according to language use would show a concentration of French and German in public places – churches, banks, government offices – and a concentration of Luxembourgese in homes and certain types of shops, but such a map, interesting as it might be, could not be used to draw formal territorial boundaries around any of the official languages, since all three cover the whole territory.[6] A territorial solution to language problems arising in a country such as Luxembourg would be absurd.

Diglossic situations are often such that the home language has limited geographical currency. It is then used to structure a local community that interacts frequently with a larger system – Swiss German in Switzerland, or Guarani in Paraguay, for example. In these cases the local language has either given up or not even attempted to express all the social roles necessary for effective interaction within the larger community; it clings to specific types of interactions. Its protection and survival depend on the frequency and vitality of these interactions, and hence to a large extent on the strength of the ethnic boundaries that the culture sets around specific roles and interactions. Romanche will continue to decline in Switzerland as long as the roles with which it is associated become more and more restricted. Inversely, some home or kitchen languages win roles previously assigned to the public domain, for example when Luxembourgese entered the literary domain through songs, poems and plays. Non-diglossic bilingual situations, by contrast, are characterized by the spread of two or more languages across all the social roles of the individuals that live within a given territorial community.

Obviously we have here ideal types that define the polar opposites of a complex continuum. Between diglossic and non-diglossic situations, the separation is not rigid; it is a matter of degree.[7] Nevertheless, most cases of language contact can clearly be assigned to the diglossic or to the non-diglossic type. In Canada, for example, English-French bilingualism is diglossic in Newfoundland and British Columbia, and non-diglossic in Quebec (not for everybody, of course, but for a large segment of the population living in the contact zone). Territorial solutions to the protection of minority languages are particularly well suited to non-diglossic bilingualism since, in such a case, the drawing of linguistic boundaries and the regulation of language use inside spatial boundaries do not cut across social roles, at least not to the same extent as in the case of bilingualism associated with diglossia.

Whether language contact leads to diglossic or non-diglossic bilingualism, it is obvious (whether one plots mother tongue or language use geographically) that all languages, even the so-called international languages, have specific geographical niches. True, the same applies to religions and races and can be explained by the friction of space over the diffusion of social and symbolic structures. However, between language and space there is a privileged association that is due to the specific geographical needs of languages. Religions and races can survive geographical dispersion; languages cannot do so as easily.[8]

Let us chart the geographical needs of a language – particularly in non-diglossic situations – by means of a theoretical proposition, the proposition that:

> *the lesser cost and greater communication efficiency of unilingualism over multilingualism leads languages to organize themselves in physical space in such a way as to avoid territorial overlaps; languages tend to coalesce into monolingual areas juxtaposed to one another.*

This proposition seems to contradict the common observation that most countries and communities are not monolingual. That seeming contradiction comes from our abstracting the behaviour of a language *qua* language from the effects of other factors with which a language happens to be associated, such as migration, conquest, expansion of economic market areas and increase in the territorial scope of new communication systems. Such abstraction is needed for theory building.

It follows from our proposition that the tendency of a socio-territorial system to remain or become monolingual is positively related to the degree of closure of that system. The United States offers a good example. Its high communication density results in the grinding of its minor languages out of existence in two or three generations; but its high degree of openness to foreign migration results in a large number of speakers of foreign languages being constantly added to its population. Thus far the rate of assimilation has been considerably higher than the rate of what Karl Deutsch called mobilization[9] – in this instance the rate at which the speakers of foreign languages enter the main stream of communication of the dominant group and acquire English as their dominant language. Diglossia (with English as a public language and a non-English language as a home or neighbourhood language) is rarely a stable phenomenon over more than two generations; it is an intermediate stage that leads newcomers from one type of unilingualism to another unless the foreign tongue be isolated socially and spatially. Note by contrast how, in a diglossic situation such as that of Luxembourg, the strengthening of French and German as a result of membership in the European Community has not resulted in the downgrading of Luxembourgese, but rather the contrary.

In the era of the global village, migration is not the only factor that prevents the territories of powerful nations, and hence powerful languages, from becoming closed systems. Not only are many countries of the industrialized West affected by very low birthrates that oblige them to import labour from outside their language pool; in addition, the very globalization of political, economic, and cultural affairs requires increased communication in foreign tongues with the outside world.

The reconciliation of the tendency towards unilingualism and of the need to communicate with other languages is achieved by: (1) the specialization of tasks through the division of labour and (2) the shifting of the cost of bilingualism onto the weaker ethno-linguistic groups. The use of immediate or delayed translation by professional translators is an application of the first principle; the lesser knowledge of the 'other' language by the dominant group, hence the avoidance of learning expenditures, is evidence of the other strategy. That second way of 'solving' the problems arising from language contact is particularly important politically since it creates asymmetrical situations: Japanese businessmen are more likely to know English than American businessmen to know Japanese. French Canadian politicians, administrators, businessmen and academics are more likely to know English than their English Canadian counterparts to know French.

The first strategy (the use of translation) reduces social tensions since it puts the communicators at the same advantage (or disadvantage) and can result in equal cost-sharing. The second strategy is on the contrary a potential source of conflict since it loads one group with the major cost of language acquisition and gives a communication advantage to the group that spends least. The Japanese businessman must invest heavily in the learning of a language that will put him at a communication disadvantage since he is unlikely ever to reach the level of fluency of his American counterpart. This need not but will often be translated into resentment, and this resentment is more likely to occur when the communicators are theoretically equal within a given community, in other words when the interaction takes place at what both interactors think of as home rather than at a location that at least one of them would consider as foreign territory. The Flemish Belgian is more likely to resent having to use French in Brussels than in Paris, and the French Canadian is more likely to feel his identity threatened by the use of English in Montreal than in Toronto or even Ottawa.

Power and Asymmetry among Languages

Genocide has weakened some languages – Armenian for example – and it may have eliminated some of Australia's aboriginal languages, but more typically languages die because of language shifts that occur from social pressure to conform or from the need to communicate quickly and effectively, and they die because of the unequal advantages that languages offer to those that know them. Most of the languages that will disappear in the next few centuries will die a quiet and natural death.

How well or how badly placed are existing languages in the worldwide competition? A precise answer would require numerous local case studies since most of the languages that will disappear will do so as a result of transfers to regionally rather than world dominant competitors. Such studies are unfortunately relatively rare. Let us thus be guided by the statistics available and let us take a global view of the hierarchy among languages. Mackey, Tsunoda and Laponce have measured the

TABLE 2.1
DOMINANT LANGUAGES IN SELECTED HIERARCHIES

Estimated population (millions), 1999		Articles indexed in *Chemical Abstracts,* 2000 (% of total)		Number of deployed strategic nuclear weapons, 1999		Language of web pages on the internet, 1999 (% of total)	
Chinese (Mandarin)	800	English	82.9	English	7,360	English	78.3
Hindi/Urdu, Punjabi	430	Chinese	6.6	Russian	5,900	Japanese	2.5
English	400	Japanese	4.2	French	440	German	2.0
Spanish	300	Russian	2.7	Chinese (Mandarin)	400	Spanish	1.7
Arabic	200	German	1.2	Hebrew	?	French	1.2
Bengali	190	Korean	0.5			Chinese	0.6
Portuguese	170	French	0.4			Others	13.7
Russian	160	Polish	0.4				
Japanese	125	Spanish	0.2				
German	120	Portuguese	0.1				
French	90	Ukrainian	0.1				

Note: Adding the nuclear weapons of India and Pakistan would add slightly to the English total if we assign the weapons, as I do here, to the actual language of government of the states concerned.

Sources: For population, John W. Wright (ed.), *The 2001 New York Times Almanac: The Almanac of Record* (New York: Penguin Books, 2000). The various regional forms of Arabic are counted here as a single language. For different population rankings, see Laponce, *Languages*. For nuclear weapons, *The Almanac*, and the International Institute for Strategic Studies, *Military Balance 1998* (Cambridge: IISS, 1999). I thank the *Chemical Abstracts* for giving me the scores of each of the 70 languages of the 573,469 articles abstracted for the year 2000. For a comparison of these scores with those of previous years, see Laponce, *Politics*. .For the languages of the web, OECD survey of 1999 as reported by the *Economist*, 11 March 2000. For other internet rankings, see Jacques Maurais 'Vers un nouvel ordre mondial?', *Terminogramme*, Nos. 99–100 (2001), pp. 7–34.

relative power of languages by comparing the number of their speakers and the weight of their economic and cultural output as well as by noting their different geographical spread.[10] Some of these measures, brought up to date, are recorded by Table 2.1, which gives the ranking of the world's most 'powerful' languages according to the number of their speakers, their military power, the percentage of 'their' articles indexed in the *Chemical Abstracts*, and their presence on the Internet.

Such measures, as well as other similar measures not included here (religious power would be particularly important for any comparison concerning Arabic) give us, rough as they be, a way of comparing the purchasing value of different languages, a value translatable into influence, status and communication benefits, since there are markets for languages as there are markets for other symbolic commodities. There are markets for first languages and markets for second or third languages as well as markets for international or local languages.

The geographical underpinnings of these markets, at least those with consequences for linguistic and political conflicts, are not so varied as to prevent our recognizing three major types of language markets:[11]

a. the dominant language borders the dominated language within the same state, for example Castilian in relation to Basque;
b. the dominant language borders the lower ranking language but is separated from it by rigid boundaries, such as the international and intra-Swiss boundaries separating French and German in Switzerland;
c. the dominant language has no territorial border with the weaker language, for example English in relation to Finnish.

If a specific minority language has a strong tie to a specific ethnos – as is frequently the case – the threat posed by the dominant language will increase as the situation moves from (c) to (a). We should expect that language contact will thus be more likely to result in conflict – ethnic as well as linguistic – as geographical proximity increases, unless the ethnic competitors be separated by a boundary, whether intrastate or international. Reducing conflict consists in bringing situation (a) to resemble (b) and to move from (b) to (c) whenever the option is available.

If India had made Hindi the dominant language of its central government and politics it would have chosen situation (a); by retaining English as its lingua franca it favoured situation (c). The same outcome occurred in Singapore when English was preferred to Hokkien, and in Senegal where Wolof did not replace French as the dominant language of the higher bureaucracy.

The Swiss way of reducing the linguistic conflicts that occur in bilingual cantons has been to move from (a) to (b) as when Vaud and Jura were separated from Bern, voluntarily in the case of Jura, under the pressure of France in the case of Vaud.[12] Similarly, Belgium evolved from a unitary into a federal state in the course of an increasingly rigid definition of linguistic areas that were given increasingly wide powers over economic and cultural matters.[13]

The territorial separation of competing languages is not always feasible. The Swedes of Finland are no longer sufficiently numerous in relation to the Finns, nor sufficiently concentrated (except in the Åland Islands and a narrow strip along the South Western coast) to justify the use of protective internal language boundaries (except again in the case of Åland where the language boundary is guaranteed by post-World War I agreements).

The partitioning of the multilingual state into unilingual zones has sometimes been considered but rejected by the dominant group. Such rejection characterizes, to varying degrees, the central government's policies in both Canada and the pre-1990 Soviet Union. Both countries objected to the creation of rigid language borders of the kind adopted by Belgium and Switzerland, the Soviet Union because it wanted Russian eventually to be the lingua franca of all the republics, Canada in the

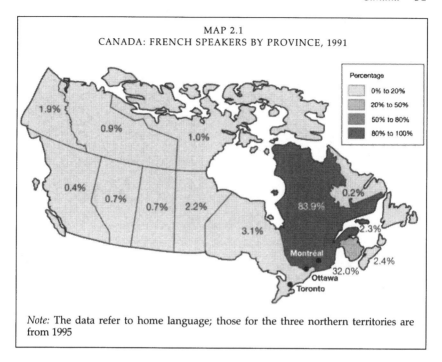

MAP 2.1
CANADA: FRENCH SPEAKERS BY PROVINCE, 1991

Note: The data refer to home language; those for the three northern territories are from 1995

name of a dream of cross-national French-English bilingualism. In both cases the policy of territorial overlap of languages kept the territories of the linguistic minorities open to penetration by the dominant language and led to conflicts. Such conflicts can be lessened by a move towards solution (b), as was done tentatively by the Soviet Union in the late 1980s when attempting to appease its rebellious republics.

In short, peace among languages in contact requires that each have a secure niche: 'role niches' in the case of bilingualism with diglossia, 'territorial niches' in the case of bilingualism without diglossia. In the first case language resembles religion and can best be protected by means of individual rights – the right to free expression in the language of one's choice, since that choice will vary according to the roles concerned. In the second case, a minority language is best protected by means of group rights and territorial boundaries – by some form of linguistic federalism.

LANGUAGE AND COMMUNITY IN CONTEMPORARY CANADA

Being still a world language of considerable power (see Table 2.1), French should be expected to have a high degree of resistance to assimilation by other languages. But in Canada it is competing with another world language of even greater power. The geographical distribution of French (measured in terms both of the percentage of the population with French

TABLE 2.2
CANADA: MOTHER TONGUE AND HOME LANGUAGE BY PROVINCE, 1991

Province	English		French		Other	
Newfoundland	98.70	(99.28)	0.42	(0.20)	0.86	(0.49)
Prince Edward Island	94.63	(97.41)	4.21	(2.29)	1.15	(0.28)
Nova Scotia	93.99	(96.49)	3.81	(2.43)	2.19	(1.07)
New Brunswick	65.41	(68.34)	33.35	(32.04)	1.22	(0.61)
Quebec	8.95	(10.71)	83.35	(83.85)	7.71	(5.43)
Ontario	77.52	(85.99)	4.74	(3.07)	17.72	(10.93)
Manitoba	76.10	(88.63)	4.46	(2.23)	19.40	(9.13)
Saskatchewan	85.16	(94.92)	2.04	(0.65)	12.79	(4.41)
Alberta	83.46	(92.21)	2.06	(0.72)	14.47	(7.06)
British Columbia	81.36	(90.35)	1.41	(0.38)	17.22	(8.26)
Total	62.15	(68.73)	24. 48	(23.43)	13.35	(7.82)

Note: The first statistic gives the mother-tongue percentage; the second, in parenthesis, the 'language spoken at home' percentage. Both statistics are provincial aggregates. For the rate of retention at the level of the individual, see Table 2.3. Because of rounding errors, total percentages may not amount to 100.0. Multiple answers (more than one mother tongue or language habitually spoken at home) are excluded from the computations. The multiple mother tongues amounted to 2.6% Canada-wide, and for the provinces, in the descending order of the columns, in percentages: 0.26, 0.84, 0.88, 2.02, 2.60, 3.06, 3.76, 2.46, 2.63 and 2.39. The corresponding statistics for multiple languages spoken at home were 1.80 for Canada as a whole, and for the respective provinces: 0.14, 0.20, 0.36, 0.84, 1.86, 2.12, 2.24, 1.21, 1.61 and 1.79.

Source: *Population by Mother Tongue; Population by Home Language* (Ottawa: Statistics Canada, code 93-317, 1991).

TABLE 2.3
CANADA: LANGUAGE RETENTION BY PROVINCE, 1991

Province	English	French
Newfoundland	100.0	50.5
Prince Edward Island	99.9	45.3
Nova Scotia	99.8	54.8
New Brunswick	98.8	87.8
Quebec	87.2	98.2
Ontario	99.2	59.2
Manitoba	99.4	45.5
Saskatchewan	99.7	24.0
Alberta	99.5	30.2
British Columbia	99.6	23.2
Total	99.0	92.8

Note: Language retention is defined as the percentage of individuals of a given mother tongue who say they speak that language habitually at home.

Source: Individual statistics computed by the author from the *Families Census 1991, 2%* sample tapes deposited at the University of British Columbia Data Library.

as mother tongue, and the percentage habitually speaking it at home) is described in Table 2.2, and illustrated in Map 2.1. While resisting the pressure of English relatively well in its strongholds of Quebec and northern New Brunswick, French does not maintain itself particularly well in the other provinces. This may be seen in Table 2.3, which reports the percentage of native speakers of English and French who still spoke that language habitually in each province in 1991.

Language and Geography

The assimilation of French outside its areas of high geographical concentration has been documented by means of both aggregate data[14] and individual statistics.[15] From these studies, three factors emerge as assisting a shift from the minority to the dominant language. The first is the degree of geographical overlap of the minority and the dominant group. Second is the level of population balance between minority and dominant group evidenced by the fact that French resists the inroads of English better in Ontario than in British Columbia (see the 1991 census measures of Tables 2.2 and 2.3). Third is the rate of endogamy of the minority population – the Chinese, who have a high endogamy rate, are more likely than Poles or Germans, who typically do not marry their language kin, to transmit their mother tongue to their children.[16] In the

TABLE 2.4
CANADA: MOTHER TONGUE ENDOGAMY BY PROVINCE, 1991

Province	English	French
Newfoundland	99.2	26.3
Prince Edward Island	95.3	50.0
Nova Scotia	96.7	58.7
New Brunswick	90.6	87.3
Quebec	65.2	96.5
Ontario	91.8	59.4
Manitoba	88.8	58.1
Saskatchewan	92.9	36.6
Alberta	92.0	33.4
British Columbia	92.1	32.5
Total	91.3	90.8

Note: Mother tongue endogamy is defined as the percentage of heads of households whose spouses have the same mother tongue. The respondents who indicated both French and English as their mother tongue are not taken into account. Adding them to the count, even on the extreme assumption that all self-declared bilinguals are predominantly French speakers, would not affect the overall pattern. Canada-wide, only 0.89% of respondents indicated both French and English as their mother tongues, only 1.8% in New Brunswick, only 1.60% in Quebec and less than 1% in the other provinces.

Source: As for Table 2.3.

case of French, the endogamy rates vary from a high of 96.5% in Quebec to lows of 26.3% in Newfoundland and 32.5% in British Columbia (see Table 2.4).

Determinants of Language Shift

Let us once again measure these effects, in particular the endogamy effect and the regional effect, by means of individual statistics, those given by a 2% sample of the 1981 census made accessible to the author, at the time, for his personal computations. A probit analysis measured, for individuals whose mother tongue is French, the statistical likelihood that they speak English at home. The following set of predictors was used: being a woman, being married, having at home at least one child between the ages of 6 and 14, being at least 35 years old, living in a household the total income of which was over $40,000 (in 1981), having a spouse whose mother tongue was either French, English or neither (as three separate variables); and living in either of the three areas of Canada where the Francophones are a numerical minority (the West, Ontario and the Maritimes). The coefficients of the canonical analysis recorded in Table 2.5 show the language of the spouse to be by far the most important factor in all three regions; so overwhelming is its effect than we can dispense with the other factors and concentrate our analysis on the territorial and marriage factors. This is done by Table 2.6, which offers a tree structure of the likelihood of a 'French mother tongue' woman speaking

TABLE 2.5
CANADA: PREDICTION OF USE OF ENGLISH AS
RESPONDENT'S HOME LANGUAGE BY REGION, 1981

Indicator	Maritimes	Ontario	West
Female	–	.07	.05
Child 6–14 at home	–	.03	–
Aged 35 or more	.10	.11	.06
Household income over $40,000	−.03	–	–
English mother tongue spouse	.87	.75	.86
French mother tongue spouse	−.29	−.44	−.32
Other mother tongue spouse	.24	.33	.51
Married	–	–	−.26
% of 'grouped' cases correctly classified	89.4	78.9	74.1
Wilk's lambda	.60	.65	.73
X2 level of significance	<.000	<.000	<.000
Canonical correlation	.58	.51	.62

Note: The elements in the above table are standardized coefficients based on probit analysis.

Source: Computed by the author from unpublished data of the Canadian census (2% individual level sample interrogated on line, 1981).

either English or French at home as a function of whether she married someone whose mother tongue was either 'French', 'English' or 'Other'.

The only significant 'protection' against a shift from French to English is in the marrying of a language kin, as Table 2.6 shows, but even that is far from being foolproof. The use of French as a home language in French mother-tongue families is only 85% in Ontario and only 69% in the West. The better 'resistance' of Francophone families in the Maritimes (95%) measures the importance of isolation for language maintenance. In the industrial centre of the country, in Ontario, the protection afforded by numbers (about half a million Francophones grouped along the Quebec border) is offset by the density of the communication network that links Francophones and Anglophones. That density affects first of all the likelihood of marrying within one's language group and it affects secondarily the home language of the Francophones who marry a language kin. The first effect – marrying across language lines – is considerable, since language cleavages are now only weakly reinforced by religion. A French Catholic in Ontario no longer has much difficulty finding an English Catholic mate if he or she so wishes.

Neither is language any longer reinforced by 'race'. It is not merely in semantics but also in perceptions that the two 'races' of Canada (the term used until recently to refer to the two original colonizers) are now increasingly perceived, simply, as two language groups. Massive immigration from Haiti and Africa to Quebec and from China to English Canada could result in Canada's duality becoming again a 'race' confrontation. The trends are in that direction but, as long as immigration to Canada remains set at about 200,000 people a year, race is unlikely to become a major factor of ethno-linguistic differentiation.

Under conditions of weak religious and non-racial reinforcement, the French language has weaker social boundaries. The Francophone who leaves the 'Montreal to northeastern New Brunswick' unilingual belt (see Map 2.1) enters a 'danger' zone, one where assimilation is likely to occur within two or three generations. Thus, whether we reason the case deductively from the theory of language contact and conflict in non-diglossic bilingual situations or whether we argue that case inductively from the evidence of language assimilation in Canada, we are led to the conclusion that language boundaries, and hence language-based federalism, offer the appropriate solution to the preservation of a minority language such as French.

LANGUAGE AND FEDERALISM

Canada is a blend of two types of federalism, the organic and the instrumental. Its federalism is instrumental in the sense that the

TABLE 2.6
ENGLISH CANADA: PREDICTION OF HOME LANGUAGE
ON BASIS OF SPOUSE'S MOTHER TONGUE BY REGION, 1981

A. Maritimes

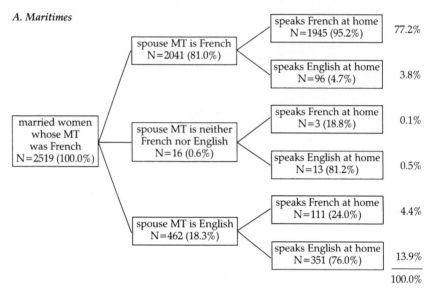

Overall retention of French = 77.2% + 0.1% + 4.4% = 81.7%
($X^2 = 81.6$, df 1, < 0.000)

B. Ontario

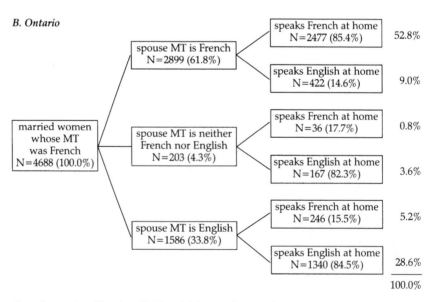

Overall retention of French = 52.8% + 0.8% + 5.2% = 58.8%
($X^2 = 631.0$, df 1, < 0.000)

TABLE 2.6 (cont.)

C. West

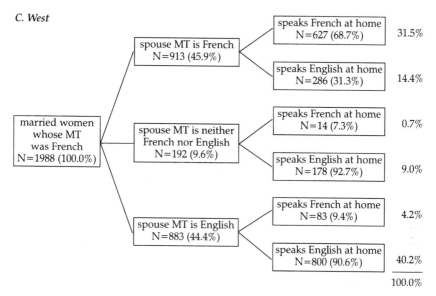

Overall retention of French = 31.5% + 0.7% + 4.1% = 36.3%
(X^2 = 333.7, df 1, < 0.000)

Note: The trees are to be read as follows: in the Maritimes, for example, out of 2519 women whose mother tongue is French, 2041 (81.0%) have a mate whose mother tongue is also French. Out of the 2041, 1945 (95.2%) speak French habitually at home, representing 1945 / 2519 x 100 = 77.2% of the original 2519 females.

Source: As for Table 2.5.

provincial boundaries are somewhat artificial and do not, in most cases, separate different societies; organic in as much as at least one of its provinces, Quebec, has a clear ethnic distinctiveness. However, even in the case of Quebec, the political and the language boundaries do not coincide. If nearly 85% of Canada's population of French mother tongue are concentrated in that province, only a roughly similar proportion of the inhabitants of Quebec have French as their mother tongue. In the past three decades, Quebec and the central government have been engaged in a tug of war, Quebec attempting to move the federation in the direction of ethnolinguistic federalism, the federal government resisting that move, especially under the governments of Prime Ministers Pierre Elliot Trudeau and Jean Chrétien.

Yet Canada came close to adopting principles that would have strengthened linguistic federalism, at least in Quebec. The Pépin-Robarts advisory Task Force had suggested in the early 1980s that the provinces be given exclusive responsibility for language policy within their spheres of jurisdiction.[17] Such power would have enabled Quebec, if not immediately then possibly at a future date, to institute what Quebec's Law 101 was pointing to: a Swiss type of language boundary. The amended Canadian constitution of 1982 pulled in the opposite direction by making language an individual rather than a group right. The inconclusive constitutional debates of the following 20 years culminated in the Quebec referendum of 1995 that saw 49.4% of the Quebec electorate vote for some form of secession (linked to Canada by an EU type of association), a solution favoured by 60% of the province's Francophone electors.[18] At the time of writing, the separation movement is at a low ebb, but a federalism based on linguistic cleavages, thus far resisted by the federal government, may become again the more obvious solution if the separatist movement regains vigour (the percentage of Quebec electors favouring sovereignty has fluctuated, in recent years between 30% and 50%).

Four Federalist Scenarios

If Quebec separates from Canada (a possibility that remains unlikely), then, obviously, the argument for ethnolinguistic federalism would cease to apply to Canada except with regard to the Aboriginal people. I shall not deal here with this last problem. Let us instead restrict the issue to that of Quebec and let us assume that the Canadian federation will survive. Given these assumptions, let us 'play' a variety of scenarios that would, over time, bring Canada closer to Switzerland and, for convenience, label these by reference to specific Swiss cantonal outcomes:

Scenario 1: Geneva
The province of Quebec becomes as unilingual as the canton of Geneva (as regards street signs, schools, provincial and local public services and legal contracts, for example).

Scenario 2: Grisons
Quebec formalizes and freezes its present de facto division at the municipal level and distinguishes a French unilingual zone from bilingual pockets.

Scenario 3: Fribourg
Quebec divides its territory into two unilingual zones, one French, the other English. The street signs, the schools, the local governments, are either French or English depending upon their location on one or the other side of an intra-provincial language border. Quebec would thus be bilingual by the juxtaposition rather than the overlap of its

languages in contact. Such a solution is that adopted by the cantons of Fribourg and Valais.

Scenario 4: Jura
Quebec is divided into two provinces, one English, one French.

To simplify the game even further, let us put the federal government on the sidelines, and retain only two players, two *Quebec* players: one Francophone, the other Anglophone. To become politically feasible, the first scenario presupposes a sharp decline in the percentage of Quebec Anglophones while the fourth is not realistic as long as the language boundary runs through Montreal. The second and third scenarios (and especially scenario 2) are more likely in the short run, but they both remain at the moment very theoretical. Let us stay at the level of theory and speculation and ask ourselves how the game of choosing among these four scenarios might be played.

The moves will depend upon whether one plays the game from a Francophone or from an Anglophone decision-maker's point of view (French or English to simplify) and will depend upon each player's expectations regarding the probable evolution of the two communities facing each other, notably their future share of the Quebec and of the Canadian populations. If the French player assumes a long-term decline of the Quebecois ethnos and if solution 4 (separation) is not politically feasible, cutting one's loses would lead to preferring solutions 2 or 3. If the same player predicts a decline in the proportion of the Anglophone population of Quebec, then solution 1 should be kept in reserve for a future date. If the French players are unable to predict, then they should insist that the constitution be reformed to give Quebec full control over matters involving language, a clear sovereign control that would go beyond the present 'notwithstanding clause' of the constitution, a clause that enables the Quebec legislator to escape some federal interventions in matters of language (some but not all: interventions concerning street signs, for example, but not those concerning the language of instruction of Canadian children coming from other provinces). A Quebec with unhindered language rights could relate the degree of constraint in its language legislation to its demographic evolution.

The English player, on the contrary, has to decide whether to guarantee the status quo (scenario 2: Grisons) or hope for a linguistic reconquest of the province. The desire to protect the status quo would lead one to the rejection of solution 4 in favour of the first three. An English assimilation strategy would lead to the rejection of all of the scenarios we outlined. In this last case we do not have a solution to the game, at least not according to our theoretical payoffs. But if the English decision maker is a pessimist and wishes to consider non-extreme solutions, then we have the possibility of a solution.

In principle, the French player has a choice of two solutions in each of two categories (total or partial unilingualism) while the English player has a similar choice in each of two categories (some or no English unilingual territory). According to the theoretical proposition we formulated earlier, a player who has minority status should prefer a unilingual to a bilingual solution and should prefer the latter to a total loss. Let us assume – not an unreasonable assumption – that, under existing constitutional arrangements, both the French and the English players feel that they are in a minority situation, the first in Canada, the other in Quebec; let us assume in other words that both are pessimistic about their future: the French player because of the Quebec birth rate and the shortage of francophone immigrants, the English player because of existing Quebec laws (particularly Laws 101 and 178) that severely restrict the use of English at work and in public places. Let us assume that each player will rank their preferences from 1 to 4 and that the French player's preference ordering will be Geneva > Fribourg > Grisons > Jura, and that the English player's will be Jura > Fribourg > Grisons > Geneva.

In principle, the French player's preference ordering makes more sense than the ordering for the English player. Would the latter actually prefer the Jura to the Fribourg solution? Possibly at the start of a negotiation, but that is probably not a reasonable objective. Under present conditions, the carving of a separate unilingual English territory out of Quebec does not make much geosociological sense. The problems posed by bilingual Montreal would thus force the game towards the Fribourg solution, a solution that has the character of a minimax outcome protecting both players from potentially severe losses. The solution emerging from an assumption of a preference for unilingual territories is thus more extreme than the proposal that Cartwright induced from his data for Eastern Ontario: a mixture of unilingual and bilingual zones.[19]

Would a real negotiation be played today as suggested by the theoretical game? That is doubtful. The present 'sovereignty is still in sight' mood of a large segment of the Quebec population should enable its decision makers to use the threat of independence in a negotiation with Ottawa. The French player is thus unlikely to select a third or even a second best solution. Are we thus led to conclude that ethnolinguisic federalism would have to be imposed rather than be the result of a mutually agreeable negotiation? Not necessarily. Pure ethnolinguistic federalism is an ideal type that one approaches more or less closely. Both Switzerland and Belgium make exceptions to the principle of territoriality, minor exceptions such as the French school in Bern or major exceptions such as a bilingual Brussels. In the Canadian case, language federalism is a model that one either rejects, as did Pierre Elliott Trudeau, or that one tries to approximate at the various territorial levels where the problems happen to arise, at the levels of schools, local governments, or provinces. The most one could expect at the moment (assuming a desire to keep Canada together) would be to give the provinces full control over their language policies, trusting that they will be kind to their linguistic minorities, but without firm guarantees of that.

I have argued the case for language federalism by giving particular attention to Quebec. The same demonstration could be made for the native languages of Canada; or, in a different context, for a United Europe à la Héraud (1963).[20] The prescription would remain the same: think federalism in terms of a language map and use either provincial or intra-provincial boundaries to protect minorities by giving them exclusive cultural control over a specific territory.

Ethnolinguistic Federalism and Secession

In conclusion, let us consider the question: would not ethno-linguistic federalism create deep cleavages favouring secession; would not the territorial mixing of different languages be a surer way of strengthening a political fabric? Answering these questions in the abstract is not possible.

Predicting the consequences of ethnolinguistic federalism requires consideration of the specificity of historical, economic, political and cultural conditions. Quantitative comparative analysis is not the most appropriate method. It is nevertheless interesting to consider here findings obtained from the comparison of a relatively large number of countries, if only to show the relevance of a factor that any case study should take into consideration when predicting the evolution of language conflicts: the degree of territorial penetration of a minority by a dominant language.

Relating the level of geographical concentration of a minority to the level of separatism, Church and his colleagues had found a lack of correlation among the 31 cases they had selected in Europe, Asia, and the Americas.[21] A re-analysis of these data leads me to a different conclusion. The authors of the study had expected a linear correlation, one that would have associated low concentration with low separatism and high concentration with high separatism. If territorial concentration created conditions favourable to separation without having an integrating effect, that is indeed what one would expect. But concentration gives security. It should thus be expected to lessen the desire for separation. The correlation between concentration and separatism should then be curvilinear. Indeed, the Church data show that low *and* high levels of concentration are associated with low levels of separatism: 18% (N = 11) and 28% (N = 10) respectively, while, at medium levels of concentration, the percentage of minorities having high levels of separatism is much greater (50%; N = 10). Intuitively, this makes sense. At a low level of concentration, separatism will seem hopeless, while at a high level of concentration, which reduces the contacts with the dominant group, one may well feel that one's culture is secure enough and thus be more willing to accept the status quo, especially so if that status quo is associated with economic benefits, such as a larger market. The Swiss technique of rigid language boundaries juxtaposing unilingual areas, beyond reducing conflicts, may well be also an anti-separatism recipe. Returning from blind quantitative measures to qualitative case by case studies, let us compare Canada not to Sri Lanka, the Sudan or the Soviet Union (countries that were included in the Church corpus) but to states such as Switzerland, Belgium, and Finland – states with a similar democratic culture, a similar level of industrialization and urbanization, and a similarly low level of group violence.

In both Belgium and Switzerland the political system has, over the last century and a half, moved ever closer to producing overlap of political, administrative and language boundaries, the latter providing the map that attracts the others. This attraction led to the separation of the cantons of Vaud and Jura from Bern and to the division of Belgium into distinct economic and cultural regions with increasing legislative and budgetary powers. In both cases the minority languages have either retained their positions, as in Switzerland, or improved them, as in Belgium. In Finland, on the contrary, where, except in Åland, the language boundaries were not fixed rigidly, the Swedish language, although a regionally dominant one, has declined dramatically, except, precisely, in Åland.[22]

CONCLUSION

The Canadian federal government has, regrettably, taken Finland as its model.[23] If the goal is to maintain the conditions favourable to the assimilation of the minority language in the long run while protecting it in the short term (by making it an official language but not giving it an exclusive territory) then the model may appear well chosen. But if the goal is survival of French into the next centuries, then a Swiss solution would be more appropriate. Ethnolinguistic federalism enables one to separate culture, where the small is often the valuable, from economics, where the big is usually preferable.

NOTES

1. J.A. Laponce 'Politics and the Law of Babel', *Social Science Information*, Vol.40, No.2 (2001), pp.179–94, note 4.
2. A. Cailleux, 'L'évolution quantitative du langage', *Societé préhistorique française*, Vol.9 (1953) pp.505–14.
3. J.C. Anceaux, *The Linguistic Situation in the Islands of Yapen, Kurudu, Nau, and Miosnum,*

New Guinea (S'Gravenhage: Nijhoff, 1961).
4. J.A. Laponce, *Languages and their Territories* (Toronto: Toronto University Press, 1987).
5. C.A. Ferguson, 'Diglossia' *Word*, Vol.15 (1959), pp.325–40; J.A. Fishman, 'Bilingualism with and without Diglossia, Diglossia with and without Bilingualism', *Journal of Social Issues*, Vol.23 (1967), pp.29–38; L-G. Calvet, *Language Wars and Linguistic Politics* (Oxford: Oxford University Press, 1998).
6. F. Hoffmann, *Sprachen in Luxemburg* (Wiesbaden: Steiner, 1979), and N. Jakob, 'Sprachplanung in einer komplexen Diglossie-situation dargestellt am Beispiel Luxemburg', *Language Problems and Language Planning*, Vol.5 (1981), pp.153–74.
7. Fishman, 'Bilingualism'.
8. J.A. Laponce, 'The French Language in Canada: Tensions between Geography and Politics', *Political Geography Quarterly*, Vol.3 (1984), pp.91–104.
9. K. Deutsch, *Nationalism and Social Communication* (New York: Wiley, 1953).
10. W.F. Mackey, *Three Concepts for Geolinguistics* (Québec: Presses de l'Université Laval, 1973); T. Tsunoda, 'Les langues internationales dans les publications scientifiques et techniques', *Sophia Linguistica*, No.13 (1983), pp.140–55; Laponce, *Languages*. For other measures of military power and GNP per head see the Laponce chapter in the first edition of this volume.
11. See a different but related classification in W.F. Mackey, 'Geolinguistics: its Scope and Principles' in C.H. Williams (ed.), *Language in Geographic Context* (Clevendon: Multicultural Matters, 1988), pp.20–46.
12. K.D. MacRae, *Conflict and Compromise in Multilingual Societies: Switzerland* (Waterloo: Wilfrid Laurier University Press, 1984); J.W. Lapierre, *Le pouvoir politique et les langues* (Paris: Presses Universitaires de France, 1988).
13. K.D. MacRae, *Conflict and Compromise in Multilingual Societies: Belgium* (Waterloo: Wilfrid Laurier University Press, 1986); F. Delpérée, 'Le fédéralisme, forme d'adaptation de l'Etat nation: le cas de la Belgique', in C. Philip and P. Soldatos *Au delà de l'Etat nation* (Bruxelles: Bruylant, 1996), pp.140–58.
14. D.C. Cartwright, *Official Language Populations in Canada* (Montréal: Institute for Research on Public Policy, 1980); R. Lachapelle and J. Henripin, *La situation démolinguistique au Canada* (Montréal: Institut de recherches politiques, 1980); Laponce, 'French Language'; C. Castonguay, 'Assimilation linguistique et remplacement des générations anglophones et francophones au Québec et au Canada', paper read at the conference on *Rethinking the Canadian Federation* (Vancouver: University of British Columbia, 2001).
15. K. O'Brian et al., *Attitudes and Behaviour of Members of Non-official Language Groups* (Downsview, Ont: York University, Institute for Behavioural Analysis, n.d.). See also Y. Corbeil and C. Delude, *Etudes des communautés francophones hors Québec* (Montréal: CROP, 1982); and J.A. Laponce, 'Conseil au prince qui voudrait assurer la survie du français en Amérique du Nord', *Cahiers québecois de démographie*, Vol.17 (1988), pp.36–47.
16. Laponce, 'Conseil au Prince'; R. Breton, W.W. Isajiv, W.E. Kalbach, and J.G. Reitz, *Ethnic Identity and Equality* (Toronto: Toronto University Press, 1990).
17. The recommendations read: 'Each province should have the right to determine an official language or official languages for that province, within its sphere of jurisdiction… Linguistic rights should be expressed in provincial statutes that *could*' (emphasis added); there followed a series of suggestions granting school, health science, and judicial language rights to French and English minorities, with the further suggestion that the *could* might be transformed into a constitutional *must*, but only if all provinces agreed to granting these rights. See the *Report of the Task Force on Canadian Unity* (Ottawa: Government Reviews, 1979).
18. R. Bernier, V. Lemieux and M. Pinard, *Un combat inachevé* (Sainte-Foy: Presses de l'Université Laval, 1997); P. Drouilly, *Indépendance et démocratie* (Montréal: L'Harmattan, 1997); J.A. Laponce 'The Quebec Sovereignty Referendum of 1995: How not to Manage a Multinational Polity', *Politikon*, Vol.26, No.1 (1999), pp.103–19.
19. D.E. Cartwright, 'Language Policy and Internal Geopolitics: the Canadian Situation', in C.H. Williams (ed.), *Languages in Geographic Context* (Clevendon: Multilingual Matters, 1988), pp.238–66.
20. See Guy Héraud, *L'Europe des ethnies* (Paris: Presses d'Europe, 1963). Admittedly a federal ethnic solution to ethnic divisions is easier in the Swiss than in the Canadian

case, because in Switzerland the linguistic cleavages criss-cross the religious and the national (national in the sense here that the cantons have their distinct historical roots and identities); but, as Belgium illustrates, by its recent move from a unitary to a federal state, one can envisage federal ethnic solutions even when there are only two or three partners.

21.　R.C. Church et al., 'Ethnoregional Minorities and Separation: A Crossnational Analysis' (paper read at the Canadian Political Science Association annual meeting, 1978).

22.　For the evolution of the Swedish minority from territorial to cultural demarcations, see J. Hätli, 'Cultures of Demarcation', in G.H. Herb and D. Kaplan (eds.), *Nested Identities* (Oxford: Bowman, 1999), pp.123–50.

23.　K.D. McRae, 'Bilingual Language Districts in Finland and in Canada: Adventures in Transplanting an Institution', *Canadian Public Policy*, Vol.4 (1978), pp.331–51.

3

Northern Ireland

Religion, Ethnic Conflict and Territory

JOSEPH RUANE and JENNIFER TODD

Ethnic conflict in Ireland is centuries old. It continues in Northern Ireland despite the peace process, the paramilitary ceasefires and the Good Friday (or Belfast) Agreement of 10 April 1998. State strategies of territorial management have been central to this conflict since the outset. In this chapter we examine the sources and changing form of the conflict: its historical origins, the changing ethnic balance, the causes of current tension, the strategies now being pursued for dealing with it, and the prospects for the future.

EMERGENCE OF THE ETHNIC PROBLEM

Ethnic division in Ireland emerged in the context of English state expansion and the beginnings of the creation of a British empire. Ireland was one piece in this imperial jigsaw. The character and intensity of internal divisions within Ireland, their articulation as ethnonational oppositions and the modes of state management of ethnic conflict were determined by this wider context.[1]

By the sixteenth century a new, highly competitive, international order had emerged in Europe. The strongest monarchs were consolidating their kingdoms and accumulating territories within Europe and beyond the Atlantic. The reformation had divided Europe in religious denominational terms, creating new bases of political alliance. English crown policy was to bring Wales, Scotland and Ireland under its control, to avoid continental entanglements, to build up its sea-power and to establish colonies and trade networks in the New World. This was the beginning of the political unification of Great Britain, the making of the United Kingdom and the first step in the creation of a wider 'British world'.[2] This placed the English crown and government at the centre of a complex web of territories each of which posed its own distinctive management problem.

The mode of acquisition was different for each territory, as were imperatives for later territorial management. English power in Wales was asserted from the end of the thirteenth century, the final Welsh uprising was crushed in 1406, and – already conquered and partially integrated – Wales was annexed in a series of acts of union between 1532 and 1539. In a process that at times was fractious, the kingdom of Scotland entered more or less voluntarily into union with England, first of the two crowns (1603), then of the parliaments (1707). The Caribbean colonies were won by victory in war. The North American colonies arose out of individual settlement. Ireland was integrated partly as sister kingdom, partly as colony. Its pre-conquest political structures corresponded more closely to the Welsh than to the Scottish model, but it was larger and more complex, and the native Old English (the descendants of medieval settlers) and Gaelic Irish were determined to remain Catholic. It was seen as underpopulated and underdeveloped, a territory ripe for settlement, a first destination for many English emigrants seeking their fortune overseas. Impossible to annex or to negotiate with, Ireland was eventually secured by renewed conquest followed by state and private colonization.[3] The province of Ulster was the last to yield to English military might but, in part as a consequence of this, it became the most thoroughly colonized.

Ireland was now a multi-stranded ethnic and cultural world, comprising Catholics of Gaelic Irish and Old English stock, Anglicans of recent English provenance and – primarily in Ulster – Presbyterians from Scotland. The Anglicans were the ruling class, monopolizing the ownership of land and political power and setting the tone of public life. On all fronts, however, their position was insecure. As a minority of the total population, Anglicans – and Protestants more generally – were demographically vulnerable. For the Catholic majority, Protestant rule of any kind lacked both religious sanction and the legitimacy of tradition; for Presbyterians – political allies, but religious opponents – Anglican rule lacked religious authority. In the face of irreconcilable difference, power was a crucial resource and ethnicity, linked inextricably to religion, formed the basis of a more or less constant struggle for political advantage and resources.

At the broader geopolitical level, the power imbalances were between Britain and Ireland, and between Protestants and Catholics within Ireland. The micro-level pattern was more uneven: the Catholic–Protestant balance varied from one local area and region to another.[4] The balance was closest in Ulster, which alone of the Irish provinces had extensive areas where Protestants were a local majority – the towns of Belfast and Derry and the valleys of the Lagan and Foyle. Catholics predominated in the more peripheral areas, with substantial zones of relatively even ethnic mix between the two. Communal conflict was shaped by both macro- and micro-level changes. A perceived slippage of ethnic position at the national level could precipitate local disturbances; purely local processes of displacement or intensified competition could have the same effect; and the worst outbreaks of ethnic conflict were the product of changes at both levels simultaneously.[5] The potential for change was inherent in this unstable balance. Catholics had been comprehensively defeated in the seventeenth century but by the mid-eighteenth century the first signs of a Catholic recovery were evident.[6] As resources came their way, Catholics offered their loyalty to the Crown in exchange for the removal of their disadvantages. A pattern developed that in time would become very familiar. Catholics would seek a remedy for their grievances and would press their case with a mixture of threats and reassurance; the British government would be open in principle to making concessions, but had to take account of Protestant fears and wider imperial interests; Protestants would oppose any concessions; and Catholic demands would eventually be met, but only in part, and not sufficiently to satisfy them in the longer term. Sooner or later Catholics would return with further demands, whereupon the cycle would recommence. Catholics had, it seemed, an unlimited store of grievances, most linked in one way or another to the injustice of the seventeenth-century displacements.

The Catholic–Protestant cleavage was a major source of conflict, but it was not the only one. There was increasing conflict between the new industrial and middle classes and the landed elite, and between British and Irish interests. In the 1790s, under the influence of the French revolution, religious, class and national tensions coalesced to produce a revolutionary movement seeking to unite 'Protestant, Catholic and Dissenter' in an Irish republic totally separate from Britain. Rebellion in 1798 was crushed, and had far-reaching constitutional implications. The British government pushed through an act of union between the two countries, taking effect in 1801. Union was in the first instance a means of securing permanent British control over Ireland; but it was also an economic measure designed to facilitate British investment in Ireland and ensure Irish manufacturers full access to British and imperial markets. It was also thought to offer a more favourable context for addressing religious conflicts and divisions.

In the event, union did not deliver on these promises. Irish economic development under the union took a markedly uneven form. The north-east underwent an industrial revolution, but elsewhere there was de-industrialization, population decline, crises of agricultural adjustment, and at mid-century devastating famine. Moreover, both in the north-east and in Dublin, industrialization was largely a Protestant affair and its benefits were directed disproportionately to the Protestant community. Initially at least, Catholic rights proved as difficult to achieve under the union as under an Irish parliament: it was not until 1829 that Catholic 'emancipation' (in particular, the right to take seats in parliament) was achieved, and then only after a campaign of mass political agitation.

By the 1830s Catholic opinion had turned against the union and the popular leader Daniel O'Connell launched a new mass campaign for its repeal. In the face of immovable British opposition, the campaign collapsed in 1844. But the issue of Irish self-government did not go away.[7] The radical 'Fenian' movement (more formally known as the Irish Republican Brotherhood, or IRB) staged a short-lived rebellion in 1867; more importantly, through the 1880s Charles Stuart Parnell mobilized the bulk of the Irish representatives at Westminster in support of 'home rule' within the union. The question of Irish self-government tapped directly into traditional ethnic divisions in Ireland. The vast majority of Catholics supported it on the principle that it would give them real power and that as the 'true Irish nation' they should be in control of their own affairs. Protestants opposed it, in part for economic reasons, in part because they feared for their liberties and privileges under a Catholic-dominated parliament.

For the British government, Irish nationalism was a threat both to the union and to the empire, but a peaceful Ireland, reconciled to the Crown, would also bring benefits. The Liberal Party supported Irish home rule for that reason; the Tories, however, continued to oppose it. The issue would dominate Anglo-Irish relations for the next 30 years and provoke the mass mobilization of both nationalists and unionists. The bedrock of unionist opposition lay in the Protestant-dominated, industrialized north-east, and it was here that mobilization took its most militant and militarist form. A home rule bill finally passed both houses of parliament in August 1914, but with two qualifications. Six north-eastern counties were excluded from its remit for six years and the bill itself was suspended for the duration of the war. A rebellion in 1916 planned by the IRB, however, radicalized Irish nationalism, its goal now being redefined as full Irish independence.

The Irish war of independence (essentially a guerrilla campaign) began in 1919 and ended with the Anglo-Irish Treaty of 1921. The Treaty confirmed the partition of Ireland, but gave southern Ireland dominion status within the Commonwealth. The new six-county northern state was given – at British insistence – devolved government within the union.[8] On both sides of the border republicans resisted the establishment of the new order, but were defeated – in the North by the new unionist government, in the South by the pro-treaty government forces. For the British government, the territorial reconstruction of Ireland evoked imperial rather than national sentiments. The secession of southern Ireland was seen not as the sundering of the British national territory but as the departure of a particularly troublesome part of the empire. Northern Ireland was retained not because a majority of its population affirmed a British identity and allegiance, but because they threatened armed rebellion if any attempt was to be made to force them into a home rule Ireland. The British priority was to secure its strategic interests in Ireland while insulating itself from Irish divisions and their capacity to disrupt the politics of the centre. As a strategy of territorial management, it was a considerable success, but it proved temporary. Irish divisions continued within the new constitutional framework, to return to British attention with explosive force in the late 1960s.

THE CHANGING ETHNIC BALANCE

The seventeenth century conquest gave the Protestant minority a monopoly of political, legal, economic and cultural power. Two centuries later they were still the dominant community. Until the end of nineteenth century they controlled the vast bulk of the land, formed the majority of political representatives at Westminster, and dominated local government. They controlled the upper echelons of the administration and security forces, the major industries and finance institutions; they were hugely overrepresented in the professions; their culture enjoyed high status and set the tone of Irish public life. But they were under increasing pressure from a resurgent Catholic community and they experienced continued erosion of their position. Land, electoral and local government reform in the 1880s and 1890s finally broke their dominance. The Liberal willingness to accede to Catholic-nationalist demands for home rule was a recognition of the changed balance of power.

The balance of Catholic–Protestant power was, however, territorially uneven. In contrast to the tendency at the level of the island as a whole, Protestants in the north-east had further consolidated their position in the late nineteenth century. The partition of Ireland in 1921 reflected this, and gave each community control in the area in which it was numerically dominant. There was an important difference, however, in the communal balance in the two parts of Ireland after partition. Protestant numbers in the 26 southern counties were 10.4% of the total in 1911; they fell to 7.4% in 1926 and to 5.2% in 1961, as may be seen from table 3.1. The Protestant minority maintained its strong economic position in land ownership, business and the professions and their high social standing, but they could make little impact on the shaping of the new state or its public culture. At the same time they posed no threat to the stability of the new state or to its nationalist priorities and experienced little direct discrimination.

The situation in the six northern counties was quite different. There Protestants were in the majority; they controlled the bulk of the economic resources, the government and state apparatus and the secu-

TABLE 3.1
NORTHERN IRELAND AND REPUBLIC OF IRELAND:
RELIGIOUS COMPOSITION, 1911–91

Year	Northern Ireland Catholic	Republic of Ireland Protestant
1911	34.4	10.4
1926	33.5	7.4
1936–37	33.5	6.6
1946–51	34.5	5.7
1961	35.6	5.2
1971	36.8	4.3
1981	38.5	3.7
1991	42.1	3.2

Note: The data are percentages and refer to the territories of the two states that appeared in 1921. In Northern Ireland, censuses took place in 1937 and 1951; the corresponding southern data are from 1936 and 1946. Data from 1971 onwards are estimates. Statistics have been corrected to take account of those who did not declare their religion; this was a particular problem in 1981; see David Eversley and Valerie Herr, *The Roman Catholic Population of Northern Ireland in 1981* (Belfast: Fair Employment Agency, n.d. [1985]).

Source: Calculated from W.E. Vaughan and A.J. Fitzpatrick, *Irish Historical Statistics: Population 1821–1971* (Dublin: Royal Irish Academy, 1978), *Northern Ireland Census*, 1991, and John Coakley, 'Religion, ethnic identity and the Protestant minority in the Republic', pp. 86–106 in William Crotty and David E. Schmitt, eds., *Ireland and the Politics of Change* (London: Longman, 1998), table 5.1, p. 89. In estimating the corrected percentage of Catholics in Northern Ireland after 1971, we take conservative estimates following the work of Neville Douglas, Paul Compton and (for 1991) E. Jardine, see Youssef Courbage, 'Démographie et politique en Irlande du Nord', pp.335–62 in J.-L. Rallu, Y. Courbage and V. Piché (eds.), *Old and New Minorities* (London: John Libbey, 1997).

rity forces; they had a broadly based middle class which set the tone of the public culture. But Protestant demographic dominance was noticeably weaker. Catholics were 34% of the total in 1911; their numbers fell slightly in the early 1920s and then remained stable for the next four decades, as may be seen from Table 3.1. This relative stability hid a more complex dynamic: one of a substantially higher Catholic birth-rate offset by higher emigration rates. The northern state was also politically less stable: its legitimacy was rejected by nationalists, North and South, and British support for it was ambiguous and conditional.

This was the context in which unionist discriminatory practices were put into effect in the period 1921–69.[9] Catholics were discriminated against in public and private employment and in public authority housing, particularly in marginal constituencies. The unionist government eliminated proportional representation in local government and Northern Ireland regional elections in order to increase the unionist vote; they redrew local boundaries to ensure unionist-controlled councils in areas where Catholics (almost universally nationalists) were a demographic majority. The intention and effect of these practices were to limit the growth of the Catholic population and to restrict its access to power and social prominence. Protestants were aware that in so doing they were consolidating nationalist opposition to the state, but, believing this opposition to be inevitable anyway, their main concern was to limit nationalist access to power.

These policies had a measure of success. Their effect was particularly evident in the large disparities in the Protestant and Catholic socio-economic profiles in 1971, in the high rates of Catholic unemployment and emigration, in the striking imbalance between population distribution and electoral representation in key local constituencies, notably Derry City, in the very low levels of Catholic representation at the higher levels of the civil service and in the security forces, in the virtual exclusion of Catholics from public policy making, and in the low status of Catholic and Irish culture in the public domain.[10]

Despite this, there was a significant reduction in the imbalance of structural power between the communities between the 1920s and the 1960s. Several factors were responsible for this change. One was the growing dependence of the northern economy on outside forces, and particularly on the British exchequer, after the Second World War. The region's traditional industries (including shipbuilding, linen and engineering) were in decline and new industry was being sought from outside. British central spending on health, education, social services, infrastructure and housing was increasing and unionists wanted to bring its benefits to Northern Ireland, not least to reinforce the case for the union. Economic dependency, however, came with a political price. The policies of the unionist government, including discrimination, were now exposed to greater scrutiny and unionists were more susceptible to political pressure from the British government. These developments coincided with a growing political capacity among northern Catholics, who began to create effective modern nationalist political party organizations only from the 1950s.

There were also changes in the wider geopolitical context. Britain's power and prestige in the international domain were at their height in the years immediately following the First World War. By the 1960s this position had slipped dramatically: the empire was gone, the economy was growing more slowly than its European counterparts, and its international role was uncertain in the wake of the Suez crisis and the French veto on entry into the Common Market. The British government was more dependent on international opinion than before, and, in a climate of increased concern with the rights of racial and ethnic minorities, it was vulnerable to the charge that it had turned a blind eye to discrimination in Northern Ireland. This coincided with a growth in the power and effectiveness of the Irish state. The power imbalance between the two states remained stark, but it was significantly less in the 1960s than it had been in the 1920s.

These changes offered northern Catholics and nationalists an exceptionally favourable context in which to seek to express their grievances. In 1967–68 they discovered a powerful weapon – peaceful, but vigorous, public agitation in support of a demand for 'civil rights' while relegating the issue of partition to the longer term.[11] This weapon proved dramatically successful. It split the unionist party into liberal reformers and hard-liners, destabilized the unionist government, provoked British government intervention to pressure unionists to introduce a strong reform programme and brought Northern Ireland to international attention and onto the British political agenda. When the unionist government failed to achieve stability, and in the wake of a British army atrocity (Bloody Sunday) which brought Irish and international anger, the British government abandoned its attempt to restabilize the situation through rule by a reformed unionist government and established direct rule in the spring of 1972.

British involvement, and particularly direct rule, provided the context for a further reduction in the imbalance of structural power between the two communities. As early as 1970, a reform programme was set in motion in local government (including measures to end gerrymandering and to reform the electoral system), in housing, in employment practices in the public and private sectors, in the security forces, and in access to the public policy process. The British government attempted to reintroduce devolved government, this time with cross-community support and links with the South, in 1973. Following the failure of this settlement, and of a series of others in subsequent years, the British government changed tack and concluded the Anglo-Irish Agreement (AIA) with the Irish government in 1985. This gave the Irish government a consultative role in the management of the affairs of Northern Ireland and the right to act as an advocate of the nationalist community there. It also paved the way for greater cultural equality – recognition of the Irish national and cultural identity of the Catholic community and a curbing of the rights of the Orange Order to march through Catholic areas.

These measures fell far short of delivering equality to Catholics – substantial inequality continued across all areas of social life – but they contributed to the further erosion of Protestant dominance. Stronger fair employment legislation (1989) began to even up the disparity in employment profiles, while pressure built for more radical approaches to tackle the substantive inequality between the two communities. The changes also contributed to increasing cultural confidence in the Catholic and nationalist population, an increasing effectiveness in selling the nationalist position abroad and gaining external allies, an increasing role for the Irish state in finding a settlement in Northern Ireland, and increasing effectiveness in the Irish government's dealings with the British government and international actors. This in turn strengthened the nationalist

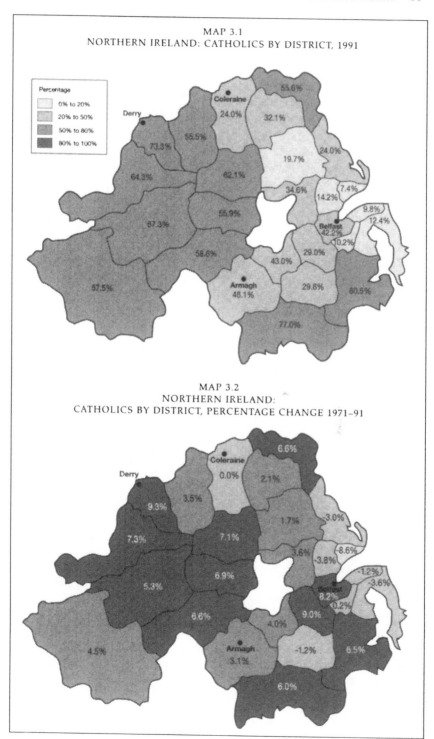

MAP 3.1
NORTHERN IRELAND: CATHOLICS BY DISTRICT, 1991

Percentage

- 0% to 20%
- 20% to 50%
- 50% to 80%
- 80% to 100%

MAP 3.2
NORTHERN IRELAND:
CATHOLICS BY DISTRICT, PERCENTAGE CHANGE 1971–91

political position. Eventually, following the Belfast Agreement of 1998, strong equality and human rights measures were implemented. 'Mainstreaming' of equality finally became a statutory duty on all public authorities in 1998.[12] A radical restructuring of the police was initiated in 2001, following the Patten Commission Report of 1999. A new Human Rights Commission was formed in 1999 and charged *inter alia* to propose a bill of rights which would respect the identity and ethos of both communities and provide 'parity of esteem'.[13] The Parades Commission was given greater powers.

The improvement in the Catholic position after 1985 also had an impact upon the demographic balance. The combination of a continued high birth rate and a reduction in the rate of emigration has led to an increase in the Catholic population – from just less than 37% of the total in 1971 to 42% in 1991 and, reportedly, to close to 45% in 2001. Demographic changes are correlated with changes in the political balance. In 1969 the vote for nationalist candidates in the Stormont election was less than 20%.[14] In 1999, the nationalist vote in the Assembly elections was nearly 40%, and in the 2001 Westminster elections, 42.7%.[15] The increased nationalist vote is only partly a consequence of the increasing Catholic population. It is also a function of the traditionally abstentionist republican constituency beginning to vote in the 1980s (with Sinn Fein's entry into electoral politics). It may also indicate increasing political apathy or lack of confidence and belief among some Protestants, who now seem to be more likely to abstain from voting.

These region-level changes have had a more complicated local patterning. The late 1960s and early 1970s saw massive population movements within Belfast as families migrated – frequently as a consequence of intimidation – into predominantly Protestant or predominantly Catholic areas.[16] This pattern has persisted, creating large tracts of territory which are now almost exclusively Protestant or Catholic (see Map 3.1). There has also been a tendency for Protestants to move from the predominantly Catholic West of the province to the predominantly Protestant East (see Map 3.2). This was accompanied and encouraged, during the 1970s and 1980s, by IRA attacks on Protestant members of the part-time security forces who often worked in rural areas or were farmers. More recently, there have been reports of systematic Protestant intimidation of Catholics and couples in mixed Catholic-Protestant marriages, forcing them to leave predominantly Protestant areas.[17]

The power balance between the two communities in Northern Ireland today is more finely tuned now than at any time in the past. The Catholic proportion of the population, about 45% by 2001, continues to rise; its position is strengthening in the economy, particularly at the middle and higher levels; the southern government is now actively involved in the management of the conflict; the economy of the Republic and its standing internationally continue to grow; northern Catholics have a sense of accomplishment and self-confidence unknown to previous generations; nationalist political support is stronger than ever before, and nationalist parties are more united on aims and policies now than at any time in the recent past.

Protestants are acutely conscious of Catholic and nationalist gains, the steadily increasing involvement of the Republic in their affairs and their own internal political divisions.[18] They continue to enjoy numerical superiority, particularly in the more strategic east of the province, but even here there is slippage. In all other respects, and particularly since 1998, their previously dominant position is being undermined. The sense of imminent defeat is reflected in unionist politics: divided and without a clear project to aim at, it is losing ground to nationalists. It is also reflected in the quality of contemporary loyalist protest: recent (2001–2002) loyalist demonstrations against small Catholic girls going to school in the Ardoyne district of Belfast – deeply counterproductive in terms of international sympathy – are indicative of a community which no longer has clear strategic aims.

THE SOURCES OF ETHNIC CONFLICT

As we have seen, ethnic conflict in Ireland has deep historical roots; it has been present in one form or another since the sixteenth and seventeenth centuries. There is continuity too in the forces that have made for such conflict – an intertwining of religious and cultural differences in a context of colonial displacement, the inscription of ethnoreligious difference in relations of power and inequality within Ireland and between Britain and Ireland, and a marked tendency towards communalist modes of identification and social organization. On the other hand, the specific form and expression of these factors has varied over time with changes in wider political, economic and cultural forces.

The current phase of ethnic conflict in Northern Ireland has to be seen within that long tradition, with both general and specific causes, historic resonances as well as strikingly contemporary themes. Each community constructs its identity out of the same set of overlapping, and in part coinciding, oppositions which have defined this conflict since the outset: Protestant versus Catholic in religion, Scottish or English versus Gaelic Irish in ethnic origin, settler versus native in geocultural provenance, and Irish versus British in national identity and allegiance. However, the oppositions which are now prioritized and the interpretations now given to them are shaped by contemporary trends in culture and ideology and by the current geopolitical context.

The religious aspects of the conflict are stressed today only by a minority within each community, notably by fundamentalist Protestants who see behind the political struggle of nationalist and unionist a much older and deeper struggle between Catholicism and Protestantism.[19] To confine the political significance of religion to this group, however, is to underestimate the importance of this dimension in the conflict. Religion permeates the conceptual understandings of both communities in Northern Ireland, including the world-views of many who see themselves as wholly secular; it is central to each community's self-definition and construction of its place in history. More than that, it is also a real and living force in the lives of a majority on both sides of the Irish border. The status of one's religion in the public domain, the extent of institutional support for it, the public respect accorded to it, and the freedom to act according to one's conscience, are not purely abstract matters or things to be taken for granted. The public sphere in both parts of Ireland is increasingly secular and pluralist, but this is a recent and still incomplete development, to be seen in the context of a virtual fusion of the political and the religious in the relatively recent past.

Ethnic origin also remains important. The communities are identified primarily using religious labels, and religion is the crucial determinant of communal membership. But religion and ethnic origin are seen as intimately intertwined. Each community has a sense of itself as of 'the same stock' ethnically, not simply religiously. This goes hand in hand with a recognition that there has been much intermixing in practice: the presence of family names in one community that 'belong' unambiguously to the other community (for example, Catholic Humes or Protestant Murphys) is testament to that. But this intermixing is seen as incidental, a matter of the idiosyncratic effects of individual life-histories, not something which counters the notion of distinct historic communities. The continued salience of ethnic origin is evident today in respect of language and cultural traditions. Each community sees itself in possession of a cultural legacy which defines its opposition to the other, which it attempts to foster and whose rights it affirms. Thus the remarkable, and highly politicized, revival in the Irish language in Northern Ireland in the last 30 years has provoked an attempt to revive, and to demand equality of status for, 'Ulster-Scots'.

The extent to which the northern communities construct their differences today in terms of the contrasting images of 'settlers' and 'natives' is more difficult to track, not least because the language of settler and native is now deemed to be 'extremist', especially in the context of the peace process. When used by Catholics, it is thought to imply an extreme republicanism with intimations of 'ethnic cleansing'; when used by Protestants, a denigratory or contemptuous attitude to Catholics is inferred. On the other hand, it is not difficult to find assumptions of settler-native distinctiveness in the ideological and emotional categories of both communities. The nationalist ideology to which many, perhaps most, Catholics subscribe in some degree views Protestant culture and religion as alien to the authentic and historic culture of the island. Popular loyalist and unionist constructions of history portray Protestants as the descendants of English and Scottish settlers who came to a barren land and developed it, despite attempts to drive them out by a backward and treacherous native population whose descendants even today refuse to live at peace with them.[20]

In contrast to the now submerged role of settler-native distinctions, the centrality of the opposition of nationalism and unionism is abundantly clear.[21] For some observers this is the only relevant distinction: the use of religious or ethnic labels to demarcate the communities is inappropriate and misleading. This, however, oversimplifies a complex reality, tending to reduce the conflict to a simple matter of opposing constitutional preferences. There is much more to both ideologies than that. Each represents a constitutional preference but also acts as a condensation of all the other oppositions. Nationalism constructs the Irish nation as predominantly – and at some level, essentially – Catholic, views the Gaelic strand in Irish culture as the dominant one and the Irish language as the native language of the island. The goal of Irish reunification and independence is not simply a constitutional preference, it encapsulates the redemptive political and cultural project of that nation. Unionism views Protestantism and Britishness as historically intertwined and both as inherently superior to Catholicism and Irishness. The British presence in Ireland – in the form of the state and a British-identifying community – is both legitimate and historically progressive, and the state (i.e. the union) is necessary to the well-being, indeed the survival, of that community. For the two communities, therefore, their nationalism or unionism represents the affirmation of a distinctive, deeply-felt, multidimensional and multilayered cultural and historic identity.

Conflict is, however, not simply about, or the product of, cultural difference. Now, as in the past, difference is inscribed in relations of power and inequality. That inequality is now diminishing, undermined by ever-stronger reform legislation and continued nationalist pressure. However, still today communal inequality may be seen in employment profiles and still more in the disproportionate unemployment among Catholic men, in membership of the security forces, in cultural capital and in the public culture, most notably in loyalist parades.[22] Contemporary struggles to overcome (or protect) this entrenched inequality highlight the salience of cultural differences, at the same time as they are interpreted in terms of the cultural oppositions.

Historically the power-inequality nexus was triangular in shape, involving the British state, Irish Protestants and Irish Catholics. The British government established and supported Protestant settlers in a dominant position in Ireland in exchange for their loyalty; Protestants as a vulnerable minority depended on British support to maintain their privileges and ensure their survival. Since partition, the structure of the conflict has been more complex: Protestants are still a minority at the level of the island as a whole, but are a majority in Northern Ireland; the majority of Catholics on the island are free of British rule and of Protestant dominance; the British government no longer has strategic interests in Ireland, or an interest in perpetuating Protestant dominance in Northern Ireland. But within Northern Ireland the old contradiction continued within the new framework: Catholics struggled to achieve (at the very least) equality in a context of Protestant dominance and insecurity, and of ultimate British control.

This contradiction is intensely experienced. Consciousness of inequality takes on multiple historical meanings. Whether focussed on blatant acts of discrimination, as in the civil rights period, or on the more pervasive lack of 'parity of esteem' for nationalists and republicans today, the northern Catholic community has a deep sense of grievance with roots in the distant past – northern Catholics see themselves as the group that suffered most from the colonizations of the seventeenth century, and from generations of economic discrimination and political oppression. When the rest of Ireland went on to independent statehood, they were faced with partition, endured the iniquities of the Stormont system and were reduced to the status of 'second-class' citizens in a state set up simply to accommodate the sectarian demands and threats of a minority community. 'Off our knees' was one of the slogans of the civil rights movement; 'No return to Stormont' has been the shared point of departure of all nationalist politics since the abolition of Northern Ireland's regional government and parliament in 1972. There is hope that some day Irish reunification will be achieved, but in the meantime and as a matter of priority the imperative is to undo the legacy of the past and remove the inequalities which still exist in the present.[23]

Northern Protestants bring to the conflict an opposed set of historical and contemporary understandings.[24] If they are in an advantaged position today – and not all accept that they are – it has nothing to do with the displacement of, or discrimination against, Catholics: it is the just reward for generations of hard work and enterprise, which Catholics could equally have engaged in if they so chose. On this view, the northern state is fully legitimate, the democratic creation of the majority in the north-east of the island of Ireland, a country without claim to a historic or 'natural' unity, which was only ever unified under British rule. If Catholics have experienced hardship in the past, on the unionist view, it is something they have largely brought upon themselves – by their unwillingness to work hard, their refusal to accept the legitimacy of the state, and their subversive or lawless activities. On its own understanding, from its establishment in Ireland, the Protestant community has been repeatedly threatened and attacked by Catholics and nationalists. This threat has never ceased: the Catholic demand for equality is seen as ultimately a demand for control in Northern Ireland, as a first step towards ending its very existence. With the disappearance of Northern Ireland as a distinctive political entity will go Protestants' last line of defence.

This intensely communal conflict – at once economic, political and cultural – is further complicated by the ambiguities and uncertainties that surround the role of the British state in Northern Ireland. This is both external and internal to the conflict.[25] Britain identifies with neither community, not even with the Protestant community which affirms both its loyalty and its Britishness. Since the 1970s, it has presented itself as a neutral arbiter of conflict; through the 1990s, it emphasized that it had 'no selfish strategic or economic interest' in Northern Ireland.[26] At the same time, the British state is an internal player of the greatest importance. Direct rule did not signal a radical departure from all aspects of previous practice. The British government continued to support and depend on local Protestant power to maintain stability: through police and reserve forces which were respectively over 90% and over 95% Protestant and whose role in security was extended by British policy from the mid-1970s; and by means of a judiciary and civil service both of which have been disproportionately manned by Protestants at the highest levels and which are only now in process of change – a process that is still incomplete.[27]

Moreover, even while the policies of the British state became more even-handed, particularly after 1985, this was much less true of the cultural and institutional consequences of its presence. This underwrote the British character of Northern Ireland evident in the functioning of its public institutions and its prevailing cultural tone and style. The national symbols and aspirations of northern nationalists might be formally recognized and accorded legitimacy, but the official culture and the dominant strain in the public culture remained British, even if state institutions in Northern Ireland have a somewhat different cultural form and style than in Great Britain.[28] As in every society, the state plays a central role in defining what constitutes cultural capital; in Northern Ireland, it did this in ways that meshed with the UK valuation of cultural capital, which defined British culture as superior to Irish culture. Since the Belfast Agreement of 1998, this has come more into public focus and dispute. Both communities are well aware of what is at stake. It is implicit in the unionist argument that their Britishness is inextricably bound up with and dependent upon the state being British. Nationalists may now be less likely to have Britishness imposed upon them, but it remains the context within which they must work.

At the level of policy, the British government has – for the most part – attempted to be even-handed between conflicting aims and demands. However, this has fed the conflict as much it has diminished it, encouraging each community to make stronger and more urgent demands on the assumption that it would at best get a part of what it asked for. Security policy deeply divides the communities. Unionists saw little need for reform of the security forces – indeed they saw such proposals as a betrayal of those who gave their lives to defend Northern Ireland. Nationalists insisted that the security forces be radically reformed or even disbanded. The outcome was a compromise, in which the police service was renamed, given more politically neutral symbols, and placed on course to become more representative of the population in terms of personnel.[29] Fair employment policy has been in contention between the communities, as has been a whole array of cultural policies, from the display of flags and emblems, to the proper role of the state broadcasting media, to the control of Orange marches through nationalist areas. At the same time the British government's policy of constitutional neutrality – its declared willingness to withdraw if that is the wish of the majority of the population of Northern Ireland – constitutes an arena for further communal struggle. If the increase in the Catholic population continues – as nationalists hope and unionists fear – it holds out the possibility of majority support for Irish unity while large sections of the Protestant community remain deeply hostile to it.[30]

Southern Ireland, and the goals and policies of the Irish government, form a further part of this jigsaw. At one level the Republic is outside the conflict: it is not the sovereign power and its primary concern as a government is the well-being of its own citizens. But it forms an integral part of the conditions of conflict: it represents the embodiment of one side of the set of cultural binaries which defines the conflict between the two northern communities; it is the state with which northern nationalists wish to unite; and it is the major power-holder on the island as a whole. In the recent period, and particularly in the Belfast Agreement of 10 April 1998, it has undertaken a wide range of initiatives to reassure unionists of its commitment to democratic principles and its respect for cultural pluralism, but the predominant relationship between unionists and the South – both at the level of government and of the wider public – is one of mutual antipathy. The South aspires to Irish unity despite, not because of, the presence of unionists; for their part the numbers of northern Protestants supporting Irish unity is of the order of 3%.

Nor is the impact of the Republic of Ireland on the conflict reducible to its northern policies. The Republic is a society in rapid change with many of the old certainties falling away. A decade of rapid economic development has called into question a host of traditional assumptions both about its economy and its culture, which is today increasingly consumerist and, at least in its public expression, 'post-Catholic'. It is not clear whether this process will continue or how far it will advance, and it is easy to exaggerate its progress thus far. But if it continues, its impact will be felt not simply in Northern Ireland, but throughout the British Isles. For much of its existence, the Republic's poor record as an independent state has disappointed northern nationalists while comforting unionists. It has also served as a cautionary tale to Scots contemplating an independent Scotland; today Scottish nationalists use Ireland to back their case for independence within the framework of the European Union. If Scotland seceded from the union, the status of Northern Ireland within it would inevitably come into question.

All of this makes the power balance between the two northern communities unstable. Apart from changes within Northern Ireland, cultural trends in Britain, Ireland and internationally have cast doubt on the traditional 'national' allies of the communities and opened new possibilities of international alliances, with Catholics and nationalists benefiting most from new allies in the European Union and the United States.[31] British reform programmes have affected the balance of power between the communities and, indirectly, the demographic and political balance, while the increasing role of the Irish government has functioned as a power resource for nationalists. These developments have eroded the Protestant and unionist position during the past two decades, but as the institutions of the Belfast Agreement begin to function, international support for nationalists may well become more attenuated. One way or another, however, the balance of power appears set to remain unstable, dependent on such volatile factors as communal self-confidence and organizational unity, on the interest and commitment of external allies, and on the direction and speed of reform and the complexion of government in Britain and Ireland.

So unstable a power balance contributes to conflict. Conflict in the past has been at its most intense when an increase in Catholic structural power (demographic, organizational, military and economic) has led to pressure for changes in political institutions to take account of this; it has come to an end when Catholic institutional and structural power have again been brought into line.[32] The most recent example of this was the civil rights movement of 1968-70 when Catholics harnessed the shift in the power balance which had taken place since 1921 to bring down the 1921 settlement. The crisis that followed inaugurated a period of uncertainty and instability; much of the recent conflict has been about determining the nature of the new power balance and its implications. The Belfast Agreement of 10 April 1998 initiates a period of stable equilibrium around a relatively equal power balance between nationalists and unionists (and between the two governments), but the extent of unionist opposition to the Agreement, and the difficulty of achieving agreement on specific policies even among the pro-Agreement parties, point to the limits of that stability.[33]

For the moment, therefore, the communal struggle goes on, among the pro-Agreement parties about the terms of the Agreement, and among the anti-Agreement parties about whether it should exist at all. Alongside this, sectarian conflict continues unabated at local level in the form of violence, intimidation and, in some areas, the forced movement of families to create ethnically homogeneous neighbourhoods. At this level, communal opposition is stronger now than it was 30 years ago, and in many respects it has increased since the peace process began.[34] Communal identification remains intense, and there is still evidence of the mechanisms of 'representative' violence or intimidation and 'communal deterrence' which Frank Wright identified as provoking self-perpetuating cycles of conflict.[35]

THE STATE RESPONSE: TERRITORIAL MANAGEMENT

The ethnic conflict in Ireland was initially constituted and later reproduced as one facet of a wider strategy of British territorial management. From the outset Ireland was just one of a network of territories, to be managed in its own terms and to the benefit of the Crown; later it formed part of a vast territorial domain, by far the largest empire of the modern period. The ethnic division was the consequence of the strategies employed by the English/British government to secure Ireland in the early modern period, and above all of the process of native displacement and colonial imposition. Once this had taken place, and once it was inevitable that the settlers and their descendants would remain a minority, ethnic conflict was deeply embedded – at once a problem to be managed, but also a resource to be used for purposes of territorial control.

The constitutional and political strategies used to manage Ireland and Irish divisions have varied with the evolution of constitutional forms in Britain and in the modern world, the resources available to the British government, and the immediate exigencies of the situation in Ireland. The flexibility of the constitutional frameworks used is a function of the British political tradition: constitutional unity – either within the empire or within the kingdom – was never a central virtue in British politics. One characteristic of British management of Ireland is, however, particularly striking: the extent of ambivalence and ambiguity about whether Ireland should be made part of the domestic or imperial domain. The dominant tendency has been to keep Ireland at one remove from the domestic sphere: the exception to this was the period of the union (1801–1921), though even then Ireland was treated as a distinct political and administrative entity. Before this Ireland was established as a separate kingdom with its own (subordinate) parliament; since 1921 southern Ireland has gone its separate way, and Northern Ireland has been kept at one remove from mainstream British politics.

This has remained the central thrust of British territorial policy. The British government's re-entry into the 'Irish situation' in 1969 was something forced upon it by the depth of the crisis and the possibility of political destabilization in both parts of Ireland. The initial hope of the then Labour government, and of the Conservative government which came to power in 1970, was to help the northern government to overcome the crisis, speed up the process of reform, and then return to the arm's length policy of the preceding period.[36] But the worsening of the security situation ruled this out, and as the British army became more and more deeply implicated in a steadily worsening security situation, direct political control from London became an imperative. At that point the whole settlement of 1921 came back onto the agenda.

There was, however, one important difference from the situation in 1921. There was now another established, fully independent, state system on the island with its own ethnic character and national and territorial imperatives. In the decades after 1921, the Irish state had harboured strong irredentist designs on the North, denying the legitimacy of the northern state and in its 1937 constitution declaring the island as a whole to be part of its national territory. On the other hand, apart from criticisms of unionist policies and of its treatment of the Catholic minority, and calls for reunification, the Irish government did not interfere in the North, and assisted in the suppression of republicans who attempted to subvert it. The southern desire for reunification and resentment at the mistreatment of northern nationalists were genuine, but in the face of unionist opposition to unity and British refusal to curb unionist excesses it was not clear what could be done. In any case there were more pressing concerns at home. From the 1920s to the 1960s, the southern government and wider society insulated itself from the North; the crisis of 1969 was as traumatic a development for the Republic as it was for Britain.

When the crisis first broke, the British government did not envisage any role for the Republic, other than cooperation on security. Britain was concerned that the Republic might try to exploit the opportunities created by the crisis to pursue its own agenda, as indeed some in the Irish government wished to do. The British view was that Northern Ireland was internal to the United Kingdom and a matter for the British government alone; the crisis was to be resolved within the existing framework of devolved government. It was only when the political and security crisis deepened, and it was clear that the Catholic community could neither be persuaded nor coerced back into a modified version of the status quo ante, that the British government accepted that something more radical would be needed. The abolition of the devolved Stormont institutions in 1972 and the establishment of direct rule was a recognition that the constitutional experiment of 1921–72 was over.

After 1972, the British government had four main options: complete withdrawal from Northern Ireland, full integration of Northern Ireland into the United Kingdom, repartition, or constructing a new form of devolved government. Withdrawal was not seriously contemplated. The British government had few if any emotional ties to Northern Ireland, or strategic reasons for being there. But it was the sovereign government in a territory which was not formally a colony – it could not allow itself to be driven out by the armed campaign of a small minority, in defiance of the wishes of the majority and with the likelihood of an ensuing civil war. Full integration into the UK was also unattractive: it would be strongly opposed by the Irish government, and in any case Northern Ireland was thought to be too different in political character from the rest of the UK to be absorbed into it. Nor was repartition a viable option, given the highly ethnically mixed character of Northern Ireland and the inevitability of leaving a large Catholic population in west Belfast in any reconstructed northern state.[37] Furthermore, repartition was opposed by all sides in Northern Ireland.

This left some form of devolution as the way forward. Successive British governments laid down two principles for a new devolved administration: on the one hand, a constitutional guarantee that Northern Ireland would remain part of the United Kingdom as long as that was the wish of a majority of its population; on the other hand, insistence that any new form of devolved government be acceptable to both communities.[38] Since nationalists would give this support only if a new settlement included power sharing, explicit recognition of their Irish identity and institutional linkages with the South of Ireland, 'power sharing plus an Irish dimension' became the effective goal of British policy.

Initially, this was conceived within the normal framework of British territorial management: as a form of local control within the British system which insulated British politics from the conflict in Northern Ireland. Power sharing might be innovative in normative terms (in involving both communities in Northern Ireland) but as a management strategy it involved no more than a change in the local administrators of the region. It was believed to require no more internal reform or reconstruction of Northern Ireland than had already been accomplished since 1969. The Irish dimension was seen by British governments at this time as largely symbolic: the British government had no principled objections to it as long as it did not infringe British sovereignty.[39]

For its part, the Irish government was positive about taking on a role in Northern Ireland. Its northern policy in the 1960s centred on reaching an accommodation with the unionist government and developing closer linkages with the North. The crisis of 1969 threw this policy into disarray and forced it back into the role of a putative defender of the nationalist community. But the resurgence of republicanism on a scale not seen since 1919–23 caused it to fear for its own stability and security. It had initially supported the attempts by northern nationalists to organize themselves and to procure arms to defend themselves against loyalist attack; in 1970 some government ministers went beyond this and were implicated in an attempt to import arms illegally for use in the North. But the tactics of the Provisional IRA and the scale of its campaign frightened the southern government. It could no longer ignore events in the North; but, in the face of general disorder and loyalist anger and violence, its traditional policy of reunification had to be set aside. A policy that delivered power-sharing within the North and gave the Irish state a role in northern affairs, without ruling out unity in the longer term, was an attractive alternative.

Any attempt to put such a settlement in place had, however, to reckon with the depth of unionist opposition to both power sharing and an Irish dimension. The first attempt to put such a settlement in place – the power sharing executive of 1973–74 – was brought down by an industrial strike organized by the Ulster Workers Council (UWC) backed by an open display of Protestant paramilitary strength. In the face of this challenge, the British government preferred to let the executive fall. But if it was unwilling to impose a settlement on unionists, neither was it willing to allow unionists to write their own. The result was a political stalemate that lasted for more than 20 years. This did not, however, prevent other policy initiatives. While awaiting the conditions for compromise, the British government pursued a dual strategy involving, on the one hand, intensified security using predominantly local Protestant security forces, and, on the other, measures (initially ineffective) to revive the northern economy and to address Catholic grievances about discrimination and inequality.

The need to fill the political vacuum thus remained. In the absence of a form of devolution that would be acceptable to both nationalists and unionists, the British and Irish governments began discussions in 1980 on a common way forward at intergovernmental level. The initiative came from the Irish government and was part of a wider attempt to reconceptualize the northern conflict as a joint Irish–British, rather than a solely British, concern.[40] The most ambitious Irish proposals envisaged the creation of a joint authority administration. These were firmly rebuffed by the British government, but senior British officials, and even Prime Minister Thatcher, were open to an increased Irish input into the policy-making process.[41]

Negotiations would prove difficult, due in part to intergovernmental differences unrelated to Northern Ireland, and US pressure on the British government was eventually to play a role in their resolution. But they finally bore fruit in the Anglo-Irish Agreement (AIA) of 1985. In addition to formalizing links between the two governments and providing the government of the Republic with a direct input into policy making in Northern Ireland through the Anglo-Irish Inter-Governmental Conference, the AIA marked a further shift in the terms in which the conflict was conceived and a solution was to be sought –

from an internal United Kingdom matter with an Irish dimension, to a joint British–Irish policy matter (though not one involving a shared constitutional responsibility).[42] It also helped speed up the reform process; legislation followed which focussed on remedying economic and cultural inequality.

The AIA was critical in breaking the political impasse, even if this did not happen immediately, by providing an incentive for both unionists and republicans to enter negotiations. Unionists deeply resented what they termed the 'diktat' of the AIA, the imposition of Irish influence on policy making (and therefore that of the moderate nationalist Social Democratic and Labour Party who were briefed by the Irish government), with no corresponding provision for unionists. They spent two years trying to bring it down (though not resorting to the extreme measures adopted to bring down the Sunningdale Agreement in 1974). When it became clear that the British government would not abandon the Agreement under duress, unionists determined to negotiate for its removal.[43] Republicans likewise saw the Agreement as a threat: they feared that the other parties would now negotiate a settlement which would make their own marginalization permanent. The increasingly important Irish role in Northern Ireland from 1985 onwards also suggested to them the possibility of a gradualist, incrementalist strategy towards Irish unity.

What began as a consultative process between the two governments regarding policy making thus developed into a more full-blooded binational process, in which the two governments set about working out the conditions for a settlement in association with the representatives of the two communities. This was the framework for the inter-party talks that took place between 1991 and 1993 involving the two governments and the 'constitutional' parties (those which were not associated with paramilitary groups). These talks ended in failure, but they soon gave way to the 'peace process' conceived again at two levels – the two governments and the two communities – but this time involving the political representatives of the main republican and loyalist paramilitary organizations and with the promise of ceasefires. The 1994 ceasefire of the IRA was broken in February 1996, but it was renewed in July 1997 and full negotiations got underway, resulting in the Belfast Agreement of April 1998.

The Belfast Agreement is a highly complex arrangement designed on the one hand to offer an interim settlement and on the other hand to provide a framework within which the conflict can be resolved in the longer term. As an interim settlement, it follows the broad parameters first set out in the 1970s: a guarantee of no constitutional change without majority consent, a power-sharing executive and an Irish dimension. However the detail and context make this a much more ambitious constitutional experiment than any of its predecessors.[44] The principle of majority consent to constitutional change is now enshrined in the Irish constitution, while there is provision for periodic referenda in Northern Ireland so that the majority will can be ascertained. There is a devolved assembly elected by proportional representation, with complex safeguards for minority rights, including parallel consent and weighted majority voting procedures to ensure cross-community consent on contentious matters. The new Northern Ireland executive includes a first and deputy first minister with identical powers elected by parallel consent (thus guaranteeing that the positions will be filled by a unionist and a nationalist acceptable to a majority on both sides) and ten ministers (the ministries are distributed in proportion to party strength in the Assembly by the d'Hondt mechanism). This is a broadly consociational structure which also leaves openings for non-communal political voices. The settlement is backed by strong equality legislation which, if fully implemented, promises to transform the structural inequality between the communities in Northern Ireland, and strong guarantees of protection of human and minority rights.[45] Equivalent guarantees of rights within the Irish state (and implicitly in any future united Ireland) are promised.

The Agreement also specified procedures to begin the process of reforming the police, as mentioned above, releasing paramilitary prisoners, demilitarization and decommissioning of parliamentary weapons. These are combined with a North–South Council and implementation bodies which, at least potentially, can allow gradual economic and administrative integration North and South, thus opening the possibility of a transition to Irish unity at some stage in the future. Meanwhile the Irish government maintains an influence on policy on non-devolved issues in Northern Ireland through a new British–Irish Inter-Governmental Conference. A British–Irish Council has been set up which (partially) balances the North–South Council in providing the potential for further integration and harmonization within the British Isles. In short, the Agreement provides at once for strong guarantees of individual rights, cultural and communal equality and rights, regional autonomy and an opening for further Irish national integration and a potential path to Irish unity; and it does this while guaranteeing unionist constitutional preferences for as long as they remain a majority in Northern Ireland.

The Belfast Agreement was ratified by large majorities in referenda North and South. Implementation was slow; the main institutions only began to function in December 1999, and thereafter suffered successive crises. Even with the beginning of IRA decommissioning in autumn 2001 the crises did not subside. Support for the Agreement remains very strong within the Catholic community in Northern Ireland, although their initial hopes that it may bring lasting peace have waned.[46] Protestants are much more divided. One of the major unionist parties opposes it, and support within the Protestant community has decreased since 1998.[47] The institutions are suspended for the fourth time, at the time of writing (November 2002) and even when they have functioned, continuing conflict and discard prevented them from functioning to their full potential.[48] Even more problematic are the contradictory foundations on which the Agreement rests: republicans believe that it weakens the union and hastens Irish unity, while unionist supporters of the Agreement believe that it strengthens the union.

These conflicting perspectives make all the more pressing the second level at which the Agreement is conceived: that of creating the conditions for the deeper resolution of the conflict. In the Agreement itself, this longer-term process is left vague: the Agreement is a 'new beginning' which may start what one of its main architects called 'a healing process'. More specifically, however, the provisions of the Agreement, if fully implemented, might be expected to produce wide-ranging changes in identities and allegiances in Northern Ireland. The harmonization of North and South, and the provision for strong equality legislation and a common human rights culture in each jurisdiction, could decouple the issues of national loyalty and allegiance from material fears and interests. The release of paramilitary prisoners, reform of policing, decommissioning and demilitarization should remove the war culture which characterized Northern Ireland for 30 years and added emotional intensity to national concerns. Voting procedures and referenda allow demographic change to be easily and smoothly translated into institutional and constitutional form. The reform programme, cultural equality and demilitarization promise to make the British state's role in Northern Ireland less a focus of conflict. All of these factors can encourage change in identities, interests, incentives for compromise and perhaps even allegiances.

CONCLUSION

In this chapter, we have traced the interactions between changing forms of territorial management and the character and intensity of ethnic conflict in Northern Ireland. In this case study, ethnic conflict is determined in a multiple way. Its sources include differences of religion, ethnic origin, settler/native provenance and nationality, structures of inequality, and the role of the British (and more recently Irish) state. The development of ethnic conflict has been crucially affected by the changing ethnic power balance; we have emphasized in the chapter that while the demographic balance is important it is only one part of (and is in fact responsive to) the wider balance of and struggle for ethnic power resources. These resources are only partially 'internal' to Northern Ireland: they implicate both the British and Irish states, and are constituted by wider state policies, international alliances and global processes.

All of these factors are relevant to the conditions for successful territorial management of conflict. Incentives for negotiation depend in part on the changing ethnic balance but this can be affected and stabilized by institutional innovation and international alliances. In Northern Ireland, the key factor underpinning the conditions for a settlement was the adoption of a binational approach by the British and Irish governments. The direct and indirect effects of this strategy were profound. It stimulated more radical reform within Northern Ireland and thus affected the internal power balance; it gained wider international support; it clarified the limits of power of each party; and it provided a means of countering the entrenched modus operandi of the British state in Northern Ireland.

The Belfast Agreement represents the culmination of these and other conjunctural factors – the new incentives to negotiate given at once by the Anglo Irish Agreement and by the changes in and clarification of the power balance; the wider international (particularly American) involvement in seeking a settlement; the increasing prosperity, status and pluralism of the Republic of Ireland, which contributed to a lessening of unionist fears; the election of a Labour government in Britain with a clear majority which removed from unionists the hope of holding the balance of power at Westminster; and the new constitutional changes in Wales and Scotland which allowed Northern Ireland to appear less anomalous (for unionists) and the union to appear weaker (for nationalists). These favourable British and Irish contexts and the helpful American conjuncture (identified with President Clinton's interest), together with the changed incentives for negotiation for the Northern Ireland parties, allowed an agreed settlement to emerge.

This does not mean that the conflict is now at an end. Far from it. The restoration of the devolved institutions and the stability of the Agreement are by no means assured. We have stressed the historic depth and structural embeddedness of this conflict. Present modes of territorial management have (partially) succeeded only because of the favourable balance of power and conjuncture; as these change, the chances of successful management of conflict are no longer guaranteed. The longer-term project of undercutting the conditions of conflict remains.

NOTES

1. For an extended discussion, see Joseph Ruane and Jennifer Todd, *The Dynamics of Conflict in Northern Ireland: Power, Conflict and Emancipation* (Cambridge: Cambridge University Press, 1996), pp.16–48, 204–14.
2. See Hugh Kearney, *The British Isles: A History of Four Nations* (Cambridge: Cambridge University Press, 1989), pp.106–27.
3. See Nicholas Canny, 'Early Modern Ireland, c. 1500–1700', in R.F. Foster (ed.), *The Oxford Illustrated History of Ireland* (Oxford: Oxford University Press, 1989), pp.104–60.
4. Louis Cullen, *The Emergence of Modern Ireland 1600–1900* (London: Batsford, 1981), pp.19–22.

5. Ibid., pp.210–33.
6. Thomas Bartlett, *The Fall and Rise of the Irish Nation: The Catholic Question 1690–1830* (Dublin: Gill and Macmillan, 1992), pp.45–65.
7. For outlines of the history of nationalist mobilization in Ireland, see Tom Garvin, *The Evolution of Irish Nationalist Politics* (Dublin: Gill and Macmillan, 1981); D. G. Boyce, *Nationalism in Ireland* (London: Croom Helm, 1982); and John Hutchinson, *The Dynamics of Cultural Nationalism: The Gaelic Revival and the Creation of the Irish Nation State* (London: Allen & Unwin, 1987).
8. For a discussion of the negotiation of the Anglo-Irish Treaty and the making of the Northern state, see Nicholas Mansergh, *The Unresolved Question: The Anglo-Irish Settlement and its Undoing 1912–1972* (London: Yale University Press, 1991).
9. John Whyte, 'How Much Discrimination Was There under the Unionist Regime?', in Tom Gallagher and James O'Connell (eds.), *Contemporary Irish Studies* (Manchester: Manchester University Press, 1983), pp.1–35.
10. See Ruane and Todd, *Dynamics*, pp.119–22, 139–44, 153–57, 166–70, 179–84.
11. For an account of the emergence, organization and actions of the civil rights movement in Northern Ireland, see Bob Purdie, *Politics in the Streets: The Origins of the Civil Rights Movement in Northern Ireland* (Belfast: Blackstaff, 1990).
12. Christopher McCrudden, 'Equality and the Good Friday Agreement', in Joseph Ruane and Jennifer Todd (eds.), *After the Good Friday Agreement: Analysing Political Change in Northern Ireland* (Dublin: University College Dublin Press, 1999), pp.96–121.
13. *Agreement Reached in the Multi-Party Negotiations*, 1998, section on Rights, Safeguards and Opportunities, paragraph 4.
14. The figure rises to 23% if we include all civil rights and Republican Labour candidates as nationalist (a description some of them would have resisted). For an analysis of voting figures over time, see Brendan O'Leary and John McGarry, *The Politics of Antagonism: Understanding Northern Ireland* (London: Athlone, Press, 1993), pp.170, 186.
15. Paul Mitchell, Brendan O'Leary and Geoffrey Evans, 'Northern Ireland: Flanking Extremists Bite the Moderates and Emerge in Their Clothes', *Parliamentary Affairs*, Vol.54 (2001), pp.725–42, at pp.733–4.
16. John Darby, *Intimidation and the Control of Conflict in Northern Ireland* (Dublin: Gill and Macmillan, 1986), pp.58–9.
17. See, for example, *Irish Times*, 3 July 1999.
18. See many of the interviews in Susan McKay, *Northern Protestants: An Unsettled People* (Belfast: Blackstaff, 2000).
19. For explicit religious motivations for conflict, see John D. Brewer with Gareth Higgins, *Anti-Catholicism in Northern Ireland 1600–1998: The Mote and the Beam* (Houndsmills: Macmillan, 1998). For the more pervasive effects of religion, see John Fulton, *The Tragedy of Belief: Division, Politics and Religion in Ireland* (Oxford: Clarendon, 1991).
20. The popular loyalist religio-political societies like the Loyal Orange Order or the Apprentice Boys of Derry explicitly refer to such settler origins in their symbolism.
21. For different interpretations of the significance of nationalism, see John McGarry and Brendan O'Leary, *Explaining Northern Ireland: Broken Images* (Oxford: Basil Blackwell, 1995), chapter 9, and Joseph Ruane and Jennifer Todd, 'Irish Nationalism and the Conflict in Northern Ireland' in David Miller (ed.), *Rethinking Northern Ireland: Culture, Ideology and Colonialism* (London: Longman, 1998), pp.55–69.
22. For analysis of the extent of inequality in Northern Ireland in the 1990s, see Ruane and Todd, *Dynamics*, pp.139–44, 166–70, 194–200. On the diminishing economic inequality in employment in 2000, see Equality Commission for Northern Ireland, *Monitoring Report no.11: A Profile of the Northern Ireland Workforce: Summary of Monitoring Returns 2000* (Belfast: Equality Commission, 2001).
23. Indeed, it is largely because of its strong equality provisions that republicans accepted the Good Friday Agreement of 10 April 1998.
24. For different aspects of the Protestant perspective, see D.P. Barritt and Charles F. Carter, *The Northern Ireland Problem: A Study in Group Relations* (Oxford: Oxford University Press, 1962), especially chapter 6; Tom Wilson, *Ulster: Conflict and Consent* (Oxford: Basil Blackwell, 1989), especially chapter 12; John Doyle, 'Workers and Outlaws: Unionism and Fair Employment in Northern Ireland', *Irish Political Studies*, Vol.9 (1994), pp.41–60.
25. For an overview of British policies see Michael J. Cunningham, *British Government*

Policy in Northern Ireland 1969–2000 (Manchester: Manchester University Press, 2001). For analyses of different aspects and periods of those policies, see O'Leary and McGarry, *Politics of Antagonism*; Paul Bew, Peter Gibbon and Henry Patterson, *The State in Northern Ireland 1921–94: Political Forces and Social Classes* (London: Serif, 1995); Ruane and Todd, *Dynamics*, pp.223–31.

26. The phrase was first used by Secretary of State Peter Brooke in the early 1990s; it was later incorporated into the 1993 Downing Street Declaration.
27. At the highest level of the Northern Ireland Civil Service (those on salaries exceeding £35,000 per year), only 14.6% were Catholic; see *A Profile of Senior Staff in the Northern Ireland Public Sector: Survey of Employment Patterns*, Fair Employment Commission Report (Belfast: Fair Employment Commission, nd [1990]), table 3, p.7. By 1995 this figure had improved, but only to 21%. Comparable figures are not available for the contemporary period, but in 2000, SOC 1 (professional) category, Catholics were 37.8% and in SOC 2 (managerial and administrative) category, Catholics were 28.9% of the overall workforce. See Equality Commission, *Monitoring Report No.11*, Table 25, p.28.
28. Especially after 1985, the public and official culture of Northern Ireland self-consciously diverged from the British 'mainstream', and this had been true of the media from the late 1960s; see David Butler, 'Broadcasting in a Divided Community' in Martin McLoone (ed.), *Culture, Identity and Broadcasting in Northern Ireland* (Belfast: Institute of Irish Studies, 1991), pp.99–103.
29. See *A New Beginning: Policing in Northern Ireland: The Report of the Independent Commission on Policing for Northern Ireland* (Belfast: HMSO, 1999). After much political debate in Northern Ireland, this report has been partially implemented.
30. In surveys between 1998 and 2000, Protestant resistance to a united Ireland appears to be moderating. Only about a quarter say they would find a united Ireland, should a majority in Northern Ireland so choose it, impossible to accept, while around the same percentage would happily accept it. See Life and Times Surveys, Political Attitudes module, Futures 1, www.qub.ac.uk/ss/csr/nilt.
31. Since September 2001, there are some indications that the Bush administration has been distancing itself from nationalism and showing a level of sympathy with unionist views. See 'Remarks by Richard N. Haas to the National Committee on American Foreign Policy', 9 January, 2002, New York City, in *Irish Times*, 10 Jan. 2002.
32. Joseph Ruane, 'The End of (Irish) History? Three Readings of the Current Conjuncture', in Ruane and Todd, *After the Good Friday Agreement*, pp.145–70.
33. See Joseph Ruane and Jennifer Todd, 'The Politics of Transition? Explaining Political Crises in the Implementation of the Belfast (Good Friday) Agreement', *Political Studies*, Vol. 49 (2001), pp.923–40.
34. Bernadette Hayes and Ian McAllister, 'Ethnonationalism, Public Opinion and the Good Friday Agreement', in Ruane and Todd, *After the Good Friday Agreement*, pp.30–48.
35. Frank Wright, *Northern Ireland: A Comparative Analysis* (Dublin: Gill and Macmillan, 1987).
36. For changing British strategies and assumptions, see Bew, Gibbon and Patterson, *The State in Northern Ireland*, pp.145–226; O'Leary and McGarry, *Politics of Antagonism*, pp.171–85.
37. Liam Kennedy, *Two Ulsters: A Case for Repartition* (Belfast: the author, 1986). State papers released by the British government in January 2003 showed that the repartition option had been briefly considered in 1972.
38. Cunningham, *British Government Policy*, pp.45–49; O'Leary and McGarry, *Politics of Antagonism*, p.194.
39. Just how substantive the Irish dimension was to be was neither prejudged by the British, nor agreed between British and Irish governments. A relatively substantive Irish dimension in 1973–4 was subsequently trimmed to a negligible role in the later 1970s. The Anglo-Irish Agreement of 1985 marked a new level of institutionalized Irish involvement. See Cunningham, *British Government Policy*.
40. From 1921, unionists tended to see the two states in Ireland as symmetrical, between which healthy competition was appropriate. The British political elite, too, had a tendency to see southern Ireland as a somehow 'semi-detached' part of the British system, not a real international actor. Initial cooperation between the governments in the 1970s did not mark a radical break from these assumptions. It was the later engage-

ment between the governments in the 1980s which marked the emergence of a binational approach, where the Republic of Ireland (in this respect) was seen as on a par
with the British rather than on a par with Northern Ireland and its regional administration.

41. Bew, Gibbon and Patterson, *State in Northern Ireland*, pp.192–226. For the Irish government perspective, see Garret FitzGerald, *All in a Life* (Dublin: Gill and Macmillan,
1991), pp.494–575.

42. McGarry and O'Leary, *Politics of Antagonism*, pp.220–76; Tom Hadden and Kevin
Boyle, *The Anglo-Irish Agreement: Commentary, Text, Official Review* (London: Sweet and
Maxwell, 1989).

43. In fact there was provision within the Anglo-Irish Agreement for the withdrawal of
the role of the Anglo-Irish Inter-Governmental Conference, and thus the role of the
Irish government, in sectors where devolution of power was agreed (Anglo-Irish
Agreement, article 2b). This was intended as an incentive for unionists to accept power
sharing devolution (see Fitzgerald, *All in a Life,* pp.533–4). Thus, nationalists, and in
particular the Irish government, willingly joined negotiations with unionists albeit
with the (different) understanding that they were aiming to fulfil, rather than to
replace, the Anglo-Irish Agreement.

44. See Brendan O'Leary, 'Assessing the British-Irish Agreement', *New Left Review*, No. 233
(1999), pp.66–96; Joseph Ruane and Jennifer Todd, 'The Belfast Agreement: Context,
Content, Consequences', in Ruane and Todd, *After the Good Friday Agreement*, pp.1–29;
Rick Wilford (ed.), *Aspects of the Belfast Agreement* (Oxford: Oxford University Press,
2001).

45. Christopher McCrudden, 'Equality and the Good Friday Agreement' in Ruane and
Todd, *After the Good Friday Agreement*, pp.96–121.

46. See for example, poll conducted by the *Belfast Telegraph* and *Independent*, and reported
in *Belfast Telegraph*, 25 May 2001.

47. Hayes and McAllister, 'Ethno-nationalism'.

48. Arthur Aughey, 'A New Beginning? The Prospects for a Politics of Civility in Northern
Ireland', in Ruane and Todd, *After the Good Friday Agreement*, pp.122–44.

4

Belgium

From Regionalism to Federalism

LIESBET HOOGHE

Ethnic conflict in Belgium has been intense, but peaceful. Its roots are linguistic: a majority of the population speaks Dutch, but the official language in the nineteenth century was French. Ethnic demands and conflict management strategies were initially non-territorial, but increasingly acquired a territorial aspect. The fact that Dutch- and French-speakers were to a large extent territorially segregated facilitated this evolution. At a later stage, ethnic conflict also acquired a socio-economic dimension. The increased territorial emphasis in ethnolinguistic politics had made the emergence of economic ethnonationalism easier and was in its turn reinforced by these later developments.

Each of the two forms of nationalism demanded a slightly different type of territorial settlement. This made the ethnic challenge ambivalent in two ways. First, language and socio-economic interests were treated as separate criteria in drawing and redrawing boundaries. Which was to have priority? Second, the two were to some extent contradictory. Was a territorial solution really the better choice for the management of ethnic conflict in Belgium, or did the nature of ethnic conflict call for a non-territorial solution? This ambiguity gave ammunition to those who sought to postpone or prevent territorial devolution.

Hence, political actors in Belgium had considerable leeway in dealing with the ethnic issue. This leeway was a consequence of the structure of the conflict, and the actors used it to their political advantage. Thus they were likely to change definitions of the groups-in-conflict when political opportunities altered. Furthermore, actors who favoured a territorial position on one occasion might be found to take a much less radical or even a non-territorial stand in another situation. Put differently, political actors in Belgium were prepared to draw and redraw boundaries such that inter-group contact was lessened, but only when it was to their advantage.

This chapter starts with a short historical introduction and data on the current ethno-linguistic balance. It continues with an analysis of the principal sources of ethnic conflict and change over time. The following section tries to show why the territorial approach became the dominant strategy for conflict management and how Belgium evolved from regionalism to federalism. Finally, this approach is placed in the broader context of political conflict management in Belgium. It is argued that federalism is an attempt to continue the traditional consociational approach by other means, but that the legacy of consociationalism is strong.

EMERGENCE OF THE ETHNIC PROBLEM

Belgium was created in 1830 when it seceded from the Netherlands after only 15 years of union. The national question in Belgium was initially defined as a language issue. Cultural deprivation spurred a Flemish movement, whose roots are to be found in the nineteenth century. After 1945 divergent economic developments between north and south gave rise to a Walloon nationalism. Finally, in the 1960s and 1970s the lines of conflict converged in and around Brussels, where a Francophone 'nationalist' movement became articulate.[1]

These different types of nationalism developed against the background of early industrialization and liberal democracy on the one hand and relatively late mass democracy on the other hand. This had important consequences. First, nationalism and the emergence of a modern society evolved quite independently in Belgium. In many European countries nationalist movements were pivotal in the break-up of the old regime and the diffusion of liberal democratic ideas. The Belgian state, however, was created by a coalition between traditional groups (nobility or landowners, and the Catholic Church) and new middle classes (industrialists and the intelligentsia). When this coalition broke down shortly after independence, politics rapidly became competitive. Nation-wide political parties were formed along the conservative (or, more precisely, Catholic)–liberal cleavage. Put differently, modern political cleavages and modern politics came first; nationalist movements appeared afterwards. New middle classes in search of political incorporation turned more readily to politics defined by the conventional Catholic–liberal or capital–labour cleavage than to nationalism. Hence nationalist movements took root only slowly in Belgian political life, and the older cleavages continued to cause divisions within them.

Second, the retarded breakthrough of mass democracy inhibited popular mobilization on the nationalist issue. Suffrage was limited to the upper classes until the last decade of the nineteenth century; the first elections according to the 'one man, one vote' principle were held in 1919.[2]

Third, the combination of early liberal democracy and late transition to mass democracy influenced the agenda of the early nationalist movements and has marked nationalist conflict to this day. Nationalists had little chance of becoming the major advocates of civil rights or social rights and democratization, let alone of monopolizing these issues. The Liberal Party had defended civil rights and the liberal secular state since the creation of Belgium.[3] Universal suffrage and better labour conditions were advanced by leftwing elements within the two traditional parties, and from the 1880s onwards also by a small socialist party. Nationalists played only a marginal role in this debate, especially since social and cultural grievances did not coincide geographically. The socio-economic cleavage was most salient in Wallonia, which was assimilated fairly smoothly to the Francophone culture of the Belgian state; the capital–labour conflict was much weaker in rural, Dutch-speaking Flanders.

Flemish nationalism was provoked by language grievances and remained very weak on the labour and agrarian issues throughout the nineteenth century. This thwarted mass mobilization. However, the small group of Flemish nationalists, most of them intellectuals or members of the higher middle class,[4] was successful in its narrow political agenda: by the end of the nineteenth century the Dutch language was accepted in Flemish public life and gradually replaced French in Flanders. Flemish nationalism 'imagined its community'[5] predominantly along cultural-linguistic lines. When universal suffrage was introduced, the Flemish nationalists again failed to reap the expanded mobilization potential. Democratization strengthened the Belgian Socialist Party and the Christian Democratic labour wing in the Belgian Catholic Party instead, groups that monopolized the socio-economic cleavage.[6] But democratization was also a deathblow for unilingually Francophone Belgium: a Flemish public life, complete with its own elite, emerged parallel to the Francophone one. Flemish nationalists had been demanding this since the 1850s, and have continued to imagine their community mainly in terms of these successful cultural-linguistic criteria.

After 1945 the industrial decline of Wallonia became apparent, and this sharpened Walloon regional consciousness (as distinct from a consciousness based on language). Walloon nationalism imagined its community primarily along socio-economic lines, and continues to do so.

THE ETHNO-LINGUISTIC BALANCE

In the Belgian census of 1846, 42.1% reported French as the language they spoke most frequently, 57.0% Dutch and 0.8% German.[7] In the Flemish provinces 2–4% reportedly spoke French only (most of these belonged to the upper classes).[8] The most recent official figures on language usage date from the census of 1947, and demonstrate how little the situation had changed by then.[9] Its general findings are reported in Table 4.1 and are illustrated in Map 4.1. It may be seen that Flanders and Wallonia were to a large extent linguistically homogeneous in 1947, especially when the 'unknowns' (most of them infants under two years) are disregarded. The 5% Francophone minority in Flanders was widely dispersed. However, critical masses were to be found in large cities (notably Antwerp, Ghent, Bruges and Louvain) and in some villages along the border with France or Wallonia. Detailed studies of their socio-economic background are lacking, but most Francophones reportedly belonged to the aristocracy, the upper bourgeoisie or the liberal professions.[10] In Wallonia, the most sizeable minority in 1947 was German speaking. The great majority of this group was to be found in the so-called East Cantons, which were acquired from Germany after the First World War. The Flemish minority in Wallonia consisted mostly of immigrants of lower economic status in a process of cultural assimilation. By contrast to the two larger regions, Brussels (within its current boundaries) had undergone significant changes since Belgian independence. Until well into the nineteenth century the Brussels area was predominantly Dutch speaking, but with urbanization and expansion Dutch was rapidly losing ground to French, which had clearly overtaken Dutch by 1947.

Language usage became a sensitive issue after 1947, to such a degree that subsequent population censuses no longer provided data in this area. It is therefore a rather risky enterprise to assess the current linguistic balance in the three regions. Linguistic homogeneity has

TABLE 4.1
BELGIUM: LINGUISTIC COMPOSITION BY REGION, 1947

Language	Flanders		Wallonia		Brussels		Belgium	
	000s	%	000s	%	000s	%	000s	%
Dutch	4,184.0	90.4	59.5	2.0	231.7	24.2	4,475.2	52.6
French	225.4	4.9	2,671.2	90.8	675.0	70.6	3,571.6	41.9
German	8.2	0.2	67.0	2.3	3.4	0.4	78.6	0.9
Unknown	198.6	4.3	145.4	4.9	45.9	4.8	389.9	4.6
Total	4,616.2	100.0	2,943.1	100.0	9,560.0	100.0	8,515.3	100.0

Note: Respondents were asked which language they spoke only or most frequently. Absolute figures are in thousands. More than 80% of the 'unknown' category were infants under two years of age; if included, the linguistic composition would be something like 55% Dutch-speaking and 44% French-speaking.

Source: Computed by the author from Nationaal Instituut voor de Statistiek (NIS), *Algemene Volkstelling op 31 december 1947: indeling naar de gesproken landstalen* (Brussels: NIS, 1954), pp.58–63, 72–3, 152–3.

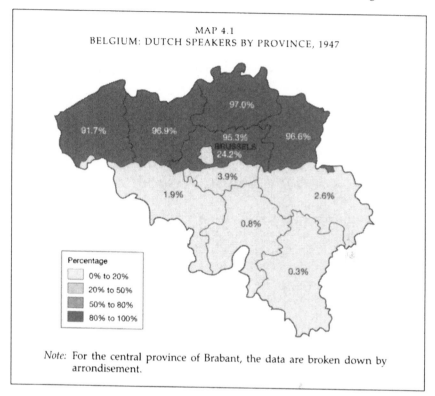

MAP 4.1
BELGIUM: DUTCH SPEAKERS BY PROVINCE, 1947

Note: For the central province of Brabant, the data are broken down by arrondisement.

undoubtedly increased in Flanders and Wallonia, and, of equal importance, the formally unilingual character of the two regions is no longer a political issue. This is to a large extent the result of the language law of 1963, which transferred 25 communes (with some 87,000 inhabitants) from Flanders to Wallonia, and 24 communes (with some 24,000 inhabitants) in the opposite direction. Many more meticulously defined bits of territory were transferred one way or the other across the linguistic border. The development of mass society also stimulated homogenization. In Wallonia, the Flemish immigrants quickly integrated. In Flanders, most Francophone families of elite backgrounds quietly adjusted to the change of language patterns: Dutch has become their working language, but their cultural identity seems to have remained primarily French-orientated. The one significant exception concerns Flemish municipalities adjacent to Brussels, where the Francophone presence has undoubtedly increased since the last census.

Language usage is still a sensitive question in and around the Brussels region. Many efforts were made to develop alternative measures of language use.[11] None of them seems to be reliable, although it is clear that *verfransing*, or assimilation to French culture, has continued in Brussels since 1947. Current estimates of the proportion of Dutch speakers fluctuate between 10 and 20% for the 19 municipalities that constitute the Brussels Capital region.[12] Passions run particularly high in six Flemish municipalities adjacent to Brussels (especially south of Brussels), where French-speakers constitute up to 30–50% of the population. These areas, formally part of the Flemish region, form a narrow territorial corridor between the predominantly French-speaking Brussels metropolis to the north and the unilingually French-speaking Walloon region to the south.

PRINCIPAL SOURCES OF INTER-ETHNIC TENSION

Interethnic conflict in Belgium does not resemble a simple two-actor game. There are three major games, each with a limited number of parties involved: Flemish nationalism versus French-speakers on cultural identity, Walloon nationalism versus Flanders and Brussels on socio-economic grievances, and (Francophone) Brussels versus the rest of the country on centre–periphery matters. Each game is played by rather distinctly defined actors. But the distinctions are small, making it hard to keep the games separate all the time. A singular feature of ethnic politics in Belgium is that the three games collapse regularly into a single game of Flemish against Walloons or Flemish-speakers against French-speakers.

Flemish Nationalism

While the constitution of 1831 guaranteed linguistic liberty, French became the only official language.[13] Soon after independence, however, some intellectuals in the Flemish provinces began to advance language grievances.[14] The first issues were purely linguistic and literary, but gradually the language grievances reached out to broader aspects of social life. Under Flemish pressure, language policy in Belgium evolved gradually from laissez-faire to language planning.

The first series of language laws of the late nineteenth century imposed asymmetrical bilingualism.[15] Flanders became bilingual, while the rest of the country remained unilingual. The legislation was limited in scope. The most important act symbolically was the Equalization Act of 1898, which made Dutch an official language on equal footing with French.[16]

The second wave of language laws, adopted in the 1930s, moved towards territorial unilingualism in Flanders and Wallonia and bilingual institutions in Brussels and in areas with linguistic minorities. The laws were more comprehensive than their nineteenth century predecessors. The switch to territorial unilingualism allowed Flemish and

Francophones (and especially French-speaking Walloons) to preserve their interests. Many Flemish feared that French would remain a highly attractive language for the leading classes in Flanders. The spread of French as 'the language spoken only or most frequently', in the terminology of the census reports, reached a maximum in the 1920s and 1930s: between 6 and 14% in the urban centres of Flanders.[17] Territorial unilingualism was to isolate this small, but strategic, Francophone minority in Flanders from Brussels and Wallonia. Walloons and Francophone Brussels residents feared that the alternative to territorial unilingualism, nation-wide bilingualism, would take jobs away from Francophones because of their poor knowledge of Dutch. Territorial unilingualism secured the essential: a unilingual Wallonia.

After the core law of 1932, which regulated the use of languages in the administration and in its dealings with the public, parliament passed language laws on education, judicial matters and the army. The different pieces of legislation rested on the same broad principles. First, official unilingualism was introduced in Flanders and Wallonia, but the boundaries could be adjusted after each language census. Municipalities with a significant official language minority offered certain public services in the minority language. Second, the general rule for the central public service was bilingualism of services but unilingualism of employees. Unilingual working units were created where possible, in order to restrict the number of bilingual positions. Third, Brussels was declared bilingual.

The law of 1932 and others in the 1930s were pivotal in transforming Flemish society into a Dutch-speaking community with a Dutch-speaking elite.[18] Flemish nationalists now perceived a Francophone threat on their boundaries. After each language census some Flemish territory was lost, especially around Brussels. In 1960–61 the language questions in the census were boycotted on a large scale by Flemish local government authorities.

These grievances, along with gaps in the previous language laws, led to the last series of laws, which were passed in the 1960s. They refined and hardened territorial unilingualism. Most significant was the 1963 law, which divided Belgium into four language areas: unilingually Dutch-speaking (Flanders), unilingually French-speaking (Wallonia) and unilingually German-speaking areas, and the bilingual area of Brussels.[19] Some municipalities on the two sides of the Flemish–Walloon border, six communes around Brussels and the German-speaking area retained some limited bilingual facilities. The 1963 law froze the linguistic frontier between Dutch-speaking Belgium, French-speaking Belgium and bilingual Belgium. But many Francophones have never accepted the freezing of the linguistic frontier around Brussels. Attempts to negotiate a permanent settlement for boundaries and linguistic minority rights around Brussels have failed consistently, most recently in 2001. The other contested area is Voeren, a conglomerate of six villages of altogether 5,000 inhabitants, the majority of whom now speak French, which was transferred from Wallonia to Flanders.

In the process of interaction with the Belgian-Francophone state and the emerging Francophone-Walloon movement the Flemish movement became nationalist. After the First World War cultural autonomy became the most urgent demand of the nationalist movement. In 1919 a genuine Flemish nationalist party, the *Frontpartij*, gained its first electoral success. In the 1930s, the *Vlaams Nationaal Verbond* (VNV) succeeded it. Its success forced the Catholic Party in Flanders to support demands for some form of cultural autonomy. Several Flemish nationalist leaders collaborated with the German occupiers during the Second World War. The Flemish movement made a fresh start in 1954, when a new Flemish party, the *Volksunie* (VU), entered parliament on a federalist platform. However, its breakthrough came only in 1965. The VU obtained its highest share of the vote in 1971 with 19.4% of the Flemish vote. The success of the Flemish nationalists at the polls gradually heightened Flemish–Francophone tensions in the traditional parties, which split along linguistic lines after 1968. The Flemish Christian Democrats and Socialists wrote federalism into their party programmes in the 1980s, while the Liberals remained more reluctant. The VU was damaged by this co-optation of their primary issue, and it has been declining since, obtaining its lowest result since 1965 in the November 1991 parliamentary elections: a mere 9.4% of the Flemish vote. Since then, its fortunes have waxed and waned; it obtained just over 10% of the vote in 1999 and ceased to exist in 2002. The VU also suffered from the defection of more extreme elements: in 1978, a breakaway group, the *Vlaams Blok*, entered parliament on a separatist and traditionalist platform. In the 1980s, elements moved the party to the radical right, espousing an anti-immigrant stance, Euro-scepticism, support for law and order, and for traditionalist values. These radical-right views overshadow its traditional Flemish separatist stance. Its support jumped from 3% of the Flemish vote in 1987 to 10.4% in 1991 and 15.5% in 1999.[20]

Walloon Nationalism

The breakthrough for Walloon nationalism came only after the Second World War,[21] and it was a reaction against Wallonia's economic decline in the twentieth century. The Walloon economy was dependent on the heavy steel and coal industries, which were rapidly losing importance after 1945. Light industry lagged behind in modernization or moved out of Wallonia and new industry tended to avoid the region.[22]

Uneven patterns of economic development and an increasingly negative demographic balance caused widespread resentment. First, Belgian high finance, which had made considerable profits in the heyday of

TABLE 4.2
BELGIUM: EVOLUTION OF GROSS DOMESTIC PRODUCT
AND GROSS REGIONAL PRODUCT, 1955–98

Year	Flanders	Wallonia	Brussels	Flanders	Wallonia	Brussels
	Share of GDP			*GRP per capita*		
1955	44.2	34.2	21.6	87.3	100.6	140.8
1963a	46.0	30.8	23.2	89.6	93.3	147.8
1963b	49.8	31.3	18.9	90.0	93.2	169.7
1970	53.9	29.1	17.0	96.0	88.9	152.6
1980	56.9	27.6	15.5	99.6	84.4	152.4
1988	58.7	26.3	15.0	101.9	80.8	152.6
1998	56.6	24.0	19.3	97.5	73.5	206.4

Note: The data refer to the share of each region in Gross Domestic Product (GDP), Gross Regional Product (GRP) per head (national=100), average yearly growth of GRP and average yearly increase of GRP per head. The Brussels region was reduced in 1963 and Flemish territory was expanded; the two series of figures on 1963 refer to the positions before and after this change.

Source: Computed by the author from NIS, *Statistische studiën*, No. 91 (Brussels: NIS, 1991), pp.76–83; for recent data: http://statbel.fgov.be/indicators/home_nl.asp.

Wallonia's industry, made few new investments and turned instead increasingly to Flanders. Flanders overtook Wallonia between 1963 and 1966 in terms of gross regional product (GRP) per capita (based on residence), and by the end of the 1980s had established a considerable lead, as may be seen from Table 4.2. This gap widened in the 1990s. Wallonia felt abandoned by high finance in Brussels and by Flanders.

Second, many Walloons were afraid of political domination by the Flemish, because the latter held a majority of the seats in the national parliament.[23] Table 4.3 shows that the Walloon population increased at a much slower pace than the Flemish. Until the 1970s this was mainly due to a significantly higher birth rate and higher life expectancy in Flanders. Although the two rates of natural increase have converged (the Flemish birth rate was even lower than the Walloon one for several years in the 1980s), it is expected that the share of Flanders in the total Belgian population will increase further due to earlier high birth rates in Flanders and to divergent migration patterns.

Walloons feared that in a unitary state the necessary restructuring of their economy would be done on Flemish terms. Political preferences in Wallonia have traditionally been more supportive of state intervention than in free market-oriented Flanders or Brussels. This was due to a larger socialist movement, but it can also be explained by divergences in the economic structure of the three regions. The general pattern of development was analogous in the two larger regions: near-disappearance of agriculture, decline of the industrial sector, and growth in the

TABLE 4.3
BELGIUM: DEMOGRAPHIC EVOLUTION BY REGION, 1947–2001

Year	Flanders	Wallonia	German Region	Brussels	Belgium
1947	4,552 (53.5)	2,950 (34.6)	54.8 (0.6)	956 (11.2)	8,512.2 (100.0)
1961	5,064 (55.1)	3,045 (33.1)	57.7 (0.6)	1,023 (11.1)	9,189.7 (100.0)
1971	5,417 (56.1)	3,102 (32.1)	62.0 (0.6)	1,075 (11.1)	9,650.9 (100.0)
1981	5,630 (57.2)	3,156 (32.0)	64.9 (0.7)	997 (10.1)	9,848.6 (100.0)
1991	5,769 (57.8)	3,188 (31.9)	67.6 (0.7)	954 (9.6)	9,978.7 (100.0)
2001	5,950 (58.0)	3,350 (32.6)	–	964 (9.4)	10,263 (100.0)

Note: Absolute figures are in thousands; figures in brackets are percentages. The 2001 projections for Wallonia include the German region.

Source: NIS, *Volkstelling, 1947, 1961, 1971, 1981; Belgisch Staatsblad,* 15 October 1991 (for 1991); www.statbel.fgov.be/figures/d21_fr.asp (for 2001).

tertiary sector. In 1966 the industrial and tertiary sectors were almost equally important in terms of their contribution to the GRP of Wallonia (46 and 48% respectively) and of Flanders (44 and 51%). By 1988 the tertiary sector accounted for 64% in Wallonia and the secondary sector had dropped to 35%. In Flanders the evolution had been less dramatic: 61% for the tertiary sector and almost 39% for industry. By 1995, the tertiary sector in Wallonia constituted 70%, against less than 28% for industry, while the figures for Flanders were respectively 65% and 33%. The standard of living in Brussels has traditionally been highly dependent on the tertiary sector (71% in 1966; 84% in 1988; and 81% in 1995). However, the evolution within each region has been different. Walloon industrial production has depended heavily on three sectors (the metallurgical industry, iron and steel, and construction), and all three experienced abrupt recessions in the 1970s or 1980s. Flemish industrial production was more diversified, was more often based in advanced sectors (the car industry, the chemical industry and electronics) and did not experience comparable setbacks. Similarly, the tertiary sector has developed differently in the three regions. In Wallonia, growth has been most pronounced in the services category (public services and education especially). Increase in Flanders has been more evenly spread over different categories. In Brussels, financial services and insurance have boomed. In a nutshell, tertiary growth in Flanders and Brussels has depended more on private initiative than in Wallonia.

The first serious challenge to the Belgian unitary state came from the Walloon movement. At a conference of all major Walloon and

Francophone leaders in 1945 an overwhelming majority opted for an autonomous Wallonia in a federal Belgium. However, the dust settled quickly and very little changed. Walloon nationalist party formation did not take place until the 1960s. In 1961, a popular Walloon labour leader broke away from the socialist party. His popular movement, *Mouvement populaire wallon*, carried a radical federalist and socialist platform. Four years later two Walloon nationalist parties each won a seat in the national parliament. In 1968, a new party, the *Rassemblement wallon* (RW), suddenly won 11% of the regional votes. However, in the 1980s the RW became almost completely absorbed by the Francophone socialists (PS) and Christian Democrats (PSC). In the 1980s the PS endorsed a radical federalist programme for economic autonomy. The nationalist parties in Wallonia obtained less than 2% of the regional vote in the elections of 1991, and they have disappeared since then.

The economic expansion programme of the 1950s and 1960s and subsequent decentralization of industrial policy and regional development in 1970 were in part a response to Walloon nationalist demands. The new structures respected the linguistic border between Flanders and Wallonia and became the first regional (as opposed to local) policy instruments. But genuine regional autonomy was not realized until the state reform of 1980.

The Defensive Reaction of Brussels

In the 1960s and 1970s the Flemish and Walloon movements transferred the battle about the appropriate state structure to Brussels, although there was also an independent Brussels component.[24] The two most significant features of the development of Brussels since independence are its expansion into the Flemish countryside and its becoming increasingly French-speaking, especially since the 1950s. Nearly one out of ten Belgians is an inhabitant of Brussels, approximately 85% of whose population is solidly French speaking. Approximately a quarter of French-speaking Belgians live in Brussels, but fewer than 3% of the Dutch-speaking Belgians do so.

As Flanders became solidly Dutch speaking in the 1960s and 1970s, the Flemish movement shifted its attention to Brussels. It seemed a logical step, because the expansion and *verfransing* of Brussels echoed the earlier Francophone threat to Flemish culture in Flanders. The Flemish movement won the first round in the 1960s. Expansion was stopped by the 1963 law, which defined the linguistic frontier. Creeping *verfransing* was made more difficult by the establishment of more rigid rules and more effective control mechanisms on the implementation of official bilingualism in the capital. But the Francophones reacted against this *cordon sanitaire* and the restraints upon their majority position in the capital. Brussels produced its own Francophone nationalist movement, the *Front démocratique des fran-*

cophones (FDF, founded in 1964), which at the height of its success in the 1970s obtained more than 35% of the votes in the Brussels metropolitan area. By 1991, however, its support had been reduced to approximately 12%, and in 1993 the party entered into a federal relationship with the local Liberal party. In 2002, the two parties merged.

Flemish and Francophones diverged on the appropriate institutions for bilingual Brussels, and its place in the Belgian constitutional structure. The Francophones of Brussels favoured an autonomous Brussels region. They found support in the Walloon nationalist movement, which wanted to transform Belgium into a federation of three regions. The Flemish movement was reluctant to accept a tripartite federal model. In an autonomous Brussels region the Flemish minority would be cut off from Flanders, which might put pressure on them to assimilate. At the national level Flanders could be pushed into a permanent minority position by a Francophone Brussels region and a Francophone Walloon region. It argued instead for federalism based on the two large communities.

Only in 1989 were Flemish and Francophones able to agree upon autonomous regional institutions for Brussels with special minority guarantees for the Flemish. The boundaries of the Brussels metropolitan area were confirmed without granting additional rights to the Francophones in the adjacent municipalities. However, for many Francophones from the Brussels area the debate is not closed, and by late 2002 the issue had not been resolved.

FROM REGIONALISM TO FEDERALISM

Belgium's unitary state structure resisted ethnic pressure until 1970, when the government declared before parliament that 'the unitary state, its structure and functioning as laid down by law, had become obsolete'.[25] Reform then came in three waves. In 1970 the existence of different territorial and cultural identities and the right to autonomy were constitutionally recognized. The second wave came in 1980, when the state was regionalized. The third wave of federalization began in 1989. The constitutional reform of 1989 stopped short of creating a federal state, but the 1993 reform formally characterized Belgium as a federal state. A mini-reform in 2001 further deepened federalization.

Intergroup Conflict Recognized, 1970

The constitutional revision of 1970 was the first significant institutional response to regionalism (or nationalism). The modification of the unitary state followed two distinct tracks: regionalization on the one hand, and acknowledgment of regionalist (or nationalist) aspirations in national-level institutions on the other. The reform attempted to protect the principle of unity of authority, which had for so long been characteristic of the Belgian state.

The first track concerned the recognition of the principle of language group rights at state level. The constitution entrenched four measures of power sharing between the two language groups. First, from 1970 on the government was to consist of an equal number of Dutch- and French-speaking ministers, taking decisions by consensus. Second, members of the national parliament were subdivided into separate Dutch and French language groups. Third, language policy legislation and certain constitutional laws were subject to special voting requirements (the presence of a majority of each language group, support by a majority within each, and an overall two-thirds majority of yes-votes). Fourth, an 'alarm bell procedure' was approved: if 75% of a language group judged a legislative proposal harmful to relations between the Flemish and French communities, the measure would be postponed and referred to the national government.

On the other hand, two models of devolved government were entrenched in the constitution: recognition was given to three distinct communities for cultural autonomy (French, Dutch – later renamed Flemish – and German) and to three regions for socio-economic autonomy (Flanders, Wallonia and Brussels). The proposed regional socio-economic autonomy was not implemented during the 1970s, but a limited form of cultural autonomy was put into effect in 1971 with the establishment of cultural councils for the communities, each with its own executive.

This cultural devolution was peculiar. First, it was the language groups in the national parliament that acted as the communal legislative bodies; the cultural councils were not elected separately. Second, the community executives remained part of the national government, which collectively was still fully responsible for the implementation of cultural policy legislation. The communities thus did not get a separate administrative apparatus.[26] Although Belgium gave up its formal unitary structure, the new system tried to maintain unity of authority by a conscious intertwining of central and regional/community levels.[27] This conflict management tactic of blending these two levels in personal, institutional or policy domains was repeatedly tried out in later reforms.

Regionalization, 1980

The reform of 1980 opted more unambiguously for regionalization. The cultural communities gained new competences, the socio-economic regions were given institutional infrastructures and regional autonomy in general was strengthened. But nationalist pressures, as in 1970, pushed the reform in conflicting directions: regionalization preserved unitary features, but at the same time adopted some federal or even confederal attributes. Communities and regions obtained separate institutions, including a separate executive and civil service.[28]

The regional reform of 1980 went beyond regionalization in several respects. First, legislative acts of the regional and community councils were given the same legal status as national laws. Second, Belgium opted for a devolution in which most competences of regions, communities or the national state were exclusive instead of concurrent. Regionalization established also a jurisdictional rather than a functional division of labour: a government would combine legislative authority and implementation. Each level had its field of interest, which was reserved exclusively for it. This is different from Germany, where the federation often sets the broader legislative framework but leaves more detailed legislation and administrative implementation to the *Länder*. The intention of this combination of separate institutions, equal legal status, exclusive competences and jurisdictional division of labour was to create 'watertight compartments', and this was meant to keep conflict low.

But at the same time, there were several features that continued to compel close interlocking between central and regional levels. For one thing, the regional and community councils were not directly elected, but continued to consist of the members of the language groups in the national parliament. So the same people exercised political control over national and regional executives. Second, the financial resources of the new structures, which were modest (less than 10% of public expenditure by 1988), came predominantly from block grants. Regions and communities had no significant financial responsibility. Third, policy areas were divided into thin slices that were then distributed among two or three arenas (central state, community or region) – not in coherent policy packages. Fourth, regionalization in Belgium combined constituent units based on the principle of territoriality (regional economy: two regions) and on the principle of nationality (language: three communities). Ethnoregional interests were thus institutionalized in two ways.[29] This made it more difficult for a unified regionalist counterforce to emerge.[30] Thus the blending of central, community and regional levels not only restricted regional autonomy; it also forced the different arenas to consult or collaborate to render policy making effective.

The 1980 reform combined efforts to segregate and equalize central and regional arenas with attempts to link them and maintain some hierarchy. The result was an unstable and destabilizing mechanism. The distribution of competences necessitated collaboration, but each arena's exclusive control over 'its' thin slice of a policy area complicated this. Furthermore, the divergent forms of institutionalization of ethnoregional interests created divisions: Flemish, Francophones, Walloons and

Bruxellois disagreed on whether the territorial or the nationality principle should take priority. These clashes contaminated the central level, which was divided along language lines.

Proto-Federalization, 1989

The reform of 1989 attempted to strike a new balance between centrifugal and centripetal tensions by opting for federalization. But similar tensions were built into the new model: a process of cooperative federalism was promoted in a constitutional framework of predominantly dual federalism (with exclusive competences and jurisdictional division of labour).

The reform gave effect to a considerable transfer of powers, with a division of labour between the federal level and the constituent units of the federation (community, region).[31] Allocation – that is, the delivery of public goods – was almost completely transferred to regions and communities. Communities or regions could now, for instance, subsidize cultural events, organize and pay for education, invest in a cleaner environment (within national and European norms), undertake public housing, and seek to attract industrial investment (within ceilings for aid or subsidies set at the federal and the European levels). The federal level retained control over the largest public utilities (such as the railways, telecommunications, postal services, the national airline, nuclear power plants and electricity). Stabilization – that is, manipulation of inflation, employment and economic growth levels through budgetary, fiscal and monetary policy – remained federal (or European). Redistribution (meaning, in effect, social security) continued to be fully federal.

The state reform of 1988–89 opted for a more systematic implementation of the dual federalism ('two worlds') model than that of 1980, but with a peculiar twitch. As usual under dual federalism, very few competencies were concurrent; most were exclusive. This reduces opportunities for the federal level to interfere with the regions and communities and vice versa. But the second component of dual federalism, according to which the division of powers runs along jurisdictional rather than functional lines, was weak. In several areas from environment to health to energy policy, the federal government retained control over the general legislative and fiscal framework, while detailed legislative and executive work was transferred to regions or communities.

Two more features induced cooperation. First, the 1989 reform intentionally limited fiscal devolution.[32] Regions and communities obtained only circumscribed fiscal autonomy: some fiscal powers, a mechanism for automatic funding and a solidarity mechanism, but no powers over tax scales and tax base. But they received considerable financial autonomy. That is, they gained limited powers to tax, but they received considerable discretion to spend their share of the total national budget, which was increased from less than 10% in 1980 to one-third in 1990. This fiscal power provided the national government some leverage over subnational policy.

Furthermore, the regional and community parliaments were composed of the members of the national parliament. For example, the Walloon regional council consisted of all members of the national parliament elected in Walloon constituencies. The French community council consisted of all members of the national parliament elected in Walloon constituencies as well as all French-speaking members of parliament elected in the Brussels bilingual region.

Relations between central and subnational were thus bound to be extensive, and effective policy making would necessitate mechanisms for cooperation. The state reform of 1989 created a deliberative structure to stimulate a cooperative federal process. The central institution for federal–regional–community relations was the Deliberation Committee (*Overlegorgaan* or *Comité de concertation*). The composition of the 12-member committee conformed to the 'double parity' rule: parity between federal and community/regional levels, and between Dutch and French speakers.[33] The German community voted on matters of its concern. The Deliberation Committee established more than a dozen Interministerial Conferences (IMCs) of functional ministers. They were authorized to conclude collaboration agreements, which are legally enforceable. Each IMC could set up working groups and commissions to prepare political meetings or handle technical decisions. These bodies consist of public servants or political aides of the minister (members of their *cabinet*), often assisted by experts. They may also include representatives from interest groups.

Federalization, 1993

With the constitutional reform of May 1993, Belgium finally became a federal state *de jure*. The revisions put in place the full panoply of institutions and mechanisms typical of a modern federation: direct election of regional councils; a senate representing constituent units' interests; residual competencies vested within constituent units; fiscal federalism (changes in financing mechanisms and more fiscal autonomy); constitutional autonomy for each level over its working rules; international competencies and treaty power; and coordination and conflict-resolution machinery.

The list of subnational competencies is extensive. Regions have competencies with a territorial logic. These consist of regional economic development, including employment policy; industrial restructuring; environment; nature conservation and rural development; housing, land-use planning and urban renewal; water resources and sewage; energy policy (except for national infrastructure and nuclear energy);

road building; waterways; regional airports and public local transport; local government; agriculture; and external trade. However, as under the 1989 rules, framework rule making remains federal in most of these areas. The communities have responsibility for matters related to individuals: culture (including arts, youth policy, tourism); language policy (except in communes with a special language regime); education (three-quarters of the community budget); health policy and welfare (but not social security); and international cooperation in these areas. The communities set the normative framework for culture and, with some exceptions, for education, autonomously. The list of exclusive federal competencies is short, though substantial: defence, justice, security, social security, and fiscal and monetary policy. Under European monetary union (EMU), monetary policy has largely shifted to the European Union and fiscal policy is considerably constrained by EMU criteria.

The basic blend of autonomy (exclusive competencies) and cooperative incentives (functional division of labour) remained unchanged. This is a blend that increases rather than reduces the chance of conflict. The lawmaker provides four arenas in which federal versus subnational or Flemish versus Walloon/Francophone interests can be addressed.

Federal institutions remain the prime venue for the resolution of much horizontal Flemish–Francophone conflict. Federalization has left the constitutional recognition of language group rights at the national level unchanged. The most important provision is that the federal cabinet must have an equal number of Flemish- and French-speaking ministers. And because the federal cabinet decides by consensus, this ensures the two large linguistic groups a veto at the federal level. The other non-majoritarian measures introduced by the 1970 state reform are also still in place: the two federal chambers are organized in language groups, sensitive legislation needs to pass with super-majorities, and an aggrieved language group can invoke the alarm bell procedure.

The second arena is the reformed senate, a hybrid of the American Senate and the German Bundesrat. It is composed of three groups: 40 directly elected senators (25 elected in the Flemish community and 15 in the French community); 21 delegated from regional and community councils, with 10 Flemish, 10 French-speakers and one German member; and six Flemish- and four French-speaking individuals appointed by the previous two groups. The Senate advises on conflicts of interest between the various governments. Although its decisions are not binding, its advice carries considerable political weight. It is not involved in ordinary legislation, in budgetary control, or parliamentary control over the federal government, but it plays a full role, together with the House of Representatives, in constitutional reform and legislation on the organization of the state.

The third arena for conflict regulation is the complex maze of intergovernmental relations, created in 1989 and strengthened in 1993.

Regional, community, and federal executives are intertwined through an elaborate network of collaborative agreements. The central institution in this executive network, the Deliberation Committee for the Government and the Executives, takes decisions by consensus. Although its decisions are not legally binding, its recommendations are difficult to reject because it consists of the political heavyweights of each government. The 1993 reform extended the scope of this network to international relations.[34] The core component is a 1993 cooperation agreement in the Interministerial Conference for External Affairs by the federal government, the three regional and the three community governments. It lays down the composition of the Belgian representation in the EU Council of Ministers and decision rules concerning negotiation strategy and voting in the absence of agreement among the governments from Belgium. Regions and communities are fully competent to regulate international cooperation within the scope of their competencies. This includes the power to conclude treaties. Detailed machinery arranges the coordination of a partitioned Belgian foreign policy. For EU policy, for example, the agreement divides the meetings of the council of ministers into four categories, depending on the relative importance of federal and regional competencies in a policy area. This categorization is then used to determine whether federal or subnational officials represent Belgium in the Council of Ministers and related council working groups. For areas with regional or community competence, regions and communities handle affairs on a rotation basis.

A final arena for territorial conflict resolution is the Court of Arbitration (set up in 1980, but significantly strengthened in 1989), a quasi-constitutional court composed of an equal number of judges or legal authoritative figures and former politicians (and an equal number of Dutch- and French-speakers.) It guards the legal division of competencies between the various levels of government, and it checks the conformity of federal laws and regional or community decrees with specific constitutional provisions (equality of all Belgians, protection of ideological and philosophical minorities, and freedom of education). However, it is considerably less powerful than the German, Canadian or US constitutional courts. For example, it cannot scrutinize the constitutionality of laws and decrees beyond the aforementioned three provisions.

Unlike the three previous reforms, the 1993 reform was presented as the final round in ethnic conflict management. Indeed, the intensity of Flemish–Francophone conflict has abated, and the pace of centrifugal change has slowed down. Nevertheless, senior politicians on either side still plead for further devolution, and some do not exclude full independence. Particularly among Flemish politicians of the right and centre-right, separatism is discussed as a viable option. A broad consensus has emerged among the political parties on either side of the linguistic divide to siphon off a few additional policy segments – in areas as diverse as education, agriculture, external trade and immigrant policy – from federal to regional or community control. This would strengthen the jurisdictional features of federalism. In June 2001, the parliament passed a near-complete regionalization, including rule making, of agriculture and external trade. Yet the most important changes are financial: regions obtain extensive fiscal autonomy, and the budget for the communities has increased considerably. Most financial changes will be phased in, but the bottom line is that the Belgian centre is set to shrink further, and federalism is due to take a decidedly dual-type turn.

INSTITUTIONAL PERSISTENCE:
THE CONSOCIATIONAL LEGACY AND TERRITORIAL SOLUTIONS

How does one make sense of this durable mix of cooperative and autonomist features in Belgian nationalist conflict management? Why has this mix been so resilient? This last section argues that the consociational tradition in Belgian politics is responsible for this.[35]

The Consociational Legacy: Cooperation and Separation

Consociationalism is a particular way of combining autonomy (or separate existence) with power sharing (or cooperation). The literature on consociationalism usually emphasizes power sharing, or to use the typical consociational term, elite accommodation. However, this underestimates the extent to which the incentives for a centrifugal, separatist course are embedded in a consociational logic. When the conflict is territorial, these centrifugal features may lead elite conflict managers to hollow out the centre.

Classical consociational devices to constrain majority rule specialize in maximizing benefits to the groups while minimizing loss of the centre. These mechanisms were initially developed to deal with religious and class conflict in Belgium, but from the 1960s they helped to contain nationalist conflict.

Carving up the centre: One way to achieve peace among competing groups is to give each group control over those central policies that matter most to them. Belgian conflict brokers traditionally applied this technique to the allocation of ministerial portfolios. They often gave big expenditure departments like defence, public works, or public housing to Walloon Socialist ministers, who could thereby create jobs for the declining Walloon economy. They allocated agriculture and culture to Flemish Christian Democrats, who wanted to satisfy their sizeable rural constituency or felt pressure from cultural nationalists.

Mutual checks: Mutual checks may be used when parties are not keen to vacate a central policy area. This technique was introduced first in education policy after the 'school war' in the 1950s to alleviate tensions between the Catholic private school network and the secular state network. The solution was to appoint a deputy minister for education from the side of the religious cleavage opposite to that of the minister. When in the early 1970s the ministry of education was divided along linguistic lines, this mutual check system was simply extended one level down. A non-Catholic became minister for education in the Flemish community with a Catholic deputy-minister at his side; in French-speaking Belgium, a Christian Democratic minister had a non-Catholic deputy. In this way, non-Catholics in Flanders were assured that they would not be discriminated against by the powerful Catholic network, while Catholics in Wallonia gained the same assurance with respect to the dominant non-Catholic state system. In the 1960s and 1970s, mutual checks became a more general feature when several ministerial departments introduced linguistic deputy ministers.

Allocating new resources: The centre may also buy off disaffected groups by putting more resources on the table. This technique was used to settle educational conflict after the school war in 1958, and at a high financial cost. It quickly became a widely used technique for buying nationalist peace as well. The Belgian centre released additional resources to fund linguistic quotas in public service and public procurement. One famous package deal was the construction of a new university in Louvain-la-Neuve to put to rest Flemish – Francophone conflict over the bilingual university of Leuven in the late 1960s. Another, in the 1980s, concerned the construction of a highway connecting two Walloon towns in exchange for a Flemish kindergarten in Comines (a Francophone commune with special language rights for Flemish speakers).

Each of these three techniques affects political cohesion differently. The first two – carving up policy, and mutual checks – make competing groups more interdependent. One cannot move without the consent of the other; this is *interlocking*. The latter strategy – to share out new resources – allows groups to go separate ways; this is *unlocking*. While the former two manipulate the balance of power *at the centre*, the latter manipulates power *between centre and groups*.

There is one catch to this system. These consociational devices are expensive. Partly as a result of this, Belgium has the highest public debt per head in the European Union. Public finance ran out of control in the late 1970s, a period of chronic nationalist conflict and social friction, governmental paralysis, and expensive deals between parties in power. As money ran out in the late 1970s, conflict managers introduced a new currency for making deals: while they used to trade goods (jobs, subsidies, infrastructure), penury forced them to start trading competencies (slices of authoritative decision making in such areas as culture, education, regional policy and environmental policy). It is not difficult into understand why this transition from goods to competencies occurred. In the late 1970s, nationalist conflict appeared close to descending into violence. Consociational techniques had successfully abated potentially violent religious conflict; they promised to achieve the same for potentially violent nationalist conflict.

But this consociationalist style of conflict management created an incentive structure in which nationalism became an attractive strategy. Even non-nationalist actors were tempted to raise the nationalist banner to bolster their case. This conflicts with the traditional argument of consociationalism scholars, who assume that elites always prefer compromise to conflict unless constituents force them into conflict. It is their prudent wisdom that justifies elitist governance in consociational regimes. In contrast, as George Tsebelis has argued forcefully, given a certain incentive structure it may be rational for elites to initiate nationalist conflict so as to maximize electoral utility. By the late 1970s, this situation had emerged in Belgium.[36] Nationalist demands became part of the standard competitive game between regional parties in Belgium.[37]

The consociationalist legacy was crucial in Belgian elites' capacity to contain nationalist conflict. They successfully exported consociational devices from religious to nationalist conflict, and they flexibly changed the currency for compromise from goods or money to competencies. The upshot of this is that nationalist conflict in Belgium avoided violence. However, this efficient and flexible response made it profitable for contending groups to perpetuate nationalist conflict. Consociational cooperation and group benefit became intimately linked to group separatism. As a result, the centre was being hollowed out.

Consociationalism and the Transition to Federalism

Why did the major parties in Belgium finally replace consociationalist devices by federal rules? One reason is that federalism offered them an opportunity to curb the creeping separatism embedded in consociationalist politics. Federalism became Belgium's best chance for survival. Another reason is that unchecked nationalist conflict had become a threat to the major parties' predominant position in Belgium. It is useful to remind oneself that Belgium has been a partitocracy, with a preponderant role for Christian Democrats and Socialists since the first half of the twentieth century. Party leaders – not governments, the electorate, or societal actors – have been the architects of all major reforms.[38] A top-down federal reform would allow these party leaders to design the rules in ways that would help them sustain their positions in authority.

From the standpoint of party leaders traditional consociational devices appeared less effective in contending with nationalist conflict than federalism. First. of all, consociational conflict resolution requires that elites represent relatively monolithic segments; opposition within a segment is destabilizing. Yet interparty competition within the regional or linguistic 'segments' undermined the dominant parties' authority. The Flemish Christian Democrats' capacity to deliver a deal was threatened by nationalist parties, and even by the nationalist outbidding from the Liberal and Socialist parties. The Walloon Socialists faced similar challenges in Wallonia from the regionalist movement and nationalist factions in the other mainstream parties. In a federal system, opposition within a region is institutionalized. Governments backed by a simple majority rather than near-unanimous support make and break deals. The Flemish Christian Democrats and the Walloon Socialists could anticipate being major coalition partners in governments of their respective regions.[39]

Second, consociationalism works best when government is limited. This is why consociational elites usually seek to hive off functions to semi-private segmental organizations. Yet nationalists ordinarily demand an expanding role for public authority – not limited government. Federalism can accommodate such demands for greater authoritative autonomy. The Flemish Christian Democrats wanted and received extensive community autonomy in education and cultural policy; the Walloon Socialists wanted and obtained extensive regional autonomy in economic development policy, industrial policy and public housing. The extent of federalization has been to a large extent a function of the particular policy preferences of these two dominant parties.

Finally, consociationalism requires a secure equal status among the segments. If the institutional mechanisms to prevent one segment from dominating the other are insecure, consociationalism may become a control regime.[40] A potentially destabilizing situation emerged in the 1970s, when the end of Flemish linguistic discrimination and the reversal of economic fortunes briefly tempted the Flemish demographic majority to pursue a majoritarian logic within a unitary Belgian framework. Federalism blocked these ambitions.

CONCLUSION

Federalism is Belgium's best chance for survival. Yet the political logic of dual federalism is stacked against the Belgian centre. The costs of unresolved territorial conflict are relatively low for regions and communities, while they are potentially considerable for the federal level. A weak federal level, composed of Flemish and Francophone representatives,

has an interest in preventing deadlocks. In a framework of dual federalism, it can do so most easily by shifting more competencies to regions
or communities. For example, throughout the 1990s Flemish politicians
have demanded the federalization of health insurance funds on grounds
of the principle of dual federalism. Since health policy is a competence
for the Flemish and Francophone communities, they argue, it is simply
more efficient to devolve all levers of health policy, including national
health insurance, to the communities. While the federal government has
held out so far, the logic of the Flemish argument is a powerful one in a
context of dual federalism with a non-existent autonomous federal level.
In 2001, the federal level gave way in two contentious policy areas – agriculture and external trade – but, more importantly, it was willing to take
out a mortgage on its hard-won financial solvency in return for placating
intense subnational demands for greater financial resources for education policy and greater fiscal autonomy. The financial deal, observers
agree, constitutes a total victory for communities and regions at the
expense of the federal treasury.[41] The hollowing of the Belgian centre is
likely to continue – if at a slower pace than under consociationalism.

NOTES

1. This account is largely based on L. Hooghe, *A Leap in the Dark: The Belgian Federal Reform* (Ithaca, NY: Cornell University Occasional Papers of Western Societies Program, No.27, 1991).
2. In 1893 suffrage was extended to all male citizens, but its democratizing effect was tempered by a system of plural voting based on educational and economic status.
3. The secular state was contested by one part only of the Catholic Party.
4. For an analysis of the social bases of early Flemish nationalism see M. Hroch, *Die Vorkämpfer der nationalen Bewegungen bei den kleinen Völkern Europas: eine vergleichende Analyse zur gesellschaftlichen Schichtung der patriotischen Gruppen* (Prague: Universita Karlova Praha, 1968), pp.103–12. Hroch categorized the Flemish nationalist movement among the unsuccessful cases, because it did not develop into a mass movement.
5. See B. Anderson, *Imagined Communities* (London: Verso, 1991).
6. The Flemish nationalists tried to build a fourth pillar (*zuil*) next to the christian, socialist and liberal *zuilen* in the interwar period, but the repression of Flemish nation-alism immediately after the Second World War thwarted these efforts. Hellemans defined a *zuil* as 'an ideological and subcultural, integrated network of several (more than two) organizations that are task-specific and enjoy a monopoly in the movement. One of these organizations is a political party'; see S. Hellemans, *Pleidooi voor een inter-nationale en tegen een provincialistische benadering van verzuiling* (Leuven: K.U. Leuven, Sociologisch Onderzoeksinstituut, 1990), p.26.
7. Infants were either classified in the language group of their parents or not counted at all; K. McRae, *Conflict and Compromise in Multilingual Societies: Belgium* (Waterloo: Wilfrid Laurier Press, 1986), pp.36–7.
8. McRae, *Conflict and Compromise*, p.40.
9. More recent population censuses do not have questions on language usage. During the 1947 census Flemish politicians accused census takers of pressuring Dutch-speakers to report themselves as French-speakers. In the subsequent census in 1960–61, grassroots mobilization among Flemish local authorities effectively boycotted the language questions in the census. The national government was forced to drop questions on language usage from subsequent population censuses.

10. McRae, *Conflict and Compromise*, pp.276–85.

11. For a discussion of alternative measurements see M. De Metsenaere, 'De taalver-houdingen sinds Hertoginnedal', *Taal en Sociale Integratie: het probleem Brussel sinds Hertoginnedal (1963)* (Brussels: VUB-Press, 1990), pp.37–57.

12. A figure somewhere in between these was suggested by the first direct election of the Council for the Brussels Capital Region in 1989, when the Dutch-speaking parties obtained 15.3% of the vote. All parties were required to submit unilingual lists. Due to the salience of linguistic issues in capital politics at that time, very few voters crossed linguistic lines, so that it seems reasonable to extrapolate this 15:85 proportion among voters to the population. This is more difficult for subsequent elections in 1994 and 1999, where there are signs of some linguistic crossvoting. Note that the figures refer here to Belgian citizens only; close to 30% of the Brussels population is non-Belgian, and most of this group prefers French in public life. In October 2000, EU citizens among these non-Belgians were able to vote for the first time in local elections, but only 10% of eligible voters registered. Mainly because of potential electoral implications in and around Brussels, the Flemish parties were extremely reluctant to support the 1993 Treaty of European Union, which grants non-national EU citizens voting rights in local and European elections. They finally agreed, though not before the Belgian government negotiated some exemptions. Registration for participation in these elections was extremely laborious, which helps explain why so few eligible voters registered.

13. This decision was taken by the Provisional Government, which was formed after the secession, on 16 October 1830.

14. See H. Elias, *Geschiedenis van de Vlaamse gedachte* 4 vols. (Antwerp: De Nederlandsche Boekhandel, 1970–71).

15. See P. Berckx, *150 jaar institutionele hervormingen in België* (Antwerp: Kluwer Rechtswetenschappen, 1990).

16. The official Dutch version of the Belgian Constitution obtained legal force under the law of 10 April 1967.

17. McRae, *Conflict and Compromise*, p.278.

18. W. Dewachter, 'Elite-circulatie en maatschappelijke ontvoogding. De Belgische elite tegenover de Vlaamse Beweging', *Tijdschrift voor Sociologie*, Vol.11, No.3–4 (1981), pp.199–258.

19. These were incorporated in the Belgian constitution in 1970.

20. B. Maddens, R. Beerten and J. Billiet, *Ethnocentrism and Nationalism: Towards a Contextual Approach* (Leuven: Departement Sociologie, ISPO, 1996); B. Maddens, J. Billiet and R. Beerten, 'National Identity and the Attitude towards Foreigners in Multi-National States: The Case of Belgium', *Journal of Ethnic and Migration Studies*, Vol.26, No.1 (2000), pp.45–60.

21. L. Genicot (ed.), *Histoire de la Wallonie* (Toulouse: Univers de la France et des pays francophones, 1973); H. Hasquin, *Historiographie et politique: essai sur l'histoire de Belgique et la Wallonie* (Charleroi: Institut Jules Destrée, 1982); C. Kesteloot, 'Stratégies wallonnes et francophones à Bruxelles', *Taal en sociale integratie* (Brussels: VUB, 1982), pp.445–80; A. Mommen, *The Belgian Economy in the 20th Century* (New York: Routledge, 1994); A. Murphy, 'Belgium: Regional Divergence along the Road to Federalism', in Graham Smith (ed.), *Federalism: The Multi-Ethnic Challenge* (London: Longman, 1995).

22. M. Quevit, *Les causes du déclin wallon* (Brussels: Editions vie ouvrière, 1978).

23. Kesteloot, 'Stratégies', pp.448–80; J. Tyssens, 'De *Mouvement populaire wallon* en de kwestie Brussel (1961–1964)', *Taal en sociale integratie* (Brussels: VUB, 1989), pp.373–401.

24. For the Brussels situation see especially the series *Taal en sociale integratie* from the *Centrum voor Interdisciplinair Onderzoek van de Brusselse Taaltoestanden*, Vrije Universiteit Brussel.

25. *Parlementaire Handelingen, Senaat, 1969–1970*, 18 Feb. 1970, pp.777–8.

26. In the meantime the central public service was increasingly reorganized along language lines. The public service had begun to create unilingual working units from the 1930s. It had also adopted a division of labour along language lines; for instance, Dutch-speaking public servants usually dealt with dossiers originating in the Dutch language area or drawn up in Dutch. This strategy was generalized through the 1960s and 1970s. The evolution was most drastic for the ministry of education and culture, which in 1963 was entirely restructured along language lines. In 1966 the two 'wings'

drew up separate budgets for the first time. In 1969 a French and a Dutch ministry of education and culture were established. Semi-federalization in 1980 transferred cultural policy almost completely to the communities; the administrative units for cultural matters were subsequently regionalized. The two national ministries were slimmed down to the ministry of Dutch-speaking education and the ministry of French-speaking education. Finally, in 1989 these two ministries were transferred to the Flemish and Francophone communities respectively. Note that partition in the 1960s preceded the first major move towards regionalization in 1970.

27. Berckx, *150 jaar*, p.150.
28. The Brussels region was not given separate institutions because the parties could not choose between the bipartite or tripartite model. They 'left Brussels in brackets', i.e. a subcabinet within the national government took care of the regional affairs of Brussels. The institutions of the Flemish region were merged with those of the Flemish (previously Dutch) community.
29. The third path was the national arena, where rules for linguistic parity in parliament, cabinet, national public service and most policy areas protected the linguistic groups.
30. The nationality principle did not mean that the communities had no territorial boundaries. Territorial delineations were fairly unambiguous; only in Brussels could persons or institutions choose their community adherence. To the Flemish community belonged the citizens of the Flemish region (including those who did not speak Dutch) and the Dutch-speakers in the Brussels region. The French community united the citizens of the Walloon region (including those who did not speak French) and the Francophones in the Brussels region. The German community consisted of a limited number of predominantly German-speaking municipalities in the east of the country. It was part of the Walloon region for regional matters.
31. D. Heremans and P. Van Rompuy, 'Economische beleidsautonomie voor Vlaanderen in het Europa van morgen', in P. Van Rompuy (ed.), *Vlaanderen op een kruispunt: sociologische, economische en staatsrechterlijke perspectieven* (Tielt: Lannoo, 1990), pp.152–74.
32. For an overview of fiscal policy since the 1989 reform, G. Stienlet, 'Institutional Reforms and Belgian Fiscal Policy in the 90s', in Rolf R. Strauch and Jürgen von Hagen (eds.), *Institutions, Politics and Fiscal Policy* (Boston/Dordrecht: Kluwer Academic Publishers, 1999), pp.215–34.
33. The committee consists of a six-member federal delegation headed by the prime minister and containing an equal number of Dutch and French speakers; two members of the Flemish executive (which represents both region and community), including its president; the presidents of the Walloon regional executive and of the Francophone community executive; and the French-speaking president and a Dutch-speaking member of the Brussels regional executive. The German community does not have a permanent seat, but takes part as a voting member on matters of concern to it.
34. Y. Devuyst, 'De omzetting van EG-richtlijnen in de Belgische rechtsorde en de Europeanisering van de Belgische politiek', *Res Publica*, Vol.35 (1993), pp.39–54; L. Hooghe, 'Belgian Federalism and the European Community', in Barry Jones and Michael Keating (eds.), *Regions in the European Community* (Oxford: Clarendon Press, 1995), pp.135–65; F. Ingelaere, 'The New Legislation on the International Relations of the Belgian Communities and Regions', *Studia Diplomatica*, Vol.47 (1994), pp.24–45.
35. This section is based on L. Hooghe, 'Hollowing the Center: Managing Territorial Conflict in Belgium', in Nancy Bermeo and Ugo Amoretti (eds.), *Does Federalism Matter? Political Institutions and the Management of Territorial Cleavages* (Baltimore, MD: Johns Hopkins University Press, forthcoming).
36. G. Tsebelis, 'Elite Interaction and Constitution Building in Consociational Democracies', *Journal of Theoretical Politics*, Vol.2, No.1 (1990), pp.5–29; see also M. Covell, 'Ethnic Conflict and Elite Bargaining: The Case of Belgium', *West European Politics*, Vol.4, No.3 (1981), pp.197–218; M. Covell, 'Agreeing to Disagree: Elite Bargaining and the Revision of the Belgian Constitution', *Canadian Journal of Political Science*, Vol.15 (1982), pp.451–69; M. Covell, 'Regionalization and Economic Crisis in Belgium: The Variable Origins of Centrifugal and Centripetal Forces', *Canadian Journal of Political Science*, Vol.19, No.2 (1986), pp.261–82.
37. K. Deschouwer, 'Falling Apart Together: The Changing Nature of Belgian Consociationalism 1961–1998', Paper prepared for presentation at the Conference *The*

Fate of Consociationalism in Western Europe, 1968–98, Harvard University, 29–31 May 1998.

38. See Deschouwer,' Falling Apart Together'; also K. Deschouwer, 'Waiting for the "Big One": The Uncertain Survival of the Belgian Parties and Party Systems', *Res Publica,* Vol.38 (1996), No.2, pp.295–306.

39. This proved to be a miscalculation for the Flemish Christian Democrats, who were relegated to the opposition benches after the 1999 election. But few would have anticipated their electoral demise at the time of the negotiations for federalization in the late 1980s and early 1990s.

40. Ian Lustick, 'Stability in Deeply Divided Societies: Consociationalism versus Control', *World Politics,* Vol.31 (1979), pp.325–44; see also B. Barry, 'The Consociational Model and its Dangers', *European Journal of Political Research,* Vol.3 (1975), pp.393–412.

41. See Jerry van Waterschoot, 'De verzwegen aderlating van Lambermont', *De Standaard,* 8 August 2001.

5

South Africa

The Failure of Ethnoterritorial Politics

ANTHONY EGAN and RUPERT TAYLOR

As the spotlight of international interest in ethnic conflict moves from one part of the globe to another in the early part of the twenty-first century, it tends to focus only fleetingly on South Africa. It is easy to forget that as recently as the 1990s South Africa was rarely out of its glare. The struggle for a new democratic political order that then reached its climax had simmered on for decades, with the rulers of the old South African regime having given a new word to the English language: *apartheid*.[1]

Apartheid represented a pernicious system of differentiation and domination; it was a system in which a privileged white minority – representing under a fifth of the total population – held sway over a disenfranchised black majority. For many years, under the old order, the promotion and defence of an ethnoterritorial agenda was central to the white minority rule of the National Party (NP) – first in informing the development of apartheid, then in charting an evolutionary consociational power-sharing reform agenda in the 1980s, and finally in influencing the NP's negotiating position on constitutional structures and mechanisms for a new South Africa. This chapter critically traces these developments, and highlights the circumstances associated with the failure of the National Party's strategy.

At the heart of apartheid thinking was a group-based philosophy of Afrikaner nationalism, rooted in Calvinism and German Romanticism, which viewed South Africa as a deeply divided society in which the existence of different ethnic groups 'was a God-given reality'.[2] As differing ethnic groups were seen to lack common cultural attributes, it was argued that 'separate development' had to be pursued, so as to reduce the potential for ethnic group contact and friction. 'Separate development', it came to be realized, could be implemented not only in terms of territorial considerations but also in broader terms of consociational social engineering, as the latter also assures that ethnic group identity and autonomy are recognized as being foremost. It is in this context that former President F.W. de Klerk strongly believed 'that in multicultural societies the assurance of group security was the key to inter-group peace. I was convinced that... offering a high degree of autonomy to the various population groups, was the best way to defuse the tremendous conflict potential in South Africa's complex society'.[3]

The National Party's approach, however, could not be defended in theory or practice; it served to perpetuate white minority privilege and was consistently incompatible with the demands of the main opposition movement – the African National Congress (ANC) – which through a non-racial politics that rejected the primacy of racial and ethnic group identity advocated a unitary, non-racial, democratic South Africa.[4] In fact, under apartheid, ethnoterritorial politics did not result in a genuine conflict resolution strategy, but actually created ethnic divisions where none had previously existed, and generated widespread opposition to ethnic politics such that today there is a general aversion to coupling ethnicity and territoriality. The bantustan strategy, which endeavoured to foster ethnic nationalism through the creation of homogenous national states ('black homelands'), simply served to deepen social inequalities and fuel political resistance. Likewise, the subsequent consociational agenda, which sought to develop corporate consociationalism alongside an embryonic territorial federalism, not only led to more intense resistance, but also effectively undermined any prospects for a strong federalist outcome to the constitutional negotiations of the 1990s.

COUPLING ETHNICITY AND TERRITORY: THE OLD SOUTH AFRICA

In the 1948 'whites-only' election the National Party, led by D.F. Malan, came to power on an electoral programme of apartheid. The essence of apartheid was segregation, but a more total form of segregation than had gone before; it was an ideology of exclusion and economic exploitation, which effectively instituted white privilege through the statutory differentiation of whites, Coloureds, Indians and Africans. More than this, through later appropriating concepts such as 'ethnic groups' and 'nations', Prime Minister H. F. Verwoerd moved to consolidate segregation into a rigid 'ethnonational' racially-based grand design. This had two strands, one territorial, the other non-territorial.

The Territorial Approach

Viewing history in terms of the God-given rights of the Afrikaner *volk* and other organic 'national' communities for ethnic self-determination,

Verwoerd redefined South Africa's population in terms of ethnic groups so as to develop the policy of 'separate development' whereby existing 'tribal reserves' could be transformed into sovereign 'national states', which in time could come to form a constellation of southern African states. Amongst Afrikaner leaders it was believed that this policy was 'the only means of avoiding the conflict that had been the cause of so much inter-ethnic violence in so many other plural societies throughout the world'.[5]

The clearest expression of the rationale for creating culturally homogenous national states, the so-called 'homelands' or bantustans,[6] was laid out in the 3,755-page Tomlinson Commission Report of 1955. This report stressed that there was a lack of common interests among African people, and argued that there were a number of 'Bantu' national organisms falling into various main ethnic groups, each of which should be able to run its own affairs.[7] Moreover, it was recommended that £104 million should be spent over ten years to finance the development of separate 'homelands', to make them economically viable.[8] On becoming Prime Minister in 1958, Verwoerd drew on aspects of this report, and without fully consulting the cabinet, formulated the 1959 Promotion of

MAP 5.1
SOUTH AFRICA: THE FORMER BANTUSTANS, TO 1994

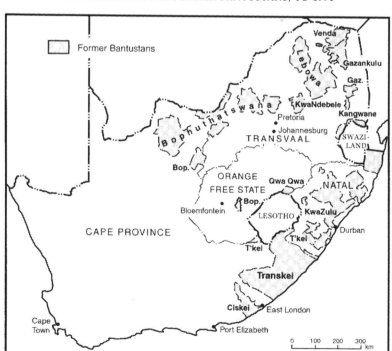

Bantu Self-Government Act. This act identified a number of distinct 'nations' that could progress through to political independence, thereby serving as a political alternative to granting citizenship rights within South Africa (and enabling apartheid functionaries to 'repatriate' those without work).

In time, building on the 'tribal reserves' of the early years of the twentieth century, and using the register of property rather than the census to determine boundaries,[9] ten bantustans were identified (see Map 5.1). Four of these – Transkei (1976), Bophuthatswana (1977), Venda (1979) and Ciskei (1981) – were granted 'independence'. The other bantustans were defined as 'self-governing states'. True to the ideology of apartheid, each of the bantustans was given its own national symbols, flag and emblems; as the Minister of Bantu Administration and Development stated to the House of Assembly in May 1963, 'It is one of the basic desires of the Bantu to have his own flag'.[10]

National Party policy dictated that all African people be allocated to their 'own' ethnic bantustan, even if they had never lived there. As Table 5.1 shows, there was a marked disjuncture between the *de facto* and *de jure* population of the bantustans; in Transkei, for instance, only 39% of the *de jure* population was located in the bantustan. None of the bantustans came close to being an ethnically homogenous 'national state'. Map 5.1 also shows that almost all bantustans were comprised of multiple and fragmented pieces of territory – bits and pieces that were allocated with little attention to serious economic planning criteria.[11] The demarcation of bantustans was supervised by the government, with the co-optation, wherever possible, of African traditional leaders, few of whom actually

TABLE 5.1

SOUTH AFRICA: MAIN ETHNIC GROUPS IN THE BANTUSTANS, c. 1976

Bantustan	Population	Ethnic Group	No. of ethnic group in bantustan	Population of ethnic group	% of group in bantustan
Bophuthatswana	1,154,000	Tswana	600,000	2,103,000	29
Ciskei	475,000	Xhosa	n.a.	872,000	n.a.
Gazankulu	333,000	Shangaan and Tsonga	234,000	814,000	29
Kangwane	209,000	Swazi	82,000	590,000	14
KwaNdebele	150,000	Ndebele	n.a.	n.a.	n.a.
KwaZulu	2,691,000	Zulu	2,057,000	5,029,000	41
Lebowa	1,388,000	North Sotho	946,000	2,234,000	42
QwaQwa	91,000	South Sotho	24,000	1,698,000	1
Transkei	2,391,000	Xhosa	1,651,000	4,250,000	39
Venda	339,000	Venda	239,000	449,000	53

Source: Adapted from Barbara Rogers, *Divide and Rule: South Africa's Bantustans* (London: IDAF, 1980), pp.36–7.

accepted the borders as satisfactory (although where the designated bantustan areas coincided with historical 'tribal' areas – such as Zululand or Transkei – there was greater acceptance).

Clearly, the bantustan strategy cannot be seen as a case of ethnic groups making territorial demands on the state; rather, it was a means by which the state carved up territory to insulate white rule. F.W. de Klerk has acknowledged that 'if the world and human beings did not conform to our vision, National Party ideologists would use their political power and all the devices of social engineering to force them to do so'.[12] When the bantustan strategy was first implemented the majority of African people did not live in their designated bantustan, but by the 1980s the bantustans housed over half of the country's African population.[13] This was achieved through large-scale population removals and resettlements.

Fundamental human rights were violated through the policy of forced removals. Regulated by the 'scientific' classifications of government ethnologists, millions of African people were uprooted to bantustan locations. Over a period of 25 years nearly four million people were forced to move, many of them several times over. Forced removals aimed to ensure that certain categories of African people were permanently placed in the bantustans: women and children, the old and sick, and the unemployed. In reality, bantustans were a dumping ground for white South Africa; as A.J. Christopher has suggested, this was a form of 'ethnic cleansing' by another name.[14]

National Party strategy resulted in African people being subject to severe inequalities. Social and economic conditions in the bantustans were dire; in general around '70% of households fell below the generally accepted poverty datum line, and disease and malnutrition were commonplace'.[15] Part of the problem was that African people constituted over 70% of the total population, yet the bantustans were disproportionately granted just under 14% of South Africa's surface area. Much of the land falling within the bantustans was significantly less fertile and considerably less industrially developed than that found in non-bantustan areas.

Mounting population densities in the bantustans accentuated problems, especially as apartheid urbanization policies resulted in the African population being bottled up within bantustan borders. During the 1960s the population of the bantustans increased from 4 million to 6.9 million, and by 1985 the figure stood at 14 million. With ever more people crowding onto the land, subsistence farming declined to a dramatic extent. An extensive study found that 'In many cases people are too poor to farm, they cannot afford protective fencing or even to buy seed and fertiliser. Tractors may be too expensive to hire and oxen too weak to plough'.[16] In QwaQwa, for example, in the early 1970s it was clear that only 15% of the area was suitable for farming, and much of that was used for resettlement camps. Attempts by bantustan authorities to rectify the situation, through the coercive implementation of soil conservation and land rehabilitation policies, failed to work and were often met with violent resistance. Beyond this, employment opportunities in the bantustans were few and far between.

The Tomlinson Commission recommended that employment opportunities be created in the 'Bantu areas', but there were only limited and far from adequate moves towards the creation of small-scale industries.[17] In the early years, the National Party only invested around a third of the sum that had been recommended by the Tomlinson Report. Little attempt was made to develop power and communication networks, and the Development Bank (through which central government controlled the pace of economic growth in bantustans) did little to encourage independent bantustan capital accumulation. Although bantustans came to attract some overseas investors and industries – notably from Taiwan – who were able to extract high profits from employing ultra-cheap unskilled labour and by taking full advantage of government subsidies, the bantustan policy was never economically viable.[18] The bantustans never accounted for more than around 5% of gross domestic product.[19] Not surprisingly, with such appalling agricultural and industrial conditions, bantustans were financially dependent on the South African parliament for over 70% of their budgets.[20] In return, the bantustans served South Africa with a huge army of cheap migrant labourers, numbering, at any one time, more than 1.5 million workers.[21]

Politically, the governmental structures of the bantustans were unilaterally imposed by the central state, and had 'no real power to affect the key issues within South African society'.[22] Internationally, none of the 'independent' bantustans was ever recognized. Within the bantustans power rested not with the people, but with the bureaucratized authority of chiefs and officials.[23] Popular support proved minimal and the cohesion of bantustan rule had to be engineered through 'patronage, nepotism, bribery, emergency regulations, developmental benefits and force'.[24] On the ground, possession of the ruling party membership card was 'the quickest and safest way of acquiring housing, land, business rights, jobs, pensions and disability grants'.[25] At a higher level bantustan leaders, despite inflated salaries and luxury extras, embezzled millions of rands in public funds; in the Transkei, for example, over 100 million rands went 'missing'.[26] Wide-ranging powers, including emergency laws, existed to curtail dissent and opposition. In Venda, for instance, the 'opposition' party won two elections in a row, but was kept out of office through detentions. All the same, the 'independent' bantustans became increasingly susceptible to military coup attempts. In sum, as Nelson Mandela recognized from the start: 'There is no sovereignty then. No autonomy. No democracy. No self-government. Nothing but a crude, empty fraud'.[27]

The workings of patronage, welfare provision and resource distribution did, however, play an important part in fostering class stratification and gave certain groups of people benefits and a stake in the bantustan system. In particular, the chiefs, party bureaucrats, local traders and small-scale entrepreneurs (in both 'formal' and 'informal' sectors) all gained from the bantustan policy.[28] Thus, the bantustan strategy worked to give ethnicity a material basis, and it is important to recognize that to some extent the National Party succeeded in enhancing ethnic consciousness. This was especially the case with regard to KwaZulu, where since 1975, under the leadership of Mangosuthu Buthelezi, Inkatha came to play a significant part in instilling and mobilizing a Zulu ethnic consciousness for political gain.[29] In the final years of apartheid KwaZulu was being subsidized by Pretoria to around 1,800 million rands per annum, and those millions of Zulu-speakers who wanted to qualify for KwaZulu welfare and employment schemes had little choice but to join Inkatha.[30]

Significantly, though, Buthelezi refused to accept 'independence' for the KwaZulu bantustan, claiming that he was concerned to challenge the system from within. Most anti-apartheid activists, however, entirely rejected participation in the bantustan structures on the grounds that the inherent divisiveness of NP strategy closed off the space for any progressive potential. Ethnonational politics was seen to perpetuate the ethos of apartheid, suppressing a broad inclusive nationalism and undermining efforts to create a genuinely egalitarian non-racial society. As Steve Biko, the Black Consciousness leader, wrote in the 1970s, 'No bantustan leader can tell me that he is acting at his own initiative when he enters the realms of bantustan politics. At this stage of our history we cannot have our struggle being tribalized through the creation of Zulu, Xhosa and Tswana politicians by the system'.[31] The divisiveness of the bantustan strategy was most apparent in the way in which ethnic discrimination came to the fore within bantustans – where, because bantustans were not ethnically homogenous, members of other ethnic groups faced discrimination in terms of access to jobs and social services. In the Winterveld area of Bophuthatswana, for example, the non-Tswana population were constantly harassed by Bophuthatswana police on the grounds of being 'illegal squatters'.[32]

Altogether, there can be no doubt that the bantustans were highly unstable entities, which increasingly became counter-productive to the interests of the apartheid state. In practice, the bantustans were resisted by the majority of their artificially-designated 'citizens', and NP strategy created conditions under which anti-apartheid resistance could only intensify. All major African movements – the ANC, Pan-Africanist Congress and Black Consciousness Movement – refused to accept the imputed political saliency of ethnic differences amongst African people. The ANC, in particular, strongly and consistently emphasized the building of a unitary non-racial South Africa which would safeguard individual rights.[33] Supporting this, sociological research into perceptions of ethnic identity has consistently revealed widespread rejection of ethnicity as a basis for political activity; many African people have not and do not see themselves as ethnic subjects.[34] The ethnonational project of 'separate development' failed to win the hearts and minds of those at whom it was directed. Given that the National Party's understanding of ethnicity was contrived, and that the bantustan strategy violated the Universal Declaration of Human Rights, this is not difficult to understand. The bantustans were not a basis for national self-determination but a means of turning an African majority/white minority relationship into one of a 'nation of minorities', so that around five million whites could maintain rule over 24 million Africans.[35]

Not surprisingly, once F.W. de Klerk removed the ban on the ANC in 1990 and the negotiations for a new South Africa began, many bantustans imploded.[36] The first of the 'independent' bantustans to collapse was the Transkei, which even before the ANC's unbanning was ruled by a pro-ANC leader, Bantu Holomisa (who had come to power in a military coup in 1987). In the Ciskei, the regime of Brigadier Oupa Gqozo voluntarily gave up power after civil servants went on strike. In Venda, a military coup in 1990 brought the pro-ANC Gabriel Ramushwana to power; and in Bophuthatswana, the last to hold out, local leader Lucas Mangope was bought down by a strike by civil servants and police in early 1994. Adrian Guelke has written that 'De Klerk's unbanning of the ANC... had much the same impact on the homelands as Gorbachev's abandonment of the Brezhnev doctrine had on the communist regimes of Eastern Europe',[37] but a crucial difference between nationalist movements in Eastern Europe and the bantustans was that whereas the former sought independence the latter sought re-incorporation.

As the transition from apartheid to democracy unfolded, the ANC called for the dismantling of the bantustans and their re-incorporation 'back' into South Africa, and the bantustan strategy was officially abandoned by the National Party. In particular, the ANC accepted that in order to carry through the process of re-incorporation they needed to identify and win over new partners within the bantustan structures, so as to counter the emergence of a conservative NP-led alliance comprised of traditional chiefs and the bantustan leaders. To this end, Nelson Mandela worked hard to attract notable chiefs and leaders towards the ANC, a task made smoother through the Congress of Traditional Leaders of South Africa (Contralesa) which since 1987 had sought to broaden the ANC's support base in rural areas.[38]

In the 'independent' bantustans it was the 'internal' security forces which played a crucial role in overthrowing the erstwhile regimes. Generally, though, the social dynamics of change revolved around the fact that because bantustan leaders operated 'less as middle class agents, than as intermediaries in a clientelist chain emanating outwards from Pretoria', they were out of touch and often in conflict with a pro-incorporationist middle class.[39] It was this disjuncture between the bantustan leadership and this section of the middle class that helped swing the 'battle' for political allegiance firmly towards the ANC. Would the end of the bantustans, though, signal the demise of ethnoterritorial politics?

The Non-Territorial Approach

The failure of the bantustan strategy was not unexpected to National Party leaders. Over the years there had been a growing recognition that an alternative strategy was needed. Behind the scenes, from the 1970s onwards, there was much serious debate over the future political structure and constitution of South Africa. From the National Party's perspective the primary objective was to avoid majoritarianism, and hence the ideas of consociational democracy were most attractive in charting a reform agenda. Importantly, within the realms of consociational social engineering, 'consociation can be defined as asymmetrical federalism, which is either territorial or nonterritorial'.[40] Consociationalism opened the potential for developing a form of group-based power sharing at the centre, alongside a form of federalism in which bantustan and non-bantustan areas could constitute states which are as ethnically homogenous as possible.

Consociational thinking strongly informed the constitutional changes that were put forward by the National Party following the Soweto Uprising of 1976, particularly in the P.W. Botha era.[41] The centrepiece of the reform agenda was a corporate and non-territorial blueprint; the 1983 Constitution which established a multi-racial tricameral parliament comprising the House of Assembly (the established white parliament), the House of Representatives (for Coloureds) and the House of Delegates (for Indians). The 1983 Constitution was advanced to deal with the problem of how to include the apartheid-designated Coloured and Indian racial groups in the political process, as the bantustan strategy could not feasibly be applied to these categories.[42] In terms of consociationalism, as the racial groups were predetermined and imposed from above, and because this design provided no opening to those people the state labelled black, the 1983 Constitution was a 'sham'.[43]

The 1983 Constitution, however, was also advanced in the context of developing a new approach to ethnoterritorial politics that sought to move away from bantustan boundaries. Not only was the political instability of the bantustans a cause for concern, but the impact of new patterns of capital and labour location dictated a more rational regional planning approach, especially with regard to urbanization. Thus, in 1983 the National Party, drawing on the work of the Development Bank, presented nine new 'development regions' demarcated in terms of 'nodal cores'. To hasten the development of this new framework, the NP also moved to create Regional Services Councils which placed African townships within bantustan areas in the same local government structures as adjacent non-bantustan metropolitan areas. This whole approach was presented in terms of being technocratically engineered, though it was still very much informed by ethnic criteria and largely embraced individual bantustans.[44] Gradually, leading *verligte* ('enlightened') NP politicians (notably Chris Heunis and Stoffel van der Merwe) moved to consider broader federal principles which would grant blacks and whites a shared common South African citizenship, but as events transpired the ethnoterritorial federal options were not given as much attention as they could have been.[45]

For, at the non-territorial level, the 1983 Constitution generated massive resistance. A broad oppositional alliance, the United Democratic Front (UDF), emerged and through being linked to ANC politics embarked on a national campaign to wreck the tricameral parliament and to force the apartheid state to institute non-racial democracy.[46] In reaction, states of emergency were declared from 1985 to 1990. In this period the police and military patrolled the townships, thousands of activists were detained without trial (often for up to two years), and death squads targeted opponents. On the ground, an intricate network of information gathering and political repression, the National Security Management System, was set up. At the top, the President's National Security Council often bypassed cabinet and parliament alike. For many opponents of apartheid, this became the real face of 'sham consociationalism'. Resistance did not abate. The ANC engaged in more and more armed action, and international economic sanctions damaged a weakening economy. Accordingly, from the mid-1980s onwards an uneasy 'stalemate' emerged which pushed senior National Party politicians towards making tentative covert and informal negotiations with the ANC. By the end of the 1980s the cabinet was split between hard-line 'securocrats' who sought a military solution and those who wanted negotiations.[47] The latter helped to oust President P.W. Botha (who was identified, at least publicly, more with the 'securocrats' than with the reformers) in late 1989 in favour of a negotiator, F.W. de Klerk, who, as earlier stated, on 2 February 1990 announced the unbanning of the ANC and other opposition movements.

DECOUPLING ETHNICITY AND TERRITORY: THE NEW SOUTH AFRICA

As the journey towards a negotiated settlement began, one of the most difficult and crucial questions was over the extent to which the new

South Africa would have a federal or unitary system.[48] The National Party entered the constitutional negotiation process at the Conference for a Democratic South Africa (Codesa) seeking to maintain the initiative by advocating a more genuine form of consociational power-sharing along with federal models within the context of a single national South African state.[49] F.W. de Klerk believed that strong regional government was 'the only way in which we can successfully accommodate the heterogeneous nature of our society in a meaningful manner'.[50] To this end, the National Party looked to building regional alliances with conservative bantustan leaders.

Reflecting the centrality of ethnic mobilization to Inkatha politics, the federalist position was taken furthest by Buthelezi, who advocated strong and wide-ranging devolution of powers to the provinces and special recognition of the Zulu monarchy. Inkatha argued that the country be called the 'Federal Republic of South Africa', and threatened secession if its demands were not met. In addition, there were proposals – often sounding like threats in some cases – from the white right-wing for a separate white state, a *volkstaat*.[51] In fact, in 1993, Inkatha (along with bantustan parties from Bophuthatswana and Ciskei) and far right-wing white parties came to form an *ad hoc* pressure group, the Freedom Alliance.[52] As it turned out, the basis for support of the Freedom Alliance was seriously undercut once the bantustan governments began to implode.

The ANC's position supported a majoritarian and strongly centralist constitutional structure. It argued that it was not so much a case of needing to recognize and protect ethnic diversity, but rather that such issues could best be dealt with through granting greater powers to centralizing authorities.[53] The ANC rejected the National Party's federal position because it was seen as 'a way of depriving majority rule in South Africa of any meaning, by drawing boundaries around race and ethnicity', and thereby preventing 'any economic restructuring of the country'.[54] For the ANC, the crucial point was that the new constitution should be a tool of transformation and social justice, not of conservation and inequality.[55]

In the negotiations, the debate over the federal versus unitary state form was resolved by a mutual recognition that there was a need for some degree of regional authority (with powers delegated from central government), and that, given the economic realities of South Africa, it did not make sense to take the bantustans as the basis for administrative units. It was resolved that the best starting-point would be to take the nine 'development regions' that had been drawn up by the Development Bank in the early 1980s. The outcome was that completely new provinces were created, the powers of which were subject to hard bargaining well into the final phases of the constitution-writing process. The issue of national versus provincial powers was the source of most

MAP 5.2
SOUTH AFRICA: NEW PROVINCES, 1994

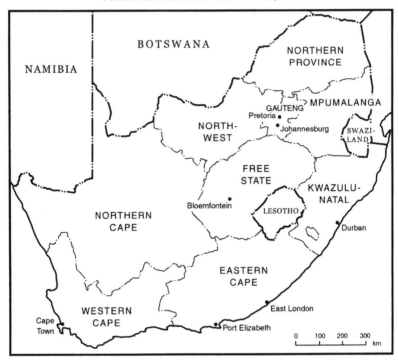

controversy for the Constitutional Court during the certification of the 1996 Constitution.

After much dispute, agreement was reached between the NP and ANC over the delimitation of nine provinces (see Map 5.2).[56] Of the four provinces that constituted the Union of South Africa, the physically large Cape and the numerically large Transvaal were split up into smaller geographical units. The Cape Province was split into the Western Cape, Northern Cape, and Eastern Cape (incorporating Transkei and Ciskei). The Transvaal was divided into the Northern Province (renamed Limpopo Province in February 2002), Gauteng (the Johannesburg-Pretoria area) and Mpumulanga, and its western parts were merged with part of the northern Cape and Bophuthatswana to become the province of North West. Natal became KwaZulu-Natal, and the Orange Free State was simply renamed the Free State.

This process was facilitated through the work of the Commission on the Demarcation/Delimitation of States, Provinces and Regions, which was established in late May 1993 and was given six weeks to hold public hearings and make its recommendations on new regional boundaries.[57] As the Commission saw it, the aim of provincial delimitation was 'the

reduction of territorial disparities in social and economic development...
and the prevention of negative forms of competition between regions',
particularly with regard to 'ethnic and chauvinistic' forces.[58] To what
degree, then, are the new South African boundaries based upon ethnic
considerations? Here, the closest approximation that can be offered is an
analysis of provinces according to home language.[59] The figures
according to the 1996 census are shown in Table 5.2.

Clearly the crude ethnoterritorial approach of the National Party, as
shown in Map 5.1, was swept away by the new provincial boundaries.
The consolidation of ethnonational politics was not the primary motiva-
tion behind regional delimitation. If it had been, demographic patterns
suggest that the current Western and Northern Cape Provinces would
have been joined into a more predominantly Afrikaans-speaking region,
with eastern parts of the Western Cape ceded to the mainly Xhosa-
speaking Eastern Cape and northern parts of the Northern Cape ceded
to North West, which might also have gained north-west Free State and
far-western Gauteng. Gauteng would have been more ethnically homogenous if it had been merged with Mpumulanga and possibly even with
KwaZulu-Natal. Following an overtly ethnic line, the new South Africa
would have looked very different. The nine new provinces are far less
congruent with the apartheid designated ethnic groups than were the
bantustans, and the degree of subnational heterogeneity is relatively
high. Although the Western Cape and Northern Cape did not incorporate any bantustans, in general there was no ethnically contrived
pattern. For example, the Northern Province incorporated three former
bantustans, and Gauteng none.

There were certainly no territorial concessions to the white far right.
Demands for a separate ethnic Afrikaner *volkstaat* were confounded by 'a
disorganised muddle of maps' attempting to locate *volkstaat* territory.[60]
The position of the extreme right, which coalesced around the Freedom

TABLE 5.2
SOUTH AFRICA: MAIN LANGUAGE GROUPS BY PROVINCE, 1996

Province	1st Language Group		2nd Language Group		3rd Language Group	
Eastern Cape	IsiXhosa	83.8	Afrikaans	9.6	English	3.7
Free State	Sesotho	62.1	Afrikaans	14.5	IsiXhosa	9.4
Gauteng	IsiZulu	21.5	Afrikaans	16.7	Sesotho	13.1
KwaZulu-Natal	IsiZulu	79.8	English	15.8	Afrikaans	1.6
Mpumulanga	SiSwati	30.0	IsiZulu	25.4	IsiNdebele	12.5
Northern Cape	Afrikaans	69.3	Setswana	19.9	IsiXhosa	6.3
Northern Province	Sepedi	52.7	Xitsonga	22.6	Tshivenda	15.5
North West	Setswana	67.2	Afrikaans	7.5	IsiXhosa	5.4
Western Cape	Afrikaans	59.2	English	20.3	IsiXhosa	19.1

Note: All figures are percentages.

Source: Statistics South Africa, *Census in Brief* (Pretoria: Statistics South Africa, 1998), p.11.

Front, was at first moderated by ANC openness in conceding space for the election of a *volkstaatraad*, a statutory council of 20 people, to look into the feasibility of a *volkstaat*. Subsequently, when in 1996 the ANC rejected a proposal for such a tenth province, the idea of an Afrikaner *volkstaat* had lost much of its appeal to most Afrikaners.[61] Reflecting this, the Freedom Front, which had received 2.2% of the national vote in the 1994 election, managed to secure only 0.8% in the 1999 election.[62]

Moreover, unlike the bantustan strategy, the new territorial politics has not created and fuelled ethnic antagonism. The one serious territorial flashpoint that has emerged is the area of Bushbuckridge, where the majority of people are Pedi- or Tsonga-speakers. Here there have been incidents of violent protest against the area's inclusion in Northern Province as opposed to Mpumulanga (where the majority are Swazi-speakers). The roots of this conflict lie in the fact that Mpumulanga is the richer province, better able to provide basic services to the community.[63] Bushbuckridge illustrates the extent to which material interests are more important than questions of ethnic identity.

It would be inaccurate, though, to conclude that purely technocratic considerations pertaining to natural and economic resources were uppermost in the drawing of the boundaries of the new provinces. The process was far more complex, and strategic calculations of the potential for racial and ethnic regional bloc voting and electoral alliances did play a part.[64] In particular, there was little attempt to territorially divide the bantustans, and the demographic composition of three of the new provinces – KwaZulu-Natal, Western Cape, Northern Cape – favour ethnically based politics. In KwaZulu-Natal support for Inkatha has been strong; in the 1994 election Inkatha won 50.3% of the regional vote to the ANC's 32.2%.[65] In the 1994 election, the National Party won the provincial ballot in the Western Cape with 53.3% of the vote, and came a strong second in the Northern Cape with 40.5% of the vote. Both of these provinces have a large Afrikaans-speaking population, the majority of whom were designated as Coloured by the apartheid state.[66] Here, the NP was able, in the context of the post-apartheid loss of preferential labour treatment, to exploit 'the dominance of ethnic chauvinism'.[67] The results of the June 1999 election indicate, however, declining electoral support for ethnically based politics; the ANC increased its share of the vote in KwaZulu-Natal by 7.2%, in the Western Cape by 9.1%, and in the Northern Cape by 14.6%.[68]

In any event, of fundamental import is the fact that the powers of the provinces as determined in the 'final' Constitution of 1996 are not designed to encourage ethnic politics, but are subject to a complex set of checks and balances between regional and central authority. Each of the provinces was granted a provincial legislature with executive powers with the scope to adopt its own constitution (including the right to establish provincial monarchs), and provincial governments can influence national legislation through a new 90-member second house of parliament, the National Council of Provinces; yet the overriding policy-making powers of the National Assembly are considerable. The 1996 Constitution does not describe the national and provincial levels of government as 'federal', but rather as 'cooperative government'. In fact, the 1996 Constitution does not conform to key consociational principles. Over the course of the constitutional negotiations the consociational agenda of the National Party collapsed. The NP moved away from its commitment to an ethnically defined group-orientated view of South African politics and society, and came to accept that a constitutional state in which individual rights are protected by a Bill of Rights provides sufficient safeguards for human liberty.[69] Apart from an openness in principle for Cultural Councils, recognition of traditional leaders, and provision for traditional structures of government (for those provinces which incorporated former bantustans), the 1996 Constitution does not reflect collective rights of a non-territorial kind.[70] In sum, the new South Africa is best characterized in terms of territorial centralism with some regionalism; the state has devolved some powers to the new provinces, but not for reasons of protecting ethnic group rights.[71]

CONCLUSION

As ethnic groups, ethnic identities and ethnic divisions have been insidiously constructed through apartheid, the South African case indicates that it is highly problematic to take it for granted that the starting-point for political and sociological understanding must be in terms of ethnic groups and 'ethnic conflict management'.[72] In South Africa under apartheid, it was not the case that subordinate ethnic groups demanded an equality rooted in territorial separation. Rather, ethnonational territorial division was imposed from above in the professed interests of equality, but in the real interests of continuing white rule. In the new South Africa equality has actually been premised on establishing formal equality before the law in terms of individual rights and a common citizenship, not in terms of ethnic group demands for recognition of separateness.

It remains to be seen as to whether political demands for ethnic group rights will re-emerge in the new South Africa, but given the history of past failures it is unlikely to be a major feature of the country's future. As Inkatha has moderated its ethnonationalism since the advent of democratic rule,[73] notably with Buthelezi being given a stake in national and non-racial politics (by being appointed Minister of Home Affairs), and as electoral support for the white far-right has all but collapsed, demands for ethnic group rights are no longer on the agenda. In the new South

Africa, ethnonationalism is not a primary and determining factor in people's political attitudes. A recent comprehensive attitude survey found that 63% of respondents argued that South Africa would eventually become a united nation, and a further 14% suggested that 'We are becoming a united nation', whereas only 22% agreed that 'South Africa will always be divided'.[74] In post-apartheid South Africa the political keywords are not ethnicity and nationalism, but non-racialism and transformation.

ACKNOWLEDGEMENTS

The authors wish to thank John Coakley, Adrian Guelke, Thabisi Hoeane, Tom Karis, Meshack Khosa and Stephen Louw for their comments on a draft version of this chapter.

NOTES

1. For historical background see Leonard Thompson, *A History of South Africa* (New Haven: Yale University Press, 1990); William Beinart, *Twentieth-Century South Africa* (Oxford: Oxford University Press, 1994).
2. See T. Dunbar Moodie, *The Rise of Afrikanerdom* (Berkeley, CA: University of California Press, 1975); Allister Sparks, *The Mind of South Africa: The Story of the Rise and Fall of Apartheid* (London: Heinemann, 1990), Chapter 7.
3. F.W. de Klerk, *The Last Trek – A New Beginning: The Autobiography* (London: Macmillan, 1998), p.108.
4. The ANC's struggle against apartheid involved South Africans of all racial and ethnic groups designated by the apartheid system; see Julie Frederikse, *The Unbreakable Thread: Non-Racialism in South Africa* (London: Zed, 1991).
5. de Klerk, *Last Trek*, p.16.
6. The term 'bantustan' is used, in this chapter, to indicate critical distance from the apartheid state's preferred term of 'homeland'.
7. The assumptions the report made were sweeping and historically inaccurate. The so-called 'Bantu' national organisms were themselves largely artificial constructs of European missionaries and colonial administrators.
8. See *Summary of the Report of the Commission for the Socio-Economic Development of the Bantu Areas within the Union of South Africa*, UG 61/1955 (Pretoria: Government Printer, 1955).
9. A. J. Christopher, 'Post-Apartheid South Africa and the Nation-State', in Anthony Lemon (ed.), *The Geography of Change in South Africa* (Chichester: Wiley, 1995), p.5; as Christopher adds, this is 'a situation only paralleled by the partition of Palestine in the 1940s'.
10. M. C. de Wet Nel quoted in Ben Maclennan, *Apartheid: The Lighter Side* (Cape Town: Chameleon, 1990), p.126.
11. In 1980 the ten bantustans comprised a total of 67 pieces. The apartheid state had long-term plans for consolidating the bantustans, but this encountered opposition from white farmers who wished to keep their profitable land.
12. de Klerk, *Last Trek*, p.40.
13. Laurine Platsky and Cherryl Walker, *The Surplus People: Forced Removals in South Africa* (Johannesburg: Ravan, 1985), p.18.
14. Christopher, 'Post-Apartheid South Africa', p.9.
15. Martin Murray, *The Revolution Deferred: The Painful Birth of Post-Apartheid South Africa* (London: Verso, 1994), p.63. Also see World Health Organization, *Apartheid and Health* (Geneva: World Health Organization, 1983).

16. Francis Wilson and Mamphela Ramphele, *Uprooting Poverty: The South African Challenge* (Cape Town: David Philip, 1989), p.41.
17. See Govan Mbeki, *The Peasants Revolt* (London: IDAF, 1984).
18. Primary emphasis was placed on establishing border industries in the existing urban areas, at considerable cost to the apartheid state. In the mid-1980s such activity cost Pretoria over 500 million rands; see Bertil Egerö, 'South Africa's Bantustans: From Dumping Grounds to Battlefronts', Discussion Paper 4 (Uppsala: Nordiska Afrikainstitutet, 1991).
19. Christopher, 'Post-Apartheid South Africa', p.10.
20. South African Institute of Race Relations, *Race Relations Survey* (Johannesburg: South African Institute of Race Relations, annual).
21. The migrant labour system severely undermined social and personal relationships; see Colin Murray, *Families Divided: The Impact of Migrant Labour in Lesotho* (Cambridge: Cambridge University Press, 1981).
22. Richard Turner, *The Eye of the Needle* (Johannesburg: Ravan, 1980), p.123.
23. Thomas G. Karis and Gail M. Gerhart, *From Protest to Challenge: A Documentary History of African Politics in South Africa, 1882–1990. Volume 5: Nadir and Resurgence, 1964–1979* (Pretoria: Unisa Press, 1997), pp.222–30.
24. Johann Graaff, 'Towards an Understanding of Bantustan Politics', in Nicoli Nattrass and Elisabeth Ardington (eds.), *The Political Economy of South Africa* (Cape Town: Oxford University Press, 1990), p.63.
25. Barry Streek, 'Disunity through the Bantustans', *South African Review Two* (Johannesburg: Ravan, 1984), p.261.
26. *Race Relations Survey, 1988/89*, pp.74–84.
27. Nelson Mandela, *No Easy Walk to Freedom* (London: Heinemann, 1965), p.73.
28. Alf Stadler, *The Political Economy of Modern South Africa* (Cape Town: David Philip, 1987).
29. Gerhard Maré and Georgina Hamilton, *An Appetite for Power: Buthelezi's Inkatha and the Politics of 'Loyal Resistance'* (Johannesburg: Ravan, 1987). In 1990 Inkatha was renamed the Inkatha Freedom Party (IFP).
30. *Race Relations Survey, 1988/89*, pp.61–74; Mzala, *Gatsha Buthelezi: Chief with a Double Agenda* (London: Zed, 1988), pp.128–33.
31. Steve Biko, *I Write What I Like* (Harmondsworth: Penguin, 1988), p.101.
32. William F. Lye and Colin Murray, *Transformations on the Highveld: The Tswana and Southern Sotho* (Cape Town: David Philip, 1980), p.100. Also consider National Land Committee, *The Bantustans in Crisis* (Johannesburg: National Land Committee, 1990).
33. See Maria van Diepen (ed.), *The National Question in South Africa* (London: Zed, 1988).
34. Philip Mayer, 'Class, Status and Ethnicity as Perceived by Johannesburg Africans', in L. Thompson and J. Butler (eds.), *Change in Contemporary South Africa* (Berkeley, CA: University of California Press, 1975), pp.138–67; Lynette Dreyer, *The Modern African Elite of South Africa* (London: Macmillan, 1989), pp.97–107.
35. This is to cite official apartheid population statistics; Bureau of Information [South Africa], *South African Profile*, July 1987.
36. Jeff Peires, 'The Implosion of the Transkei and Ciskei', *African Affairs*, Vol. 91 (1992), pp.365–87.
37. Adrian Guelke, 'Ethnic Rights and Majority Rule: The Case of South Africa', *International Political Science Review*, Vol. 13, No. 4 (1992), p.426.
38. Ineke van Kessel and Barbara Oomen, '"One Chief, One Vote": The Revival of Traditional Authorities in Post-Apartheid South Africa', *African Affairs*, Vol. 96 (1997), pp.561–85. Thus, for example, both Holomisa and Ramushwana were given ANC seats in Parliament (1994).
39. Leslie Bank, 'Between Traders and Tribalists: Implosion and the Politics of Disjuncture in a South African Homeland', *African Affairs*, Vol. 93 (1994), pp.75–98. The quotation is taken from p.76.
40. Arend Lijphart, 'Federal, Confederal, and Consociational Options for the South African Plural Society', in Robert I. Rotberg and John Barratt (eds.), *Conflict and Compromise in South Africa* (Cape Town: David Philip, 1980), p.62. Lijphart argues that federalism can be viewed as a consociational device when it is applied to an ethnically diverse society and is asymmetrical in form (meaning that the subnational units must be significantly more homogeneous than the society as a whole).

41. On Soweto in 1976 see John Kane-Berman, *Soweto: Black Revolt, White Reaction* (Johannesburg: Ravan, 1978); Baruch Hirson, *Year of Fire, Year of Ash* (London: Zed, 1979).
42. Consider Aletta J. Norval, *Deconstructing Apartheid Discourse* (London: Verso, 1996), Chapter 4.
43. Frederik van Zyl Slabbert, 'Sham Reform and Conflict Regulation in a Divided Society', *Journal of Asian and African Studies*, Vol. 18, No. 1–2 (1983), pp.34–48; Arend Lijphart, *Power-Sharing in South Africa*, Policy Papers in International Affairs 24 (Berkeley, CA: Institute of International Studies, University of California, 1985). Also see Rupert Taylor, 'South Africa: Consociation or Democracy?', *Telos*, Vol. 85 (1990), pp.17–32.
44. William Cobbett, Darryl Glaser, Doug Hindson and Mark Swilling, 'South Africa's Regional Political Economy: A Critical Analysis of Reform Strategy in the 1980s', in *South African Review 3* (Johannesburg: Ravan, 1986).
45. Consider de Klerk, *Last Trek*, Chapter 10.
46. The UDF was an umbrella body made up of hundreds of affiliated organizations, and involving (at its height) around three million people. See Tom Lodge and Bill Nasson, *All, Here and Now: Black Politics in South Africa in the 1980s* (New York: Ford Foundation, 1991); Anthony W. Marx, *Lessons of Struggle: South African Internal Opposition, 1960–1990* (New York: Oxford University Press, 1992).
47. Centre for Policy Studies, *South Africa at the End of the Eighties* (Johannesburg: Centre for Policy Studies, 1989).
48. de Klerk, *Last Trek*, p.281.
49. Codesa Working Group 2 dealt with constitutional principles, including the issue of federalism; see Steven Friedman (ed.), *The Long Journey: South Africa's Quest for a Negotiated Settlement* (Johannesburg: Ravan, 1993), pp.60–85.
50. Speech by the Leader of the National Party, Mr F.W. de Klerk, at the Congress of the National Party of Natal, Durban, Friday, 25 September 1992, verbatim transcription.
51. B. M. du Toit, 'The Far Right in Current South African Politics', *Journal of Modern African Studies*, Vol. 29, No. 4 (1991, pp.627–67.
52. The Freedom Alliance was preceded by a Concerned South Africans Group, which was formed in October 1992; see Martin Meredith, *South Africa's New Era: The 1994 Election* (London: Mandarin, 1994), Chapters 4 and 5.
53. In this regard, consider Charles D. Tarlton, 'Symmetry and Asymmetry as Elements of Federalism: A Theoretical Speculation', *Journal of Politics*, Vol. 27, No. 4 (1965), pp.861–74.
54. Albie Sachs, *Protecting Human Rights in a New South Africa* (Cape Town: Oxford University Press, 1990), p.152.
55. Consider Siri Gloppen, *South Africa: The Battle over the Constitution* (Aldershot: Ashgate, 1997).
56. Yvonne Muthien and Meshack Khosa, 'Demarcating the New Provinces: A Critical Reflection on the Process', in Meshack Khosa and Yvonne Muthien (eds.), *Regionalism in the New South Africa* (Aldershot: Ashgate, 1998), pp.23–56.
57. The name of this Commission (with its catch-all reference to 'States', 'Provinces' and 'Regions') indicates the highly contested nature of the debate.
58. Yvonne G. Muthien and Meshack M. Khosa, '"The Kingdom, the Volkstaat and the New South Africa": Drawing South Africa's New Regional Boundaries', *Journal of Southern African Studies*, Vol.21, No.2 (1995), p.322. Also see *Report of the Commission on the Demarcation/Delimitation of States, Provinces and Regions*, 31 July 1993.
59. The apartheid-designated ethnic categories are no longer employed in official statistics.
60. Mervyn Bennun and Malyn D. D. Newitt, *Negotiating Justice: A New Constitution for South Africa* (Exeter: University of Exeter Press, 1995), p.183.
61. Adrian Guelke, *South Africa in Transition: The Misunderstood Miracle* (London: I. B. Tauris, 1999), Chapter 4.
62. Rupert Taylor and Thabisi Hoeane, 'Interpreting the South African Election of June 1999', *Politikon*, Vol. 26, No. 2 (1999), p.141.
63. Jim Day, 'Bush Buck riot blamed on ANC indifference', *Electronic Mail & Guardian*, 9 May 1997 (www.mg.co.za); Maano F. Ramutsindela and David Simon, 'The Politics of Territory and Place in Post-Apartheid South Africa: The Disputed Area of

Bushbuckridge', *Journal of Southern African Studies*, Vol. 25, No. 3 (1999), pp.479–98.

64. Roddy Fox, 'Regional Proposals: Their Constitutional and Geographical Significance', in Lemon, *Geography of Change* (1995), pp.19–41.
65. Nationally, however, the Inkatha Freedom Party won only 10.5% of the vote, with less than 50% of Zulu-speaking support.
66. In terms of apartheid racial categorizations, the combined white and Coloured population for the Western Cape is 75.0%, and for the Northern Cape it is 65.1%; see Statistics South Africa (1998), p.9. The Western Cape and Northern Cape are the only two provinces in which African people do not form a majority of the population.
67. Wilmot James, 'Identity shrinks in shadow of dread', *Democracy in Action* (Idasa), 18 April 1995, pp.19–20.
68. Taylor and Hoeane, 'Interpreting the South African election', pp.139–40.
69. Kader Asmal, 'Making the Constitution', *Southern African Review of Books*, Vol. 5, No. 3 (1993), p.3.
70. *The Constitution of the Republic of South Africa, 1996.*
71. For an assessment of the prospects for cooperative government, see Roger Southall, 'A Deepening of Democracy? Establishing Provincial Government in South Africa', *Africa Insight*, Vol. 28, No. 1–2 (1998), pp.5–18.
72. Compare the analysis here with that, for example, of Milton J. Esman, *Ethnic Politics* (Ithaca, New York: Cornell University Press, 1994).
73. Laurence Piper and Kerri Hampton, 'The Decline of "Militant Zulu Nationalism": IFP Politics after 1994', *Politikon*, Vol. 25, No. 1 (1998), pp.81–101.
74. Roger Friedman, Karen MacGregor, Eric Ntabazalila, Judith Soal and Simon Zwane, 'Here is your reality, South Africa', *The Star* [Johannesburg], 19 April 1999, p.11.

6

Israel

Ethnic Conflict and Political Exchange

ALEX WEINGROD

In keeping with the overall theme of this volume, this chapter provides a broad survey of the issues of 'territorial management' as they relate to Palestinians and Jews in Israel, the West Bank and Gaza territories, and the city of Jerusalem. This affords a brief general overview, emphasizing in particular spatial and other types of separation, as well as majority–minority political relationships, between Jews and Arabs. Attention is then focused upon the various forms of political exchange that came into being in Jerusalem in the period between 1967 and the present. Jerusalem is important not only since it has both practical and symbolic significance in the overall Israeli–Palestinian conflict, but also because of its position as a large city where Jews and Arabs live and interact on a continuing, daily basis.

In the lexicon of the lengthy Arab–Jewish or Israeli–Palestinian dispute, the term 'territorial management' has essentially meant partition into separate Arab and Jewish states.[1] Based upon the belief that a single state composed of approximately equal numbers of Jews and Arabs would be so conflict-ridden as to make its very existence impossible, the advocates of partition proposed dividing Palestine into two states. The 1947 United Nations resolution called for the formation of separate Arab and Jewish states, while Jerusalem, which was to remain united, would have the special status of an 'international city'. Although the United Nations plan was never implemented, the events of the Arab–Israeli war of 1947–48 themselves led to a de facto partition and practically total separation of populations. Israel was proclaimed a Jewish state that included a Jewish majority and a small Arab minority; Jordan, itself a new state, absorbed the West Bank region that was entirely Arab in population, with no Jews remaining; and instead of becoming internationalized Jerusalem was divided into two separate cities, the one Israeli and the other Jordanian.

This entire constellation changed again when, in 1967, during the course of the Six-Day War waged between Israel on one side and Egypt, Syria and Jordan on the other, Israel captured and established control over the West Bank, Gaza, the Golan Heights and Sinai, and Jerusalem, divided since 1947, was also unified by Israeli forces. As a consequence, Israel established military rule over the territories it had occupied, and having formally annexed the Jordanian sections of Jerusalem the Israeli municipality enlarged its jurisdiction to include the entire city.[2] In addition, under these conditions of Israeli military control, Jewish settlers began building new communities in all of the areas held under military rule; Arabs continued to be the majority group, but a Jewish minority was also established in the occupied territories.[3] Active resistance to the Israeli occupation began in late 1987 with the outbreak of the *intifada*, or Palestinian popular uprising, and the violence continued sporadically until 1991. Following the Oslo peace process which began in 1993, the newly established Palestinian Authority was awarded political control over the main Palestinian population centres in the West Bank and Gaza. The Israeli settlements remained, however, and the entire area was divided into separate geographic zones under either Palestinian or Israeli military control. This situation has continued to the present (2002), with brief moments of Israeli–Palestinian cooperation followed by lengthy periods of communal antagonism and growing armed violence.

RELATIONS BETWEEN JEWS AND ARABS

The events briefly outlined above are well known, and there is no need to expand upon them further. What is important for present purposes is to recognize that, over time, one consequence of the continuing Israel-Palestinian conflict has been to bring into being new contexts in which Jews and Arabs, previously 'partitioned', have been drawn together within the same political structures.[4] Overall, in these regimes Jews exercise preponderant political as well as military and police power, while Arabs either are a minority or, if a majority, are in a dependent, controlled political position (see Map 6.1). The exception to this rule are the Palestinian cities and towns in the West Bank and Gaza which, following the Oslo agreement, came under the jurisdiction of the Palestinian Authority. Nonetheless, everyday realities are likely to involve some types of interaction (economic and social exchange, political conflict and cooperation as well as violence) between members of the two groups. In addition, in areas under its control the dominant Jewish group has consistently adopted policies of centralized state control, and has opposed devolving or otherwise permitting authority to be independently exercised by members of the Arab minority. This has been the case in Israel, the West Bank and Gaza, as well as in Jerusalem. Given these circumstances, the major problem is to understand the patterns of political relationships that developed between Israelis and Palestinians who presently live within these shared political frameworks.

Israel

The term 'Israeli Palestinians', which emphasizes their group identity as well as solidarity with other Palestinians, has in recent years been adopted by many Arabs living in Israel, and it will be used throughout this essay. Israeli Palestinians comprise a growing minority within the Jewish state; amounting to about 14% of the Israeli population in 1948, their numbers have increased over the years so that in 2000 Israeli Palestinians composed about 18% of the total Israeli population.[5] They are citizens of Israel, and have the same political rights as Israeli Jews – for example, they vote in elections, may be elected to the Knesset, or parliament, and in principle are able to fill roles throughout the political

MAP 6.1
ISRAEL AND THE PALESTINIAN TERRITORIES, 2000

and economic systems. With the exception of the small Druze and Bedouin populations, however, Israeli Palestinians are not conscripted into the Israeli army, and they are therefore ineligible to receive those state-allocated benefits that are conditional on completion of military service. Moreover, in a variety of respects there is an overall separation between Israeli Palestinians and Jews. This division has both territorial and institutional features. A relatively small number of Israeli Palestinians reside in mixed Arab-Jewish towns, while the majority (about 85%) live in towns and villages whose populations are entirely Palestinian. While there are exceptions, Palestinians living in mixed towns also tend to be concentrated in separate, homogeneous neighbourhoods. Beyond this residential segregation, what in Israel is referred to as the 'Arab sector' (*migzar ha'Aravi*) is also differentiated within the overall state system. There is, for example, a separate Arab school system whose language of instruction is Arabic, and issues of marriage and divorce are determined by separate Muslim or Christian religious authorities. Hence, while there is no devolution of authority to Arabs as a minority group, the state has recognized certain special features or needs of the Arab minority.

Although political equality is formally accorded to all Israeli citizens, a significant degree of structural inequality exists between members of the majority Jewish and minority Palestinian 'sectors'. Stated in terms of social stratification, Palestinians tend to hold unskilled and semi-skilled occupations, their incomes are significantly lower in comparison with Jews, and Arab educational training is also generally inferior to that of Israeli Jews. Overall, the level of community services is also poor in comparison with the Jewish majority; this is the case with regard to medical facilities and educational opportunities, as well as other basic services such as roads, waste-disposal systems and recreational facilities provided by the state. With regard to political activity and participation, at the local level mayors and village or town council members are elected, and the growing Palestinian minority has also been active in national politics and political parties, including several political parties that are entirely or largely based upon Arab voters. Indeed, since Israeli Palestinians presently number close to 20% of the total population their electoral strength has grown significantly.

While Israeli Jews and Palestinians enter into various exchange relationships – notably in the contexts of work, and, to a lesser extent, in politics – the overall contacts between them have tended to be circumscribed and more antagonistic and tense. The majority of Israeli Palestinians are secular, although there also is a significant minority whose practices and outlooks are religious and increasingly fundamentalist. The continuing Israeli–Palestinian conflict has further strained ties between Israeli Jews and Israeli Palestinians. Many express demands for equality with the Jewish majority, while others have proposed instituting some form of separate 'communal autonomy' for the Palestinian minority living in Israel.

The West Bank and Gaza

Mention should also be made of the Palestinians and Israelis living in the West Bank and Gaza regions. Beginning in 1967, these areas had the status of 'occupied territories' – they were directly governed by the Israeli military authorities, and the Palestinians living there continued to hold their Jordanian or Egyptian citizenship. In economic terms, to a large extent both the West Bank and Gaza became appendages of the Israeli economy, providing pools of unskilled and semi-skilled workers employed within Israel or by Jewish employers in the territories. Palestinian political organization was also tightly controlled by the Israeli military regime – Arab civil authorities were appointed and supervised by the military government, and independent political activities, which tended to oppose the Israeli occupation, were also prohibited. As noted previously, the Palestinian popular uprising, or *intifada*, challenged continuing Israeli control of these territories, and following the Oslo accords (1995) the Palestinians have held civilian and military jurisdiction over the major population centres in the West Bank and Gaza.[6]

In the period since 1967, groups of Jewish migrants established settlements in these regions, and consequently the territories include a Palestinian majority and a small Israeli minority. The settler population has subsequently grown in size, but the Palestinian population has grown even more rapidly (see Table 6.1). These groups reside entirely separately from each other, and they do not share services to any significant degree. They are also distinct in respect to legal jurisdiction – the Israeli settlers are subject to Israeli law and appear before Israeli courts, and the majority of Palestinians, who previously were under Jordanian

TABLE 6.1
ISRAEL, JERUSALEM AND WEST BANK-GAZA TERRITORIES:
ETHNIC COMPOSITION, 2000

Ethnic group	Israel Number	%	Jerusalem Number	%	West Bank-Gaza Number	%
Jews	5,180,600	81.3	448,800	68.3	200,000	5.7
Arabs	1,188,700	18.7	208,700	31.7	3,300,000	94.3
Total	6,369,300	100.0	657,500	100.0	3,500,000	100.0

Source: For Israel and Jerusalem, *Statistical Yearbook of Jerusalem* No.18-2000, Jerusalem, 2001. Figures for the West Bank and Gaza are an estimate based upon newspaper reports.

law and Israeli military government regulations, have since 1995 been under the jurisdiction of Palestinian courts and law. Relationships between these groups have steadily deteriorated, and the economic links between them have also narrowed as the violence has grown more intense.

Jerusalem

We turn now to a more detailed analysis of political relationships between Israelis and Palestinians in Jerusalem. This focus is particularly instructive since, in contrast with the others that have been described, Jerusalem is composed of an Israeli Jewish majority and a sizeable Palestinian Arab minority; it is the only instance of a large population centre that includes significant numbers of both Arabs and Jews living within the same political system. An ancient city holy for Jews, Muslims and Christians, Jerusalem was divided by the 1947–48 war into two cities, the one Jewish and the other Arab. Separated by walls and barbed wire erected along the armistice line where the fighting ended, the two cities developed their own separate economic, administrative and political systems, just as both, over time, grew outward away from the dividing line and from one another (the only city service that they continued to share after 1948 was the underground sewer system.)

This entire context changed suddenly and unexpectedly in June 1967. By the fourth day of the Six-Day War all of Jerusalem was under Israeli control, and days later the walls dividing the city were torn down. For the triumphant Jews, Jerusalem had become reunited under Israeli rule; but for the Arabs this represented not just defeat, but worse, occupation under the control of Israeli forces. The overall contour of an inter-ethnic political system then swiftly took form. Late in June 1967, the Israeli parliament passed a law expanding the borders of Jerusalem and annexing the Arab sections of the city; Israeli rule and laws henceforward prevailed throughout all of the 'Eastern', or Arab, as well as 'Western', or Jewish, sections of the city. The Israeli municipal authorities assumed responsibility for the entire city and its enlarged, mixed, and deeply divided population – the Israeli mayor and municipal council undertook to provide city services and passed ordinances that were to be observed both in the Arab Old City and in Jerusalem's rapidly expanding Israeli Jewish sections.

In response to these new circumstances, the Jordanian Arab mayor and his council members resigned in protest. What is more, under the terms of the annexation law the 65,000 or so Arabs then living in the city did not become Israeli citizens, but were instead placed in the category of 'resident'; they were issued with Israeli identity cards, but in almost all cases they also retained their Jordanian passports and Jordanian citizenship.[7] As 'residents' Jerusalem Arabs were, for example, required to pay

Israeli taxes and entitled to receive Israeli social security and other benefits, and, in addition, they could vote in local municipal elections but not
in Israeli national elections. The Arabs rejected the claims of Israeli sovereignty, and yet under the new circumstances they often needed to deal
with official Israeli government agencies. They continued to be
Jordanian citizens – but at the same time they were Israeli 'residents'
who were frequently required to display their Israeli identity cards. Their
situation was, to say the least, complex, ambiguous and problematic.

The overall context was, in fact, even more complicated. Immediately
following Israel's occupation and annexation, the Arab municipal
employees – including hundreds of teachers, clerks, technicians and
others – refused to return to work under the new circumstances of Israeli
control. Later, however, they did go back to their previous tasks, even
though they had been incorporated within the Israeli municipality. On
the other hand, the Arab judges refused to serve in the Israeli legal
system, and Arab lawyers also went on strike against the occupation.
What is more, the numerous Arab officials employed by the Jerusalem
waq'f, or religious trust, continued to be employees of the Jordanian
government, and they received their monthly salaries from Amman,
Jordan's capital. The lawyers and judges who were on strike, as well as
various others, also received salaries from the Jordanian authorities;
from their point of view they were Jordanians serving Jordanian interests in a city now temporarily under Israeli control. If, as the Israelis saw
it, Jerusalem was a 'united city under Israeli sovereignty', these Arabs
could also imagine themselves to be maintaining the Jordanian or the
Palestinian presence in *Al-Quds*, their Holy City.

There is an additional element that needs to be set into this political
context; each group developed its own beliefs, assumptions and
ideology regarding the new circumstances of Jerusalem's unification. For
the Palestinians, it was clear that they were living in a situation of foreign
military occupation – just as in the West Bank and Gaza areas, Jerusalem
had been conquered by Israeli military force and they were therefore
under the hegemony of an occupying power. They did not recognize the
moral or legal basis for Jerusalem's unification under Israeli control; on
the contrary, they insisted that it was both illegal and morally wrong.
The agonizing question facing them was, what could be done under the
circumstances? Agreeing to take a direct part in Israeli political and legal
institutions was clearly out of the question since this would, in effect, be
a tacit acceptance of Israeli sovereignty. For this reason, Jerusalem Arabs
typically did not take legal cases of complaint or injury before the Israeli
courts. On the other hand, in those many areas where there were no
alternatives, it was deemed legitimate for Palestinians to avail themselves of Israeli government agencies and services. To cite several examples, Palestinians who owned automobiles had no choice but to register
them with the Israeli authorities, taxes had to be paid to the municipality,

and if one wished to have a telephone installed there was no option other than the Israeli phone company. In addition to these individual matters of everyday practical necessity, Arab political forums that had previously existed during periods of foreign domination were revived. The best example is the Supreme Muslim Council which, in an earlier era, had represented Arab interests when Palestine was under British mandatory control. The Supreme Council was again reconstituted, and its members occasionally met with the Israeli authorities.

In a broader sense, however, the viewpoint that informed Arab behaviour in the post-1967 period was expressed by the ideology of *sumud*, or, in English, 'steadfastness'. To 'remain steadfast' meant refusing to leave Palestinian soil (in contrast with those who had fled during both the 1948 and 1967 wars with Israel), and, at the same time to seek to build Palestinian institutions that would sustain the occupied population until its final liberation. *Sumud* was not a doctrine of active or violent opposition – Israeli military control was considered to be too potent, and the dangers of yet another Palestinian disaster too great, to encourage direct revolt. On the other hand, the *sumud* doctrine enjoined the Arab population to build from within in order to endure and, ulti- mately, triumph. In keeping with this orientation, during the mid-1970s and 1980s Palestinian schools, hospitals, newspapers, universities, labour unions, mortgage programmes for home construction, and other activi- ties were encouraged and developed. Indeed, for a variety of reasons Jerusalem became the hub of these Palestinian activities.[8]

The Israeli viewpoint was, of course, entirely different. Their percep- tion was that Jerusalem was not merely 'united', but rather 'reunited' under Israeli sovereignty; it was the extraordinary culmination of a historical process reaching back to biblical days. The critical fact was that Jerusalem was under their sole control, and that they were in charge of the state apparatus. Since this was the case, it was also possible (in fact, often desirable and probably wise) to develop pragmatic policies regarding the Arab minority; compromise and pragmatism with respect to Arab interests were desirable so long as they did not impinge upon or seriously challenge Israeli sovereignty over the entire Holy City. With this as its basic premise, an ideology was developed that conceived of Jerusalem as an 'ethnic mosaic' in which over the centuries many different groups had lived together side by side. Arabs and Jews were only two large categories in this mosaic, which also included Christian and Muslim Arabs of different church and other affiliations, as well as ultra-orthodox and secular Jews, all of whom lived in their own residen- tial neighbourhoods, followed something like an ethnic division of labour, and maintained their own separate customs and institutions. Jerusalem was seen as always having been 'pluralistic'; in keeping with this vision, during the 1980s the Jerusalem municipality designed colourful posters that showed a Jerusalem of mosques and churches, minarets and Stars of David, all linked together in an interwoven pattern. What is more, the desirable relationship between Arabs and Jews was defined in Hebrew as *du kiyum b'shalom*, or peaceful coexistence. This was the municipality's major ideological message – Jews and Arabs might not wish to live in the same city system, but since Jerusalem was now 'reunited' they had no real alternative except to recognize facts, avoid dogma, be pragmatic and thereby seek to solve everyday problems, and 'coexist peacefully'.

Remarkably, these orientations and ideologies persisted until the beginning of the first Palestinian *intifada*, or popular uprising, in 1987. Since then, and continuing to the present, repeated confrontations and violence have produced a much different set of outlooks and behaviour: the *sumud* doctrine has been replaced by more active and often violent opposition to Israeli control, and the Israeli vision of 'peaceful coexistence' has equally given way to a deeper separation between Israelis and Palestinians, as well as the increased Israeli police and military control over the Palestinian population. These events and their consequences will be considered later in this essay.

THE POLITICAL SYSTEM IN JERUSALEM

What kinds of political exchanges developed between the Jewish majority, who controlled the state apparatus, and the minority Arab population that rejected the political status imposed upon them? Even more directly, since Arabs refused to take part in Jerusalem's governance, how were decisions made regarding their day-to-day problems or longer-term requirements?

Informal Brokerage

During the two-decade period between 1967 and 1987, a largely informal system of political interaction came into being. This system operated at two different levels. First, networks of Arab and Jewish brokers were engaged in dealing with the everyday needs and problems facing the Arab minority. This range of Jewish–Arab contacts can be thought of as comprising a 'patronage system'. Second, a small number of Arab and Jewish political notables and leaders met from time to time to consider various matters of general policy, and this format can be termed the 'elite system'. These brokers and elites – classic roles in political analysis – became major actors in the system of inter-ethnic political exchange.

The patronage system grew out of the myriad practical issues and daily concerns that faced the Arab population under the post-1967 conditions of Israeli control. These included many of the same kinds of problems that periodically confronted Jerusalem's Jewish population – for example, a complaint about a faulty sewer or a water bill, a request for permission to add a room or enclose a porch, or registering a child in a particular school. In addition, Arabs also faced more complex problems such as finding the whereabouts of a family member who had been arrested for alleged terrorist activity, or requesting permission to cross the bridges to Jordan in order to attend a wedding or complete a business transaction. Since the Israeli bureaucracies and the Hebrew language were unfamiliar to them, they often turned to an intermediary or broker for assistance. The local Arab *mukhtars*, or neighbourhood head men, soon became principal avenues of inter-ethnic contact (Arabs employed by the municipality also served as sources of information, and occasionally, intervention). The role of *mukhtar* had a long historical tradition. *Mukhtars* had responsibility for maintaining local order under the Ottomans, had served under the British and later during Jordanian rule in Jerusalem, and the Israeli municipality quickly sought to revive the position.[9] One or more *mukhtars* were appointed in each of the East Jerusalem Arab neighbourhoods; typically they were older men of modest status, members of the leading or the largest local family groups.

The *mukhtars* (who numbered about 60 in the 1980s) could frequently be seen in the various Jerusalem municipality and other Israeli government offices, attempting to resolve problems that they, or their family members and neighbours, were contending with. Usually, however, their contacts with the Israeli authorities were funnelled through the mayor's advisor on East Jerusalem Affairs. Established after 1967, and modelled after the Israeli Prime Minister's advisor on Arab Affairs, the mayor's advisor maintained a small office designed to assist local Arabs with their municipal and other related problems. The *mukhtars* typically sought to enlist the advisor's advice and intervention; to cite several examples, faced with a request by a *mukhtar* to obtain a building permit, admit a sick or injured family member to a particular hospital, or obtain permission for a Palestinian to establish residence in Jerusalem and thereby receive an Israeli identity card, the advisor might make a series of telephone calls, write a letter, or, upon reflection, conclude that 'nothing can be done in this case'. The advisor was appointed and served directly under the mayor of Jerusalem, and he was constantly in touch with the mayor on a variety of issues concerning Jerusalem's Arab minority.

It can readily be seen that brokers on both sides, including Arabs and Jews, were in continuous contact; messages, assistance, favours, information, and the like, were exchanged between them. What made this into an operative patronage system was the fact that the Arabs were entitled to vote in local elections, and that, not surprisingly, both the Arab *mukhtars* (as well as others) and the advisor were periodically involved in organizing the Arab vote. In the four local elections held in Jerusalem between 1967 and 1988 only a minority of Arabs chose to vote (for example, in the 1983 election about 18% did so).[10] However, those who did overwhelmingly cast their ballots for Teddy Kollek, who was Jerusalem's mayor from 1965 until 1993. In fact, these Arab voters not only helped to re-elect Kollek but also gave him a majority in the municipal council. This was, in short, a patronage system that appeared to work effectively.

Mention of Mayor Kollek brings us to the second arena of Arab–Jewish political exchange – namely, the elite system. The reasons for the development of this system and its results are of central importance to this analysis.

Israel's rapid military victory in the 1967 war left the Jerusalem Palestinian Arab political leadership in a state of shock. Some influential persons fled, others were banished into exile in Jordan, and those who remained steadfastly refused to enter into joint municipal activities with the Israelis. However, a small number of Arabs who held responsibility in various non-municipal organizations and institutions remained in the city. In particular, they were persons who headed offices that were connected with the Jordanian government authorities in Amman, or who represented the Jordanians, or both. To cite several examples, they included the heads of the Muslim *waq'f* responsible for supervising the Muslim Holy Places as well as the extensive property holdings controlled by the *waq'f*; the head of the East Jerusalem Chamber of Commerce, the body that concerned itself with commercial links between Arabs in Jerusalem and Jordan; the chairman of the board of the East Jerusalem Electric Corporation, the largest employer in Arab Jerusalem; and a number of others, including the former Jordanian governor of the Jerusalem region as well as the heads of several professional associations. Unlike the Arab mayor of Jerusalem and his fellow councillors, there was no reason for these Arab office holders to resign from their positions – the offices they held were not controlled directly by or under the aegis of the Israeli authorities.

In addition to these Arab notables, post-1967 Jerusalem also included the heads of the many Christian churches that are located in this Holy City. Nearly all of the important Christian Holy Places are situated in East Jerusalem, and the Jerusalem municipality (as well as various Israeli government ministries) quickly entered into contact and negotiation with the church leaders. Several of these groups, notably the Greek Orthodox and Armenians, have a comparatively large resident population, and church leaders who represented the interests of their constituents and their churches were also numbered among Jerusalem's political leadership.

The actors or participants in the 'elite political system' therefore included the heads of the Jerusalem-based Christian churches, and, more importantly, the small number of notables, mainly Muslims, who held local positions of political and economic significance. On the other side, the number of Israeli participants was more limited. Indeed, it is fair to say that Mayor Kollek was the principal actor, and that, depending upon the issues being considered he was joined by his advisor on East Jerusalem Affairs or by other specialists.

These were the principal actors; but what contacts were established between them? How did the elite system work?

Briefly described, this system of contact and exchange operated in something like the following manner. In the years following 1967 Mayor Kollek sought out Arab influentials with whom he could informally raise and consider local issues that were of concern to the Arab population. Over time some of the Arab notables, who were also concerned about the condition of local Arab affairs, responded to these initiatives. Periodically, one of the parties initiated contact with the other, and a private meeting was arranged between them. At the meeting – say, between the mayor and the chairman of the East Jerusalem Electric Corporation, or the mayor and the heads of the *waq'f* – views might be exchanged regarding recent political events, and then particular requests as well as broader issues of policy were discussed. To cite several examples, at various times the mayor and one of the notables considered issues such as the tax rate on *waq'f* property, permission to build a new Arab hospital or school, whether the Jordanian or the Israeli curriculum would be followed in East Jerusalem schools, or the level of taxation which the city authorities would assess upon merchants in East Jerusalem. These discussions, or, rather, negotiations, typically unfolded in a series of steps. During his meeting with the mayor a notable might express his point of view, or simply seek to obtain information regarding the Israeli viewpoint. In either case, the Arab notable would then meet with Jordanian or Palestinian national-level authorities in order to convey the information to them.

This is a critical point: while they had their own understandings and perhaps strategies, the notables did not have an independent base of authority but rather needed to consult and convey the decisions of the Jordanian and Palestinian leadership. In order to do this they travelled to Amman to meet with the Jordanian officials. For many years following 1967 the Jordanian government maintained an entire ministry whose task was to continue active involvement in the affairs of the West Bank and Jerusalem. The notables met with these and other authorities, reported to them regarding their discussions with the mayor and Israeli officials, and then took part in the debates and exchange of views aimed at establishing the Arab position. Upon returning to Jerusalem, they typically met again with the mayor and others in order to continue the negotiating. In some instances these exchanges resulted in agreement and a mutually acceptable policy, while in others the negotiations continued or were set aside since the two sides were unable to find a suitable resolution.

Quiet discussions along these lines were carried out for practically two decades. In order to understand this system more fully, two additional points need to be made. First, the cast of characters engaged in these deliberations hardly changed – as noted, Teddy Kollek was mayor of Jerusalem from 1965 until 1993, and for much of this time the Palestinian notables with whom he consulted and negotiated also included many of the same personages. Second, it should not be concluded that these were the only forms of ethnic political activity; exchange and elite-level negotiation were one format, and various expressions of Palestinian protest, including strikes, demonstrations, rioting and intermittent acts of violence and terror, were another. It would be correct to say that terrorist acts, such as placing bombs on buses or attacking civilians, were mainly carried out by members of the Palestinian minority; at the same time, Israeli Jews also initiated acts of aggression and terror, and consequently Jerusalem was periodically shaken by explosions of ethnic violence.

Shadow Games

'Shadow games' is a useful way to characterize the main contours of this political system. The term refers to certain of the interactions, mutual perceptions and political negotiations that were characteristic of relations between Palestinians and Israelis in Jerusalem. These may be termed 'games' since they were played according to a set of mutually accepted rules and proceeded according to scripts that were understood by both parties. To cite several examples, the rules recognized that the elite-level negotiators might consult with others outside of the municipal arena, and they stopped short of setting explicit limits regarding the parties with whom the other side might meet or consult. To designate these exchanges as 'games' is not to suggest that they were trivial pursuits; on the contrary, they were serious encounters involving the most complicated issues, negotiated by persons who had considerable stature, political experience, intelligence and influence. It is the regularized, rule-like, give-and-take nature of these interactions and negotiations that gave them the format of 'games'.

But why 'shadow'? First, negotiations entered into between Arab and Jewish elites were always private and hidden from view; they were held 'in the shadows', set in darkness where they could not be seen. Meetings between the mayor and an Arab notable or church leader were typically conducted as private affairs; when, as sometimes happened, a meeting was reported in the media or publicly noted in some other fashion it was immediately denied by those who presumably were involved. These were quiet conversations, whispers in the dark, between politicians representing two peoples who were in deep conflict; no stenographic record was kept, and, in fact, the success of the system depended upon a certain mutual interest and begrudging personal trust. Both sides wished to maintain secrecy about the exchanges. Privacy was useful since it allowed each to test the other; real bargaining might then take place, and the absence of observers opened the possibilities for a process of give-and-take in which neither party would be forced to follow its traditional positions. Besides, these meetings were potentially dangerous – Arab notables known to be meeting with Israeli officials faced the serious charge of being collaborators and traitors, and although the physical danger was not as great for the Israelis they too were open to criticism and attack from their political opponents. The shadows, it was clear, provided the best place for these encounters to take place.

Second, they were not only held in dark places; by denying that exchanges took place or that another side even existed each group could maintain a series of vital fictions. Shadows were important since they provided the darkness or convenient cover that was needed to keep a certain make-believe alive. Some Arabs might conclude that the Jordanian presence in Jerusalem – as represented by the various Palestinian Arab institutions, hundreds of persons who were receiving monthly salaries paid by the Jordanian government, and could travel to Jordan and other countries on Jordanian passports – was actual and significant, whereas signs of Israeli rule could whenever possible be avoided, disregarded or even willed out of sight. For their part, Jews typically considered the crowds of tourists strolling through the Arab Old City markets, or the tens of thousands of Arabs who daily came to work in Jewish factories and building sites, as evidence that Jerusalem was truly united under their control. They too filtered out the many signs that indicated that the city was, in fact, deeply divided. These were also shadows, and they covered realities and produced a kind of fictive world.

Finally, these were shadow games since they might be taken as the reflections of some basic, long-run processes. The actors cast large shadows, and this lent the illusion that an Arab–Jewish political system was working and on the way to becoming permanently institutional-ized; the *mukhtars* went busily about their tasks, the mayor's advisor rushed from one meeting to the next, while the mayor and the elite nota-bles carried on quiet negotiations. Were these real forces, the expressions of a viable inter-ethnic political system, or, in the end, merely shadows? However strained and tenuous it may have been, this Arab–Jewish polit-ical system persisted in the two-decade period following 1967. Before turning to examine how it changed, the question of why this particular framework emerged and remained in place needs to be considered. What made these 'shadow games' so effective?

To put it succinctly, this form of exchange came into being since it served the interests of both parties. In effect, each side had a consider-able stake in this political format. Let us begin with the Israeli side. The problem that faced Mayor Kollek and his associates following the 1967 war was how to effectively govern a city that included a large, hostile minority population. One alternative was to convince Arab leaders of the need to take an active, formal role in governing Jerusalem. On various occasions the mayor apparently sought to persuade politically moderate Palestinians to become candidates for election to the municipal council, but his offers were never accepted. He may not, however, have been over-enthusiastic about Arabs actually taking part in council affairs; at public meetings they inevitably would have taken uncompromising positions, and formal sessions would quickly turn into emotional debates between the Israeli majority and the Palestinian minority.[11] From his point of view it would be preferable to hold private negotiations with members of the Arab elite in order to consider practical matters, such as building permits and taxes, rather than engage in lengthy debates about 'sovereignty'. The patronage system was certainly advantageous – a political arrangement in which Jerusalem Arabs were encouraged to make use of the local *mukhtars* and the advisor meant that the mayor could acquire political capital that became valuable during elections. Besides, it was an arrangement that permitted Arabs to manage some of their own affairs and also to receive services from the Jewish municipality. In brief, a system that emphasized Arab brokers and periodic quiet consultations between elites had practical advantages as far as the mayor, and more generally, Israeli interests, were concerned.

The same can be said regarding the Palestinians – they too found certain advantages in this system. Their problem was how to manage affairs and persevere while under Israeli occupation. As was emphasized, Jerusalem Arabs could not hold a formal Israeli public office. On the other hand, there were real needs and pressing issues confronting them, and the problem was to find a political mechanism that would serve local interests without appearing to accept Israeli hegemony. The system of Arab brokers and notables offered a way to accomplish these ends; the *mukhtars* dealt with technical urban matters that needed solutions, and members of the elite could be depended upon to represent Jordanian and Palestinian interests in secret negotiations whose existence was always denied. To be sure, these arrangements did not change the facts of Israeli occupation; but, under the circumstances, they could assist the Arab population to achieve its goal of remaining steadfast.

In addition to serving the interests of both sides, it can also be seen that this rather peculiar, *ad hoc* arrangement was also an effective system. By empowering the various brokers, it offered the Arab population an avenue for dealing with their everyday urban problems, and the elite system also provided a forum for making decisions about specific policy matters.[12] It brought together leaders from both sides who were, presumably, both moderate and pragmatic, and they did at times succeed in introducing changes or opening new opportunities for the Arab minority. What is more, in the face of wars (1973 and again in 1981), recurrent ethnic violence and endless provocations, the system of elite consultations was sustained for more than two decades; different Israeli political parties, as well as different Jordanian governments and Palestinian leaderships, held power during this period, yet all of them continued to take part in these quiet conversations about Jerusalem issues. Given the history of the Arab–Israeli dispute, and of political conflicts more generally in the Middle East, this was no small feat.

At the same time, however, it was also a deeply flawed political framework. The patronage system obviously had the result of increasing Arab dependence – having to turn to brokers, either Jewish or Arab, meant that Arabs were always at a disadvantage. What is more, by basing itself on the same tiny set of notables, the elite system could never evolve into a wider Arab–Jewish political process involving larger numbers of actors. This would only have come about by Arabs taking a direct role in governing Jerusalem; to be sure, this would raise difficult problems for both groups, and yet in the long run it is the only way to establish more durable political arrangements.

Moreover, the fact that this system was entirely personal and informal had both advantages and pitfalls. Thoroughly *ad hoc* and *ad hominem*, founded upon personal understandings and bargaining rather than a legal code, constitution or a permanent set of rules, the political system did have a maximum of flexibility; whatever was finally agreed upon became the order of the day. This was, however, its ultimate weakness; there were no long-run guarantees, only short-term understandings, and consequently decisions and agreements could easily be disregarded or torn up as it suited one or both parties. These were, even in the short run, only temporary devices by which members of antagonistic groups maintained a minimum of contact and exchange.

This brings us back to 'shadow games'. This format of hidden meetings between pragmatic representatives was a useful tactic. To have conducted these negotiations in the open would have doomed them to failure. The system depended upon parading make-believe, while, back-stage, discussions were actually taking place. But in the end this was hardly enough; after two decades of playing shadow games it became clear that Jerusalem was not, as the Israeli view had it, just a mosaic of different cultures, and that 'pragmatic policies' were not an acceptable substitute for self-determination, just as the Palestinians found that Israeli control of the entire city was determined and real, and their attempts to separate themselves were unsuccessful. Fictions may have their usefulness in contexts as complicated and explosive as Jerusalem, but they delay moments of truth rather than transforming reality.

Jerusalem during and after the Intifada, 1987–2002

Events taking place during the late 1980s and throughout the 1990s brought about a number of deep, fundamental changes. While it is not possible to summarize all of these in detail, special attention will be given to three developments. First, during this period the level of violence between Jews and Arabs in Jerusalem grew significantly. Second, among both Palestinians and Israelis a new leadership took office, and the new spokesmen and leaders expressed viewpoints and ideologies that differed from the past. Third, the knotty issue of 'sovereignty over Jerusalem' grew more salient, particularly as the East Jerusalem Palestinian neighbourhoods came under the influence of the Palestinian Authority located in the nearby West Bank.[13]

The Palestinian *intifada*, or popular revolt, that began in 1987 and continued through 1990, had a profound effect upon the patterns of Arab–Jewish relationships. The *intifada* did not begin in Jerusalem, but it quickly spread to the Holy City.[14] To be sure, terrorism and communal violence had also marked the earlier period, but the *intifada* initiated a broader scaled, more intense level of antagonism. The previous Palestinian doctrine of *sumud*, or 'steadfastness', that implied a kind of passive resistance, was replaced by direct, often violent opposition to Israeli control. Mass demonstrations and rioting broke out intermittently in the East Jerusalem Arab neighborhoods, and attacks were also made on Israeli cars and government offices in East Jerusalem. In response, the Israeli police and, at times, the Israeli army, actively patroled the Palestinian neighbourhoods, frequent curfews were announced, and the police clashed with demonstrators and arrested many of them. The Israeli slogan of 'the Jerusalem mosaic', or 'peaceful coexistence among all groups', was replaced by repeated statements that 'undivided Jerusalem was and would remain Israel's eternal capital', thereby implying that the entire city would be forcibly maintained under Israeli control.

Throughout this tense period the Old City markets and Arab stores throughout East Jerusalem were frequently shut down, schools were closed on the 'strike days' proclaimed by the *intifada* leadership, and many Palestinians (including those employed by the Jerusalem municipality) did not go to work. In response, during much of this period the municipality essentially stopped providing services to the Palestinian neighborhoods – faced with hostility and rioting, garbage was not collected for weeks and longer, roads were left in disrepair, government offices were closed, and so forth. On a number of occasions groups of Jews also attacked Arabs in West Jerusalem. The extent of violence (as indicated by the number of persons killed and wounded) was less in Jerusalem then in the West Bank and Gaza – but at the same time the continuing violence, as well as the mutual fear, rage and mistrust, deepened the schism dividing Israelis and Palestinians. Later, in the mid-1990s, when the Oslo peace process led to a reduction in violence and a certain revival of Palestinian–Israeli interchange, communal tensions were to some extent lessened. Even then, however, Israelis and Palestinians continued to draw apart from one another – few Israelis shopped or visited in the Old City markets, and in Jerusalem, as elsewhere in Israel, many employers replaced their Palestinian workers with foreign workers or newly-arrived Russian immigrants. Needless to say, the crisis in relations following the failure of the Camp David conference in 1999, and the new outbreak of violence that followed (the 'al-aksa *intifada'*), have only deepened the mutual antagonism and divisions. If, in the two decades following 1967, Jerusalem could be described as a 'deeply divided' city, after 1987 it could more aptly be called a 'city torn apart'.

How did these changes affect the Israeli–Palestinian political system that was previously described? The local Arab *mukhtars* and the Palestinian elite, on the one side, and the mayor and his advisor on East Jerusalem Affairs, on the other, were the principal actors in the post-1967 political system. In the period following the *intifada* some of the Arab *mukhtars* continued to represent their family and neighborhood to the municipal authorities – but others resigned or simply stopped playing the role, and in various neighborhoods the municipality no longer recruited or appointed new *mukhtars*. What is more, the previous system of elite-level negotiations also changed. The Arab notables who formerly met with the Israeli mayor or his advisor no longer played that role; leadership passed to a younger generation of persons who were not interested in particular programmes or so-called 'practical measures', but who instead were striving to achieve Palestinian political independence. The notables had close ties with – or were in effect representing – the Jordanian government; however, in the 1990s the Jordanian government largely withdrew from its direct involvement in Jerusalem and the West Bank, and representatives of the Palestine Liberation Organization (PLO), and later the Palestinian Authority, replaced them as leaders and spokesmen.

Important leadership changes also took place on the Israeli side. Although Teddy Kollek was again re-elected to office in the 1989 elections, for the first time since 1965 his party lost control of the municipal council. This loss foreshadowed the outcome of the 1993 election, in which the candidate of the Likud Party, Ehud Olmert, defeated Kollek and was elected mayor of Jerusalem. A relatively small number of Palestinians voted in these elections (for example, in 1993 only 6% of the eligible Palestinians voted), and this was an important factor in the transfer of power from Labour to the Likud Party. Olmert was re-elected in 1998 elections which the Palestinians again boycotted. Thus, in brief, the 'patronage system' that had for two decades benefited Kollek and the

Labour Party was no longer relevant, and although the new mayor also met with Palestinians he did not actively court their votes. Even though quiet negotiating between the Israeli and Palestinian leadership continued to take place, 'shadow games' had been replaced by an active conflict in which the Israelis sought to maintain their control over the entire city and the Palestinians struggled to establish their political authority over East Jerusalem.

Kollek's electoral defeat was not only the end of an era – he had been Mayor of Jerusalem for 28 years – it also ushered in a different agenda in the relationships between Palestinians and Israelis. Jerusalem became a main arena for conflict or competition between the Palestinian Authority and the Israeli government, and issues of sovereignty as well as control over the Holy Places were repeatedly emphasized. As mentioned earlier, already in the 1980s East Jerusalem became the centre for Palestinian national activity; the PLO and various of its offshoots established their offices and based their activities there, and they also became the leading group in important East Jerusalem institutions such as the Muslim *waq'f*, local hospitals, and the East Jerusalem Electric Company. Faisal Husseini, a member of one of Jerusalem's most distinguished Arab families, became a major figure and chief spokesman for Palestinian interests in the city. Under his leadership an old and gracious family building called 'Orient House' became the non-official centre for Palestinian national representation in Jerusalem. Diplomats from many countries and important guests from around the world began to visit Orient House, where Husseini and other Palestinians greeted them, at first as a spokesman for 'the Palestinian people' and later, in the mid-1990s, as the representative of the Palestinian Authority that was then negotiating peace agreements with Israel.

These activities appeared to pose serious problems for the Israelis: how could a Palestinian official openly receive diplomats from foreign countries in Jerusalem, the capital of Israel? If, as Israeli politicians repeated, 'Jerusalem would always be undivided and under Israeli sovereignty', how could the Palestinian flag fly over Orient House where Palestinian officials carried on discussions with foreign diplomats? To be sure, under the previous Kollek regime the local Arab schools were allowed to follow the Jordanian rather then the Israeli school curriculum, and in various other ways Israeli officials had quietly acquiesced in expressions of Palestinian symbols in Jerusalem. The Palestinian activities at Orient House continued to challenge Israeli politicians and government officials, and throughout the 1990s efforts were made to entirely ban or place limits on them. Notwithstanding these coercive efforts, the issue of sovereignty remained divisive; for example, following lengthy negotiations in 1995 Palestinians living in Jerusalem were allowed to vote and choose their representatives in the Palestinian National Assembly. What is more, as the West Bank area immediately north of Jerusalem (in particular the city of Ramallah and its environs) became the official centre of Palestinian political activity, the Arab neighborhoods bordering on the West Bank increasingly came under the influence of the Palestinian Authority. The Palestinian police were at times active in these neighbourhoods, and in various other ways these sections of Jerusalem were essentially cut off from Israeli control.

Finally, during the 1990s the struggle over Jerusalem increasingly took on religious dimensions. The Jerusalem issue became, in other words, not just a conflict waged between two national groups, Palestinians and Israelis, but was also phrased as a confrontation between opposed groups of religious believers, Muslims and Jews. Religious fundamentalism had grown more powerful among members of both groups, and the decades of violent opposition also strengthened the hand of religious extremists. In Jerusalem, authority over the Holy Places located in the Old City became a cardinal issue; Palestinians were in control of the Temple Mount (the *haram el-sharif*), while Jews controlled the Western Wall located immediately below, and periodic tensions and occasional violence flared between them. This was hardly a new problem – it has been a flash point for centuries – and yet the rising tones of religious fundamentalism made pragmatic efforts aimed at resolving conflicts and 'living together' even more difficult.

It is clear that deep and radical changes have taken place. There is no reason to suppose that the previous political format will be revived. Moreover, it is apparent that there can be no resolution of Jerusalem's ethnic conflict without an overall settlement of the complicated issues that divide Israelis and Palestinians. Indeed, the oft-repeated 'political wisdom' has it that Jerusalem issues are the most thorny and intractable, and that they should therefore be left for the last stage in negotiations between Israelis and Palestinians. In the meantime, mutual hostility and sullenness, punctuated by outbursts of violence, continues to divide the two populations.

The Prospects for Jerusalem

Are the conflicts between Jews and Arabs so primordial that any attempt to share their Holy City will inevitably be doomed to failure? Or, returning to the major theme of this volume, might some form of 'territorial management' offer a possible resolution in this as in other cases of persistent ethnic conflict?

If 'territorial management' is translated to mean building walls between the different sections of the city, then neither Palestinians nor Israelis have shown any interest in returning to a physically divided Jerusalem. On the contrary, if there is any agreement at all it is that Jerusalem should not again be divided into two cities separated by walls and barbed wire. Neither side recalls the time when the city was physically divided with anything like nostalgia or pleasure; the wall was an unnatural imposition, an ugly, threatening scar drawn in the midst of what is otherwise a bustling, overly-dramatic city. There are other reasons too. The Israelis, who presently control the city, find no reason to physically divide what they already have; the costs of continued Arab opposition and violence may be substantial, yet Israelis of all political outlooks apparently agree that Jerusalem should not again be physically divided. The Palestinians also have not proposed that new walls be built; they wish to regain full control over their parts of the city, but they have not seen the solution as requiring that walls be built and that the populations be physically separated.[15]

The alternatives need not, of course, be limited to physical partition. Practically since the city's 'unification' in 1967, various proposals have been made for resolving the 'Jerusalem problem' by allocating separate authority to both Israelis and Palestinians; rather than to physically divide the city and its antagonistic populations, these plans recommend that both groups divide or share sovereignty over the city.[16] For example, the oft-cited Borough Plan (modelled after London's system of local boroughs coupled with an overarching Greater London Council) called for re-dividing an expanded Greater Jerusalem into five autonomous administrative units or boroughs; based upon residence, most of the units would be ethnically homogeneous, although several would include both Arabs and Jews. Each of the boroughs would be self-governing with regard to providing local services, and, in addition, this plan provided for the formation of a Greater Jerusalem Council that would include representatives from both the Israeli and the Jordanian, or Palestinian, sovereignties.[17]

The recent negotiations related to the Oslo peace process have spawned a number of new proposals. One plan recommends that rather than expanding the city to include a larger population, Jerusalem's borders should be re-drawn in such a way that the Palestinian neighborhoods on the northern and southern peripheries be incorporated within the Palestinian Authority, and ultimately, into the Palestinian state. The Palestinian minority remaining in the city would have administrative control over their own neighborhoods, and Palestinians would also be included in an expanded city council. A second proposal – known as the 'Beilin/Abu-Mazen understanding' – seeks to combine the Borough Plan with a practical level of sovereignty for both groups. According to this plan not only would Jerusalem's boundaries be expanded, the city would also become a capital for two states, Israel and Palestine. Each of the boroughs would elect its own mayor, an over-arching city council would be formed, and the council would also elect a mayor for the entire city. In addition, both Palestinians and Israelis would continue to control their own holy places, and as a symbol of 'sovereignty' the Palestinian flag would fly over the Muslim holy places on the Temple Mount.[18]

Finally, the outline of a plan – since called 'the Clinton plan' – was also put forward by US negotiators in late 2000. As a way to break the deadlock in Israeli–Palestinian negotiations, US President Clinton proposed that sovereignty in Jerusalem be divided between Israelis and Palestinians: Jerusalem would become the capital for two states, each side would have sovereignty over its own neighborhoods, and in the Old City where the holy places are located each would have sovereignty over its own sacred sites. This proposal also called for joint Israeli–Palestinian municipal councils, but the emphasis was on a division of the city between the two groups.

Needless to say, none of these proposals has been adopted or, for that matter, widely discussed or jointly considered. The Palestinians are not interested in receiving 'local autonomy' over their own neighborhoods, or securing minority rights in a city in which Israelis continue to be the majority and the sovereign power – and the Israelis are opposed to sharing the sole control they have had since 1967, or weakening their independent sovereign right to make and enforce decisions throughout the city. What is more, all of the plans have been criticized as being much too complicated and therefore unworkable. If there were to be two independent sovereignties in Jerusalem, would each have its own currency, system of taxation and police force? Why imagine that these separate sovereignties, which only yesterday were violent enemies, would choose to cooperate with one another in a single urban system? Why would the Palestinians agree to a borough system if the Jews, the numerically larger group, would always have a majority on the upper-level council? Moreover, a divided city might be so cumbersome that it would quickly turn into an urban nightmare of underground tunnels and overhead bridges, mutual check-points and disputed crossing areas, as each 'sovereign' stubbornly protected its own territory as it grudgingly linked with the other. Rather then a glorious Holy City, Jerusalem might then become an ugly mess of petty dispute and missed opportunity.

Granted that the practical problems of designing a system of shared sovereignty are daunting, it should also be recalled that the present system for governing Jerusalem is also exceedingly complex. Where else do persons with different nationalities (Israel and Jordan), some of whom are citizens with full political rights and others who are 'residents' and take no part in the political process, all reside within the same urban system? Indeed, it can be argued that the issues of sovereignty and political control have historically been complicated in this ancient Holy City. For example, during the nineteenth century the Turkish-appointed governor of Jerusalem shared power with the European consuls, and Arabs and Jews served together on a municipal council.[19] The problem is not just complexity (although the practical problems should not be underestimated), but more fundamentally the absence of an interest on both sides to compromise their opposed dreams and ambitions.

However complex they might be, the particular mechanisms for sharing power could be designed – but first both Palestinians and Israelis must wish to move from their present-day conflicts to a different system in which understandings could be reached and conflict resolved.

CONCLUSION

As we have seen, the issues of Jerusalem's future are inseparable from the wider problems of Palestinian–Israeli relationships. Not only are the topics immensely complicated, the recent outbursts of violence have undoubtedly made them even more intractable. Nevertheless, in bringing this chapter to a close it may be worthwhile to briefly identify and comment upon some of these wider issues.

Two topics are especially important – first, the ties between Israeli Jews and Israeli Palestinians, and second, the shape of possible relationships between Israel and the Palestinians living in the West Bank and Gaza. Once again, these issues are closely connected, and yet it is useful to consider them separately.

With regard to Israeli Jews and Israeli Palestinians, the principal question is how the rising volume of Israeli Palestinian expectations and demands will be met by an increasingly apprehensive Israeli Jewish majority. These groups have by now lived side-by-side for more than 50 years. Even though their experience has been vastly different, members of both groups have already begun their third generation as 'Israelis'. Generally speaking, over time many Israeli Palestinians have become 'more Israeli', just as they also have become 'more Palestinian'. That is, in many features of everyday life and behavior Jews and Arabs share some common Israeli values, outlooks and expectations, while, at the same time, as the latter adopt a Palestinian identity they have become more critical of and alienated from the dominant Jewish majority. Despite repeated government promises to allocate the substantial resources needed to bring the physical infrastructure and educational opportunities of Israeli Palestinians on a par with or closer to Israeli Jews, these programmes have rarely been implemented and consequently the deep occupational, educational and other inequalities persist and become more severe. What is more, even though the Israeli Palestinian minority has grown in size it has not yet been able to translate its numerical strength into effective political power. In contrast with religious Jews or Sephardi Jews, who in recent decades have successfully mobilized and made coalitions with other political blocs, the large Israeli Palestinian minority has not yet been able to enter into (or, alternatively, it has been kept apart from) the kinds of political influence and government coalitions that presumably would lead to power, economic resources, and, ultimately, legitimacy. These trends serve to accentuate the growing crisis in relationships between Israeli Palestinians and Jews. Will the Jewish majority permit the minority to become more fully integrated as equal citizens and partners? Equally, however complicated the process, will the Palestinian minority seek out a place for itself within the often frustrating, contradictory contours of Israeli society?

The answers to these questions in many ways depend upon the future course of Arab–Jewish, Palestinian–Israeli, relationships. If the past hundred years are any guide, then the prospects are dim: the Israel–Palestine conflict has continued to defy solution and grown ever more bitter and violent. Events may lead to a 'two-state solution' in which the 1967 borders will become the border between the Palestinian and Israeli states. For that to happen Israel needs to withdraw its settlements from the West Bank and Gaza, and the Palestinians and other Arab states need to recognize Israel's right to exist within secure borders. There are, to be sure, other issues in dispute – the Palestinian refugees' right to return and Jerusalem's future are certainly among the most difficult. The broad dimensions of a political resolution can perhaps be seen; but this hardly guarantees that either side will be prepared to make the necessary compromises. Another hundred years of violence is certainly not inevitable. Movement towards an ending of violence, and finally to a treaty of peace between two sovereign nations, will no doubt depend upon sustained international involvement, wise leadership, and perhaps the exhaustion that follows endless personal and national tensions and traumas. It will not take place overnight, nor in a brief period of time – but, as has often been said, for better or worse, Palestinians and Israelis will ultimately need to share this ancient Holy Land.

NOTES

1. The issues, problems, plans and strategies involved in partitioning Palestine have been discussed in many books and articles. See, for example, B. Kimmerling, *Zionism and Territory* (Berkeley, CA: Institute of International Studies Research Series, No.51, 1983), pp.49–65.
2. This is described in M. Benvenisti, *Jerusalem: The Torn City* (Minneapolis, MN: University of Minnesota Press, 1976), pp.79–127. See also M. Romann and A. Weingrod, *Living Together Separately: Arabs and Jews in Contemporary Jerusalem* (Princeton, NJ: Princeton University Press, 1991), pp.19–23.
3. Jewish settlements in the Occupied Territories were established as a direct result of Israeli government policies and support. The issue of continued Jewish settlement in these areas, and particularly the West Bank and Gaza, has divided the Israeli electorate and the two major political parties, Likud and Labour. Nevertheless, when in control of the government both of these parties sponsored new Jewish settlements in the Occupied Territories. See Kimmerling, *Zionism*, pp.147–82.
4. The exception to this process is the Sinai Region. When, as a result of the 1977 Camp David Agreement, Israel returned Sinai to Egyptian sovereignty, all of the Jewish settlers who had moved there left the area and their settlements were dismantled.
5. These figures include Jerusalem Arabs who are not Israeli citizens.
6. There is a rich literature that describes and analyzes the *intifada*. See D. Peretz, *Intifada*

(Boulder, CO: Westview Press, 1990); D. Grossman, *The Yellow Wind* (New York: Farrar, Straus and Giroux, 1988); E. Yaari and Z. Schiff, *Intifada: The Palestinian Uprising* (Jerusalem: Shocken Books, 1990).

7. Arabs who were 'residents' of Jerusalem could formally apply to become Israeli citizens. In the period between 1967 and 1987 only a small number – about 200 persons – changed their citizenship from Jordanian to Israeli. In the late 1990s there appears to have been a revived interest in obtaining Israeli citizenship – largely due to the uncertain character of the Palestinian Authority – but the number of those who applied for and received Israeli citizenship is not clear.

8. Paradoxically, Jerusalem became the major centre for Palestinian nationalist activities since, unlike the Occupied Territories, Israeli law prevailed there. The Israeli Military Government could more easily curtail Palestinian newspapers and other activities when they took place in the Occupied Territories, whereas the legal requisites were more stringent in Jerusalem. In addition, Jerusalem has been a more newsworthy, politically sensitive place, and openness to the media has made it easier for Palestinian nationalist groups to operate there.

9. The traditional roles of the *mukhtar* are described in J. Migdal, *Palestinian Society and Politics* (Princeton: Princeton University Press, 1980).

10. Romann and Weingrod, *Living Together Separately*, p.207.

11. This is cited by Benvenisti, who was himself involved in the events. See Benvenisti, *Jerusalem*, p.115.

12. Comparable processes termed 'hegemonial exchange' are depicted by Rothchild in his analysis of 'soft' African states. See D. Rothchild, 'Hegemonial Exchange: An Alternative Model for Managing Conflict in Middle Africa', in D. Thompson and D. Ronen (eds.), *Ethnicity, Politics and Development* (Boulder, CO: Lynne Rienner Publishers, 1986), pp.65–104, esp. p.94.

13. Events during the 1990s and the changes they produced are described and analyzed in a number of excellent studies. See, for example, Amir Cheshin, Bill Hutman and Avi Melamed, *Separate and Unequal: The Inside Story of Israeli Rule in East Jerusalem* (Cambridge, MA: Harvard University Press, 1999); Roger Friedland and Richard Hecht, *To Rule Jerusalem* (Cambridge: Cambridge University Press, 1996); Michael Dumper, *The Politics of Jerusalem Since 1967* (New York: Columbia University Press, 1997); Scott Bohlens, *On Narrow Ground: Urban Policy and Ethnic Conflict in Jerusalem and Belfast* (Albany: State University of New York Press, 2000); and Menachem Klein, *Jerusalem, The Contested City* (London: Hurst, 2001).

14. Some of the results of the *intifada* are described in Romann and Weingrod, *Living Together Separately*, pp.238–41.

15. See T. Prittie, *Whose Jerusalem?* (London: Frederick Muller, 1981), pp.171, 186.

16. There are obvious differences between 'sharing' and 'dividing' sovereignty. The latter is something like erecting political 'walls' without actually putting up a real physical structure.

17. This proposal is also referred to as the 'Benvenisti plan', since it was originally drawn up by Meron Benvenisti in 1968. The plan is described at length in Benvenisti, *Jerusalem*, and also in his *Conflicts and Contradictions* (New York: Villard Books, 1986). Prittie also describes the proposal in his study (*Whose Jerusalem?* p.175).

18. These proposals are detailed in Menachem Klein's recent book on negotiations regarding Jerusalem. See Klein, *Jerusalem*, especially Chapter 8.

19. See Y. Ben Aryeh, *A City Reflected in Its Times: Jerusalem in the Nineteenth Century – The Old City* [in Hebrew] (Jerusalem: Yad Izhak Ben-Zvi, 1979).

7

Pakistan

Ethnic Diversity and Colonial Legacy

CHARLES H. KENNEDY

At the beginning of 2002, Pakistan faced two monumental threats to its existence. The first was the so-called 'war against terrorism' being waged by the United States and its coalition partners against the remnants of the Taliban and wholly, up to this point, confined to activities within Afghanistan. Pakistan has been obliged to provide support to US and coalition efforts to destroy the Taliban regime. But Pakistan's decision to support the United States has been quite a difficult one for the country's leadership, and it has been far from universally popular – so unpopular that this observer would argue that Pakistan could only pursue such a policy during a period of martial law. In this sense it may be fortunate that General (now President) Parvez Musharraf has ruled Pakistan as a military dictator since October 1999. In effect, Pakistan has been forced into conflict with Pashto-speaking 'Islamists', many of whom were or are residents or citizens of Pakistan.[1] This episode also forced Pakistan to side with the forces of westernization and globalization (never popular in non-western states); that is, the US–Afghan war has forced Pakistan to take a stand which challenges its ethnic loyalties as well as its ideological rationale.

Second, and directly related to the US–Afghan war, has been the resultant deterioration of relations with India over Kashmir. The mid-January 2002 mobilization of troops on both sides of the border and along the Line of Control was the largest and most dangerous since the 1971 Indo-Pakistan war. Unlike 1971, however, when Pakistan suffered military defeat and the dismemberment of its state at the hands of the Indian Army, both India and Pakistan now possess nuclear weapons. The main cause of such unprecedented sabre-rattling is the Indian contention that the 'principles' of the war in Afghanistan – to combat terrorism – should be applied to the Kashmir dispute. That is, Pakistan should suspend any aid to Kashmiri nationalists (read 'terrorists') and should rather seek to weaken their activities within Azad Kashmir. Of course, Pakistan has long contended (since 1948) that India has illegally occupied Kashmir and that resistance to Indian occupation (particularly since the late 1980s) is a valid expression of nationalism. In their view, resistance to Indian occupation is not an act of 'terrorism' but of 'nationalism.'

Both of the foregoing challenges to Pakistan's integrity are related to the country's troubled ethnic landscape. In ethnic terms there is little meaningful distinction between Pashto-speaking 'Pakistanis' living in Pakistan and Pashto-speaking 'Afghans' living in eastern Afghanistan. The Durand Line that separates the two states has always seemed unnatural, and during the USSR–Afghan war (1979–89) the creation of millions of refugees blurred the distinction still further. Pakistan's troubled relations with India are also rooted in ethnonational conflict. The main rationale for Pakistan's creation was the acceptance of 'Muslim' as opposed to 'Indian' nationalism. Tragically the subsequent Indo-Pakistan wars (1947-48, 1965 and 1971) and the current problems are all related to sorting out this still unsettled issue.

THE EMERGENCE OF ETHNIC PROBLEMS

Pakistan has suffered, before and since its emergence as an independent state, from ethnic group demands upon the state and from ethnic conflict. The sources of these problems are complex, and may be difficult to identify definitively; but two stand out as being of exceptional importance. The first is the diverse ethnic character of the state itself. The second is the inheritance of the pre-independence period and the legacy of colonial policy.

Ethnicity and the State

The creation of Pakistan was fuelled by the spectre of prospective second-class citizenship for Muslims in a would-be Hindu majority independent India. Indeed, Mohammed Ali Jinnah, the 'father' of Pakistan, generated much popular support for his Muslim League by increasingly insistently invoking the refrain of 'Islam in danger' to receptive Muslim audiences worried about the nature of post-colonial India. From partition (1947) until the dismemberment of the state in 1971, Pakistan served as the ideological battleground for antithetical visions of West Pakistani (Punjabi and Muhajir) and East Pakistani (Bengali) forms of nationalism. The resultant civil war, which came to a rapid conclusion following the Indian Army's occupation of Dhaka, split Pakistan into two states – Pakistan (formerly West Pakistan) and Bangladesh (formerly East Pakistan). Ominously, since the 1971 civil war ethnic demands, some separatist, have been voiced by Sindhi, Muhajir, Baloch and Pakhtun (Pathan) leaders.

Pakistan's decision-makers have addressed such demands through a variety of policies. Arguably (at least to actual or would-be secessionists), Pakistan has consistently pursued policies that Donald Rothchild would term 'ethnic subjection'.[2] Indisputably, Pakistan has also attempted cultural assimilationist strategies at several points – the Urdu language policy (1947–52); the 'One Unit Plan' (1955–69) which administratively unified West Pakistan; and currently the Islamization programme (1979–).[3] Indeed, the Islamic response to ethnic diversity is inherently assimilationist, with its reliance on the unity of the *ummah* (community of believers) and its commitment to radical egalitarianism.

More extensive and comprehensive, however, have been Pakistan's attempts to manage ethnic demands through policies of regional preference. Since 1949, Pakistan has instituted comprehensive regional quotas for recruitment to federal and provincial bureaucratic posts, and to openings in public sector enterprises. Similar regional quotas with numerous variations have been applied to the admission policies of educational institutions. To the extent that such policies of preference have a regional base (the relevant criterion of selection is the candidate's province of domicile), it can be argued that they are a variant of a territorial strategy to manage ethnic conflict. That is, Pakistan's decision-makers have addressed ethnic demands for greater political authority in the state by proportionally inducting relevant 'ethnic nationals' into the civil bureaucracy and professional elite. We argue here that Pakistan's experiment with such a strategy has proved to be less than successful.

The Colonial Heritage

Pakistan's ethnic dilemma was largely structured as a consequence of British colonial policy. By the mid-nineteenth century, save for remote and sparsely settled tribal territories and a handful of tiny princely states, the territory that was to become Pakistan was under the direct administrative authority of the Crown. But, with few exceptions, such territories were not central to Britain's colonial enterprise. Britain's incursions into the subcontinent had originated in the settlement and development of three coastal enclaves – Bombay, Madras and Calcutta. From such beachheads British influence spread along the coasts and eventually to the interior. The British presence, as a consequence, arrived relatively late and relatively unenthusiastically to northwest India; and in the northeast, British administration was concentrated in the area of Bengal that was to emerge as West Bengal (India), not East Pakistan.

Therefore, to borrow Donald Horowitz' concept, the peoples of the territories that were to become Pakistan did not benefit from the 'locational advantage' of close geographical propinquity with the colonial power.[4] Few Bengali Muslims, still fewer Punjabis, and virtually no Pakhtuns, Sindhis, or Baloch were able to avail themselves of the benefits of British mission schools or western education. Consequently, few became clerks and still fewer became senior administrators in the British colonial apparatus.[5] Members of such groups were also largely excluded from careers in international commerce.

Such ethnic outcomes were reinforced by the British penchant for imputing group characteristics to India's ethnic communities. Perhaps the most important such imputation was that concerning the existence of the so-called 'martial races'. Subsequent to the failed Revolt of 1857, the British propagated a widely held theory that members of some ethnic communities (coincidentally those that had remained loyal during the Revolt) were better suited to be soldiers than members of other (less loyal) ethnic communities. Under this schema, Punjabis and Pakhtuns were deemed 'martial' and Bengalis 'non-martial'. Largely as a consequence of such ethnic bias, Punjabis and to a lesser extent Pakhtuns became disproportionately overrepresented in the colonial military; Bengalis were disproportionately underrepresented.

Indeed, by the time of partition ethnic stereotypes, still relevant to contemporary Pakistan, had been established. The British considered Bengalis clever, but untrustworthy; Punjabis none too bright, but loyal; and, save for occasional romantic paeans to the straightforward manly virtues of the Pakhtun and Baloch tribesmen, they did not give much consideration to other prospective Pakistani ethnic communities at all.

Also, of extraordinary importance to the eventual ethnic composition of Pakistan was the mass transfer of populations associated with partition. During 1946–47, approximately 12 million individuals migrated from India to Pakistan or vice versa. Perhaps as many as 1 million more lost their lives in the attempt. The overwhelming majority of such migrants undertook the journey for communal reasons – Muslims fleeing India, Hindus and Sikhs fleeing Pakistan. By far the largest component of such transfers (80% of the total) occurred with respect to West Pakistan. For our purposes two consequences of this mass migration are of crucial importance. First, most of the Muslim immigrants ('Muhajirs')[6] settled in West Pakistan, particularly in Sindh. Second, the Urdu-speaking component of this community had benefited far more from the cumulative effects of colonial policies; and its members arrived in Pakistan, as a consequence, disproportionately advantaged relative to the indigenous population, particularly in comparison with Sindhis. Each of these consequences has helped to determine the contours of Pakistan's ethnic landscape.

THE ETHNIC LANDSCAPE

At partition, newly independent Pakistan consisted of an amalgamation of six politically significant ethnic groups.[7] In numbers, the largest of these groups were the Bengalis (52%), followed by the Punjabis (28%), Pakhtuns (7%), Sindhis (6%), Muhajirs (5%), and Baloch (2%).[8]

Each of these ethnic groups is defined by an admixture of linguistic and territorial attributes. Bengalis are Bengali-speaking and are concentrated almost exclusively in East Pakistan (formerly Bengal). Similarly, Punjabis are defined as Punjabi or Siraiki-speaking and they are territorially based in Punjab province; Pakhtuns are Pashto-speaking and are linked to the Northwest Frontier Province (NWFP); Sindhis are Sindhi-speaking and inhabit Sindh province; Baloch are Brahvi or Balochi-speaking and are centred in Balochistan province. 'Muhajirs' are a

TABLE 7.1
PAKISTAN: MOTHER LANGUAGE BY PROVINCE, 1998

Language	Punjab		Sindh		NWFP		Balochistan		Pakistan	
	All	*Urban*	*All*	*Urban*	*All*	*Urban*	*All*	*Urban*	*All*	*Urban*
Urdu	4.5	10.1	21.1	41.5	0.8	3.5	1.6	5.9	7.8	20.5
Punjabi	75.2	78.8	7.0	11.5	1.0	4.6	2.9	10.6	45.4	47.6
Pashto	1.2	1.8	4.2	8.0	73.9	73.5	23.0	19.7	13.0	9.6
Sindhi	0.1	0.1	59.7	25.8	–	0.1	6.8	6.9	14.6	9.3
Balochi	0.7	0.1	2.1	2.7	–	–	58.5	46.7	3.5	2.6
Siraiki	17.4	8.4	1.0	1.7	3.9	3.1	2.6	4.1	10.9	5.5
Others	0.9	0.8	4.9	8.8	20.4	15.1	5.1	6.1	4.8	4.8
Total (%)	100.0	100.0	100.0	100.0	100.0	100.0	100.0	100.0	100.0	100.0
Population (millions)	73.6	23.0	30.4	14.8	17.7	3.0	5.7	1.4	127.5	42.2

Source: Compiled by the author from Government of Pakistan, Population Census Organisation, Statistics Division, *1998 Provincial Census Report of Punjab* (Islamabad: Census Organization, January 2001); *1998 Provincial Census Report of Sindh* (Islamabad: Census Organization, May 2000); *1998 Provincial Census Report of NWFP* (Islamabad: Census Organization, October 2000). The data for Balochistan (the report had not been released as of March 2002) was compiled by the author from the 21 individual district census reports relating to that province. The material for Quetta District was extrapolated from the 1981 district report.

residual category; the word is used to describe those individuals who had migrated to Pakistan as a consequence of partition. Punjabi-speaking Muhajirs quickly integrated into the Punjabi mainstream, and ceased to be considered an immigrant community, but Urdu and Gujarati-speaking Muhajirs, many of whom settled in Karachi, Hyderabad, and Dhaka, did not fully integrate and in time came to be considered a separate community. Subsequent to partition the overwhelming majority of each linguistic community were Muslims.[9]

In 1971, after a lengthy nationalist struggle that culminated in a civil and later an international war, East Pakistan seceded from Pakistan, and became Bangladesh. Consequently, Bengalis ceased to be a constituent component of Pakistan's ethnic landscape. Also, subsequent to partition there has been considerable interprovincial and intraprovincial migration within West Pakistan. Table 7.1 describes the ethnic composition of Pakistan by province in 1998, the date of Pakistan's most recent census, and this is illustrated in Map 7.1.

Two patterns deserve note. One has been the phenomenon of rural to urban migration, spurred by brighter employment opportunities in the cities. The urban population of Pakistan grew by 19.2 million (83%) from 1981 to 1998. A second phenomenon, also largely fuelled by employment prospects, has been the interprovincial shifting of Punjabis and Pakhtuns to Balochistan and Sindh. These phenomena have had two major consequences: the major urban areas of Pakistan have become far more ethnically diverse, and the indigenous population of the smaller provinces, particularly Sindh and Balochistan, have become threatened by the prospect of outside domination. For instance, Quetta, the capital of Balochistan, has more Pakhtun and Punjabi residents than local Baloch; and Sindhis constitute less than 10% of the population of the four districts of Karachi (Sindh's largest city).

Given the diversity of communities, ethnic stereotypes remain plentiful and widely held in Pakistan. Punjabis view themselves as the rightful heirs of the martial tradition, providing the society with fine soldiers, efficient administrators, yeoman farmers and pious Muslims. Outside communities view Punjabis as arrogant, deceitful and domineering – and resist their 'dominance' of the state's institutions. Muhajirs consider themselves the intellectual and professional elite of the society – and indeed they are disproportionately represented in the universities, professions, big business, and until recently civil administration. Other communities view the Muhajirs as an effete and somewhat illicit commercial class, at times doubting their patriotism, owing to their former ties to India. The Pakhtuns consider themselves a pure tribe of consummate warriors following the ancient and manly path of *Paktunwali* (way of the Pakhtun – hospitality, honour, and revenge). Outsiders view the Pakhtuns as lawless, rough and anti-intellectual. Since 1979, Pakistani Pakhtuns have become increasingly identified with the closely affiliated Pashto-speaking Afghan refugees. The latter in turn, as evidenced by the rise of the Taliban, have helped to reinforce this stereotype. Sindhis take great pride in the antiquity of their culture and the purity and beauty of their language. They also claim a connection to the font of mystical Islam and Sufi orders. Outside communities view the Sindhis as peasants, dominated by perverse feudal chieftains. Finally, the Baloch trace their ancestry back to ancient times and are proud of their accomplishments as warriors and as independent

MAP 7.1
PAKISTAN: MOTHER LANGUAGE BY PROVINCE, 1998

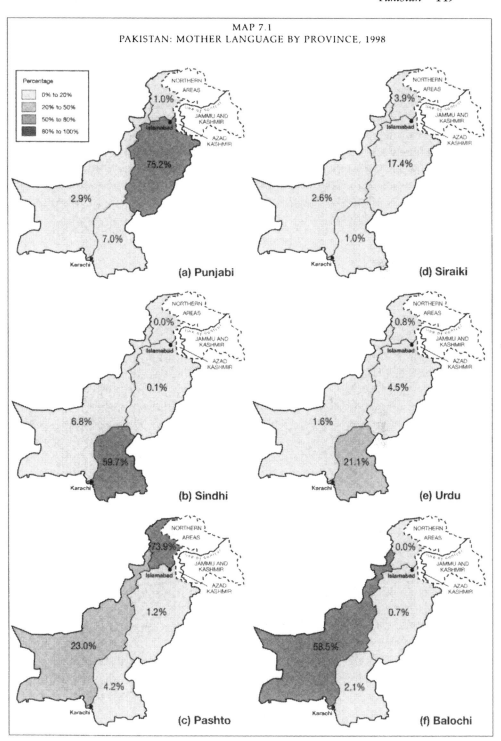

(a) Punjabi

(b) Sindhi

(c) Pashto

(d) Siraiki

(e) Urdu

(f) Balochi

survivors of their harsh environment. Outside communities view the Baloch as archetypes of stumbling, backward provincials.[10]

Of course, such ethnic stereotypes in part reflect the colonial attitudes and policies of the British. They also bespeak what Horowitz has described as invidious comparisons of 'backward' and 'advanced' ethnic communities.[11] Clearly, employing this criterion, Muhajirs and Punjabis are often typified as 'advanced' communities, while Sindhis and Baloch are typified as 'backward.' As imprecise as such stereotypes may be, they provide a potent rationale for the most persistent and virulent theme of ethnic conflict in Pakistan. This is the insistent refrain voiced by members of indigenous 'backward' communities that their communities (Bengalis, Sindhis and Baloch) are being overrun by 'advanced' outsiders (such as Punjabis and Muhajirs).

SOURCES OF ETHNIC CONFLICT

As we have seen, the homeland for the Muslims of South Asia was formed with little concern for the ethnic homogeneity of its peoples. This section examines the sources of ethnic conflict in the state by tracing the major grievances, perceptions, and political responses of Pakistan's ethnoregional actors.

Bengali Secession

Much has been written concerning the rationale and process of dismemberment of Pakistan and the creation of Bangladesh.[12] For our purposes, four arguments against the continuation of united Pakistan – political, administrative, economic and linguistic – seem compelling.

First, at partition, East Pakistan contained a majority of Pakistan's people (54%), and Bengalis were by far the largest ethnic community (52% of the total; 96% in East Pakistan.) But their political authority did not reflect their majority status in the new state. None of the major national leaders of the post-independence government based in Karachi was Bengali-speaking, nor was Pakistan's Constituent Assembly eager or willing to enshrine the principle of majority rule in Pakistan's first constitution. Indeed, the issue of the political representation of the two wings of Pakistan was the major factor that delayed the adoption of Pakistan's first constitution until 1956.[13]

Second, Bengalis were also underrepresented in the civil and military bureaucracies. Such underrepresentation was largely a legacy of colonial policy. For example, in 1947 only one of the 95 members of the Indian Civil Service (ICS) who opted for Pakistan was a Bengali.[14] Similarly, less than 1% of the military officers inherited by Pakistan were Bengalis. By

1949, Pakistan had adopted recruitment policies designed to ameliorate the underrepresentation of Bengalis in the civil bureaucracy,[15] but policies of ethnic preference were never implemented with respect to military recruitment. Indeed, as late as 1955 less than 4% of Pakistan's military officers were Bengali.[16]

Third, Bengalis were also aggrieved by the much-publicized contention that West Pakistan was absorbing the lion's share of development expenditure in the state while East Pakistan, through the export of jute, was providing the bulk of Pakistan's foreign exchange. Such contentions were supported by relevant economic data at least until the early 1960s.

Fourth, and perhaps of greatest importance, was the issue of language. The founding fathers of Pakistan, including Mohammad Ali Jinnah, advocated that Urdu be made the national language of Pakistan. This ill-conceived decision, controversially justified on the grounds of promoting cultural assimilation, was universally despised in East Pakistan. In the first place, the adoption of Urdu as the national language was seen as an invidious slight against the Bengali language and the Bengali people. It also placed Bengali speakers at a disadvantage in regard to access to the national elite. Furthermore, it elevated the influence of Urdu-speaking 'outsiders' in the East Wing at the expense of the indigenous Bengalis. Indeed, the selection by the central government in 1947 of the Urdu-speaking Khwaja Nazimuddin as the first chief minister of East Pakistan was widely interpreted as constituting proof of a plot to deny Bengalis their political birthright. Given the symbolic importance of the language issue, it is not surprising that the first expressions of Bengali separatism revolved around the language disturbances of 1948 and 1952 in Dhaka.

To make a long story short, the politicization of such grievances, coupled with the inability or unwillingness of the central government to devolve authority to Bengali nationalists, resulted in increasingly insistent and radical calls for autonomy and separatism, including Sheikh Mujibur Rehman's 'Six Points' programme.[17] When Mujib and his Awami League received a majority of seats in the 1970 election, the central government was loath to transfer power to forces that it feared would weaken the integrity of the state. The refusal of the centre to accept the results of the election led to the civil war and to the subsequent intervention of the Pakistan Army, the ethnic bloodbath that followed, and the eventual creation of Bangladesh. One long-lasting legacy of the war was the creation of 300,000 or so Urdu-speaking 'stranded Pakistanis', usually known as Biharis, who remained loyal to West Pakistan (Pakistan) during the war and have never been fully repatriated to Pakistan following the war nor integrated into Bangladesh. The status of the Biharis remains an important issue in Muhajir and Sindhi politics, as described below.

Punjabi Domination

At the core of ethnoregional sentiment in Pakistan is the perception by Punjabis and non-Punjabis alike that the Punjabi community dominates the politics and society of the state. There is considerable objective support for this perception. First, Punjabis constitute a majority of the population when one includes closely affiliated Siraiki speakers (see Table 7.1). Second, Punjabis have long dominated membership of the civil and military bureaucracy,[18] and in recent years they have increasingly come to dominate the business community as well. Third, Punjab is by far the wealthiest and most developed province in the state. Indicators of such advantage include differentials in per capita income, life expectancy, levels of industrialization and urbanization, and literacy rate. In the face of such facts, nationals of the smaller provinces perceive themselves as threatened by the spectre of Punjabi domination. This issue was particularly contentious during Prime Minister Nawaz Sharif's second government (1997–99): he was Punjabi, and so too were the President (Rafiq Tarar) and the Chief of Army Staff (Jehangir Karamat). This ethnic monopoly was broken in 1999 when Parvez Musharraf, a Muhajir, took over as Chief Executive; he succeeded as President the following year.

Sindhi Regionalism

Sindh, to a greater extent than any other province in Pakistan, has experienced an extensive influx of immigrants, first from India (Muhajirs), and then, after partition, from the other provinces of Pakistan.[19] Exacerbating the tensions occasioned by this invasion of ethnic 'outsiders' has been the fact that such newcomers were typically better educated, wealthier, more cosmopolitan, and better able to compete in a modernizing state than Sindhi sons of the soil.[20] Particularly galling to the indigenous Sindhis has been the rapid commercial growth of Karachi, fuelled by the influx of Muhajirs and later by Punjabi money and talent, with relatively little corresponding benefit to the indigenous Sindhis. Indeed, the rural areas of Sindh have remained largely unaffected by the rapid growth of Karachi, and the social patterns that have prevailed in Sindh for centuries have remained substantially unchanged. The perception of Sindhi subordination in the rural areas has been encouraged by governmental policies that award tracts of reclaimed agricultural land in Sindh to retired civil and military officers, the majority of whom are Punjabi or Pakhtun.

Originally, the demand for 'Sindhudesh' (Sindhi homeland) was directed primarily at the Muhajir community, which controlled the commercial and industrial life of Karachi. Aggravating such sentiments in the early years of Pakistan's statehood were the aforementioned Urdu language policy and the One Unit Plan (1955–70). This plan integrated West Pakistan's four provinces into 'one unit' and moved the capital to the Punjab, first to Lahore and later to Islamabad.

But the greatest impetus for Sindhi regionalism is linked with the career and demise of the late Prime Minister Zulfiqar Ali Bhutto (1971–77). Bhutto was the scion of a very prominent Sindhi landholding family. During his regime he encouraged Sindhi sentiments by empathizing with the grievances of the Sindhis and by promising to rectify past injustices. Among the policies pursued by his government were land reforms, the purposes of which were to favour the Sindhi masses at the expense of the landlords in Sindh and to end non-Sindhi ownership of Sindhi agricultural land. Bhutto also nationalized heavy industry, banks and insurance. Each of these actions was perceived in Sindh as a challenge to the interests of the Muhajirs. Similarly, Bhutto's civil and military reforms were perceived as detrimental to non-Sindhi interests. Following Bhutto's overthrow by a military coup and his eventual execution, Sindhi ethnic sentiment gained a focal point, perhaps even a martyr, and has correspondingly proliferated.

During President Zia-ul-Haq's regime (1977–88), Sindh became the most aggrieved of all of Pakistan's provinces. Many Sindhis perceived Zia's government as Punjabi inspired – at best, oblivious to the grievances of Sindhis, at worst conspiring to strengthen further the position of the Punjabis at the expense of the Sindhis. Perhaps the most serious challenge to Zia's rule was the Movement for the Restoration of Democracy (MRD), which inspired the disturbances of 1983 that originated in, and for the most part remained confined to, rural Sindh. During the heyday of the 1983 disturbances, Sindhi separatists voiced grievances reminiscent of Bengali leader Sheikh Mujibur Rehman's Six Points. These dissidents called for increased provincial autonomy, and insisted on reducing disparities in economic development. They also charged the federal government with inadequate allocation of federal government funds; claimed underrepresentation in the military, bureaucratic, entrepreneurial, and political elite of the state; and charged that Sindhis were second-class citizens, even in their own province. The assassination of President Zia in August 1988 and the subsequent election of Benazir Bhutto as Prime Minister dramatically changed such perceptions. Sindhi grievances remained, but there was widespread confidence that Benazir's regime, led by a woman from Sindh, would be more accommodating to Sindhi interests.

As the daughter of the late Prime Minister, Benazir inherited the mantle of Sindhi leadership. This has been both a benefit and a liability. Competing nationalist demands (Sindhi and Punjabi) have largely come to define the Pakistani political arena since 1988. Benazir Bhutto and the Pakistan People's Party (PPP) have become increasingly associated with Sindhi interests, and Nawaz Sharif and the Pakistan Muslim

League–Nawaz (PML–N) with Punjabi interests. For instance, in the 1997 National Assembly elections, the PPP failed to win a single seat in any province save Sindh, and the PML-N was the only political party to win a seat in the Punjab. This led one perceptive observer of Pakistani elections to assert that the PPP had 'become solely a regional party.'[21] After leaving office for the second time Benazir Bhutto was charged with numerous crimes, tried in absentia, and sentenced to a 14-year prison term for corruption. She currently lives in exile, dividing her time between the Middle East and England. Sindhi nationalist politics has become more muted since her departure.

Muhajir Nationalism

The recent emergence of Muhajirs as a full-fledged ethnic group constitutes a pure case of what could be termed the creation of an 'acquired' as opposed to a 'primordial' ethnic identity. For most of Pakistan's history, Muhajirs were a residual category, in effect newcomers to the country who had abandoned their respective primordial ethnic affiliations when they opted for Pakistan. It is true that non-Muhajir communities, particularly Sindhis, defined 'Muhajirs' as a group which was able to take unfair advantage of state policies. But the overwhelming majority of so-called Muhajirs rejected such definitions, preferring rather to be called 'Pakistanis.' Such self-definition underwent rapid transformation following the communal riots in Karachi in December 1986.

During the riots, Muhajirs organized by the fledgling Muhajir national movement (*Muhajir Qaumi Mahaz*, MQM), and its leader Altaf Hussain, participated on the side of 'indigenous Sindhis' (defined in 1986 to include both Muhajirs and Sindhis) against 'outsiders' (Pakhtuns, Punjabis, and Afghans). Muhajir militancy continued after the riots and resulted in the forceful expression of several demands by the MQM on the central government. Three demands are salient. The first was a call for the repeal or significant revision of Pakistan's ethnic quota system for government employment. According to the MQM, the size of the 'urban Sindh' quota (7.6%) unfairly restricts Muhajir entry into Pakistan's elite. Second, the MQM demanded the repatriation of the approximately 300,000 Urdu-speaking Biharis, many of whom languish as stateless people in refugee camps in Bangladesh. Third, Altaf Hussain also advocated the idea that Muhajirs should be treated as a 'fifth subnationality', a status commensurate with that of the Punjabis, Sindhis, Pakhtuns and Baloch. Fourth, the MQM insisted on holding a 'fair' national census. Muhajir nationalists claimed that the 1981 census underreported the population of Karachi, hence underreporting the size of the Muhajir community. Each of these demands is anathema to Sindhi interests. Sindhi leaders do not favour a revision of the ethnic quota as it currently disproportionately favours Sindhi candidates; nor does Sindhi leadership look with favour upon the repatriation of the 'Biharis', who they fear will take up residence in Karachi. Also, Sindhis fear that Muhajir attempts to be considered a fifth subnationality masks their real goal of claiming a territorial right to Karachi. Finally, the Sindhi leadership does not favour the holding of a 'fair' census that is likely to disclose that Sindhis are a minority in several districts of 'their' province.[22]

Despite such obvious conflicts of interest, the MQM joined the PPP's coalition government following the national elections of 1988. The PPP had promised to pursue the MQM's demands in exchange for such support. Benazir's government, however, proved unable or unwilling to keep its promises. The immediate consequence was that the MQM left the coalition government and joined the opposition *Islami Jamhoori Ittehad* (IJI) led by Nawaz Sharif. The IJI-MQM accord held firm throughout the course of the 1990 elections; MQM candidates swept the polls in both Karachi and Hyderabad; and the MQM helped to form the government both at the centre and in the Sindh provincial assembly. However, following a military crack-down in Sindh province during the summer of 1992, which targeted alleged illegal activities of MQM activists (such as torture cells, kidnapping and extortion gangs, and drug running activities), the MQM severed its ties with the IJI. Consequently, Altaf Hussain and other prominent MQM leaders have either absented themselves from Pakistan or gone underground to escape arrest.

Since then, MQM–Sindhi as well as MQM–Punjabi relations have continued to deteriorate and have been major contributors to the ethnonational violence that has plagued urban Sindh (particularly Karachi) ever since. Three times in the 1990s – in 1992, from 1994 to 1996, and again in 2000 – successive governments have been forced to the desperate expedient of inviting the Pakistan Army into Karachi in order to carry out police duties. Ethnic violence reached a peak in the 1994-96 period, claiming over 5,000 lives according to official figures.

Pakhtun Provincialism

In the NWFP the call for an independent entity of 'Paktunistan' predates independence. Paktunistan means different things to different people, ranging from the demand for the formation of a new state incorporating Pakhtun areas on both sides of the Pakistan–Afghanistan border to a mere change of nomenclature for the NWFP. Near consensus has emerged in recent years, at least among Pashto-speakers, that the NWFP should be renamed 'Pakhtunkhwa'. In any event, the call for a Pakhtun entity stems from the perception of the common ethnic, cultural, and linguistic background of the Pakhtun communities on both sides of the border.

Before partition, the demand for a separate Muslim state was weaker in the frontier regions of Pakistan than in the more settled areas.

Undoubtedly, one reason for such a distinction was the fact that few Hindus lived in the frontier regions. Hence the grievances of the Pakhtuns at that time were with the British, and not with the confluence of British and Hindu domination, as in the Sindh and Punjab. Consequently, the pre-partition sentiments of the Pakhtun leaders found a natural ally in the policies of the Indian National Congress, and few took part in the Pakistan Movement. Indeed, Khan Abdul Ghaffar Khan (1890-1988), the most prominent pre-partition Pakhtun leader, was referred to as the 'Frontier Gandhi' for his espousal of an undivided India and his use of non-violent civil disobedience.

After partition, development in the NWFP was slow and uneven. Building upon a foundation of grievances reminiscent of Mujib's Six Points and the eventual secession of Bangladesh, Khan Abdul Ghaffar Khan formed the West Pakistan portion of what in 1957 became known as the Awami League Party (NAP). This party never gained much support in Sindh or Punjab, but it took firm root in the NWFP and Balochistan. Indeed, in the 1970 election the NAP emerged as the most significant party in the NWFP. In 1974, Khan Abdul Wali Khan (the son of Ghaffar Khan), the leader of the NAP, ran afoul of Zulfiqar Ali Bhutto and the PPP. Consequently, Wali Khan was arrested for the murder of H.M. Sherpao, a PPP Minister in the NWFP government, and the NAP was banned. The charges against Wali Khan were dropped in 1977 following Bhutto's overthrow.[23]

The Soviet–Afghan war and its aftermath complicated issues connected to Pakhtun provincialism. Afghanistan has never accepted the validity of the Durand Line, which demarcates the Pakistan –Afghanistan border. Cross border raids by Soviet-Afghan airplanes, common during the period of Soviet occupation (1979–89), highlighted this fact. A further complication is the status of the Afghan refugees who have taken up residence in the NWFP. Chronic sectarian clashes between the two main groups of Muslims – the Sunnis and the Shias – have been exacerbated by the influx of Afghans, most of whom are Sunnis. There is considerable sentiment in the NWFP (particularly in the urban areas) to the effect that the Afghans constitute a drain on the already limited resources of the province. From the Soviet withdrawal in 1989 until the hostilities of 2001, these issues were finessed by successive regimes through a combination of tacit non-involvement in Pakhtun tribal affairs and extensive domestic and international financial subsidies to the refugee communities.

The US–Afghan war that began in 2001 has exacerbated Pakhtun–Pakistan relations. The target of the US activities, the Taliban regime, was primarily made up of and supported by Pashto-speaking Afghans, close ethnic affiliates of the Pakhtuns on the Pakistan side of the border. The defeat of the Taliban, coupled with President Musharraf's support for the US actions, has created the impression that Pakistan is 'fighting against' Pakhtun nationals. Largely for this reason Musharraf's government was obliged to ban the activities of the militant Islamic movement, *Jamiat-ul-Ulema Islami* (JUI), and to place its leader, Fazlur Rahman, under house arrest in October 2001. The JUI had organized mass protests against Pakistan's support for the US-led war effort. Of course, the war has also created hundreds of thousands – and perhaps millions – of additional refugees, many of whom will seek to live in the NWFP or Balochistan when the dust settles. Many of these new refugees will be opposed to the Karzai regime in Kabul, further complicating an already complicated ethnic morass in the province.

Baloch Marginalism

Balochistan is Pakistan's largest, poorest, and most sparsely settled province. It constitutes roughly 40% of Pakistan's territory but has less than 5% of its population. Balochi-speakers are a minority in eight of Balochistan's 22 districts. Pashto speakers predominate in six of these and Brahvi speakers in the other two districts. In Quetta, Balochistan's capital and by far largest city, Balochi speakers constitute only around 5% of the population. These figures do not reflect the million or more Afghan refugees (mostly Pashto speakers) who live in the province, their camps clustered near Quetta.[24]

At partition, Balochistan was only partially incorporated into Pakistan. British colonial policy had treated Balochistan as a large buffer zone and had granted local Baloch leaders wide autonomy within their traditional sphere of influence. In 1955, Pakistan incorporated such territories as part of the One Unit Plan and the tribal leaders in 'merger agreements' ceded their territories to Pakistan. In practice, however, the Baloch tribal leaders maintained considerable autonomy over their former domains.[25] But the merger sparked demands by the masses for significant social change. Such incipient politicization found expression in the 1970 elections, and Balochistan, like the NWFP, elected the NAP to power.

Tensions between the Baloch NAP government and the PPP central government came to a head in 1973, when a cache of arms, allegedly destined for Baloch separatists, was discovered in the residence of the Iraqi military attaché in Islamabad. The government reacted by confiscating the arms, dismissing the Baloch provincial government, and arresting its leaders. As a result of such 'provocations', Baloch guerrillas began to ambush army convoys. The war rapidly escalated; at its peak between 80,000 and 100,000 Pakistani army personnel were in Balochistan. Despite considerable loss of life the results of the conflict were inconclusive. Fighting continued intermittently until Zulfiqar Ali Bhutto was removed from government in 1977. Upon assuming power, Zia released thousands of Baloch from jail and declared an amnesty for the guerrillas who had taken refuge in Afghanistan or Iran.[26]

Since the civil war, most Baloch nationalists have tempered their demands for separation from the state but have continued to stress the need for greater provincial autonomy. Such autonomist demands have been countered with increasing fervour during the 1990s by Balochistan-domiciled Pakhtuns who call for the partition of Balochistan along ethnic (Baloch–Pakhtun) lines. During the past decade small-scale violence between the two communities has become endemic, particularly in Quetta. It is important to note that it is likely that the outcome of the US–Afghan war will further exacerbate Pakhtun–Baloch relations in the province. As mentioned above, the war has created a continuing flow of Afghan refugees (mostly Pashto-speaking) to the province. Moreover, most of the support for Fazlur Rehman's JUI, the party most vocal in its opposition to Pakistan's participation in the war, comes from Pakhtun areas of Balochistan.

Kashmiri Disputed Partition

Technically, Azad Kashmir ('free Kashmir', also known as Pakistan Occupied Kashmir) is not part of Pakistan.[27] Azad Kashmir has its own political institutions: its own constitution, its own court system, and its own legislature. However, in a de facto sense the 'state' is hardly sovereign with respect to Pakistan – though its 'independence' is a logical consequence of the long-standing Pakistani claim that Kashmir is disputed territory. This dispute can only be settled, according to Pakistan, when the UN-sponsored referendum is held in the 'whole of Kashmir', including the Indian state of Jammu and Kashmir, and this will determine the status of the entire territory. In lieu of such a referendum, Kashmir has remained the focal point of Pakistan–Indian conflict since partition.

At first, the conflict was seen in its original terms – that is, one solely between India and Pakistan. Kashmir could either become part of India or part of Pakistan, the outcome to be decided by the aforementioned referendum, rather than being partitioned between the two countries (as happened in fact). Since the mid-1980s, however, the issue has become far more complicated as the so-called 'Third Option' of Kashmiri independence has gained increasing salience. What such independence would entail in practice remains problematic. The minimal boundaries of such an independent state could be confined *only* to Srinagar and the Vale of Kashmir (within Jammu and Kashmir); the maximal boundaries would encompass the whole of Jammu and Kashmir (including Ladakh), Azad Kashmir, and Pakistan's Northern Areas.

Nevertheless, the conflict in Kashmir has become increasingly violent in recent years owing to the Indian government's brutally repressive policies, as well as Pakistan's complicity in supporting Kashmiri 'nationalist' (India would use the term 'terrorist') activities in the Vale of Kashmir. Conservatively speaking, more than 50,000 people have died in the conflict since 1988 – the overwhelming majority Muslims.

The long-standing Indian position that the conflict is at heart a 'terrorist uprising' led by Pakistan has been given theoretical support by the actions of the United States and its coalition partners during the 'war against terrorism' that began in 2001. That is, if the justification for destroying the Afghan government is that it 'harboured terrorists' it follows that Pakistan should be obliged to crack down on those supporting the Kashmiri uprising. If Pakistan fails to follow through, the Indian government argues, Pakistan's government should suffer the same fate as the Taliban. Pakistan has countered that such a comparison is inappropriate, as the Kashmir uprising is a legitimate indigenous nationalist movement, not akin to the Taliban's relation with external terrorists. Such Indian claims and Pakistani counter claims led to the mass mobilization of troops along the India–Pakistan border following the 13 December 2001 attempted attack on the Indian parliament, which India blamed on Pakistani-supported Kashmiri insurgents.

It is important to note in conclusion that Kashmir, however defined, is ethnically complex. The overwhelming majority of Azad Kashmiris are Punjabis (85%). Jammu and Kashmir is ethnically divided between Kashmiri (52%), Dogri (23%) and Tibetan (around 10%) speakers.[28]

POLICIES OF ETHNIC PREFERENCE

As we have seen, Pakistan's attempts at promoting cultural assimilation through the ill-fated Urdu language programme (1948–52) and the One Unit Plan (1955–69) failed and were abandoned. Similarly, the assimilationist benefits of the Islamization programme that began in 1979 have been modest at best, and this policy has been placed on the back burner since the mid 1990s.[29] Clearly, as the proliferation of ethnic conflict in Pakistan attests, the salience of ethnic factors in the politics of the state continues to increase.

Development of Ethnic Quotas

Since 1949, the central government has embarked on a parallel track that seeks to manage ethnic conflict through mandating proportionality of ethnic representation in Pakistan's administrative, professional and business elite. The vehicle to give effect to this end is a system of ethnic quotas.

The catalyst for the formation of the quota was the jarring reality of Bengali underrepresentation in the civil bureaucracy. As mentioned above, Pakistan inherited only one Bengali officer from the Indian Civil Service; the overwhelming majority of the others were either Muhajir or Punjabi. Accordingly, in 1949, the central government established a quota for recruitment into the 'Central Superior Services' (CSS – the then elite cadre of Pakistan's civil bureaucracy). The provisions of the policy stipulated that 20% of such vacancies were to be filled by 'merit' as determined by the CSS examination process. The remaining 80% would be filled by the following formula: East Pakistan, 40%; Punjab and Bahawalpur, 23%; Karachi, 2%; and Sindh, Khairpur, NWFP, Frontier States and Tribal Areas, Balochistan, Azad Kashmir and Kashmir refugees, 15%.[30] The aims of the quota were modest. Its thrust was to prudently increase the representation of Bengalis in the elite ranks of the civil bureaucracy, while not compromising the quality of its membership. Moreover, advocates of the quota considered it a temporary remedial expedient, which would be phased out within ten years of its introduction.

However, the quota grew and matured in the fertile soil of regional animosities between East and West Pakistan. By 1956, the quota policy, which had originated as an administrative directive, had grown to the status of a statutory exception to the non-discrimination clause of the constitution. This status was reiterated in the 1962 constitution.[31] Perhaps more importantly, however, its range also underwent steady expansion. By the early 1950s the quota had been made applicable to vacancies filled by interview through the Federal Public Service Commission. Eventually, it was applied to departmental and attached departmental recruitment in the central government as well. Indeed, by 1971 the quota had application to approximately 2000 entry level positions in the central government each year.[32]

Despite the rapid growth of the quota system, the grievances of Bengalis proved too great to be overcome by such administrative expedients. The resultant civil war left Pakistan dismembered. Ostensibly, the secession of Bangladesh made moot the original rationale for the quota. Since 1971, however, instead of dying, the quota system has become increasingly vibrant. In August 1973, the quota re-emerged in its present form: 10% merit; 50% Punjab; 7.6% urban Sindh (Karachi, Hyderabad and Sukkur); 11.4% rural Sindh; 11.5% NWFP; 3.5% Balochistan; 4% Northern Areas and Centrally Administered Tribal Areas; and 2% Azad Kashmir.[33]

During the 1970s the ambit of the quota continued to expand. The catalyst for such expansion was the economic policies of Zulfiqar Ali Bhutto. Between 1972 and 1975 Bhutto nationalized numerous industries (banks, insurance, mining, heavy machinery, rice, cotton, textiles, and so forth). Consequently, such concerns, formerly in the private sector, became subject to the terms of federal employment. That is, thousands of additional entry-level positions became subject to the federal quota. Parallel to such developments in the public sector was the introduction and rapid proliferation of ethnic quotas governing admission to educational institutions. Such quotas began to make their appearance in the early 1950s, at first in an *ad-hoc*, temporary manner. By 1980, however, admission to virtually every institution of higher education and professional school in the state was subject to an ethnic quota.[34] It is important to note that despite the near-universality of ethnic quotas in respect to recruitment to the civil administration, public sector enterprises and educational institutions, no comparable quotas have ever been applied to the recruitment of Pakistan's military. The officer corps of the military is composed overwhelmingly of Punjabi and Pakhtun nationals.

The Ethnic Consequences

Understandably, assessments of the efficacy of quota systems are shaded by partisan ethnic concerns. Policies of ethnic preference by their very nature favour the interests of certain groups at the expense of others. Pakistan's experience with the operation of its ethnic quota system substantiates such observations. Tables 7.2, 7.3 and 7.4 present data relevant to officers' provincial domicile in the federal bureaucracy, in the Secretariat Group (the elite cadre of the federal bureaucracy) and in public corporations, respectively.[35] An examination of these tables leads to three major findings.

First, Punjab and ostensibly ethnic Punjabis dominate membership in the bureaucracy and in the business elite; such dominance is roughly proportional to the respective population of the province. However, the most recent data for the civil bureaucracy indicates that Punjab representation has become disproportionately high. Second, 'urban Sindhis' (predominantly Muhajirs) have traditionally enjoyed greater representation in such elite groups than their quota allotment would allow (7.6%); but their disproportionate advantage is declining and had disappeared with respect to the senior bureaucracy by 2001 (see Table 7.3). It is likely to have declined or disappeared in other elite groups as well. Third, the provincial representation of less advanced areas (rural Sindh, Balochistan, Northern Areas, Azad Kashmir) has continued to expand. That is, traditionally advantaged groups have been limited by the operation of the quota, which has tended to favour traditionally disadvantaged groups. Therefore, the quota system is working in the direction anticipated by its founders. More importantly, in the absence of the quota ethnic representation in the bureaucratic and business elite would be far less equitable than is currently the case.[36]

Despite such success, however, ethnic demands and ethnic conflict have proliferated in Pakistan. Paradoxically, there is ample evidence to suggest that the quota system itself is a contributory factor to such developments. For instance, it is undoubtedly the case that the creation and growth of the Muhajir community as an ethnic actor has been

TABLE 7.2

PAKISTAN: DOMICILE OF OFFICERS IN THE FEDERAL BUREAUCRACY,
1973–86

Domicile	1973		1983		1986	
	All	Senior	All	Senior	All	Senior
Punjab	49.3	53.5	54.9	55.8	55.3	57.7
NWFP	10.5	7.0	13.4	11.6	12.6	12.1
Rural Sindh	3.1	2.7	5.4	5.1	7.2	6.7
Urban Sindh	30.1	33.5	17.4	20.2	18.2	18.3
Balochistan	2.5	1.5	3.4	3.1	3.6	3.1
Northern Areas	2.6	1.3	3.6	3.4	1.4	1.5
Azad Kashmir	1.8	0.5	1.9	0.9	1.7	0.7
Total (%)	100.0	100.0	100.0	100.0	100.0	100.0
Number	84,749	6,011	134,310	11,816	187,925	17,652

Note: 'Senior' refers to officer-level rank.

Source: Adapted by the author from Government of Pakistan, *Report of the Fourth Triennial Census of Federal Government Services as of 1st January 1973* (Islamabad: MPCPP, 1976); *Federal Government Civil Servants Census Report, January 1983* (Islamabad: MPCPP, 1984); and *Federal Government Civil Servant Census Report, January 1986* (Islamabad: MPCPP, 1987).

TABLE 7.3

PAKISTAN: DOMICILE OF OFFICERS OF SECRETARIAT GROUP, 1989–2001

Domicile	1989 Grades		2001 Grades	
	19–22	20–22	19–22	20–22
Punjab	62.1	59.6	67.1	67.4
NWFP	10.1	10.3	13.4	11.4
Rural Sindh	6.1	8.9	7.9	7.6
Urban Sindh	14.8	14.3	4.1	6.0
Balochistan	3.3	4.2	2.4	3.3
Northern Areas/FATA	2.3	1.7	3.4	2.2
Azad Kashmir	1.2	1.0	1.7	2.2
Total (%)	100.0	100.0	100.0	100.0
Number	663	406	417	184

Note: The 'Secretariat Group' is the elite cadre of Pakistan's bureaucracy.

Source: Adapted by the author from Government of Pakistan Cabinet Secretariat, *Gradation List of Secretariat Group BPS 19-22* (Islamabad: Cabinet Secretariat, Establishment Division, 1989); Cabinet Secretariat (Establishment Division*) Posting List of the Secretariat Group BS 19-22* (Islamabad: Cabinet Secretariat, July 6, 2001).

TABLE 7.4
PAKISTAN: DOMICILE OF SENIOR EXECUTIVES IN PUBLIC CORPORATIONS,
1974–83

Domicile	1974: salary greater than Rs. 1000 per month	1983: salary greater than Rs. 3000 per month
Punjab	41.3	47.9
NWFP	6.2	9.6
Rural Sindh	3.6	6.8
Urban Sindh	46.8	31.5
Balochistan	1.2	1.9
Northern Areas	0.4	1.0
Azad Kashmir	0.5	1.2
Total (%)	100.0	100.0
Number	16,501	29,845

Source: Adapted by the author from Government of Pakistan, Statistics Cell, *Provisional Data on Distribution of Employees of Autonomous Organizations and Taken-over Establishments by Grade, etc.* (Islamabad: Unpublished photocopy, 1976); and *First Census of Employees of Autonomous/Semi-Autonomous Corporations/Bodies Under the Federal Government* (Islamabad: Public Administration Research Centre, 1986).

largely conditioned by the politicization of issues relevant to the quota system. Muhajirs view the quota as placing unwarranted restrictions upon their career opportunities. The declining representation of Muhajirs in the civil administration provides bitter evidence that they are losing influence in Pakistan's national elite. But most galling to Muhajirs is the perception that the quota denies Muhajir youth the opportunity to succeed or fail on the basis of merit. Muhajir nationalists argue that far more Muhajirs would be inducted into the civil administration and into the professional elite if the quota were abolished. It is important to note in this context that Altaf Hussain formed the All Pakistan Muhajir Student Organization (the lineal forbear of the MQM) after he failed to gain admission to the graduate pharmacy programme at Karachi University owing to the operation of the federal quota. Accordingly, one of the central demands of the MQM has been for the abolition of the quota system, or, failing that, an increase in the percentage of seats allotted to 'urban Sindh'. The MQM's continuing demands for a 'fair' census, and for consideration as a 'fifth subnationality', are also linked to the operation of the quota.

Groups that have been traditionally underrepresented in Pakistan's elite, particularly Sindhis and Baloch, have also been none too happy with the operation of the quota. Members of both groups have consistently contended that their nationals have been prevented from fully benefiting from the operation of the quota owing to 'domicile fraud'. It is often alleged that clever Muhajirs, Punjabis or Pakhtuns, with the connivance of ethnic co-conspirators, forge respective domicile certificates and stand for seats reserved for Sindhis and Baloch. Although hard evidence of such fraud is scanty, such arguments have prompted both Sindh and Balochistan to enact strict provincial residency requirements, and law suits challenging domicile have become commonplace, particularly in regard to admission to educational institutions.[37] In this sense, therefore, the quota system has provided yet another vehicle through which ethnic conflict can be expressed.

It is also important to note that the quota system has done nothing to counter the perception of Punjabi domination. In fact, the provisions of the quota actually ensure a Punjabi majority in all realms of its application. As demonstrated by Table 7.3 the dominance of Punjabis in the most senior ranks of the bureaucracy seems to be increasing. Similarly, as non-Punjabi critics of the quota system are quick to point out, the quota has never been applied to recruitment to the military, the ethnic preserve of Punjabis.

Finally, it should be stressed that the operation of Pakistan's ethnic quota reinforces invidious comparisons between ethnic groups. The system's reliance upon a small merit reservation encourages the perception that job seekers from advantaged ethnic communities have borne the brunt of the government's attempts to equalize access to the bureaucracy and the professions. Conversely, members of disadvantaged ethnic communities must reconcile themselves to the fact that they are perceived to be less qualified than their Punjabi or Muhajir counterparts. Indeed, the very existence of the quota provides statutory verification of the perception that there are profound ethnic differences between the peoples of Pakistan.

DEVOLUTION AND THE LOCAL GOVERNMENT PLAN

The long-term prognosis for Pakistan's troubled ethnic relations is not favourable. Without a significant restructuring of Pakistan's federal system to provide a true devolution of power to competing ethnic groups, the prospect of continuing ethnic conflict seems a near certainty. At the core of Pakistan's ethnic dilemma are perceptions of Punjabi domination. Punjabis constitute over 56% of the population of the state, and they are becoming increasingly dominant in each of Pakistan's most significant national elite groups – the civil bureaucracy, the military and business. Current policies of ethnic preference do not address this concern; indeed, they may exacerbate the problem.

A more useful approach to the dilemma of ethnic conflict would involve the structural reform of Pakistan's federal system. Such prospective reforms would redraw Pakistan's territorial boundaries to make them accord more closely with the ethnic landscape of the state. They would also devolve considerable authority to such newly crafted sub-state units. Zia's government contemplated two such structural reforms, but neither was implemented. The first, suggested by the Ansari Commission, recommended that the federal system be abolished and replaced by one in which the then 21 administrative divisions would serve as newly constituted provinces. The Commission reasoned that such a restructuring would dilute the perceived domination of the Punjab and consequently tame interprovincial and interethnic conflict.[38] Similarly, in early 1988 the government was working on the formulation of a policy that would have decentralized Pakistan into eight administrative units. Punjab would have been carved into three units (two predominantly Punjabi, one Siraiki); Sindh into two units (one predominantly Muhajir, one Sindhi); Balochistan into two units (one predominantly Baloch, one Pakhtun) and the NWFP with minor territorial adjustments would have remained Pakhtun dominated. There is compelling evidence that Zia contemplated promulgating this measure or a close variant after he dissolved the national assembly in 1988, but his death in August precluded such an action.[39] Indeed, when civilian rule was restored and the national and provincial assemblies were reconstituted in 1988, there was little if any support for revising boundaries or the devolution of authority. Civilian politicians in Pakistan derive their authority from specific constituencies; it is clearly not in their collective interest to change the basis of their support.

However, 11 years later (October 1999), following a military coup which placed General Parvez Musharraf (a Muhajir) in the position of 'Chief Executive' and later 'President and Chief Executive' of the state, objective circumstances had changed. Musharraf dissolved the national and provincial assemblies and placed severe restrictions upon political party activity. He also established the National Reconstruction Bureau (NRB), empowered to develop plans to reconstruct Pakistan's political system in order to make it more efficient and democratic.

The NRB responded with the 'Local Government Plan, 2000' in May 2000, which was revised and re-issued in August 2000, and later codified into provincial ordinances in August 2001. The closely related devolution plan was also introduced in August 2001.[40] The main features of the plan are:

1. To dissolve the divisional tier of government. The division level (introduced in the nineteenth century in colonial India) was designed as a vehicle of central governmental control strategically located between the provincial and local governmental levels.
2. To devolve authority from the provinces to the districts. The plan calls for the transfer of six provincial ministries (Agriculture, Education,

Finance and Planning, Health, Revenue, and Works and Services) to the districts. This is a monumental shifting of authority and resources, constituting around one-half of the budgetary value of services heretofore performed by the provinces.

3. To elect district *nazims* who will serve as executive heads of each district (akin to district governors). Such *nazims* are given authority over 'Distict Coordination Officers' (civilian bureaucrats – formerly district commissioners) who formerly administered programmes at the district level. District *nazims* were elected in 97 of Pakistan's 104 districts in August 2001.

Obviously, such reforms are revolutionary and if fully implemented would radically restructure ethnic relations in Pakistan. The reforms target the authority of the civilian bureaucracy – an institution dominated by Punjabis. But, more importantly, the reforms transfer authority from the provincial level to the districts, undercutting and modifying the importance of ethnic politics at the provincial level. Instead of four relevant units (Punjab, NWFP, Sindh, and Balochistan) each with attendant ethnic 'sons of the soil', the reform empowers 104 districts. If the plan is fully implemented ethnic politics will be completely transformed.

Table 7.5 presents data concerning the ethnic composition of the districts. Several points stand out from a consideration of this table. First, districts are far more ethnically homogenous than provinces. Fifty-five of the 104 districts possess populations in which 90% or more of the inhabitants are of a single ethnic group. Similarly, 84 districts have populations in which the dominant ethnic community constitutes 70% or more of the respective populations. Such ethnic homogeneity, ostensibly, would allow district level governments to specifically tailor their policies to fit the needs of their respective populations. Indeed, the main principle guiding the devolution plan is that local government, where feasible, is more efficient and democratic than direct government from the centre. Second, political representation along district lines increases the number of relevant national actors – ten 'nations' have majorities in at least one district, as opposed to four in the provinces. Third, the devolution of authority to the districts weakens the spectre of Punjabi dominance. Ostensibly, Punjabis will be dominant in only the 26 districts in which they constitute a majority of the population. The scope for Punjabi dominance from the centre via the civilian bureaucracy and/or from the largest province has been reduced. Fourth, the rationale for ethnic conflict will be reduced as a consequence of devolving authority to the districts. Competition between 'nations' for resources and postings will be reduced to the extent that devolution takes place. Finally, the rationale for separatist movements should be reduced by devolution. A truly federal arrangement extends stake-holding to minorities at the centre who are majorities at the district level.

Unfortunately, there are significant hurdles to be crossed before the

TABLE 7.5
PAKISTAN: DISTRICT POPULATION AND PREDOMINANT LANGUAGES, 1998

Language	90%+	70–89%	50–69%	Plurality	Total
Punjabi	18	7	1	0	26
Pashto	20	5	0	2	27
Sindhi	8	6	2	1	17
Urdu	0	1	1	2	4
Siraiki	0	5	5	0	10
Balochi	6	2	5	0	13
Brahvi	0	1	1	0	2
Hindko	1	2	0	0	3
Khowar	1	0	0	0	1
Kohistani	1	0	0	0	1
All languages	55	29	15	5	104

Note: The districts grouped above are as follows:

90%+ (Punjabi) Khusab, Bahawalnagar, Jhang, Sheikhpura, Chakwal, Jhelum, Gujranwala, Gujrat, Pakpattan, Toba Tek Singh, Okara, Sialkot, Hafizabad, Mandi Bahauddin, Faisalabad, Narowal, Sargodha, Sahiwal. (Pashto) Hangu, Bannu, Mardan, Swat, Lower Dir, Swabi, Malakand, Nowshera, Upper Dir, Lakki Marwant, Shangla, Buner, Karak, Killa Saifullah, Killa Abdullah, Charsadda, Pishin, Ziarat, Loralai, Zhob. (Sindhi) Jacobabad, Larkana, Dadu, Tharparkar, Thatta, Shikarpur, Khairpur, Ghotki. (Balochi) Panjgur, Gwadur, Kech, Kharan, Awaran, Dera Bugti. (Hindko) Abbottabad. (Khowar) Chitral. (Kohistani) Kohistan.

70–89% (Punjabi) Mianwali, Attock, Vehari, Lahore, Kasur, Khanewal, Rawalpindi. (Pashto) Kohat, Tank, Peshawar, Batagram, Musakhel. (Sindhi) Sanghar, Badin, Naushero Feroz, Sukkur, Nawabshah, Umerkot. (Urdu) Karachi – Central. (Siraiki) Muzzafaragarh, Dera Ghazi Khan, Rajanpur, Bhakkar, Dera Ishmail Khan. (Balochi) Mastung, Barkhan. (Brahvi) Kalat. (Hindko) Mansehra, Haripur.

50–69% (Punjabi) Islamabad. (Sindhi) Hyderabad, Mirpurkhas. (Urdu) Karachi –East. (Siraiki) Layyah, Lodhran, Multan, Bahawalpur, Rahim Yar Khan. (Balochi) Chagai, Nasirabad, Bolan, Jaffarabad, Jhal Magsi. (Brahvi) Khuzdar.

Plurality: (Pashto) Sibi: 44%, Quetta: 40% est. (Sindhi) Malir: 25%. (Urdu) Karachi West: 40%, Karachi South: 26%.

Sources: Derived by the author from the individual district census reports, 1998. Four have not been released as of March 2002: Quetta, Islamabad, Karak, and Rawalpindi. Their inclusion above is based upon extrapolations of the 1981 census data.

devolution plan can be heralded as a success. First and most immediate is the anticipated political resistance from the provinces. On 12 October 2002 elections were held to the national and provincial assemblies; governments were duly established in late November. It is likely that the newly constituted provincial governments will attempt to reclaim authority devolved to the districts during the period in which the operation of the provincial assemblies was suspended. Second, civilian bureaucrats will continue their efforts to sabotage the reforms. Third, the district is hardly an ideal administrative unit to provide equal democratic representation. The respective size of districts in Pakistan varies tremendously. In terms of population the smallest district, Ziarat (Balochistan), has only 33,000 inhabitants, while the largest district, Lahore (Punjab), has 6.3 millions – a ratio of 191:1. Indeed, Lahore district has a larger population than Balochistan's twenty-two districts combined. Fourth, districts vary widely with respect to resources – including literacy, level of urbanization and income.

But the most crucial problem facing the implementation of the devolution plan is the fact that districts are dependent upon the provinces and federal governments for revenue. In Pakistan over 90% of tax revenue is collected at the federal level; 7-8% at the provincial level; and only 2-3% at the district or local level. Therefore, given current arrangements, the rapidly expanding functions of district and local governments will have to be met by prospective fiscal transfers from provincial and federal governments. Indeed the 'Fiscal Decentralization Task Force' established Provincial Finance Commissions (PFCs) in late 2000. The task of such PFCs is to make 'awards' to the districts. Their task will be difficult. First, PFCs will have to deal with the issue of equality of expenditures between districts. Currently, per capita governmental expenditures in Pakistan's districts vary widely. Residents of the wealthier districts receive per capita government expenditure several times greater than residents of the poorer districts. Such expenditures are closely linked to respective degrees of urbanization.[41] Second, the PFCs will have to come to grips with the prospect of autonomous decision-making at the district level. When the devolution plan is fully implemented, the districts collectively will have larger budgets than their respective provinces. Third, given the foregoing, PFCs will have to decide to what extent district governments can revise budget guidelines set at the provincial level. District governments have very little latitude to change provincial guidelines in the current administrative set-up, but the devolution plan demands district autonomy. Fourth, PFCs must decide whether district governments can apply surtaxes or surcharges to existing provincially administered taxes (such as sales and land taxes). They must also decide whether such surtaxes or surcharges can vary from district to district within provinces. Fifth, and finally, PFCs must finesse the question of whether districts can introduce and administer their own local taxes.

Ultimately, an accommodation will have to be reached in a contest where the battle lines are clearly discernible. The advocates of rapid implementation of the devolution plan call for a wholesale revision of Pakistan's tax system which would allow districts to substantially increase their tax base at the expense of provincial and/or federal governments. Those less wedded to the devolution plan stress the prudence of maintaining the system as it exists. Advocates of the current system argue that the province should serve as the policy-making arm of government; and that it would be unwise to devolve too much authority to the districts – the provinces should continue to hold the purse strings. They also argue that the federal government, and to a lesser extent the provincial governments, are far better suited to collect taxes than the local or district governments. But, clearly, meaningful devolution will only occur if and when the district governments have at least a partially independent tax base, an outcome that cannot be taken for granted.[42]

CONCLUSION

Pakistan's policies of ethnic preference have largely failed, if one looks at the bottom-line criteria of ethnic conflict. During Pakistan's 54-year history it has suffered a successful violent secessionist movement in which it lost over 50% of its population. It has been unable to fully integrate Azad Kashmir and the Northern Areas into the state owing to the continuing ethnonational dispute with India over Kashmir. It has fought a civil war in Balochistan. Karachi (Pakistan's largest city) has become known as one of the most dangerous cities in the world owing to chronic ethnonational conflict. And there remain lingering and disturbing problems with the western borderlands, which led indirectly to the formation of the Taliban and the attendant travails of the Afghanistan war.

In my view the recently introduced devolution plan, however flawed or difficult to implement, offers the best hope for addressing Pakistan's serious ethnic problems. Of course, Pakistani decision-makers are 'under the gun' both figuratively and literally. There is little time to implement decisions. Paradoxically, this may be an advantage. The radical reforms contemplated by the devolution plan are a bitter pill for many in the Pakistani establishment, a pill that will only be swallowed from a position of desperation. The detrimental side effects of the cure may be severe; but the recourse of leaving the disease untreated is far worse.

NOTES

1. Most of the Taliban were drawn from the ranks of the Afghan refugee community that resides in Pakistan's western borderlands. The overwhelming majority of such refugees are Pashto speaking, and are largely indistinguishable from the Pakhtuns of Pakistan's NWFP and Balochistan provinces. Since the early 1980s over two million (at times nearly four million) refugees have lived in Pakistan. Many others have settled permanently, if illegally, within Pakistan over the years as well.
2. See Donald Rothchild, 'State and Ethnicity in Africa: A Policy Perspective', in Neil Nevitte and Charles H. Kennedy (eds.), *Ethnic Preference and Public Policy in Developing States* (Boulder, CO: Lynne Rienner, 1986), pp.39–40.
3. The Islamization programme was introduced by President Zia-ul-Haq in 1979, and was pursued with greatest vigour through the remainder of his life until August 1988.

Since his death the programme has continued, despite having no clear champion. See Charles H. Kennedy, *Islamization of Laws and Economy: Case Studies from Pakistan* (Islamabad: Institute of Policy Sciences, 1997).

4. See Donald L. Horowitz, *Ethnic Groups in Conflict* (Berkeley: University of California Press, 1985), pp.151–6.

5. In 1947, of the 1,157 members of the Indian Civil Service and the Indian Political Service, only 101 (9%) were Muslim. See Ralph Braibanti, 'Bureaucracy and Judiciary in Pakistan', in Joseph LaPalombara (ed.), *Bureaucracy and Political Development* (Princeton: Princeton University Press, 1965), p.366.

6. 'Muhajir' literally means one who makes a pilgrimage. That is, the usage of the term implies that those individuals who opted for Pakistan did so for reasons associated with an Islamic obligation.

7. The term 'politically significant' and the inclusion of the six groups listed here follows the usage and meaning of Horowitz. That is, ethnic groups are included as 'politically significant' if they play a role in setting the policy agenda of the central government; see Horowitz, *Ethnic Groups*, pp.17, 51–4.

8. Percentages were calculated by the author using relevant census data. Ethnic group affiliation is defined in terms of mother language.

9. Currently 97% of Pakistanis are Muslims. Hindus constitute around 1.5% of the population and reside primarily in Sindh province; Christians around 1% of the population and reside mostly in Punjab province. For details of origins of languages and language movements see Tariq Rahman, *Language and Politics in Pakistan* (Karachi: Oxford University Press, 1996).

10. See Craig Baxter, Yogendra Malik, Charles H. Kennedy, and Robert Oberst, *Government and Politics in South Asia*. 5th ed. (Boulder, CO: Westview Press, 2002), pp.173–75.

11. See Horowitz, *Ethnic Groups*, pp.166–71.

12. Among the best known and most useful works are: Rounaq Jahan, *Pakistan: Failure of National Integration* (New York: Columbia University Press, 1972); Muhammad A. Quddus, *Pakistan: A Case Study of a Plural Society* (Columbia, MO: South Asia Books, 1982); Leo Rose and Richard Sisson, *War and Secession: Pakistan, India and the Creation of Bangladesh* (Berkeley: University of California Press, 1991); and Feroz Ahmed, *Ethnicity and Politics in Pakistan* (Karachi: Oxford University, 1998).

13. Eventually the Constituent Assembly settled on the concept of parity of representation between the two wings in the National Assembly. Otherwise, owing to their numerical advantage, it was assumed that Bengalis would have established long-term control over the government by holding a majority of seats in the National Assembly.

14. Braibanti, 'Bureaucracy', pp.365–6.

15. See Charles H. Kennedy, *Bureaucracy in Pakistan* (Karachi: Oxford University Press, 1987), pp.187–9.

16. Syed Humanyun, 'The Issue of Disparities in Pakistan Public Services: A Potent Factor Accentuating Bengali Nationalism,' *Pakistan Political Science Review*, Vol. 1, No. 1 (1991), pp.1–15.

17. The Six Points were interpreted as tantamount to a declaration of secession. For details see Baxter, et al., *Government*, pp.26–62.

18. According to Stephen Cohen, 75% of all ex-servicemen come from only five adjoining districts – three in Punjab (Rawalpindi, Jhelum, and Attock) and two in the NWFP (Kohat and Mardan). Stephen P. Cohen, *The Pakistan Army* (Berkeley: University of California Press, 1984), p.75.

19. The following treatment of Sindhi, Muhajir, Pakhtun, and Baloch politics closely follows my treatment in Baxter et al., *Government*, pp.216–21.

20. See Theodore P. Wright Jr., 'Indian Muslim Refugees in the Politics of Pakistan,' *Journal of Commonwealth and Comparative Politics*, Vol. 12, No. 2 (1974), pp.199–205; and his 'Center-Periphery Relations and Ethnic Conflict in Pakistan: Sindhis, Muhajirs and Punjabis,' *Comparative Politics*, Vol. 23, No. 3 (1991), pp.299–312. Also see Feroz Ahmed, *Ethnicity*, pp.41–158.

21. Mohammad Waseem, 'Pakistan Elections 1977: One Step Forward,' in Craig Baxter

and Charles H. Kennedy (eds.), *Pakistan: 1997* (Boulder, CO: Westview Press, 1998).

22. Indeed, a major reason for the delay in holding a national census in Pakistan was concern over prospective Sindhi/Muhajir representation in the exercise. Accordingly, the census originally scheduled for 1991 was delayed until 1998, and then was held only under pressure from the international community, and administered by the military. The results of the 1998 census remain somewhat controversial; the Quetta district and Balochistan provincial results had not been released by the government as of March 2002.

23. See Lawrence Ziring, *Pakistan: The Enigma of Development* (London: Dawson, 1980), pp.148–59; and Tahir Amin, *Ethno-National Movements of Pakistan: Domestic and International Factors* (Islamabad: Institute of Policy Sciences, 1988), pp.88–92.

24. Figures derived from 1998 district census reports of Balochistan's districts (2000–01 various dates). Quetta's data is extrapolated from the 1981 district census report as the government has not released the Quetta data yet. For more detail see Table 7.5.

25. Ziring, *Pakistan*, p.160. Privy purses were granted to rulers (as in the princely states of India and Pakistan) and to tribal leaders as compensation for their loss of revenue when the territories were incorporated into the state.

26. For a more complete description of the war see Selig Harrison, *In Afghanistan's Shadow: Baloch Nationalism and Soviet Temptations* (New York: Carnegie Endowment for International Peace, 1981); and Tariq Ali, *Can Pakistan Survive? The Death of a State* (London: Penguin, 1983), pp.115–23.

27. The best book on this topic remains Robert Wirsing, *India, Pakistan and the Kashmir Dispute: On Regional Conflict Resolution* (New York: St. Martin's Press, 1994). Also, see Ainslie Embree, Charles H. Kennedy, Howard Schaffer, Joseph Schwartzberg, and Robert Wirsing, *The Kashmir Dispute at Fifty: Charting Paths to Peace* (New York: Kashmir Study Group, 1997).

28. Kashmir Study Group, *Kashmir: A Way Forward* (New York: Kashmir Study Group, 2000), pp.10–11.

29. In any case, the Islamization programme was met with far more enthusiasm in the Punjab than in other areas of Pakistan; see Charles H. Kennedy, 'The Implementation of the Hudood Ordinances in Pakistan,' *Islamic Studies*, Vol. 26, No. 4 (1987), pp.307–19. See also Kennedy, *Islamization of Laws and Economy*.

30. Charles H. Kennedy, 'Policies of Redistributional Preference in Pakistan', in Nevitte and Kennedy, *Ethnic Preference and Public Policy*, p.69.

31. 1956 Constitution, Article 17; 1962 Constitution, Article 240.

32. See Kennedy, 'Policies of Redistributional Preference', p.69.

33. Ibid., pp.69–70.

34. Ibid., pp.70–1.

35. It is important to note that the quota is administered according to domicile as opposed to ethnic or linguistic attributes. As noted above this is a legacy of the system introduced originally for regional (West Pakistan–East Pakistan) balance rather than ethnic balance. Nonetheless, the quota has had profound ethnic consequences owing to the ethnic composition of the provinces. That is, most of the recruits selected against the 'Punjab domicile' are 'Punjabis'; most selected under the domicile 'urban Sindh' are 'Muhajirs'; and so on. However, the fit is not exact. See Table 7.1.

36. See Kennedy, *Bureaucracy in Pakistan*, pp.189–202. Also, since membership in such elites is primarily an urban phenomenon it follows that without the quota ethnic representation in the bureaucracy would closely mirror the urban composition of the respective ethnic groups. An examination of Table 7.1 indicates that 20.5% of Pakistan's urban population are Muhajirs, and over 53% Punjabis. The inescapable conclusion is that the quota has mitigated ethnic advantages.

37. Kennedy, 'Policies of Redistributional Preference', pp.76–8.

38. Government of Pakistan, *Ansari Commission Report on Form of Government* (Islamabad: Printing Corporation of Pakistan Press, 1983), pp.57–64.

39. Personal interviews, Islamabad, January 1990.

40. The main documents in chronological order are: Government of Pakistan, Chief

Executive Secretariat, National Reconstruction Bureau Local Government (Proposed Plan), *Devolution of Power and Responsibility Establishing the Foundations for Genuine Democracy* (Islamabad, May 2000); Government of Pakistan, Chief Executive Secretariat, NRB, *Local Government Plan, 2000* (Islamabad, 14 August 2000); Government of Pakistan, *The Local Government Ordinance 2001 – Promulgated by Provinces* (Islamabad, 13 August 2001); and Government of Pakistan, Chief Executive Secretariat, NRB, *Devolution: Local Government and Citizen Empowerment* (Islamabad, 14 August 2001).

41. A useful attempt to analyse the distinctions in district development has been presented by S. Akbar Zaidi (ed.), *Regional Imbalances and the National Question in Pakistan* (Lahore: Vanguard Books, 1992).

42. This argument is more fully developed in Charles H. Kennedy, 'Analysis of Pakistan's Devolution Plan,' unpublished paper presented to Wisconsin South Asian conference, October 2001.

8

Sri Lanka

Ethnic Strife and the Politics of Space

A. JEYARATNAM WILSON†

Arend Lijphart, the great theorist of consociationalism, advocated federalism and consociational democracy as solutions to the problems of
plural societies. He defined consociational democracy in terms of four
principles which deviate from the Westminster model of majority rule:
grand coalition, mutual veto, proportionality and segmental autonomy.[1]
But he emphasized that for any of these principles to become opera-
tional, 'the political elites of the rival parties would have to cooperate,
not compete.' In the present essay, we shall examine the failure of the
consociational principle to provide a lasting solution to problems of
ethnic conflict in Sri Lanka (known as Ceylon until 1972). While we do
not suggest that there was a conscious effort at emulation of the model,
it seems to have been followed unconsciously to a limited extent for
some years, though without much success.

In looking at the Sri Lanka experience of ethnic minority management, we begin by outlining the ethnic balance. This is followed by an
overview of the evolution of ethnic policy and by an examination of the
issue of territoriality. We conclude with an analysis of the extent to which
ethnic relations in Sri Lanka have been aggravated by inter-communal
resource competition.

THE ETHNIC BALANCE

Sri Lanka is a multiethnic country comprising two linguistic groups –
Sinhalese (mainly Buddhists and all Sinhalese-speaking) and Tamils
(mainly Hindus and all Tamil-speaking), and a Muslim community
(mainly Tamil-speaking, but with a significant section bilingual). The
Indian Tamils of nineteenth century origin (all Tamil speaking and overwhelmingly Hindus) constitute a fourth component of the island's

TABLE 8.1
SRI LANKA: ETHNIC COMPOSITION, 1981

| Ethnic group | Northeastern Province | | Sri Lanka | |
	000s	*%*	*000s*	*%*
Sinhalese	276.5	13.3	10,985.7	74.0
Ceylon Tamils	1,359.2	65.4	1,871.5	12.6
Indian Tamils	75.5	3.6	823.2	5.5
Muslims	367.8	17.7	1,100.4	7.4
Burghers	0.0	0.0	38.2	0.3
Others	0.0	0.0	29.0	0.2
Total	2,079.0	100.0	14,850.0	100.0

Note: On the basis of their origin, the Muslims are categorized as Moors (1,056,972, or 7.1%) and Malays (43,378, or 0.3%).

Source: Department of Census and Statistics, *Census of Population and Housing, Sri Lanka, 1981: Preliminary Release, No.1* (Colombo: Sri Lanka Government Printing Press, 1981).

peoples, but their problems are different from those of the Ceylon Tamils except in matters of language. There are other minorities, including the Christians (Roman Catholics and Protestants), who are to be found on either side of the linguistic divide. The Burghers, descendants of Dutch and Portuguese settlers, are a dwindling minority (a few thousand). Table 8.1 provides a demographic picture of the island, and the geographic distribution of the major groups is illustrated in Map 8.1.

Table 8.1 must be read in conjunction with Table 8.2 (see p.188). The salient facts are that 27.4% of the Ceylon Tamil population, almost wholly middle-class and lower middle-class oriented (professionals, commerce, office workers), numbering some 511,965, live dispersed outside the predominantly Tamil Northern and Eastern provinces (hereinafter referred to as the two provinces), as do the Indian Tamils who are mainly plantation workers; the latter live in the central highlands. Some 30% of Tamil speaking Muslims live in the Northern and Eastern provinces, while the rest (mostly bilinguals) are scattered in the Sinhala districts; there is a strong concentration of Muslims in the Colombo district. There are also Christian minorities (both Roman Catholic and Protestants) within the two main communities; they number over one million and constitute 7.5% of the population.

The two main minority groups (Ceylon Tamils and Indian Tamils) continue to be exposed to racial attacks by Sinhala militants in times of stress and crises; there were pogroms in 1956, 1958, 1965 and 1977 and these became fairly regular thereafter; in particular there were terrible genocidal attacks in 1983. From 1983, particular Ceylon Tamil areas in the Northern Province were subject to aerial and, at times, naval

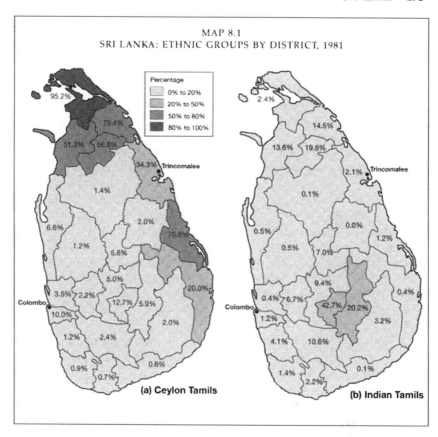

MAP 8.1
SRI LANKA: ETHNIC GROUPS BY DISTRICT, 1981

(a) Ceylon Tamils

(b) Indian Tamils

bombardment by the Sri Lankan armed forces (99% Sinhalese) in their campaign against the Ceylon Tamil militant forces led by the Liberation Tigers of Tamil Eelam (LTTE).

Up to 1977, there was periodic rioting against Tamils in the expectation that the Tamil Federal Party (FP), the principal political instrument of the Ceylon Tamils from 1956 to 1972, would be pressurized into slowing the pace of agitation against the island's Sinhala-dominated governments. Since 1977, with the LTTE staging an insurrection, the fears of Ceylon Tamils outside the two provinces have no longer had any effect because the parliamentary successor to the FP, the Tamil United Front (TUF, 1972; in 1976 re-named the Tamil United Liberation Front, TULF), was forced to withdraw from the political arena after the government's enactment in August 1983 of the Sixth Amendment, which required all Members of Parliament to take their oath to 'the unitary state of Sri Lanka'.[2] This left the TULF, which had been mandated by a majority of the Tamil electorate in the two provinces to campaign for a separate state at the general election of 1977, with no option but to withdraw from Parliament.

The Indian Tamils have also been victims but, being poor, they are less a target for loot and plunder; they live in isolated plantations, difficult of access, and their organization, the Ceylon Workers' Congress (CWC) does not support the TULF and LTTE demand for a separate state. In fact, beginning in the 1970s, the CWC became a component of United National Party (UNP) governments, and later found itself in a relatively powerful position through holding the balance of power. The CWC's demands are specific in relation to citizenship status and worker conditions; they are generally in sympathy with the Ceylon Tamils.

Of Tamil-speaking Muslims 70% live in the two provinces; in important areas of commonalty such as claims on newly irrigated lands and the use of the Tamil language for official purposes, the Muslim interest coincides with that of the Ceylon Tamils. However 30% of Muslims, all of them bilingual, inhabit the seven predominantly Sinhala provinces. Until 1977, the Muslims of the two provinces looked for political leadership to the Muslim politicians resident in the capital city of Colombo. Since 1977, the Muslims of the two provinces have had their own leadership, the Sri Lanka Muslim Congress (SLMC). They oppose the Tamil demand for a separate state, arguing that they will then be a minority within a minority.

Notwithstanding a limited convergence of interests of Ceylon Tamils, Muslims and Indian Tamils, the three groups have not, despite various attempts, forged a united front. Part of the reason lies in Sinhala-dominated political parties offering co-optation facilities to the Muslims and Indian Tamils. On other occasions Muslims have been encouraged by the Sinhala political leadership to be antagonistic to the Ceylon Tamils.

There has thus been a disequilibristic character in Sri Lanka's polity. The conflict today is primarily bi-ethnic, polarized between the Sinhalas and the Ceylon Tamils, with the Muslims more or less having greater confidence in the Sinhala leadership, while on the other hand the Indian Tamils see their ultimate lot as lying with the Ceylon Tamils. The Ceylon Tamils of the seven Sinhala provinces constitute a third force, being permanently threatened with possible retaliatory attacks from violent Sinhala Buddhist reactions to any major military or terrorist assault by the LTTE.

Two other factors have had a profound effect on the political culture of the Sinhala majority. Sinhalese elites, feudal and political, are at crucial historical turning points; they may in the national interest be prepared for compromises, but they are overwhelmed by Sinhala Buddhist pressure groups, both lay and cleric. Buddhist fronts and societies of various types can be activated and mobilized at short notice to obstruct any Sinhala government preparing to make concessions to the Tamils. More potent are the Buddhist monks who are politically active. These are not accountable to constituencies because they do not, by virtue of their calling, seek secular or political office. Hence, Sinhalese opinion can be aroused by members of the Buddhist clergy, who condemn governments seeking compromise settlements with the Tamils. More often these clerics are the instruments of politicians seeking to embarrass governments in their efforts at communal reconciliation. The irony is that this is a game played by a Sinhala political party in opposition to the Sinhala government in office; when government and opposition alternate, the very same party that opposed a settlement may offer the Tamils the compromises they had earlier condemned.

Sri Lanka's national disequilibrium is the result of a twofold factor: a Sinhala Buddhist nationalism and 'a defensive Ceylon Tamil nationalism'.[3] The Sinhalese Buddhists perceive the island as a unitary entity in which democracy is closely linked with their own politics. They view themselves as a numerocracy, implying majoritarianism. The Sinhalese Buddhist problem is embedded in a history based on the Vijayan myth and the Legend of the Buddha, which together produce an inbuilt belief that Sri Lanka is the only abode of the Sinhalese on this planet and that the Sinhalese, unlike the Ceylon Tamils who look to Tamil Nad in India, have nowhere else to go – hence the ancient Sinhalese name for Sri Lanka, 'Sihadipa', 'the island of the Sinhalese'.

The Sinhalese thus perceive that legend and myth cast a burden of responsibility on them. History's alleged investment of responsibility has prodded the Sinhalese to look on the Ceylon Tamils as obtruders from South India. Viewed as traditional foes, the Sinhalese, by and large, perceive the Ceylon Tamils as part of a South Indian Tamil threat and as a component of an enormous Tamil majority. Populist politicians and political parties among the Sinhalese exploit these age-old fears.

The Ceylon Tamils similarly insist on their own version of historical certainty. They claim that they are the co-indigenous settlers of the island with the Sinhalese, or even assert that they were the original settlers. To buttress this there is the historical record that their ancestors waged successful wars against Sinhalese kingdoms in Sri Lanka.

Yet another factor contributed to the Ceylon Tamil understanding of their perception that they are co-equals of the Sinhalese. In the distant past, Tamil incursions into the island led to parts of the island coming under Tamil rule, and by the thirteenth century a Tamil kingdom had been established in Jaffna. This kingdom lasted some four centuries after which it was captured by the Portuguese in 1616.

The two problems – Sinhala and Ceylon Tamil – are thus anchored in history and geography. The Sinhalese complain that their language (Sinhala) and religion (Buddhism) suffered neglect through four centuries of western rule (Portuguese, 1505–1658; Dutch, 1658–1796; British, 1796–1948). Britain, they allege, fostered and encouraged the deracination of the (English-educated) Sinhalese middle class at the expense of the Sinhala language and Buddhism. The Sinhalese must now therefore be compensated by the intervention of the state.

Such a view clashes with the interests of the Ceylon Tamils. The Ceylon Tamils settled in the arid and unproductive areas of the island whereas the Sinhala people live amidst rich and verdant vegetation. Consequently the Ceylon Tamils concentrated on English education provided by Christian proselytizers during the 150-odd years of British rule; previously these Tamils had functioned at the level of a subsistence economy and some trading in agricultural produce and elephants with south India – so the argument runs. The resulting fact was that the Ceylon Tamils obtained a disproportionate share of positions in the administration and in the professions which went unnoticed by their competing Sinhala counterparts for much of the British period until the Donoughmore reforms of 1931.

THE EVOLUTION OF ETHNIC POLICY

Despite these deeply ingrained historical antecedents, the islanders, during British rule, grew accustomed to constitutional models which were, on balance, secular and, within limits, democratic. These were designed to accommodate the competing claims of rival ethnic groups. However, the record from independence in 1948 to present times indicates a movement away from this position.

There was, in the early years, an attempt at consociationalism between the politically homogeneous elites of the Sinhalese, Tamils and Muslims. But parallel to this elitism was rivalry and competition within each ethnic group. Political rivalries within the Sinhalese community led competing groups there to try to outbid each other to win electoral popularity at the expense of the principal outgroup, the Ceylon Tamils. As a result populist politics gained ascendancy with the progressive mobilization by political elites of the lower and disadvantaged strata in each ethnic group. Unstated forces, such as suppressed fears (of one group by the other) and ambitious dreams (of Sinhala majoritarianism), became explicitly articulated. Political discourse and debate descended from the legislature to the market place.

The Colonial Legacy

Translated into modern idiom, the island had to contain two forms of nationalism, Sinhala Buddhist and Ceylon Tamil. The Ceylon Tamils had traditionally enjoyed certain advantages, protected under communal ratios in representation provided for in pre-1931 colonial legislatures. With universal adult suffrage, granted by Britain in 1931 under a partially self-governing system of constitutional reforms (the Donoughmore Constitution), it became clear that these advantages would be eroded, with substantial political power invested in a communal Sinhala majority. The Ceylon Tamils therefore resorted to an agitation for adequate constitutional and representational safeguards for the ethnic minorities.

Britain did not pay sufficient heed to these demands, one of which specifically asked for a legislature and a political executive which would have half its membership from among the ethnic minorities. The Reforms Commission headed by Viscount Soulbury (1944–45) rejected the plea on the score that such an artificially imposed composition would inflame the Sinhala majority and that a political atavism would prevail, with legislatures after each general election being predictably constituted in terms of ethnic structure.[4] The latter argument was not necessarily correct, as the islanders could still have been divided on party lines which cut across communal divisions. Political parties which emerged in the wake of the Soulbury Constitution of 1947 could very well have obtained candidates from among the 50% of constituencies reserved for the ethnic minorities.

In the earlier phase, the British had blunted the sharpness of possible ethnic rivalries, indirectly, for their own purposes. An immediate priority for Britain was the construction of a network of roads and railways, for movement of troops to pacify unrest. An equally important need for communications development was commerce. Apart from British consumer goods being made available to a local clientele, a British plantocracy had established itself in the central districts and their outlying areas. Its members were engaged in the production first of coffee and then of tea, as well as rubber, on a large scale, particularly in the second half of the nineteenth century and thereafter. The agricultural produce had to be transported to ports such as Colombo and Galle on the west coast, and in a few cases, to the eastern township of Trincomalee.

The improved forms of transportation enabled people from all parts of the island to move more easily, to interact and to seek employment opportunities. Such social interaction promoted a sense of 'island consciousness' among the English-educated, where earlier the village provided the frontier. Each group, however, maintained its separate identity.

A further factor was the need for the colonial power to be kept informed of the needs and views of the peoples it governed. However elementary their structure, Britain nevertheless utilized legislative and executive councils which were communally constructed and based on a restricted franchise. In this way representatives of the Sinhalese, Ceylon Tamil, European, and, later, Muslim and Indian communities met together to deliberate and then to advise the colonial governor. The experience of such political meetings engendered a togetherness and an elitism held by a sense of 'Englishness' among the westernized middle class. Governor Sir Henry McCallum created a legislative seat for this class in 1911 designated 'the Educated Ceylonese Member'. Despite a fragile Ceylonese nationalism evolving during 1911–20 culminating in the formation of the Ceylon National Congress in 1919 with a Ceylon Tamil elected as its first President, the ethnic minorities insisted on retaining communal ratios in representation in the British-imposed constitutional reforms of 1911, 1921, and 1924. Beneath the surface of this westernized class, however, there was evolving a strong Sinhala consciousness.

In 1931 British policy changed and under the Donoughmore Constitution communal representation was replaced by the territorial principle. Nevertheless the substance of consociationalism seemed to prevail in this most unusual of constitutional models. The constitution provided for a State Council, or legislature, which was to be divided into seven executive committees. Each committee was in charge of a group of subjects and had an elected chairman who became the minister in charge. The committees were responsible for the formulation of policy and, if approved by the legislature, for its implementation.[5] Each of the seven committees had representatives of the ethnic minorities so that the latter provided an input at the initial stage of legislation. Their views were considered, though the Sinhala majoritarian principle began to become increasingly manifest during the period in which the constitution functioned, 1931–47. However, the minorities had safeguards because the constitution prohibited discriminatory legislation and the governor had a reserve of powers, including the right of disallowance. In addition, the most important attributes of full internal self government such as control of the public services (recruitment and promotion), finance and legal affairs were vested in three officers of state, all British. They were appointed from the colonial civil service and were answerable to the governor.

The Soulbury Constitution of 1947 completed the process of vesting complete autonomy in internal government in the hands of the island's conservative leadership. The Reforms Commission under the chairmanship of Viscount Soulbury provided for a compromise on the distribution of seats between the Sinhala majority and the ethnic minorities, arising from the Ceylon Tamil demand for 50–50 representation in respect of seats for the Sinhalese and the combined minorities in the legislature. In addition, there were provisions in the constitution which (a) prohibited discrimination in legislation against any specific community (Section 29), (b) provided for independent public service and judicial service commissions to ensure impartiality in recruitment and promotions, and (c) instituted a second chamber, a Senate, with a suspensory veto; this chamber made further provision for the representation of ethnic minorities. Given the interethnic controversies of the time, the Soulbury Constitution was once again a vindication of the consociational principle. In 1948 Britain completed the process of transferring power and Ceylon became an independent sovereign state.

Independence and the Minorities

A majority of the Ceylon Tamils led by the All Ceylon Tamil Congress (ACTC) recorded their protest at the 1947 general elections. There were sections of Tamils who supported the constitution. During the period 1947–56, the constitution maintained the substance of its consociational character. The Prime Minister, D.S. Senanayake, the foremost conservative Sinhala leader, obtained the cooperation of the ethnic minorities including a section of the Ceylon Tamils in 1946. Two Ceylon Tamils were appointed to the cabinet. In 1948, he secured the cooperation of the Ceylon Tamil leader of the major Tamil political grouping, the ACTC. The essence of Lijphart's inter-elite consociational formula once more prevailed. The system of collective responsibility under cabinet government ensured that ministers from the ethnic minorities could voice their protests in meetings of the cabinet and these would be duly considered before a collective decision was made.

Consociationalism in Sri Lanka, however, had its snags and its road-blocks. Ideally Lijphart's theory could be made operative only if a number of pre-conditions existed. Among these, the most indispensable is the need for inter-elite cooperation to eliminate intra- and inter-ethnic rivalries. Most important in this context is a willing abstention by competing groups from indulging in electoral competition on sensitive state- or nation-building concerns such as language and religion. These *sine qua nons* are unfortunately not available in abundance in the contemporary democratic world. Today's new states, and even older ones such as those in eastern Europe and the former Soviet Union, are patchwork quilts brought together by the quirk of circumstance or because the departing decolonizer had in the first instance knitted diverse territories together on the basis of arbitrary geographical criteria. The temptations of rival power-seeking political elites to exploit inter- and intra-ethnic fears were far too alluring to be resisted. Hence the choice of the slippery slope: power in the short run, but with national ruin and economic disaster as the long-term consequence.

The circumstances of Sri Lanka were not the most conducive for consociationalism. A universal franchise was conferred by Britain in 1931; but the age-old Sinhala–Tamil wars and the Sinhala Buddhist sensitivity to contingent dangers – imaginary, real or politically exploitable – against Christian proselytizers and the historical Dravidian foe provided a happy hunting ground for unconscionable politicians. Thus despite the exercise of universal franchise in several successive general elections, the electorate did not mature as expected but instead insisted on a straightforward ethnic majoritarian principle. The latter became increasingly relevant in the context of an undiversified economy dependent on the vagaries of the international market for its primary products, with more and more people with middle-class educational orientations entering the labour force. Thus consociationalism was thwarted by a stagnant economy and the 'limited pie syndrome' (not enough jobs to go round), with fewer resources to be allocated despite generous dollops of foreign aid. This became increasingly manifest in the post-1956 phase. The first dent in the consociational armour came with the legislation of the D.S. Senanayake government to deprive the Indian Tamils of their citizenship and franchise (1948 and 1949). Some 900,000 Indian Tamils became stateless; they also lost seven seats in the House of Representatives.[6] The Tamil Federal Party (1949) soon emerged to become the defender of Indian Tamil rights, construing the denial of such rights as a first step towards reducing the overall political power of the Tamils in the island.

Political Forces in the New State

The rivalries within the ruling United National Party (UNP), formed in 1946–47 as an elite alliance of Sinhala Buddhists, Ceylon Tamils and Muslims, engendered a break-away group in 1951. Its leader, S.W.R.D. Bandaranaike, in that year formed the nationalist Sinhala Buddhist-oriented Sri Lanka Freedom Party (SLFP). The SLFP was a centrist party in contrast to the conservative UNP. On the left were various Marxist parties. At independence, the dominant Marxist groups were the Trotskyist Lanka Sama Samaja Party (LSSP, the 'Ceylon Equal Society Party') and the Communist Party (pro-Moscow). Both Marxist parties stood for a liberal solution to the 'national question'. They made no headway with the Sinhala electors because they refrained from joining the forces of Sinhala nationalism. They did not have an electoral impact on the conservative minded Ceylon Tamil electorate. In the end these parties and their splinter groups abandoned their liberal stance on language.[7] The centrist SLFP defeated the UNP at the general election of 1956, and held office with various junior partners during 1956–65 and 1970–77.

Politics followed a similar path with the Ceylon Tamils. At first, they were united under the All-Ceylon Tamil Congress (ACTC), which dominated Ceylon Tamil politics from 1944 to 1949. Then a splinter group, the Tamil Federal Party (FP), inaugurated in 1949, became the leading party of the Ceylon Tamils from 1956 to 1983; after 1972, the FP entered into united fronts with other groupings, taking the names of the Tamil United Front (TUF) and the Tamil United Liberation Front (TULF, 1976). The FP had as one of its main planks the defence of traditional Ceylon Tamil territory comprising the Northern and Eastern provinces.[8] The FP contention was that in the face of Sinhala communalism, the only fallback position for the Ceylon Tamils was to protect and develop the economy of their traditional homelands. The FP alleged that the land settlement policies of Sinhala-oriented governments were directed at diluting the demographic composition of the Ceylon Tamil homelands.

Two factors emerged from this ongoing dispute. First, ethnic federalism was for many Tamils the only safeguard against contingent Sinhala majoritarianism, even in the traditional homelands where state-aided colonization with Sinhala settlers was proceeding apace (see below). Second, if a reasonable devolution of state power for the Ceylon Tamils could not be obtained in a federal arrangement, the alternative, Tamil political groups insisted, would have to be a separate Tamil state.

The Sinhala Response

The Sinhala response to the federalist demand took diverse forms, depending on the circumstances. In the beginning (1947–56), the conservative leadership hoped to maintain consociational ties with their Ceylon Tamil collaborators notwithstanding the disfranchisement of the Indian Tamils and the Sinhala state's colonization (land settlement) policies. Ceylon Tamil 'cooptionists' willingly participated in Sinhala majority governments.

Then came the triumph of the Sinhala language movement and its vehicle the SLFP (1956). Even then, the latter's leader, S.W.R.D. Bandaranaike, hoped that the twin problems to which Sinhala majoritarianism had given rise, the Sinhala Only Act of 1956 and the Tamil insistence on a national homeland and language rights, could be resolved by a compromise settlement through regional or provincial councils and adoption of Tamil as a regional language. Bandaranaike also thought that he could balance off the rigours of the Sinhala Only Act (1956) with the Tamil Language (Special Provisions) Act, which his government enacted in 1958. The Act, however, remained a dead letter during 1958–66. In 1965, FP participation in a coalition government with the UNP, headed by Dudley Senanayake (1965–70), enabled the FP in 1966 to obtain status for Tamil as a language of administration in the two Tamil provinces.

Thus, despite the 'ethnicization' of the electorate, consociational ties were maintained during Bandaranaike's prime ministership of 1956–59, reaching their high water mark in the Pact of July 1957. The pact broadly provided for a measure of regional autonomy, for Tamil to be the administrative language in the Northern Province (NP) and Eastern Province (EP) and for an end to state-aided colonization. The Prime Minister hoped that this agreement between the two leaders would repair the broken relationship. Unfortunately for him, he was strongly opposed by extremists in his own party, forces which he himself had unleashed; his rivals in the UNP now sitting sulkily in opposition were just as rancorous in condemning the terms of the agreement as a 'sell-out' of the Sinhalese. The Prime Minister's assassination in September 1959 removed a figure of moderation in an otherwise charged atmosphere. His successor, his widow, Mrs Sirima Bandaranaike (after the general election of July 1960) was unable to rein in the Sinhala extremist forces. The relationship between the two communities reached a nadir. Sinhala Buddhist pressure groups mobilized the mass of Sinhala electors, the layers beneath the elite surface, to breach the earlier elite consociational arrangements. Neither Mrs Bandaranaike nor her advisor (Felix Dias Bandaranaike, her late husband's nephew) provided proper direction to the ship of state. The FP's civil disobedience campaigns, especially the 1961 campaign, marked a new low in the majority–minority relationship. No effort was made during Mrs Bandaranaike's prime ministership, 1960–65, to maintain consociational ties.

Consociationalism was restored when Dudley Senanayake formed his government of national reconciliation, 1965–70.[9] The relationship between the UNP and FP was sealed by the Pact of March 1965 which basically reproduced the earlier 1957 pact, with modifications.[10] The government was essentially a coalition between the UNP and the FP, with a FP representative serving as Minister of Local Government until his resignation in 1968.

The defeat of the UNP at the general election of 1970 and the runaway victory scored by the SLFP and its Marxist partners, the United Front (UF) led by Mrs Bandaranaike, brought to a virtual halt the consociational tie that had, since the FP withdrawal from the Senanayake cabinet in 1968, been threatened.[11] The failure of Mrs Bandaranaike's United Front to continue some semblance of consociational ties is difficult to explain, especially since some of the island's left wing political leaders with liberal stances on the Tamil question served as senior ministers in the cabinet.

Consociationalism returned once more with the electoral victory of the UNP in 1977 and lasted until 1983. The Executive President, J.R. Jayewardene (1977–88), made one more effort at seeking an interim resolution of the problem. He utilized the good offices of an intermediary to establish a continuing dialogue between his government and the leading Ceylon Tamil moderate party, the TULF. The exercise almost succeeded but for the President's brooding suspicion of the Ceylon Tamil parliamentarians.[12] The interminable delays in implementing the legislation of 1980 in the end proved fatal. The President was overtaken by the serious Sinhalese rioting of July 1983 against the Tamils. This was followed by a protracted war between the armed forces of the Sinhala state and Tamil militants, the LTTE. The war reached a high point with India's intervention in 1987. Thus the ever-receding line of consociationalism, the main purpose of which, at its weakest, was to maintain a dialogue between the two disputants, came to a tragic end in the latter half of 1983 with the egregious blunder of the enactment of the Sixth Amendment to the 1978 constitution. The amendment compelled all members of parliament to swear loyalty to the *unitary state* of Sri Lanka. The TULF parliamentarians refused and vacated their seats.

Constitutional Change and Political Violence

The leadership of the Ceylon Tamil movement passed on to militant groups, in particular, the Liberation Tigers of Tamil Eelam (LTTE). As damning for the Sinhala-oriented government was the internationalization of the Sinhala–Tamil problem. India became concerned about an unstable neighbouring state, while Tamil Nad, an important unit in the Indian federation, expressed sympathy and provided support for the Ceylon Tamils and their militant groups.

The TULF had, at the 1977 general election, asked for and obtained a mandate for the creation of a separate sovereign state of *Thamil Eelam* comprising the Northern and Eastern provinces. The TULF leadership had not however designed any precise strategy for the implementation of their mandate. For one thing, events on the Sinhala side moved too quickly. President Jayewardene sought to arrest the growth of popular involvement in politics by instituting a Gaullist-style executive presidency. The new political framework modified and limited the role of parliament. By providing for a stable and irremovable six-year presidency, the political executive would no longer be subject to the vicissitudes of potentially disintegrating parliamentary majorities.[13] The President would be able to devote more time to urgent tasks. In practice, this did not happen. The President operated the new system partly as a cabinet and partly as a presidential form of government. He had an intractable cabinet, in which there were individual ministers whom he could not restrain or control, with potentially disastrous consequences for the experiment.

Having reformulated the constitution on the Gaullist model, President Jayewardene banked on successfully negotiating a compromise consociational agreement with the moderate Ceylon Tamil TULF. But the President's plans failed because he allowed too much leeway to his communally disposed cabinet ministers; on the other hand, public officials were not amenable to direction on matters affecting the Tamil minority. The District Development Councils scheme which President Jayewardene devised was accepted by the TULF as a step towards their ultimate goal of a sovereign state, but these did not take off because of delay on the President's part.

President Jayewardene's tenure, however, was crisis ridden. Many components of his government had a distinct propensity to using violence against the Ceylon Tamils. Populist violence directed against the Tamils in the end enveloped his government. The President was stranded until it was time for him to relinquish his office. President Ranasinghe Premadasa, his successor, sought ways of re-opening the dialogue but negotiations with the militarized LTTE have proved more complex than with the politicians; he was assassinated in 1993 by a Tamil suicide bomber. By 1994, the SLFP was back in power as part of a broader, left-leaning coalition called the People's Alliance, with Chandrika

Kumaratunga (daughter of SWRD Bandaranaike and of the world's first woman prime minister, Sirimavoh Bandaranaike) as President. A more determined military campaign against Tamil areas followed, but the LTTE remained undefeated. At the parliamentary election of December 2001, however, the People's Alliance lost out to a coalition headed by the UNP, and Ranil Wickremasinghe (nephew of former President Jayewardene) became prime minister, opening up the prospect of an accommodation with the Tamils.[14]

TERRITORIALITY AND ETHNIC CONFLICT

During 1947–83, the FP and its various transformations had concentrated on the federal solution as the answer to the Sinhala–Tamil dispute. The FP position was tantamount to 'leave us alone'. The Ceylon Tamils would develop their territorial homeland. The Tamil sense of national pride would be restored. Tamil nationalism could be contained within the island frontiers. The Ceylon Tamils would no longer be a thorn in the side of the Sinhalese in regard to Sinhala questions. The latter would be free to develop and revive their nationalism and to preserve their language and religion in the seven Sinhala provinces. There would no doubt be sizeable Tamil-speaking minorities (Sri Lanka Tamils, Indian Tamils and Muslims) in the Sinhala provinces but federalism or a Tamil homeland would not imply an exchange of populations. Thus the status quo would not be disturbed.

The 'Colombo Tamils' formed the bulwark of an 'expatriate Ceylon Tamil community' (from the traditional Tamil areas). They had at one time wielded influence and provided leadership. With the politics of universal franchise from 1931, they gradually faded from the scene. The hub of politics moved to the heartland of the Ceylon Tamils, the Jaffna peninsula, which virtually dictated 'the party line' to the outlying areas. From 1931, the year of universal adult franchise, the Jaffna Tamils functioned as if they were under attack and as if they were beleaguered. Every act of discrimination was taken to heart by a community which was determined not to count itself as a minority. Its two foremost leaders, G.G. Ponnambalam, the ACTC leader, and the FP's S.J.V. Chelvanayakam, functioned in an ethos where elite politics prevailed.

Chelvanayakam and the FP strove, however, to change this style of politics. From the beginning, they concentrated on a widespread network of grass roots organizations which touched every nook and cranny of the Ceylon Tamil homeland. Chelvanayakam dwelt on 'the unity of the Tamil-speaking peoples' and within this wide cluster he included the Tamil-speaking Muslims of the Tamil-majority Eastern Province and the disfranchised Hill Country (Indian) Tamils of the plantation districts. He and his party were uncompromising in their goal of federalism. Any agreement in the interim, such as those of 1957, 1965 and the District Development Councils scheme of 1980 were to be only mileposts on the way to the FP destination.

There were serious contradictions and problems that were foreseeable in the FP demand. What would become of all the Tamil-speaking people outside the Tamil homeland? Would they have a place in the new firmament or would they have to relocate in the Tamil homeland? Chelvanayakam was insistent that all he was agitating for was a devolving of autonomous powers to a Tamil homeland, not a partitioning of the new state as was the case in India and Pakistan. Tamil-speaking people would be free to pursue their vocations, professions and employment in the Sinhala provinces just as the Sinhala people could voluntarily settle wherever they wanted to in the Tamil homeland. The only difference was that there had to be a termination of the state-aided colonization policies of the government. The Federal Party's aims and objectives failed to obtain support from the Colombo Tamils, the Indian Tamils and the Tamil-speaking Muslims. Table 8.2 provides evidence of the dispersal of the Ceylon Tamil population and the difficulties of negotiating a settlement without calling in question the future of Ceylon Tamils residing outside the Tamil homeland (see also Map 8.1). It gives the percentages of the Sinhala population in those Sinhala majority districts outside the Northern and Eastern provinces (the Tamil homeland) wherever over 10,000 Ceylon Tamils are resident, scattered, not ghettoized, and therefore sensitive targets to Sinhala mob violence in stressful times and periods of tension which have occurred at frequent intervals since 1977.

The strong card of Sinhala extremist groups was to organize rioting, killing and plundering of Tamils in the seven Sinhala provinces in the event of negotiations failing and/or the FP resorting to non-violent campaigns of civil disobedience. Even moderate Sinhala elites argued that if the Tamils insisted on autonomy, the Tamil areas could not expect financial subsidies from the central government.

The debate thus shifted to what the Tamils could expect in a federalized system. How strongly entrenched would their language rights be outside the Tamil homeland? Would they be eligible for equal treatment and equal access to employment opportunities? The position was advanced that a united island-wide Tamil community had more to gain and more bargaining power than if splintered under a federalized arrangement. The Indian Tamil leadership set their faces against the federalist solution, for what would then become of the Indian Tamil population? The federalist answer to their fears did not satisfy them. The Indian Tamils, the federalists said, could re-locate in the sparsely populated parts of the two provinces whenever problems of the spillover effect of unemployable population affected the plantation areas. Nor could the federalists persuade the Colombo Tamils, even when they suggested that the latter could, with increasing manifestations of Sinhala majoritarianism, have a homeland to fall back on. It was as difficult with the Muslims of the Eastern Province with whom the federalists were willing to reach a negotiated settlement.

The federalists had no satisfactory answer for the Sinhalese of the Eastern Province, who were viewed as 'Uitlanders', either to be repatriated in an exchange of populations or allowed to remain with the same language and any other rights as the Tamils in the seven Sinhala provinces. The pacts of 1957 and 1965 had arrangements on the latter lines for the Sinhala people in the Tamil homeland. Though no specific reference was made in these pacts to the status of the Sinhala language in the Tamil provinces, it was assumed that the Sinhala Only Act was in operation, and that this would protect the rights of the Sinhala people.

The Colonization Issue

However, despite the assurances contained in these agreements, they were violated, in that successive Sinhala governments and their ministers in charge of land settlement persisted in settling Sinhalese peasants in the two Tamil provinces. Table 8.3 illustrates the inroads by 1982 into the traditional Tamil provinces and the resultant demographic changes.

TABLE 8.2
SRI LANKA: DISTRIBUTION OF CEYLON TAMILS OUTSIDE THE
NORTHERN AND EASTERN PROVINCES, 1981

District	Province	Sinhalese As % of district	Ceylon Tamils	
			Number	As % of all Ceylon Tamils
Colombo	Western	77.9	165,952	8.9
Nuwara Eliya	Central	35.9	70,471	3.8
Kandy	Central	75.0	55,675	3.0
Gampaha	Western	92.2	45,807	2.4
Badulla	Uva	68.5	36,218	2.0
Puttalam	Northwestern	82.6	33,218	1.8
Matale	Central	79.9	20,936	1.1
Ratnapura	Sabaragamuwa	84.7	17,979	1.0
Kegalle	Sabaragamuwa	86.3	14,095	0.8
Kurunegala	Northwestern	93.1	13,438	0.7

Note: Only districts where the Sri Lanka Tamil population exceeded 10,000 are listed. Of a total Ceylon Tamil population of 1,871,535, 27.4% or 511,965 live dispersed outside the Tamil majority Northern and Eastern provinces. The two most highly populated Ceylon Tamil districts are Jaffna, the Tamil heartland (in the Northern Province) with 792,246 people (42.3% of the total) and Batticaloa (in the Eastern Province) with 234,348 people (12.5%).

Source: As for Table 8.1.

This table indicates that, notwithstanding the agreements of 1957, 1965 and 1979 (the District Development Councils scheme) and the undertakings given by prime ministers (in 1957 and 1965) and by a president (1979) to the effect that state-aided colonization of Sinhala settlers in the Tamil provinces would be abated so as not to disturb their demographic composition, there was a marked increase of Sinhala colonists after independence in 1948, as the data for 1971 and 1982 show. This was most noticeable in the Mannar district in the Northern Province and in all districts in the Eastern Province. The colonization schemes were deliberately interposed so as to break the geographical contiguity of the two Tamil provinces.

The Strategic Issue: Trincomalee

In claiming both provinces as their traditional homeland, the Ceylon Tamils attached considerable importance to the strategic port city of Trincomalee, which has one of the best natural harbours in the world. The electoral constituency of Trincomalee always returned a Ceylon Tamil from the time of its demarcation in 1921 through several new re-demarcations inclusive of the general election of 1977. On their electoral victory in 1956, the FP declared that the capital of their traditional homeland would be Trincomalee city, not, as would have been expected, Jaffna city, in the Tamil heartland on the Jaffna peninsula.

Trincomalee's natural harbour and the naval facilities it afforded had its attractions for major foreign powers as well. After Sri Lanka's independence, Britain was allowed naval facilities in Trincomalee, and under

TABLE 8.3
SRI LANKA: PERCENTAGE INCREASE OF SINHALESE IN
THE NORTHERN AND EASTERN PROVINCES, 1946–82

District	1946	1971	1982
Northern Province			
Jaffna	1.1	0.9	0.6
Mannar	3.8	4.1	8.1
Vavuniya/Mullaitivu	16.6	16.8	11.4
Eastern Province			
Trincomalee	20.7	29.0	33.6
Batticaloa/Amparai	5.8	17.7	21.8
Total (%)	4.9	11.0	13.2

Source: Adapted from Robert Kearney, *Internal Migration in Sri Lanka and its Social Consequences* (Boulder, CO: Westview Press, 1987) and S.V.D. Samaranayake, 'Political Violence in Sri Lanka', unpublished PhD thesis, University of St Andrews (1990) p. 148.

Mrs Bandaranaike there was speculation that China wanted to acquire a naval base in Sri Lanka in return for long-term economic assistance.[15] Mrs Bandaranaike categorically denied that Sri Lanka 'handed over Trincomalee harbour to the Chinese' under her 1963 agreement.[16]

President Jayewardene aggravated India's fear of her southern flanks being exposed to powerful foreign powers when he permitted a consortium of three western states, in which the United States was indirectly involved, to renovate 91 storage tanks in Trincomalee harbour, ignoring an Indian tender in the process.[17] The question of Trincomalee came up again for negotiation in December 1983 when Indira Gandhi's emissary negotiated with President Jayewardene an understanding that came to be known as 'Annexure C'. The strategic relevance of Trincomalee port for the Sri Lanka government was spelled out in Section 10, in which the Indian emissary agreed that Trincomalee would be placed under a Port Authority constituted by the central government.[18] Trincomalee remained of strategic interest to India. When in July 1987 Rajiv Gandhi concluded an Accord with President Jayewardene for providing a solution to the ethnic problem, Section 2 in the Letters of Exchange between the two leaders stated that 'Trincomalee or any other port in Sri Lanka will not be made available for military use by any country in a manner prejudicial to India's interests'.[19]

The aggressive Sinhalese colonization of Trincomalee district since 1946, as illustrated in Table 8.3, should therefore be viewed in the context of Sinhala Buddhist-oriented governments in Colombo seeking to gain dominance in this area.[20] The unwillingness of these governments to permit a permanent merger of the Northern and Eastern provinces can be attributed to this factor. Both Professor C. Manogaran and the late Professor Robert Kearney[21] have drawn attention to the implications of the territorial dimension of the Tamil claim for a national homeland. The latter concluded that 'the north and east, the areas of traditional Tamil homeland, have undergone major shifts in ethnic composition over recent decades'.[22] He added that Sri Lanka Tamils, once a majority of each district of the Northern and Eastern provinces, have been reduced to minority status in Amparai and Trincomalee districts and to thin majorities in Mannar and Vavuniya.[23] Kearney further noted that:

> the large eastern concentration of Sri Lanka Tamils in Batticaloa is separated from the yet larger Tamil population of the north by the Trincomalee district, in which Tamils, Moors and Sinhalese are found in almost equal numbers.[24]

The disruption of Tamil territorial contiguity was the reported objective of Sinhalese ministers in charge of irrigation and lands in the post-1960 period. Opposition to this planned Sinhala colonization was one of the principal planks of the Tamil Federal Party's platform when it was launched in 1949.[25] The FP's successors, the TUF (1972) and the TULF (1974), incorporated opposition to colonization as one of their principal objectives and in fact as a reason for their demand for the right of self-determination. By 1983, the militant LTTE proclaimed that this 'state-aided aggressive colonization ... aimed to annihilate the geographical entity of the Tamil people' as an important pretext for their continuing insurrection against the Sinhala state.[26]

The Language Issue

All four Agreements (the 1957 and 1965 Pacts, the District Development Councils scheme and Annexure 'C') had provided for Tamil as a language of administration in the two Tamil provinces. In addition, the Tamil language (Special Provisions) Act of 1958 demarcated these provinces as Tamil-speaking ones.[27] Thus the leaders of the Sinhalese and Tamil ruling elites had identified and sought resolution of the principal grounds of conflict. The solutions they envisaged proved a step forward towards promoting unity of the island.

RESOURCE COMPETITION AND ETHNICITY

Unfortunately the apex of the Sinhala political pyramid could not ensure the implementation of the agreements discussed above. There were times when inter-elite accommodation was undermined and abandoned because of populist pressures. At these critical junctures, the Sinhalese leadership became victims of their natural support base both at the elite and the middle and lower layers. At the elite level, there were prejudices against the Ceylon Tamils – their alleged 'competitiveness and cliquish-ness' and the supposed dangers of the Tamils looking towards south India's Tamil Nad for succour; in addition the Sinhalese stereotyped the Tamils for their so-called thrift, their lack of desire to interact socially with Sinhalese and their tendency in the seven Sinhala provinces to live in self-contained settlements.

The problem for the Sinhala elite was that with the availability of free education from the state from the kindergarten to the university more and more qualified Sinhalese, mostly in the liberal arts, found them-selves without the employment they desired. Because of the distribution of the population, the percentage of Ceylon Tamils was less, in compar-ison. These new Sinhala literati and intelligentsia became discontented with the lower and middle level positions they obtained in the public and private sectors. The Tamils on the other hand had already obtained appointments in the public sector or as professional people. Consequently unemployed but educated Sinhalese resented the Tamil presence. A stagnant economy and the limited pie syndrome provided issues which the political elites of both communities exploited. The Sinhalese felt that they had been denied their proportionate share. They argued that the Tamils enjoyed a larger proportion than their population warranted. The inevitable discrimination in favour of the Sinhalese for appointments followed.

To justify the policy of discrimination against the Tamils, Sinhalese politicians and ideologues contended that the Ceylon Tamils had had it so good during British rule that it was time now in a post-independent state to redress the balance. At first this policy was not acknowledged, but later it was enunciated clearly on the basis of quotas for the different ethnic groups. Merit was not to be the sole criterion; each ethnic group would obtain its proportionate share. During the second phase of SLFP/UF rule (1970–77) discrimination against Ceylon Tamils eligible for appointments became endemic.[28] Not merely was this clearly apparent in the public sector. The government extended the policy to recruitment of students to the more employment-oriented faculties of the universities – engineering, medicine and the sciences. Sinhala students with lower marks were admitted to these faculties as compared with their Ceylon Tamil counterparts, who were required to obtain higher marks. The whole scheme was given the name 'standardization of marks' and the declared intention, to avoid accusations of bias, was that the state was assisting the educationally disadvantaged and backward areas.[29]

There were such districts in the Ceylon Tamil Northern and Eastern provinces, but the hardest hit was the heartland of the Ceylon Tamils, the Jaffna peninsula, where education was a staple industry. This system of reverse discrimination in favour of the Sinhalese majority was early evidence of attempts at mass mobilization of the Sinhala electorate. The Sinhala political elite at the time (1970–77) could have managed the system so as to enable Sinhalese-Tamil consociationalism to function at the upper levels while at the same time providing concessions to the new layers of politically conscious Sinhala voters. Table 8.4 provides evidence of the policies of the state during this phase.

Consequent on these new policies, the numbers of Tamils in science courses was reduced from 35.5% in 1970 to around 21% in 1973, while Sinhalese representation rose from 75.4% in 1974 to over 80% thereafter. The United National Party government of 1977 made adjustments to the system but the changes were not of appreciable consequence.

A similar policy was followed in regard to irrigation schemes. These, the state pronounced, were intended to relieve (Sinhala) unemployment and (Sinhala) population congestion. But the same principle of 'most favoured nationality treatment' of the Sinhala people was not applied to the Ceylon Tamils, notwithstanding the heavy density of population and overcrowding in the Tamil Jaffna peninsula and the land hunger of Tamil and Muslim peasants in the Northern and Eastern provinces. Tamil polit-

TABLE 8.4
SRI LANKA: UNIVERSITY ADMISSIONS BASED ON
THE STANDARDIZATION PRINCIPLE, 1971

Area of study	Ethnic group	Minimum mark for admission
Engineering	Sinhalese	227
	Tamils	250
Medicine and Dentistry	Sinhalese	229
	Tamils	250
Bio-Science	Sinhalese	175
	Tamils	181
Physical Sciences	Sinhalese	183
	Tamils	204

Note: Marks in respect of Arts have not been listed because of low employment possibilities.

Source: C.R. de Silva, 'The Impact of Nationalism on Education: The Schools Take-Over (1961) and the University Admissions Crisis 1970–1975', in Michael Roberts (ed.), *Collective Identities: Nationalism and Protests in Sri Lanka* (Colombo: Marga, 1970), p. 486.

ical elites protested that there was adequate living space in the Sinhala provinces adjacent to the river valley irrigation tanks constructed in the Tamil provinces for resettlement of Sinhala people.

On 25 June 1986, President Jayewardene presented a statement of his government's proposals to resolve the crisis. Its most significant part was the 'Note on the Devolution of Power in Respect of Land and Settlement'. A National Land Commission was to be appointed by the Colombo government. It would have power to formulate policy on state land and in regard to the disposition of inter-provincial irrigation and land development projects. However, land required by the proposed provincial councils for the purposes of the subjects devolved to them must conform to 'national policies'. Centralized control by the Sinhala-dominated state was reaffirmed in the requirement that 'any alienation or disposition of land ... will be made by the President on the advice of the Provincial Councils'. With the soured relations between the two communities there could have been no cooperation between President and Council.[30] The 'Annexure' to the President's statement left the position of land alienation unclear.[31]

On the face of it, the three minority groups were assigned land on the basis of their proportionate due. The government appeared to take into account the Tamil concern about the disturbance of the ethnic composition of the two provinces, as the last paragraph of the 'Annexure' stated that 'it is the policy of the Government to maintain the ethnic proportions of the Trincomalee and Batticaloa districts' which prevailed at the census of 1981. Tamil political groupings were, however, cautious in their response.

The dividing line in the continuing war is territory. Questions on admissions to universities and employment in the Sinhala south will recede to the background because the Tamils are aware that there are no ideal constitutional devices to counter discrimination. Many are convinced that there is an indissoluble link between language and territory. If a demarcated Tamil homeland is recognized, the Tamils are confident that it can be developed to a point where they will not have to depend on the Sinhala government. The dispute will therefore be at its most intense when the boundaries have to be demarcated.

The Indian Intervention

In July 1987, Rajiv Gandhi and President Jayewardene signed the Indo-Sri Lanka Accord. The consociational factor ran aground in the context of the enormous resistance mounted against it by the mainly lower middle class ultra-chauvinist Jathika Vimnlethi Peramuna (the Sinhalese National Liberation Front). President Jayewardene had Parliament enact the Thirteenth Amendment to the constitution in keeping with the terms of the Accord. Provisions were made for Provincial Councils, a threefold distribution of powers as in typical federations, and for Tamil to be recognized as an official language. The LTTE jibbed at these concessions. For as long as power was concentrated in the Executive President, no amount of devolution would enhance autonomy. Officials would carry out orders from the chief executive notwithstanding any number of statutes enacted by the Provincial Council. The provincial Chief Minister and his cabinet, not having executive powers, did not have control over public officials within their jurisdictional area. The latter took their directions only from the chief executive, the President.

Apart from this impasse, the division of powers – central, provincial and concurrent – left much to be desired. The concurrent list overlapped with the provincial list. It also provided for central supervision of subjects given to the provinces. Despite the facade of a quasi-federal set-up, real power continued to be vested in the centre.

The Ceylon Tamil demand for a contiguous homeland of the Northern and Eastern provinces was partially acknowledged. The two provinces were provisionally united as a single Northeastern Province (NEP), an amalgamation that would require ratification by the people of the Eastern Province (only) at a referendum within a year. The President could, however, order a postponement of the holding of a referendum until the restoration of normalcy, and successive postponements have indeed taken place.

Recent Developments

Attempts to bring about a peaceful solution have suffered many setbacks. The Sri Lanka government realized that the second largest component of its budget was on defence and that this money could yield better peace dividends. But there was a strong Sinhala war lobby (the military complex and dealers in armaments and in such goods as food, uniforms and boots) with a vested interest in the continuation of the conflict, provided it is encapsulated in the Northern and Eastern provinces. The grave problem here was that the Tamil Tiger suicide squads began operating in the capital city of Colombo, targeting military officials and key civilians.

The important Tamil political groupings, civilian and militant, protested that the Sri Lanka government maintained merely the pretence of seeking 'peace'; the Tigers alleged that this was intensified every year when the Aid Sri Lanka consortium of powers was scheduled to meet, citing as evidence that the Sinhala numerocratic democracy was unwilling to make a meaningful move which could bring about even an interim peace. The efforts of an All-Party Conference were reduced to nought when the President unexpectedly announced that his party's manifesto did not countenance a merger of the Northern and Eastern provinces. This put paid to the exhaustive efforts that Tamil and Muslim parties had been undertaking towards working out a peaceful settlement of their differences. Furthermore, the All-Party Conference proved meaningless with the principal opposition party, the Sri Lanka Freedom Party, boycotting the proceedings. The leading Indian Tamil government minister, S. Thondaman, produced a set of proposals which could be construed as a basis for negotiations with the Tamil parties, militant and civilian, but these were rejected out of hand by Sinhala extremists, civilians and clergy. The sticking point was the merger of the Northern and Eastern provinces (the NEP) which for the Tamils was non-negotiable. The Committee proposed separate councils for the two provinces, with a single 'Regional Council' for the two provinces to deal with specific matters.

As the 1990s proceeded, the various changes in administration in Colombo were accompanied by shifts in strategy, with an alternation between political and military approaches. A further round of peace talks began in October 1994 after the new People's Alliance government came into power, but, following devastating suicide-bombing attacks in Colombo, President Kumaratunga vowed that only after the destruction of the LTTE would a political solution to the Tamil question be worked out. A major air and land offensive, involving tens of thousands of troops, commenced in October 1995, with Jaffna as its target (the Jaffna peninsula and the city itself were under LTTE control at this time; the LTTE ran its own police force, judiciary and banking system there). The LTTE was forced to retreat, but continued to control large areas of the eastern districts of Batticaloa and Trincomalee. A further military campaign that began in May 1997 was also inconclusive. Following the change in government in December 2001, however, the LTTE agreed to a ceasefire. In February 2002 this became permanent, and was intended to facilitate talks, with Norwegian mediation.[32]

CONCLUSION

The future constitutional shape of Sri Lanka remains, then, unclear. Attempts since 1983 to resolve the problem by military means have not been successful. On the one hand, the LTTE has been unable to establish the independent Tamil state for which it has been fighting; but, on the other hand, neither has the Sri Lankan government been able to achieve the kind of military victory that it set out for itself. A military stalemate need not, of itself, result in the short term (or even in the long term) in a switch towards political and diplomatic methods. But in early 2002 there were signs that the two sides were prepared to engage meaningfully with each other, and there was substantial international support, much of it possibly as a reaction to the events of September 11, 2001, for a settlement. External mediation or involvement – as was to be seen in the case of the Indian intervention in 1987–90 – is, of course, no guarantee of a lasting accommodation, and there have been many false starts in the past. But the experience of other prolonged civil conflicts suggests that there is a chance that in time elites on both sides will come to the conclusion that the material and human burden of violent confrontation is not worth bearing if the ultimate solution can be arrived at by the less costly mechanism of negotiation.[33]

ACKNOWLEDGEMENTS

This is the original text of Professor Wilson, as included in the first edition of this volume, with minor modifications by the editor (minor stylistic editing; incorporation of maps and commentary on these; and some updating at selected points). The editor acknowledges gratefully the advice of Tom Farrell in updating certain portions of the text.

NOTES

1. Arend Lijphart, 'Consociation and Federation: Conceptual and Empirical Links', *Canadian Journal of Political Science*, Vol. 12 (1979), pp.499–515. This particular piece had the Canadian Anglophone–Francophone problem in mind and is, because of the similarities, more relevant for Sri Lanka than Lijphart's many other publications. S.J.R. Noel's 'Consociational Democracy and Canadian Federalism', *Canadian Journal of Political Science*, Vol. 4 (1971), pp.15–18, in dealing with the Anglophone–Francophone situation in Canada, has much that is useful for Sri Lanka. Hans Daalder provided a broader and more flexible view of the subject in 1971 when in relation to the Netherlands and Switzerland he stated that the term 'has been increasingly used to characterize a certain pattern of political life in which the political elites of distinct

social groups succeed in establishing a viable, pluralistic state by a process of mutual forbearance and accommodation': 'On Building Consociational Nations: The Cases of the Netherlands and Switzerland', *International Social Science Journal*, Vol. 23 (1971), pp.355–70. This definition could be a more convenient yardstick, in that it is less rigid a measure than Lijphart's. We have combined Lijphart and Daalder in making our assessments.

2. The largest Tamil party, the FP, joined the Tamil Congress (TC) in 1972 to form the Tamil United Front (TUF); in 1976 with the passing by the TUF of the 'Pannakam' or as sometimes called, the 'Vaddukoddai Resolution' demanding the creation of a separate Tamil sovereign state to be called *Thamil Eelam*, the TUF changed its name to the Tamil United Liberation Front (TULF).

3. I owe the inimitable phrase, 'defensive Tamil nationalism' to Brian Pfaffenberger, a recognized political anthropologist of the Sri Lanka situation. He used it first in his 'The Kataragama Pilgrimage: Hindu–Buddhist Interaction and its Significance in Sri Lanka's Polyethnic Social System', *Journal of Asian Studies*, Vol. 38 (1979) pp.253–70.

4. *Report of the Commission on Constitutional Reform* (London: HMSO, 1945), para. 256.

5. *Report of the Special Commission on the Ceylon Constitution* (London: HMSO, 1928).

6. For further details see Sir Ivor Jennings, *The Constitution of Ceylon* (Bombay: Oxford University Press, 1953) and W. Howard Wriggins, *Ceylon: Dilemmas of a New Nation* (Princeton: Princeton University Press, 1960) for an analytical discussion of events up to 1950; Robert N. Kearney, *The Politics of Ceylon (Sri Lanka)* (Ithaca, NY: Cornell University Press, 1973) for events and analysis to 1973; and A. J. Wilson, *Politics in Sri Lanka 1947–1979*. 2nd ed. (London: Macmillan, 1979) for a comprehensive study till 1979. See also A.J. Wilson, 'Minority Safeguards in Ceylon Constitution', *The Ceylon Journal of Historical and Social Studies*, Vol. 1, No. 1 (1958), pp.73–95.

7. A.J. Wilson, *The Break-Up of Sri Lanka: The Sinhala Tamil Conflict* (London: C. Hurst and Company, 1989).

8. Ibid.

9. Robert Kearney, 'Ceylon: Political Stresses and Cohesion', *Asian Survey*, Vol. 8, No. 2 (1968), pp.105–9.

10. See Chelvadurai Manogaran, *Ethnic Conflict and Reconciliation in Sri Lanka* (Honolulu: University of Hawaii Press, 1987), Appendix II, p.190 for the text of the Senanayake–Chelvanayakam Pact of 1965.

11. A. Jeyaratnam Wilson, *Electoral Politics in an Emergent State: The Ceylon General Election of May 1970* (Cambridge: Cambridge University Press, 1976).

12. Wilson, *Break-Up*; the intermediary was the author of this essay.

13. A.J. Wilson, *The Gaullist System in Asia: The Constitution of Sri Lanka (1978)* (London: Macmillan, 1980).

14. The editor is indebted to Tom Farrell for updating the summary of political developments from 1993 onwards in this paragraph.

15. Shelton U. Kodikara, *Defence and Security Perceptions of Sri Lankan Foreign Policy Decision-Makers: A Post-Independence View* (Toronto: Centre for South Asian Studies, University of Toronto, n.d. [1990?]), p.20.

16. Ibid.

17. Ibid., p.31.

18. Annexure C is reproduced in full in Manogaran, *Ethnic Conflict*, Appendix IV, pp.192–4.

19. Shelton U. Kodikara, 'The Indo-Sri Lanka Agreement of July 1987: Retrospect', pp.161–2 in Kodikara (ed.), *South Asian Strategic Issues: Sri Lankan Perspectives* (New Delhi: Sage Publications 1990).

20. This policy of state-aided Sinhala colonization is explained in Manogaran, *Ethnic Conflict*, chapter 3, 'Tamil Districts: Conflicts over Traditional Homelands, Colonization and Agricultural Development', pp.78–114.

21. Robert Kearney, 'Territorial Elements of Tamil Separatism in Sri Lanka', *Pacific Affairs*, Vol. 60, No. 4 (1987–88), pp.561–77.

22. Ibid.

23. Ibid., p.576.

24. Ibid.

25. The Federal Freedom Party of Ceylon, *The Case for a Federal Constitution for Ceylon* (Colombo: Ilankai Tamil Arasu Kadchi (FP), 1951), p.1.

26. Quoted in Kearney, 'Territorial Elements', p.572.
27. The full text of the Tamil Language (Special Provisions) Act, 1958 is reproduced in Manogaran, *Ethnic Conflict*, Appendix III, pp.191–2.
28. Marga Institute, *Sri Lanka's Ethnic Conflict: Myths and Reality* (Colombo: Marga, 1983) contains information on the levels of discrimination against the Ceylon Tamils. Also see S.W.R. de A. Samarasinghe, 'Ethnic Representation in Central Government Employment and Sinhala–Tamil Relations in Sri Lanka: 1948–81' in Robert B. Goldmann and A. Jeyaratnam Wilson (eds), *From Independence to Statehood* (London: Frances Pinter, 1984), pp.173–84.
29. See Chandra Richard de Silva, 'Sinhala–Tamil Relations and Education in Sri Lanka: The University Admissions Issue – The First Phase, 1971–7', in Goldmann and Wilson, *Independence to Statehood*, pp.125–35 and K.M. de Silva, 'University Admissions and Ethnic Tensions in Sri Lanka: 1977–82', ibid., pp.97–110.
30. Political Parties Conference, *Statement of His Excellency The President J.R. Jayewardene ... on Wednesday 25th June 1986* (Colombo: Department of Government Printing, 1986), p.16.
31. Ibid., see 'Annexure'. This introduced the concept of a 'National Ethnic Ratio' in land alienation for the first time. In the Northern and Eastern Provinces, provision was made for land allocation on the basis of the local ethnic distribution, but the Sinhalese would be compensated by allocations in adjacent territories.
32. This paragraph has been contributed by Tom Farrell.
33. This concluding paragraph has been contributed by the editor to replace the author's original conclusion, which referred to the position at the beginning of the 1990s. For recent works on the Sri Lanka conflict, see Jagath P. Senaratne, *Political Violence in Sri Lanka, 1977–1990: Riots, Insurrections, Counter-Insurgencies, Foreign Intervention* (Amsterdam: VU University Press, 1997); Nihal Perera, *Society and Space: Colonialism, Nationalism, and Postcolonial Identity in Sri Lanka* (Boulder, CO: Westview Press, 1998); Robert I. Rotberg (ed.), *Creating Peace in Sri Lanka: Civil War and Reconciliation* (Cambridge, MA: World Peace Foundation, 1999); K.M. de Silva and G.H. Peiris (eds.), *Pursuit of Peace in Sri Lanka: Past Failures and Future Prospects* (Kandy: International Centre for Ethnic Studies, 2000); and A Jeyaratnam Wilson, *Sri Lankan Tamil Nationalism: Its Origins and Development in the Nineteenth and Twentieth Centuries* (London: Hurst, 2000).

9

The Dissolution of the Soviet Union

Federation, Commonwealth, Secession

RONALD J. HILL

In the second half of the 1980s, a bewildered world looked on as the world's largest territorial state – the successor to the Tsarist Empire – fell apart in national self-assertion and ethnic rivalry. The central authorities found themselves unable to cope with the mounting pressures, and at the end of 1991 a system that had prided itself on its capacity to embrace many different ethnic, cultural, religious and linguistic groups, and had held them together in a powerful state with significant material and cultural achievements to its credit, rapidly collapsed.

This came as a surprise to most of the world, which had, with reservations, gone along with the complacent view of the 1970s that the national question had been 'solved' thanks to the 'Leninist' nationalities policy, and that all ethnic groups lived peaceably together as 'the Soviet people'.[1] It was long understood that the Baltic nations of Estonia, Latvia and Lithuania bitterly resented their incorporation into the Soviet Union as a result of the Molotov–Ribbentrop Pact of 1939 and the subsequent Russian migration into these republics;[2] and the demographic pressures of the Muslim population were appreciated.[3] Moreover, Leonid Brezhnev's successors, Yuri Andropov and Konstantin Chernenko, had observed in the early 1980s that, although the national question had been solved 'in the form in which it reached us from the past', this did not mean that it had been entirely removed from the agenda.[4] Nevertheless, few seriously predicted that the break-up of the Soviet Union might emerge as a political issue in the 1990s.[5]

Yet the spread of ethnic tension, unrest and violence, combined with declarations of 'sovereignty' and 'independence' by sub-national units, demonstrated both the fragility of the earlier interethnic peace and the complexity of an issue that urgently demanded (and still demands) effective management.[6] By March 1991, when a referendum on the future of the USSR was held, 76 actual or potential ethnoterritorial disputes were identified, and official figures had ascribed at least 632 deaths directly to interethnic conflicts.[7] Ethnicity could clearly not be wished away, subsumed under a bland slogan such as 'fraternal family of nations',[8] or resolved simply by declaring policies of *sblizhenie* (drawing together) and eventual *sliyanie* (merging).[9] The evidence now suggested that the policies adopted by successive governments had failed, in an area of policy making in which the claims of success, however exaggerated, had appeared to possess some substance.

The issue is extremely complex, and while territorial adjustments had been attempted in the past, in the last years of the Soviet Union ancient resentments and animosities re-surfaced in violent clashes, as the 'freer' political atmosphere engendered by Gorbachev's policies allowed the expression of perceived interests on a scale previously unknown, either in the Soviet period or under the Tsars. Moreover, the collapse of the Soviet Union into its constituent republics, while assuaging some nationalist passions, actually complicated the issue still further, multiplying the problem of interethnic relations as the number of states on the territory increased, and adding an important foreign policy dimension as a result of the Soviet-era migrants now stranded outside the new republics that bore the name of their ethnic identity.

THE NATIONAL QUESTION IN THE SOVIET UNION

The ethnic question would have been a serious one for any government with responsibility for managing the territory that constituted the USSR, itself very close to that of the old Russian Empire. The problem developed as the Empire spread outwards, across Siberia to the Pacific, and indeed beyond, in the seventeenth and eighteenth centuries, towards the south and into the Caucasus in the later eighteenth century, and southeast to Central Asia in the nineteenth.[10] This expansion embraced scores – by some counts hundreds[11] – of ethnic units, which were generally treated as culturally inferior to the dominant Russians in what Lenin, among others, referred to as a 'prison of nations'. This prompted a build-up of resentments that was a significant factor in the fall of the Empire following the Bolshevik seizure of power in the 1917 revolution.[12]

By the same token, the Bolsheviks felt a special responsibility for the nationalities, who had been led to expect different treatment by the revolutionary regime from that which the Empire had meted out. Lenin, a convinced internationalist, had favoured 'self-determination' and condemned national chauvinism,[13] but nationality policy, earlier than other policy areas, came under the domination of Stalin, who was relied on principally because of his own non-Russian (specifically, Georgian) identity. As Commissar for the Nationalities (and later dictator) he pursued pro-Russian (that is, Russian chauvinist and in some cases terroristic anti-minority) policies, although with some complicated exceptions that subsequently permitted his successors to claim resolution of the nationalities question.[14] Some elements of this policy – creating a written version of some four dozen spoken languages, and encouraging interethnic mingling – may be seen as progressive, or even enlightened.

In fact, the ethnic distribution of the Soviet population, given its links with many other social issues, demanded a whole complex of policies if the problem were to be successfully managed, whatever the government's ideological disposition.[15] Indeed, the problem proved to be quite insoluble within the structures of the former Soviet state. If the various national and ethnic groups were of similar size and level of economic and cultural development and were concentrated in compact communities, management of the problem might have been relatively straightforward, through policies of genuine federalization or confederalization, or even by simply creating representative institutions that could serve each nation equally. These conditions did not apply, however, and the task consisted of 'discovering a universally accepted formula to achieve equality between unequals'.[16] Territorial adjustments and population redistribution might mitigate the difficulties, but the scale of the issues implied that even the dismemberment of the country would be insufficient to eliminate the problem, as post-Soviet experience has shown. This complexity stemmed from two main circumstances: the extent of ethnic diversity, which takes a number of forms; and the geographical distribution of ethnic groups.

Ethnic Diversity

As noted above, the number of distinct ethnic groups reflects the definition chosen, but it was common to identify 'over 100' nationalities living in the USSR.[17] These ranged in size from the large groups, including the Russians, Ukrainians, Uzbeks and Belorussians, through intermediate groups such as the Tatars, Georgians, Moldavians, Jews and Estonians, through smaller nationalities, such as the Udmurts (approximately 747,000), Komi (345,000) and Gagauz (198,000), to scores of minute ethnic groups, of which the Orochi (about 900), Aleuts (700) and Nehidaltsy (600) are examples (see Table 9.1 for a list of the larger nationalities). Indeed, in 1989, whereas 22 recognized groups had a population of more than one million, 72 had fewer than 100,000 members.[18] Because of their sheer variation in size, no policy could treat these entities as equals except in very abstract senses.

Soviet nationalities also varied in broad racial type, as expressed in identifiable physical features, including Caucasians (the majority) and

TABLE 9.1
USSR: MAJOR NATIONAL GROUPS, 1989

Nationality	Population	
	000s	%
Russians	145,155	50.8
Ukrainians	44,186	15.5
Uzbeks	16,698	5.8
Belorussians	10,036	3.5
Kazakhs	8,136	2.8
Azeris	6,770	2.4
Tatars	6,649	2.3
Armenians	4,623	1.6
Tadzhiks	4,215	1.5
Georgians	3,981	1.4
Moldavians	3,352	1.2
Lithuanians	3,067	1.1
Turkmenians	2,729	1.0
Kirgiz	2,529	0.9
Germans	2,039	0.7
Chuvash	1,842	0.6
Latvians	1,459	0.5
Bashkirs	1,449	0.5
Jews	1,449	0.5
Mordvinians	1,154	0.4
Poles	1,126	0.4
Estonians	1,027	0.4
Others	12,072	4.2
Total	285,743	100.0

Notes: The table includes national groups with a population of more than one million.

'Jews' refers to the total of four groups between which the 1989 population census distinguished: 'Jews', 'Central Asian Jews', 'Mountain Jews' and 'Georgian Jews'.

'Others' includes 103 other nationalities (including resident aliens), plus a category 'Peoples of India and Pakistan' and a residual category; percentages calculated.

Source: Narodnoe khozyaistvo SSSR v 1989 g. (Moscow: Finansy i statistika, 1990), pp.30, 32.

Orientals. While not in itself necessarily significant, a distinctive physical appearance, particularly when combined with other peculiarities such as dress and language, renders members of particular groups clearly identifiable as 'outsiders', and therefore as easy targets in times of ethnic friction and conflict.

Of greater potential importance are the wide cultural divergences, particularly those associated with language and religion. Some 130 recognized languages are spoken by the peoples of the former USSR, led by the Indo-European Slavic languages of Russian, Ukrainian and Belorussian, but with Turkic, Finno-Ugric, and a wide range of other languages. Five alphabets are in use: in addition to the Cyrillic and Roman ones, there are three that are specific to single languages (the

Armenian, Georgian and Hebrew scripts; Yiddish is written in the last of these). Many of the country's 439,000 Koreans, too, are capable of reading their own distinctive script. Without a specific language policy, the difficulties of mutual comprehension can easily be imagined, as can the resentments arising from migration patterns associated with policies of economic development or efficient state administration.

Apart from linguistic diversity, other cultural differences could be observed, including dress, a form of diversity that has been eroded but not eliminated by the standardizing effect of industrialization and urbanization, which has, in general, been associated with the introduction of European patterns of clothing, hairstyle and other forms of decoration. They also included, more particularly, religion, which frequently imposes quite distinctive group customs and practices that identify ethnic communities and clash with those of other groups.

While there were no reliable data on the number of religious believers in the Soviet Union, religion has certainly been an important form of differentiation, and in several cases it is clearly associated with ethnicity. To give some examples: religious identity links the Russians with Orthodoxy, the Lithuanians with Roman Catholicism, the Kalmyks and other groups with Buddhism, the Jewish population with Judaism, and (of particular concern) the peoples of Central Asia with Islam (and the Azeris with its Shi'ite version). While the Soviet government's policy was to eliminate religious observance and faith *per se*, in cases such as these it became an attack on a major form of identification of the nation concerned. This is especially the case with Islam, which is a greater factor of individual identity than is 'nationality'. Moreover, given that Islam and certain other sects or denominations are linked with a world-wide community, the separation of the Soviet believers from the rest added a further dimension to the Soviet state border. Religious beliefs among ethnic groups are reflected in marriage and other rites of passage, some of which also conflicted with the secular values of the ideology that was imposed by the central government in schools and through the state administration (including the legal system), frequently by state agents of a different ethnic group from the local population.

Another form of distinction lies in the varying levels of social, cultural, economic and political development – a theme that was of particular interest to a Marxist regime, although it concerns virtually all modern governments. While certain nations – the Russians, Ukrainians and Baltic peoples, for example – had reached an advanced stage of industrialization and urbanization, elsewhere the changes associated with modernization have even now barely begun. This applies in particular to the peoples of Central Asia (the Uzbeks, Kirgiz, Turkmenians, and Tadzhiks) and the small, in some cases still nomadic, ethnic groups of Siberia: the Eveny and Evenki, the Chukchi and other minuscule ethnic groups whose members have been partly inducted into the multiethnic cities produced by Soviet industrialization. Their education levels and their consequent capacity for effective political involvement similarly vary enormously.

The Soviet nationalities also differed greatly in their population dynamics. In the industrialized regions, predominantly in the west of the country, the peasantry had grown small, while the working class and white-collar segments expanded; their lifestyle became normally centred on the nuclear family, and their fertility rate fell so low that their rate of natural increase was close to zero. Elsewhere, by contrast, and notably in the Muslim communities of Central Asia, the extended family survived, and traditional attitudes to birth control combined with improved health care, housing, diet and education to produce a population 'explosion', with a crude annual reproduction rate of over 30 per thousand in the 1970s and 1980s.[19]

Broadly speaking, then, the western republics exhibited relatively low fertility, while the five 'Muslim' republics, plus Kazakhstan and Armenia, were expanding far more rapidly.[20] Whereas on a scale of 100 in 1959, the Estonians had reached 104.0 and the Latvians 107.1 in 1989, the Uzbeks had reached 278.3 and the Tadzhiks 300.0.[21] This caused a shift in the ethnic distribution, complicating the task of regional development and exacerbating the difficulties of matching labour and available jobs, with repercussions on interethnic relations. Following the collapse of a central government, the 'European' states were relieved of what they saw as a growing burden, while the newly independent governments in Central Asia have had to contend with expanding populations and a lack of resources – including natural resources such as water – to support them.

A further factor significantly affected the territorial issue. Certain groups long resident on the territory of the Soviet Union were linked with nations that possessed an independent state: Bulgarians, Greeks, Poles, Koreans, Jews, Germans, Finns and Moldavians, for instance. Where there was a common border – as between the Moldavians and Romania, for example – demands for *Anschluss* or *enosis* placed pressure on the existing system that proved difficult to resist. The same applied to the Baltic republics or Georgia, say, where contiguity with a state beyond the Soviet border offered the possibility of independence (although other factors rendered that solution difficult to concede). Ethnic groups in the interior could not enjoy genuine independence without a drastic remodelling of the state structure; this has been problematic for a number of ex-Soviet states, including Russia.

The Soviet nationality question was thus exceptionally complex, as is its legacy to the post-Soviet states. The applicability of territorial solutions is complicated by the cross-cutting distribution of the various forms of diversity and the need to tackle this issue in the context of many other policy areas, particularly economic development. Other issues have a

MAP 9.1
USSR: TITULAR NATIONALITIES BY UNION REPUBLIC, 1989

ESTONIA 61.5%
LATVIA 52.0%
LITHUANIA 79.6%
BELARUS
Minsk
Moscow
79.7%
UKRAINE
Kyiv
RUSSIA 81.5%
MOLDOVA 64.5%
72.7%
KAZAKHSTAN 39.7%
70.1%
GEORGIA
ARMENIA 93.3%
82.7%
AZERBAIDZHAN
UZBEKISTAN 71.4%
52.4%
KYRGYZSTAN
TURKMENISTAN 72.0%
62.3%
TAJIKISTAN

Percentage
0% to 20%
20% to 50%
50% to 80%
80% to 100%

bearing on the matter, some resulting from past policies. The geographical location and spread of the various groups is an obvious factor, and it has been influenced by migration resulting from investment priorities.

In addition, mention must be made of Stalin's policy of deportations of whole nations in the 1940s, ostensibly for reasons of state security (see below). This led to a further factor of enormous political significance in recent times: the ethnic issue was linked to the question of centralized communist administration. Some groups looked to a strong, ethnically neutral central authority for protection against hostile neighbours; others resented the communist regime's denial of their religious, cultural and other forms of expression; still others associated communism with Russia and added an ethnic dimension to communist repression. Communism was, in effect, deployed to serve Russian interests, and Russian nationalists such as Boris Yel'tsin and Alexander Solzhenitsyn tried to separate the two identities of the political centre, by distinguishing Moscow as the centre of oppressive Communist administration from Moscow as the capital of a more benign Russia.[22]

The Distribution of Nationalities

With certain exceptions, most officially recognized national groups of the Soviet Union were historically fairly compact; even immigrant commu-

TABLE 9.2
USSR: TERRITORIAL DISTRIBUTION OF PRINCIPAL NATIONALITIES, 1989

Nationality	Number 000s	Living within 'own' republic 000s	Living within 'own' republic %	As % of 'own' republic
Russians	145,155	119,866	82.6	81.3
Ukrainians	44,186	37,419	84.7	72.4
Belorussians	10,036	7,905	78.8	77.5
Uzbeks	16,698	14,142	84.7	71.0
Kazakhs	8,136	6,535	80.3	39.5
Georgians	3,981	3,787	95.1	69.6
Azeris	6,770	5,805	85.7	82.5
Lithuanians	3,067	2,924	95.3	79.2
Moldavians	3,352	2,795	83.4	64.4
Latvians	1,459	1,388	95.1	51.8
Kirgiz	2,529	2,230	88.2	52.0
Tadzhiks	4,216	3,172	75.2	62.1
Armenians	4,623	3,084	66.7	93.8
Turkmenians	2,729	2,537	93.0	71.8
Estonians	1,027	963	93.8	61.2

Note: The apparently irrational ordering of nationalities and republics in Tables 9.2 and 9.3 is the official order, first established in 1948, and reflecting the populations of the republics at that time.

Source: Calculated from *Vsesoyuznaya perepis' naseleniya 1989 goda*, CD-ROM version, *1989 USSR Population Census* (Minneapolis, MN: East View Publications, 1996).

nities such as the Jews and Germans existed within restricted areas. Under Soviet – and imperial – rule, however, induced migration led to significant intermingling. By 1989 some 60 million citizens lived outside their nationality's territorial unit, or had no such unit in the USSR.[23] This applies in particular to Russians (and, to a lesser extent, other Slavs), who moved around the country as administrators, educators and other specialists bringing expertise and experience to local populations embarking on modernization.[24] Since the whole country was treated as a single economic unit, workers, too, were induced to migrate to wherever the economy demanded their talents. Table 9.2 and Map 9.1 indicate the dispersal of the principal nationalities beyond the borders of their corresponding republics in 1989.[25]

Interethnic marriages, although not the norm, were seen as a 'law of developed socialism' and, as such, officially encouraged, to foster the 'consolidation and assimilation of peoples' and the 'ethnogenesis of the Soviet people as a new historic community of people'.[26] They occurred in significant numbers, and their incidence was increasing. By 1989, some 17.5% of all families were ethnically mixed, compared with 14.9%a decade earlier; the rate was even higher in urban areas (20.2%, against 18.1% in 1979).[27] According to official figures for 1988, some two-thirds of ethnic Germans (67.6% of males and 64.6% of females) who married in that year entered unions with non-Germans; high proportions of exogamous marriages were also recorded for Jews and Tatars. At the other end of the scale, only 6.6% of Uzbek bridegrooms and 5.0% of brides married partners from a different ethnic group in 1988; similarly low figures were recorded for Kirgiz and Turkmenians.[28]

When the data are examined by republic (rather than by nationality), it is clear that non-natives married outside their own group relatively frequently. Even in the predominantly Muslim areas, where members of the principal nationality tended not to marry 'foreigners', Russians showed a manifest tendency to do so. In the Baltic republics, too, where 'natives' showed a modest tendency to marry outside their nationality, Russians married non-Russians in significant numbers (though their spouses were not necessarily, of course, members of the titular nationality). Indeed, Russians were long ago recognized as 'active' participants in mixed marriages.[29] The incidence of interethnic marriage among females entering marriage rose during the 1980s in all but four republics (Lithuania, Estonia, Turkmenia and Azerbaidzhan).[30] This is significant because interethnic marriage, particularly that involving relationships between members of the indigenous population and of the 'immigrant' community, complicates both the ethnic structure of the regions concerned and the prospects of resolving tensions through a policy of population or territorial adjustment, since citizens are not at liberty to change their registered nationality. In the post-Soviet period, tensions have arisen in some states in response to this factor.

A final element in the ethnic distribution is the deportation (physical relocation) of certain ethnic groups under Stalin. The Volga Germans, the Crimean Tatars, the Chechens, Kalmyks and other groups were physically moved eastwards in the 1940s, and campaigns for their reinstatement in their traditional homelands characterized the late Soviet period, comparable with many Jews' demands for permission to leave for what they saw as their own national homeland, Israel.[31]

The complexity of the ethnic dimension of former Soviet society is thus obvious. In principle, many specific contentious issues arose, calling for various political solutions. While some nationalities might realistically aspire to separation from the Union, this was (and remains) manifestly absurd in many cases. Thus the Ukrainians, a nation of 44 million in 1989, living mainly (although not exclusively) in a well-endowed republic rather larger than France, and already possessing attributes of statehood including membership of the United Nations, clearly had the capacity to exist as a separate nation-state.[32] Its well-educated population possesses a strong sense of identity, in part associated with the knowledge that Kyiv (Kiev), the capital of Ukraine, was the centre of the first major Slavic community. The 1,719 Eskimos, the 1,278 Nganasans, the 731 Tofalars or the 190 Oroki – and many other tiny indigenous populations of the north and east[33] – cannot contemplate such an existence (although, if political consciousness rose to demand it, a form of multiethnic statehood could perhaps be devised).[34] One response in post-Soviet Russia has been to emphasize the term 'Rossiyane' (inhabitants of Russia) in place of 'Russkie' (meaning ethnic Russians) in political rhetoric addressed to all citizens of the country. This is one element in a wider task of 'forging a nation', whose identity is still uncertain.[35] The same issue of 'nation building' is faced by most other states that have emerged from the Soviet Union, and it is proving a difficult task.[36]

THE STATE AND THE NATIONAL QUESTION

The Soviet regime's response to these matters was complex, in some cases crude and in others rather sophisticated. Until the 1980s, it appeared that the problem was being managed with some success.[37] Indeed, it has been suggested that 'The Soviet state had to collapse first for the world to discover to what extent the Soviets had in fact succeeded in forming a Soviet people.'[38] While the mechanisms of federalism permitted a measure of cultural autonomy, the central state authorities used the communist party structures and certain organizational principles to prevent fragmentation, and deployed the state education system, a unified system of military training, and other similar measures, to encourage integration, harmonization and eventual assimilation.

The formally federal state, the Union of Soviet Socialist Republics, was established by a treaty of December 1922, its principles enshrined in the 1924 constitution and renewed in constitutions adopted in 1936 and 1977. Its structure was based on the allocation of territory to specific national groups, on a hierarchical basis, in which major groups on territory contiguous with an external border were granted the status of *union republic* (SSR), significant and relatively compact nationalities within such units were accorded the status of *autonomous republics* (ASSR), and other nationalities or groups were allocated an *autonomous region* or *autonomous area*. Each category of national unit had a fixed number of seats in the second chamber of the parliamentary Supreme Soviet, the Council of the Nationalities. Broadly speaking, this structure survived until the 1990s, with some adjustments over the years. The Moldavian autonomous republic, within the Ukraine, was abolished with the reincorporation of Bessarabia during the Second World War and the creation of a new Moldavian union republic; the Karelo-Finnish SSR was downgraded to the status of autonomous republic within the Russian republic (to give it its full name, the Russian Soviet Federated Socialist Republic,

TABLE 9.3
USSR: AREA AND POPULATION BY UNION REPUBLIC, 1979–89

Republic	Area, (sq. km.) 000s	Population 1979	1989
RSFSR	17,075.4	137,551	147,400
Ukraine	603.7	49,755	51,707
Belorussia	207.6	9,560	10,200
Uzbekistan	447.4	15,391	19,905
Kazakhstan	2,717.3	14,684	16,536
Georgia	69.7	5,015	5,443
Azerbaidzhan	86.8	6,028	7,038
Lithuania	65.2	3,398	3,690
Moldavia	33.7	3,947	4,338
Latvia	64.50	2,521	2,680
Kirgizia	198.5	3,529	4,290
Tadzhikstan	143.1	3,801	5,109
Armenia	29.8	3,031	3,288
Turkmenia	488.1	2,759	3,534
Estonia	45.1	1,466	1,573
Total	22,403.0	262,436	286,731

Notes: The figure for total area includes inland seas. The total population figure for 1989 does not correspond to that in Table 9.1; it refers to the 'permanent' population (total, 285,742,511) as opposed to 'resident' population on the date of the census (total, 286,730,817); figures from *Vsesoyuznaya perepis' naseleniya 1989 goda*, CD-ROM version, *1989 USSR Population Census* (Minneapolis, MN: East View Publications, 1996).

Source: Narodnoe khozyaistvo SSSR v 1989 g. (Moscow: Finansy i statistika, 1990), pp.17–23.

RSFSR) in 1956; the Crimea, formerly an autonomous republic subordinated to Russia, was transferred as a 'gift' to the Ukraine in 1954. A curiosity is the Jewish autonomous area (Birobidzhan) in the Far East, some 4,000 miles from where the bulk of the country's Jewish population has traditionally resided.

For all the apparent rationality of this arrangement in the context of the various inequalities noted above, the size of the various republics varied greatly (see Table 9.3), and the precise boundaries generated long-standing grievances which later became politically relevant. The establishment in 1924–25 of four republics in Central Asia, in what had previously been essentially a unified cultural entity in the Islamic world, has been seen as an application of the policy of 'divide and rule', in which the modern concepts and symbols of nationality and statehood were imposed so as to divert attention from common cultural and religious traditions.[39] The creation of the Moldavian republic in Bessarabia, formerly part of Romania and culturally and linguistically only marginally different from its neighbour, was a source of friction between the Romanian communist regime and the Soviet Union, and irredentism emerged. The establishment in 1923 of the autonomous region of Nagorny Karabakh, an enclave of (Christian) Armenians within (Muslim) Azerbaidzhan, caused disaffection and erupted in bloodshed in the late 1980s. In Georgia, the South Ossetian autonomous region and the Abkhaz and Adzhar autonomous republics resisted the manifestations of Georgian nationalism. Many actual or potential disputes originated in the frequent boundary changes of the 1920s, 1930s and 1950s, which failed to endow ethnic groups with the resources to match their aspirations, or to recognize their ancient attachment to particular territories.[40] At that time, any objections to the centre's policies were interpreted as manifestations of 'bourgeois nationalism' and repressed.[41]

These various grievances point to a particular feature of Soviet nationalities policy: the essential limitations to its rational application. Some national or cultural entities were divided, their populations subject to different jurisdictions, with implications lasting into the period after the break-up of the USSR. The Armenians of Nagorny Karabakh, administratively still part of Azerbaidzhan, were a clear example, where a relatively narrow strip of land separated this autonomous region from the Armenian SSR. In direct contrast was the autonomous republic of Nakhichevan, formally part of the Azerbaidzhan SSR, whose nationals occupied the territory, but which was separated from the main territory of Azerbaidzhan by a strip of the Armenian SSR. Birobidzhan offers a different extreme: the number of Jews resident in this autonomous area in 1989 was 8,887 (down from 10,166 in 1979), or 0.64% of the country's total Jewish population at that time; even within Birobidzhan itself, Jews constituted only 4.2% of the population, Russians (178,000) and Ukrainians (16,000) outnumbering them by almost 22 to one.[42]

In determining whether a given ethnic group merited the status of union or autonomous republic, a major factor was contiguity with an external border, on the logical grounds that the exercise of the constitutional right of secession could be effective only if the republic were not totally surrounded by Soviet territory.[43] Although the right of secession was a fiction never intended to be admitted, some national groups during 1990–91 unilaterally declared an upgrading of their status, while others that possessed the status of constituent republics demanded an effective right to secede; the first ever law setting out procedures for secession was passed in April 1990, and the collapse of Soviet power permitted the Baltic republics to sever their links with the Russian-dominated system.[44] In this they were undoubtedly facilitated by the fact that their incorporation into the Soviet Union in 1940, under the terms of the so-called Molotov–Ribbentrop agreement of 23 August 1939, was never recognized by the West, which regarded them as a special case among the Soviet republics.

The union and autonomous republics were given the trappings of modern statehood, including flags, anthems, coats-of-arms, supreme soviets, ministries, state committees and supreme courts, with carefully defined powers and obligations within their jurisdiction. In practice, the exercise of these rights was severely limited. First, the principle of 'democratic centralism' gave superior organs the right to annul or rescind decisions taken by lower organs. Second, the unitary Communist Party of the Soviet Union, serving as the system's principal centripetal force, maintained strict control and supervision over state organs at all levels. Even though itself nominally a federal structure, with 'branches' in all but the largest republic (until 1990), the Communist Party of the Soviet Union (CPSU) was clearly recognized as a unitary institution, with a single programme, set of rules and membership card; its officers and officials were freely transferred from one part of the Union to another. The practice developed whereby the local first secretary was drawn from the principal ethnic group, while the second secretary was normally appointed from the centre and was usually a Russian or Ukrainian.[45] The latter post carried responsibility for the recruitment system of *nomenklatura*, used for selecting individuals for appointment throughout the party and state administrative apparatus. In short, 'autonomy' was very restricted in practice, and scarcely applied even to the union republics. Two of these – Belorussia and Ukraine – may have had seats at the United Nations. This was apparently a concession by the West in establishing the UN; it was the price of bringing the Soviet Union into the organization, and less costly than conceding votes to 16 Soviet republics, as Stalin had claimed.[46] Yet their power to act independently was severely circumscribed. Even the right to use the language of the major nationality was limited, and bilingualism with Russian was promoted throughout the non-Russian areas *for those whose native language was not Russian*; Russians in non-Russian areas (principally in towns and cities) usually did not learn the local language.[47]

These experiences of attempting to manage the nationalities problem did not satisfy the needs of the various groups. In the late 1960s, living in Moldavia, this author was told that it was regarded as 'shameful' to speak the native tongue, while others abhorred the imposition of a modified form of the Cyrillic script in place of the Roman alphabet for this Romance language.[48] The influx of Russians, particularly retired army officers, into Kishinev (the capital) was resented, as they invariably had privileged access to housing. Moreover, as noted above, the populations of the independent Baltic states deplored the reduction of their status to that of union republics of the USSR. There were also stirrings of Ukrainian nationalism, apparently under the republic's highest patronage, in the 1960s and 1970s.[49]

From the mid-1980s, with the steady deterioration of the country's economic performance and the freedom granted under *glasnost* to criticize and to raise hitherto taboo subjects, various ethnic groups with increasing vociferousness expressed their dissatisfaction with their status, finding scapegoats for their plight and rejecting the authority of the centre. In 1990 serious speculation about the break-up of the system began. The independent weekly newspaper *Moskovskie novosti* (or *Moscow News*, in its English-language edition) reported 76 flashpoints of ethnic tension over the control of territory, which had either flared into open conflict with several hundred officially acknowledged deaths or were rumbling beneath the surface with open hostilities constantly threatening. By the end of October 1990, 14 of the 15 union republics had declared their 'sovereignty' and in the last (Kirgizia) parliament had approved the first reading of a similar declaration; five republics, beginning with those of the Baltic region, had proclaimed their independence, and in some cases had begun to act upon that declaration. At lower administrative levels, autonomous republics and regions unilaterally declared an upgrading of their status, and some even changed their names. Some of these changes threatened the integrity not only of the USSR but of the RSFSR and other republics.[50] Cities such as Moscow, Leningrad and L'vov, having fallen under radical control in the 1990 elections, acted on their democratically-derived mandate and passed laws that challenged the power of the all-Union authorities. This 'war of laws' between the centre and the constituent elements of the Union was the logical outcome of Gorbachev's policy of distributing power from the excessively centralized bureaucratic party and state apparatus.

THE PATH TO DISSOLUTION

The centrifugal forces set in train by democratization led relatively quickly to a formal break-up of the Soviet Union. This proceeded in a number of stages. The first centred on a new treaty of union sponsored by the central authorities in an effort to hold the Union together. As the number of territories declaring their 'sovereignty' expanded, however, a second stage was reached. Moscow proposed a Union-wide referendum on the issue of the Union itself – the first referendum in the country's history, held on 17 March 1991 under legislation rushed through in the autumn of 1990. Third, an abortive coup in August 1991 had far-reaching consequences, resulting within months in the disintegration of the Soviet Union. Finally, the end of 1991 and the beginning of 1992 saw the birth of a new political structure, the Commonwealth of Independent States (CIS). Its ultimate form took some time to clarify, and its capacity to resolve any of the territorial, ethnic and other problems of the former Soviet nationalities is in serious doubt.[51]

The New Union Treaty

Responding to the growing ethnic dissatisfaction, the centre proposed a new treaty of union, to replace that of 1922, which clearly did not satisfy the modern aspirations of the nationalities. The 'fraudulent' nature of the federal constitution, masking a highly centralized unitary state, became a topic of open debate, and at a party Central Committee plenum in September 1989 a new approach was called for. The new policy entailed renegotiation of the union treaty, plus additional measures to devolve authority from the centre, and to serve and protect the interests of national minorities – including the minute groups in remote areas, which Marxism's founding fathers held in contempt.[52] A significant measure of intra-party devolution was also contemplated; yet by the time such ideas were reiterated at the Twenty-Eighth CPSU Congress less than ten months later, the parties in the three Baltic republics had declared their independence and formal splits had followed.

After the adoption of a law on 26 April 1990 to delimit the powers of the union and the republican authorities, extensive consultations took place and many articles appeared in the press across the country, leading to the publication of the first draft of a new treaty, ostensibly intended to create a genuine federation of sovereign states.[53] However, its universal acceptance was far from certain and, according to some analysts, it was seriously flawed in retaining supremacy for federal laws over those of supposedly sovereign republics. Many republics would opt only for a looser confederation, if that.

On the principal question of the Union's sovereignty compared with that of its constituent parts, the draft was uncompromisingly federalist: the Union itself was to be a 'sovereign federative state', with common citizenship, a federal budget, a common currency, the primacy of federal law in matters of federal competence, and Russian as the state language of the federation. In addition, while the republics would determine their own administrative and political structures and levy taxes, the centre would determine defence and foreign policy and handle the adoption of the constitution. Moreover, there was considerable room for disagreement over the use of land and mineral resources and capital stock. In response to pressures from 'below', the distinction between 'union' and 'autonomous' republics was abandoned – no doubt leading to confusion, as some regions had formally redefined their status as that of autonomous republic. In any case, the latter were to remain part of – and therefore subordinate to – the union republics within which they existed. The image of a hierarchy of 'sovereign' states renders the very concept of sovereignty problematical, and may well have been designed with a political purpose in mind: to prevent secession.[54] After all, sovereignty implies 'the right to adopt one's own laws'.[55]

Some three months later, after further discussion and debate, a revised draft was published, in which the republics were accorded expanded powers and rights at the expense of the central authorities.[56] The centre was now given specific responsibility for defence and state security, foreign policy (including certain foreign economic relations), and the approval and execution of the state budget. Certain other powers were to be exercised jointly by the central and the republican authorities, including the drafting of defence and foreign policy, and the compilation of the budget. The republics were also declared to be independent members of the international community, with the right to establish diplomatic relations with other states (and presumably to apply for admission to the United Nations). They were, however, required to accept existing borders on signing the treaty; the Russian language was designated the 'official' (rather than the 'state') language; and new constitutional arrangements would, realistically, make provision for republics – rather than 'nationalities' – to participate in the law-making process.

Despite these concessions, some existing republics steadfastly refused even to engage in discussions, since they regarded themselves as already outside the USSR (a foreign state in their eyes). Even in republics and regions whose presence was absolutely vital (specifically Russia, without which the 'Union' could not effectively exist), disquiet was expressed at certain specific provisions, at the remaining lack of clarity in the institutional mechanisms for governing the new entity, and at the theoretical ambiguity inherent in a hierarchy of sovereignty.

The Referendum of March 1991

Gorbachev saw a nationwide referendum on the preservation of the Union as a 'democratic' testing of public opinion concerning his proposed new union treaty, and he called a referendum on the following question:

> Do you consider it necessary to maintain the Union of Soviet Socialist Republics as a renewed federation of sovereign republics in which the rights of each nation would be fully guaranteed?

This wording left many questions unanswered. What was meant by a 'renewed' federation? By what mechanisms would the 'renewal' take place? What 'guarantees' for the rights of each nation could be made, and how could they be upheld? If the national result was binding, how would the populations of republics that voted against the general trend be affected? Most critically, what did 'sovereignty' mean in this context: would the 'renewed federation' itself constitute a sovereign state, and what would its rights be in relation to the 'sovereign' republics that it comprised? How many republics would be members of the federation? Would acceptance freeze existing borders? The answers given referred sceptics and pedants to the draft of the new treaty, notwithstanding its flaws and weaknesses; the referendum would thus become in effect a referendum on the draft treaty.

These and further questions raised in the pre-poll debate were made all the more urgent by the political movement from below, in which four republics formally declared their independence and began to move towards complete political severance with Moscow, and other regions and autonomous republics declared their enhanced status.

Some found the question as posed so unsatisfactory that several republics modified the wording. In Kazakhstan, reference was to a 'union of equal sovereign states'; in Ukraine, voters were asked whether their republic should be part of a union of sovereign states on the principles of the declaration on the state sovereignty of the Ukraine, adopted on 16 July 1990. Similar modifications were made to the wording in Azerbaidzhan, Uzbekistan and Kirgizia. Six republics refused to hold the referendum on their territory, and instead organized their own referendum on different dates, effectively seeking endorsement of a policy of national state independence. In Lithuania on 9 February, Latvia and Estonia on 3 March and Georgia on 31 March, voters were asked their opinion of the restoration of full state independence outside the USSR, and voters in Armenia were asked a similar question on 21 September. Moreover, apart from the RSFSR and Moscow city, other republics, provinces and cities substituted their own wording or appended questions of specific local interest, ranging from the issue of land ownership in the Mari autonomous republic to the construction of an atomic power station in two regions, and the recall of an elected deputy in a district of the city of Sverdlovsk (now Yekaterinburg).[57]

The results permitted all sides to claim 'victory'. The Central Asian republics overwhelmingly supported the Union (although not all answered the same question), while advanced urbanized, industrialized areas (notably Russia, with its large population of sophisticated city-dwellers) were far less supportive.[58] On that basis, Gorbachev advanced towards the signing of a new treaty; on 23 April 1991, together with the leaders of those republics which held the all-Union referendum, he reached agreement on measures to stabilize the economic and political situation: the swift conclusion of the new Treaty of Union, to be followed by the adoption of a new constitution and elections to the organs of state power. The negotiation entailed accepting the distinction between union and autonomous republics, thereby supporting the claims of the union republics to political superiority over the autonomous republics within their borders.[59] The potential for continuing clashes remained considerable. Indeed, given the multiple ambiguities in the question, and the uncertainties in the draft treaty even as revised in March 1991, the task of devising new structures to accommodate the needs and demands of the various ethnic groups was to prove far from complete. Meanwhile, opinion among the deputies in the USSR Supreme Soviet became polarized, with the *Soyuz* (Union) group, largely comprising old-style communists and military officers, campaigning to maintain the Union at all costs. The shedding of blood in the Lithuanian capital, Vilnius, in January 1991 hardened attitudes on both sides.

The August 1991 Coup and its Consequences

The whole political situation was changed radically by the abortive coup against President Mikhail Gorbachev by traditionalist communists on 19 August 1991.[60] The Russian republic's president, Boris Yel'tsin, seized the opportunity and moved swiftly to destroy the power of the communist party, replace the old symbols of the centre (notably the red flag and its hammer and sickle emblem) by traditional Russian symbols, and take control of institutions and economic enterprises situated on the republic's territory. The communist party's activities were suspended, its assets seized, and its publications prohibited; similar moves followed in other republics; in November, the CPSU was formally banned within Russia, while in other republics it changed its name and continued a political role. Effectively, however, the Union's principal centripetal force had been destroyed, and individual republics appeared to go their own way.

During autumn 1991 Gorbachev struggled to maintain the Union in a reformed version; but his declining authority, coupled with his inability to avert economic collapse, rendered him increasingly irrelevant to the political solution of the Union's problems. The three Baltic republics formally seceded in August, and were admitted to the United Nations and other international bodies. Central power seemed increasingly incapacitated, as the Russian president issued decrees that prevented federal institutions from functioning. Faced with the refusal of republics to pay tax revenues to the federal authorities, the latter resorted to the printing press to pay for centrally-funded services and institutions: the armed forces, research and educational institutions, artistic companies, and the state service. Through the autumn, anti-Union measures became more extreme: ministries (including the Foreign Ministry) were suspended, and the state bank was taken over. In a referendum on 1 December, the people of Ukraine voted for independence of the USSR, removing any doubts about the likelihood that the republic would sign the new Union treaty: it would not. Once these developments reached a logical end-point (the disintegration of the Union), however, the process did not end, and the issue of territorial integrity has plagued a number of states in the former Soviet space.

The Birth of the Commonwealth of Independent States

Russia's opposition to the old regime, with the support of other republics, finally ensured its collapse. In early December 1991, the leaders of Russia, Ukraine and Belorussia established a new 'Commonwealth of Independent States' (CIS), which Soviet republics were invited to join. Symbolically, its headquarters were to be located outside Moscow (in Minsk, the Belorussian capital), to dispel fears of continuing Russian domination. Outmanoeuvred, Gorbachev resigned as USSR President on 25 December, and the next day the Supreme Soviet met in a sparsely attended session to suspend its activities and declare the Union of Soviet Socialist Republics dissolved. Over the following weeks and months, most former Soviet republics became members of the CIS (Georgia was the major exception, in addition to the now completely independent Baltic states, and Azerbaidzhan and Moldavia proved less than enthusiastic members). This organization originally consisted of a council of heads of state and a council of heads of government, plus a working group to prepare materials for the meetings of these. It agreed a number of economic and other matters aimed at facilitating members' continuing cooperation, drew up a charter and established some 60 institutions, most with specific coordinating functions, but no supranational authority.

In its first decade of existence, the Commonwealth proved hardly more successful than its predecessor at managing ethnic conflict: indeed, in certain respects its creation multiplied the problem. Conflicting views of the scope of the new entity – in essence, whether it was intended to 'manage' the disintegration of the Soviet Union or to facilitate its surreptitious reintegration – led to mutual suspicions and consequent substantial difficulties in coordinating policies among the various member states. The establishment of the new states on the basis of existing republican borders gave added relevance to matters that had effectively been disregarded under the Soviet regime, and the manifestation of both assertive and defensive nationalism exacerbated the problems that had led to the demise of the Soviet Union. The CIS, in effect, proved stillborn. Its constituent elements quickly ceased to function as a single economic entity, introducing their own currencies, imposing taxes against their former allies' products, refusing collaboration, seeking alternative international contacts and alliances, and generally pursuing new agendas driven by domestic considerations. In some cases that entailed civil war, ethnic strife, economic warfare, linguistic clashes and other manifestations of identity that had been 'solved' in the Soviet era by a combination of pressure and more benign policies fostering cooperation.[61]

ETHNICITY AND TERRITORIALITY IN THE SUCCESSOR STATES

The collapse of the USSR and its replacement by a 'commonwealth' of 'independent' states, whose policies in such fields as the economy, foreign relations and defence, environmental protection and the control of crime were intended to be loosely coordinated rather than determined in unison,[62] clearly did not resolve the ethnic problems. The establishment of 15 independent republics multiplied the number of governments that were faced with the problem of ethnic diversity, preventing the application of a general solution. Furthermore, the new-found independence of states formerly subordinated to the Union encouraged claims against one another over economic, territorial, defence and other issues. One study in the 1990s identified eight historical territorial disputes at the edge of the former Soviet Union, which had now become salient political issues among the successor states and their neighbours.[63] There were many other disputes *within* the territory of the former Soviet Union, which have been highly salient in post-Soviet politics.

Governing the New Republics

A real difficulty facing both the former central authorities and the regional and local administrations – and, indeed, the peoples of these territories – is that ethnic diversity combined with the pattern of distribution of resources makes a permanent and wholly rational structure difficult to attain. The central Soviet government may well have argued that all would gain if the resources of the whole country were used for the benefit of all nations and groups; this is the kind of argument that declares North Sea oil to be for the benefit of the whole of the United Kingdom. However, just as Scottish nationalists argue that the oil off Scotland's coast is a Scottish resource, so the various regions of the Soviet Union declared that the minerals and resources belonged to the inhabitants of the region. The oil wealth of Tatarstan and the diamonds of Yakutia (now renamed Sakha) are two examples of valuable assets that have permitted local elites to claim a significant measure of autonomy in their dealings with Moscow.

This factor reflects an abandonment of the Soviet practice, whereby regional boundaries were artificial, established on the assumption that for economic and most other purposes they would be disregarded. These became the boundaries of the new states, and, within Russia, of the 89 'subjects' of the federation, including constituent republics that now jealously insisted upon their 'sovereign' rights. Disagreements over ultimate ownership of such resources exacerbated the tensions between local and central authorities that have required careful negotiation between different entities. In the worst case within Russia, the republic of Chechnya has refused to sign a treaty that incorporates it into the Russian Federation, and bloody wars in 1994–96 and from 1999 onwards have characterized the attempt to settle this issue. In the transcausasian region, the authorities of the Republic of Georgia have faced virtually incessant war waged by ethnic minorities in the autonomous regions of

Adzharia and Abkhazia: this perpetual struggle has led almost to the collapse of the republic as an economic and political entity. Tensions between Azerbaidzhan and Armenia over Nagorny Karabakh, a key factor in the collapse of the Soviet Union, have remained high and appear unlikely to submit to easy resolution. In the small republic of Moldova, sandwiched between Ukraine and Romania, the largely Russian-speaking territory on the eastern bank of the River Dniester in 1990 declared its independent status as the Dniester Moldavian Republic, with the tacit – and occasionally active – support of nationalist-minded Russian politicians, and has resisted all attempts to reach a settlement, including military action in the summer of 1992. In the south of the same republic, a region occupied mainly by Gagauz (Christian Turks) also declared its autonomy, and the central authorities had to negotiate a high level of self-determination which shows every sign of not satisfying the aspirations of the local authorities in the regional capital, Comrat; a neighbouring Bulgarian minority likewise has demanded special status.

In Ukraine, one of the largest of the post-Soviet republics, arguments over the appropriate structure for this disparate state lasted several years before they were resolved. East Ukraine, with its main centre the industrial city of Kharkiv, is populated mainly by Russian-speakers of the Russian Orthodox confession who have little sympathy for the nationalist aspirations of the Ukrainian-speaking Uniates (Eastern-rite Catholics) of West Ukraine. The Crimea, 'given' by Russia in 1954, the ancestral homeland of the Crimean Tatars (deported by Stalin in 1945) but inhabited in modern times mainly by Russians, for several years refused to submit to the authority of Kyiv, and even insisted on maintaining Moscow standard time (one hour ahead of Kyiv time).

It is not obvious, in fact, that Ukraine should form a single unitary state.[64] Shortly after independence, proposals for a federal Ukraine were advanced, embracing different combinations of provincial units based variously on L'vov, Odessa (in the south), Kharkiv, and Donetsk (in the southeast), with Kyiv (the capital) as a separate unit or as the centre of a province, and with or without the Crimea as a constituent or autonomous region or republic (which might revert to membership of the Russian republic or even form a separate republic).[65] But even though the constitution of 1996 (Article 2) declares Ukraine to be a unitary state, the issue may not be resolved forever, since certain regions of modern Ukraine have historically been part of other states, including Northern Bukovina, a part of Romania between the world wars; the city of L'viv (known in Russian as L'vov, in Polish as Lwów, and in German as Lemberg) which had been part of Poland and of the Austro-Hungarian Empire; and the southern Black Sea coastal strip of Bessarabia, which might properly be part of Moldova, itself subject to possible reunification with Romania. Indeed, if historical affinities and allegiances are to be taken into consideration, Poland, Slovakia and Hungary have an interest in the borders of Ukraine, as do Romania, Moldova–Bessarabia, Belarus and Russia. Nevertheless, it appears that, despite the lack of a single state identity in Ukraine, there is strong support for maintaining existing borders.[66]

What the world witnessed in this process, then, was the collapse not just of the Soviet Union but also of what was referred to as its external empire (the communist-ruled states of Eastern and Central Europe that were linked to it in political, economic and military alliance). It can also be seen as the further dismantling of the Russian Empire, which had built up the territorial structure that was inherited by the Soviet Union. In addition, unfinished business of the collapse of the Ottoman and Austro-Hungarian empires is still being played out. But it is more appropriate, perhaps, to see recent events as part of a natural process of flux in interethnic relations in the region. Stasis in human affairs is impossible: stability is something that needs to be worked for and maintained through political processes of negotiation and careful management, rather than through the traditional resort to violence. That, in turn, requires the exercise of sophistication, wisdom and restraint on the part of leaders and peoples alike. It will often mean ignoring what are perceived as ancient grievances, and abandoning traditional claims to 'national' territory. It may also require internationally supported adjustments of boundaries, perhaps with accompanying transfers of population, funded, supervised and guaranteed by the international community.

Russia itself is now formally a federation, in which some of the constituent elements (subjects) have enjoyed a significant enhancement of their status. It stretches from the Baltic to the Pacific Ocean and the Bering Sea, and from the Arctic Ocean to the Black and Caspian Seas.[67] It is not necessarily the case that it is best administered from a single centre located in the west of the country, or that it can be effectively managed as a single economic unit. The transport costs of inter-regional trade alone are colossal. Such trade entails using the mineral and other wealth of Siberia to supply the factories of European Russia, which in turn re-supplies Siberia with manufactures and food. What sounds significantly more rational over the longer term, and could well lead to the creation of major new economic regions on a global scale, is regional economic units, with the orientation of the European provinces towards a Europe dominated by an expanding European Union and Siberia geared towards supplying Asia and the Pacific rim with energy and raw materials and drawing expertise and capital from Japan and labour from China. 'Russia' would thereby revert to its traditional aspiration of acceptance as a European power, while the remnants of its largely non-Russian hinterland would be restructured and developed as one or more separate economic and political units, perhaps as an Asian Federation. In the 1990s, there were already reports of inter-province groupings to coordinate policy, in the Urals, for example.[68]

The Issue of Territory

In such a scenario, other territories might conceivably break away from Moscow's sphere. Outside Russia, but still within the territory of the former Soviet Union, the republics of Central Asia might recombine into a federation,[69] conceivably in association with any or all of the Muslim states of the region: Afghanistan, Pakistan or Iran. Turkey, too, as a western-oriented, relatively advanced Muslim country in the vicinity, has shown strong economic and political interest in the affairs of Azerbaidzhan and Central Asia.

Any such developments could be accompanied by substantial resettlement. As early as 1990, Russians were migrating out of Central Asia.[70] Attracted there initially by a pleasant climate and prestigious jobs as administrators, teachers or doctors, they no longer felt welcome and considered their security under threat, particularly in areas where they are identified as part of the central government's imperial policy (rather than – as in Ukraine, for example – largely as linguistic or cultural minorities).[71] By the start of the year 2000, Russia had registered 960,000 refugees and forced migrants arriving on its territory since 1992–93, when registration began (although there had been significant movement in the years before that).[72] A further substantial unscrambling of the effects of induced migration and ethnic intermixing over the past several decades seems likely. Some expert assessments put the potential of mass migration at 5–6 million, while also pointing out that the Russians in the 'diaspora' (living outside Russia proper) and those who remained in their national homeland do not necessarily form a homogeneous community, even though the Russian government asserts a responsibility towards all of them.[73] A redrawing of boundaries – splitting Kazakhstan to separate the largely Russian north from the Kazakh south, for example, as advocated by Solzhenitsyn – might be workable, but it would undoubtedly offend sensibilities among some affected groups.[74] In any case, this problem is obviously not confined to Russians, although they have gained the most publicity.[75]

In short, the territorial dismemberment of the Soviet Union seems unlikely to resolve the problems. Where compact, ethnically homogeneous units could be created, either inside or outside the Union, cultural autonomy and a high degree of autonomy in economic decision making could be contemplated. However, the examples of Georgia and Moldavia suggest that such a 'solution' would not satisfy all groups, and indicate that an approach based entirely on the dismemberment of the former quasi-federal structure can lead to as many ethnic tensions as it resolves, and in fact 'internationalize' what until the end of 1991 was the Soviet Union's internal problem. Even within particular republics, and none more than the Russian Federation, the problem of 'matrioshka nationalism' – rivalries among ethnic groups within designated 'ethnic' areas – complicates an already complex situation.[76]

CONCLUSION

Plainly, then, a variety of measures is necessary, involving perhaps experiences of other multiethnic states around the world, and perhaps also some of the pre-1922 thinking; for instance, the designation of autonomous districts, towns and even villages with distinct ethnic populations could be considered.[77] The experience of other states in grappling with this issue is not particularly encouraging. Ethnic consciousness, and the preparedness to use political and extra-political measures to advance the cause of the 'nation', is not simply a given, but fluctuates over time, sometimes acquiring a salience that at other times it does not possess. Moreover, 'solutions' that effectively quell disaffection in a particular period in one society may not function when translated to different circumstances elsewhere – or even from one part of the former Soviet Union to another.

The stereotyped thinking in terms of the existing structures may have to be abandoned in favour of much more flexible solutions, which may require a degree of imagination that the traditionalist thinkers who devised Soviet policy (and their successors in the post-Soviet period) may have lacked, although academics and others have contemplated a variety of forms of linkage between the centre and the regions.[78] Unitary states, federations, a new union, such as that contemplated between Belarus and Russia, to which other former Soviet states might possibly adhere, and what might be termed 'complex unitary states' embracing various relations between centre and periphery, all need to be considered in finding effective ways of managing ethnicity and interethnic relations.[79] In the former Soviet space, ethnically pure 'nation-states' do not exist, so that thinking and acting as though they did is highly unlikely to lead to successful management of ethnic differences. In this, the former Soviet states are no different from most other states.[80] Moreover, they all wish to be part of the modern world, part of the international community and engaged in its economic dimension, which, it has been argued, renders the modern state irrelevant, at the very time when these new states came into being.[81] There may be a paradox here; but it is true that existence within a given state is a major element in modern human identity, at both the individual and the community level – and it may evoke feelings of pride, shame or resentment, depending on the circumstances of each national group.

The example of the former Soviet Union demonstrates the complexity of this area of human existence, suggesting that, without flexible and imaginative thinking, there is very little hope of even containing the problem, let alone 'solving' it. Indeed, perhaps such problems cannot be 'solved', despite claims to the contrary. Nations and states rise and fall, affecting – and affected by – the fortunes of their neighbours in the march of history. In many ways, with a number of tragic and blameworthy excesses, the experience of the Soviet Union was a positive attempt to manage a very difficult problem, and one which other political systems have not been wholly successful in controlling; nor have the Soviet Union's successors shown particular sensitivity or skill in handling the problem in the aftermath of the collapse of Soviet power. If the Soviet experiment failed, it is nevertheless an important part of human experience from which both that society and others can perhaps learn.

NOTES

1. For expressions of such views, see, for example, I. Groshev, *A Fraternal Family of Nations: A Review of Soviet Experience in Solving the National Question* (Moscow: Progress, 1967); Victor Shevtsov, *The State and Nations in the USSR* (Moscow: Progress, 1982).
2. 'Russian rule, whether Tsarist or Soviet, is deeply resented' by the Baltic peoples, according to Vernon V. Aspaturian; see his 'The Non-Russian Nationalities', in Allen Kassof (ed.), *Prospects for Soviet Society* (London: Pall Mall, 1968), pp.143–98 (p.153). See also Bohdan Nahaylo and Victor Swoboda, *Soviet Disunion: A History of the Nationalities Problem in the USSR* (London: Hamish Hamilton, 1990), p.109; Rasma Karklins, *Ethnic Relations in the USSR: The Perspective from Below* (Boston, MA: Allen & Unwin, 1986), p.51.
3. See, for example, Hélène Carrère d'Encausse, *Decline of an Empire: The Soviet Socialist Republics in Revolt* (New York: Harper & Row, 1979); Michael Rywkin, *Moscow's Muslim Challenge* (Armonk, NY: M.E. Sharpe, 1982).
4. Konstantin Chernenko, in *Pravda*, 15 June 1983, p.3.
5. Apart from Carrère d'Encausse, one observer to predict great political salience for the nationality issue was Zbigniew K. Brzezinski; see his Foreword to Vyacheslav Chornovil, *The Chornovil Papers* (New York: McGraw-Hill, 1968), p.vii.
6. It is this author's view, which will be partially elaborated below, that the ethnic structure of Soviet society is so complex that 'resolution' of the issue is probably unattainable, and effective management is the most that can be achieved. For further elaboration, based on an analysis of the significance of the Marxist-Leninist ideology for the resolution of this issue, see Ronald J. Hill, 'Ideology and the Making of a Nationalities Policy', in Alexander J. Motyl (ed.), *Sovietology and Soviet Nationalities after Perestroika* (New York: Columbia University Press, 1992), pp.50–87.
7. Figures quoted in 'Samaya politicheskaya karta SSSR', *Moskovskie novosti*, No. 11, 17 March 1991, pp.8–9.
8. The title of a propaganda book published in the 1960s: see Groshev, *Fraternal Family.*
9. The policy slogans of the Khrushchev era; see Martha Brill Olcott (ed.), *The Soviet Multinational State: Readings and Documents* (Armonk, NY: M.E. Sharpe, 1990), p.4; for

a Soviet account, see M.M. Suzhikov et al., *Razvitie i sblizhenie sovetskikh natsii: Problemy upravleniya* (Alma-Ata: Nauka, 1978), esp. pp.226–30.

10. Alaska formed part of the Russian Empire until sold to the United States of America in 1867. A Soviet joke in the crisis-ridden year of 1991 had a Chukcha (inhabitant of the Chukotka Peninsula in the Soviet Far East and the butt of many ethnic jokes among Russians) asking ruefully why the Russians did not sell Chukotka as well as Alaska.

11. Whereas at the time of the 1926 population census 194 nationalities had been identified, under Stalin's 'simplification' of the social structure only 60 national communities were identified in the mid-1930s; see Yu.V. Bromlei, 'Natsional'nye problemy v usloviyakh perestroiki', *Voprosy istorii*, 1989, No. 1, pp.24–41 (p.25). Estimates have also ranged up to 800.

12. See in particular Richard Pipes, *The Formation of the Soviet Union: Communism and Nationalism, 1917–1923*, rev. edn. (New York: Atheneum, 1974; originally Cambridge, MA: Harvard University Press, 1954).

13. Most notably in his pamphlet, *The Right of Nations to Self-Determination* (1914), excerpted in Robert C. Tucker (ed.), *The Lenin Anthology* (New York and London: Norton, 1975), pp.153–80. He had much earlier come out against national chauvinism, in his celebrated *What Is to be Done?* (1902); see ibid., p.20.

14. Including, for example, giving a written form to over 40 languages that existed only in oral form. On the distinctions between Lenin's and Stalin's attitudes towards the national question, see Pipes, *Formation*, ch. 6. For a general history of Soviet policy towards the nationalities, see Nahaylo and Swoboda, *Soviet Disunion*; an earlier study of Stalin's terroristic approach to handling certain nationalities is Robert Conquest, *The Nation Killers* (London: Macmillan, 1970); also, by the same author, *Soviet Nationalities Policy in Practice* (London: Bodley Head, 1967). For a thorough examination of the treatment of nationalities in the Soviet Union and other communist-ruled countries see Walker Connor, *The National Question in Marxist-Leninist Theory and Practice* (Princeton: Princeton University Press, 1984). A late Soviet treatment that discussed Stalin's policies is Bromlei, 'Natsional'nye problemy'. This is a much-researched theme, and a bibliography could continue for many pages.

15. For an analysis of this issue in the light of the ideology, see Hill, 'Ideology'; as John B. Dunlop put it, 'The nationalities question will represent a morass for whoever rules the USSR'; see his *The Faces of Contemporary Russian Nationalism* (Princeton: Princeton University Press, 1984), p.165.

16. Connor, *National Question*, p.485.

17. See, for example, *Sto natsii i narodnostei: Etnograficheskoe razvitie SSSR* (Moscow: Mysl', 1985).

18. This statement is based on figures in *Narodnoe khozyaistvo SSSR v 1989g.: Statisticheskii yezhegodnik* (Moscow: Finansy i statistika, 1990), pp.30–33. In addition there were two categories comprising an indeterminate number of ethnic groups: 'Peoples of India and Pakistan' (1,700) and 'Other nationalities, including those whose nationality was not listed in the census' (32,000).

19. See *Sto natsii*, p.98, Table 9.3. For a discussion of the trends, see G.P. Kisileva, *Nuzhno li povyshat' rozhdaemost'?* (Moscow: Statistika, 1979), pp.38–49. For an alarmist depiction of the trends, see G.A. Bondarskaya, *Rozhdaemost' v SSSR (etnodemograficheskii aspekt)* (Moscow: Statistika, 1977), p.93, Fig. 5; despite the alarmist graphic depiction, the author's whole argument was a complex one.

20. The Soviet demographer B.Ts. Urlanis gives the following figures for births per thousand for the decade 1959–69: Estonians – 12.3; Latvians – 12.3; Ukrainians – 15.8; Russians – 19.0; Lithuanians – 20.6; Georgians – 24.0; Moldavians – 24.8; Armenians – 20.8; Kazakhs – 41.2; Azeris – 43.7; Kirgiz – 44.0; Uzbeks – 45.2; Tadzhiks – 45.2; Turkmenians – 45.6 (cited in *Sto natsii*, p.24). For a table of comparative coefficients of fertility see B.A. Borisov, 'Vosproizvodstvo naseleniya SSSR: tendentsii i perspektivy', in *Demograficheskoe razvitie v SSSR* (Moscow: Mysl', 1985), pp.36–7. See also, for a discussion of trends based on various census data for the twentieth century, A.A. Isupov, 'Chislennost'' i razmeshchenie naseleniya SSSR', in A.A. Isupov and N.Z. Shvartsev (eds.), *Vsesoyuznaya perepis' naseleniya 1979 goda: Sbornik statei* (Moscow: Finansy i statistika, 1984), pp.111–34, esp. pp.115–18.

21. O.D. Zakharova, 'Demograficheskaya situatsiya v SSSR v 1980-e gody', *Sotsiologicheskie issledovaniya*, 1991, No. 4, pp.43–52 (p.45, Table 9.2). The same source

(p.45, Table 9.3) reveals that the Russian republic accounted for 33.0% of the natural growth in the period 1979–88 compared with 43.7% in the decade 1959–69; comparative figures for the Central Asian republics are 33.6% in the later period and 16.6% in the earlier.

22. See, for example, Solzhenitsyn's essay, 'Kak nam obustroit' Rossiyu: Posil'nye soobrazheniya', special supplement to *Literaturnaya gazeta*, 18 Sept. 1990; published in English as Alexander Solzhenitsyn, *Rebuilding Russia: Reflections and Tentative Proposals* (London: Harvill, 1991).

23. *Narodnoe khozyaistvo*, p.33. This includes, for example, Greeks, Poles, Koreans, Romanians, Czechs, Turks and others whose 'nation' possessed a state outside the USSR; it also includes some 153,000 Kurds who still possess no state.

24. Other groups that displayed relatively high migration levels are Lithuanians, Estonians and Latvians, joined in the 1970s by Kazakhs and Kirgiz; see *Sto natsii*, p.31.

25. *Sto natsii*. Further analysis of the 1989 Census reveals that, for example, 2.2 million Ukrainians lived in Russia, almost 900,000 in Kazakhstan, 600,000 in Moldavia, 291,000 in Belorussia, 153,000 in Uzbekistan, and tens of thousands in each of the other republics. With the fall of the USSR, these all became exiles in newly independent states, and not all were willing to become citizens of their host countries.

26. G.A. Slesarev, *Demograficheskie protsessy i sotsial'naya struktura sotsialisticheskogo obshchestva* (Moscow: Nauka, 1978), p.188; L.V. Luiko, *Braki i razvody* (Moscow: Statistika, 1975), p.69.

27. Calculated from figures in the 1989 USSR Population Census, CD-ROM version (Minneapolis, MN: East View Publications, 1996); figures for 1979 from *Sto natsii*, p.81, Table 9.1.

28. *Narodnoe khozyaistvo*, p.35

29. *Sto natsii*, p.82.

30. *Narodnoe khozyaistvo*, pp.35–6.

31. On the deportations, see Conquest, *The Nation Killers*. Much has been written on the Jews' campaign for emigration rights: see, in particular, Yaacov Ro'i, *The Struggle for Soviet Jewish Emigration, 1948–1967* (Cambridge: Cambridge University Press, 1991). Many, in fact, have travelled to the United States rather than Israel. For a general portrayal of Soviet Jewry see Benjamin Pinkus, *The Jews of the Soviet Union: A History of a National Minority* (Cambridge: Cambridge University Press, 1988).

32. For a brief presentation of the argument, see David Marples, 'The Case for Ukrainian Sovereignty', *Radio Liberty Report on the USSR*, Vol. 2, No. 45 (9 Nov. 1990), pp.25–8.

33. The 1989 Census recorded 184,448 citizens categorized as 'peoples of the North'.

34. There are, of course, many examples of multiethnic societies in the world, and many modern nations were created by the merging, often through conquest, of formerly distinct tribes and ethnic entities.

35. On this question see Vera Tolz, 'Forging the Nation: National Identity and Nation Building in Post-Communist Russia', *Europe–Asia Studies*, Vol. 50, No. 6 (1998), pp.993–1022. For a range of perspectives on this question, see Heyward Isham (ed.), *Remaking Russia: Voices From Within* (Armonk, NY and London: M.E. Sharpe, 1995). For a particularly perceptive account, see Valery Tishkov, 'What is Rossiya? Identities in Transition', in Valery Tishkov, *Ethnicity, Nationalism and Conflict in and after the Soviet Union: The Mind Aflame* (London, Thousand Oaks and New Delhi: SAGE, 1997), pp.246–71.

36. On this issue see, for example, Graham Smith, Vivien Law, Andrew Wilson, Annette Bohr and Edward Allworth, *Nation-building in the Post-Soviet Borderlands: The Politics of National Identities* (Cambridge: Cambridge University Press, 1998). A challenging analysis is provided in Tishkov, *Ethnicity*.

37. Notable dissenters from this view were Brzezinski and Carrère d'Encausse (see note 5 above), and in the Soviet Union Andrei Amalrik; see his *Will the Soviet Union Survive Until 1984?* (London: Allen Lane, 1970).

38. Roman Szporluk, 'Nationalism after Communism: Reflections on Russia, Ukraine, Belarus and Poland', *Nations and Nationalism*, Vol. 4, No. 3 (1998), pp.301–20 (p.317). Szporluk cites Paul Pirie, 'National Identity and Politics in Southern and Eastern Ukraine', *Europe–Asia Studies*, Vol. 48, No. 7 (1996), pp.1079–104, to argue that the identification in Eastern Ukraine is primarily 'Soviet'. In the late Soviet period, use of the ironic term 'Sovok' (Soviet Person) became popular among young sophisticates. See

also the approving commentary on an ethnically mixed (Ukrainian and Moldavian) family living in Russia and raising their children to be multilingual, in Ye. Troitskii, *Russkaya natsiya: sotsialisticheskoe preobrazovanie i obnovlenie* (Moscow: Sovetskaya Rossiya, 1989), p.210.

39. See, for example, Teresa Rakowska-Harmstone, *Russia and Nationalism in Central Asia* (Baltimore, MD and London: Johns Hopkins University Press, 1970), p.27.

40. 'Kavkaz', *Moskovskie novosti*, 1991, No. 11, p.8

41. Bromlei, 'Natsional'nye problemy', p.28.

42. Calculated from figures in the 1989 population census; see also *The Cambridge Encyclopedia of Russia and the Soviet Union* (Cambridge: Cambridge University Press, 1982), p.73. Even at the peak of Jewish settlement in 1936, they constituted only 23% of the population of Birobidzhan; see Pinkus, *Jews*, p.75.

43. See Nahaylo and Swoboda, *Soviet Disunion*, p.360. This argument is not without significance, and was applied by critics of the Republic of South Africa (RSA) to its policy of creating 'national homelands' such as Bophuthaswana and Transkei, surrounded by the territory of the RSA and thereby deemed to be at the mercy of the government in Pretoria.

44. This was not the only example of constitutional provisions that lacked the formal legislative backing to make their exercise possible; another case in point was the referendum, which in 1991 became a crucial event in managing the nationality issue (see below).

45. See John H. Miller, 'Cadres Policy in Nationality Areas: Recruitment of First and Second Secretaries in Non-Russian Republics of the USSR', *Soviet Studies*, Vol. 29, No. 1 (1977), pp.3–36.

46. See Adam B. Ulam, *The Rivals: America and Russia since World War II* (New York: Viking, 1971), pp.17–18, 26, 54.

47. On bilingualism see, for example, D.I. Marinesku, *Dvuyazychie – faktor sblizheniya sotsialisticheskikh natsii i narodnostei* (Kishinev: Kartya Moldovenyaske, 1975); *Sto natsii*, pp.69–80. The official line was always that the peoples of the Soviet Union had 'voluntarily' chosen Russian as the language of interethnic communication. A sophisticated argument that sets out the advantages and inevitability of such a use of Russian is to be found in E. Glyn Lewis, *Multilingualism in the Soviet Union* (The Hague and Paris: Mouton, 1972).

48. On 31 August 1989 the Roman alphabet was restored.

49. See Ivan Dzyuba, *Internationalism or Russification? A Study of the Soviet Nationalities Problem* (London: Weidenfeld & Nicolson, 1968); also Chornovil, *Chornovil Papers*, and Borys Lewytzkyj, *Politics and Society in Soviet Ukraine, 1953–1980* (Edmonton: Canadian Institute of Ukrainian Studies, 1984), esp. ch. 4.

50. For details see Ann Sheehy, 'Fact Sheet on Declarations of Sovereignty', *Radio Liberty Report*, Vol. 2, No. 45 (Nov. 9, 1990), pp.23–5. This process continued into 1991 and still threatens the integrity of some states of the former Soviet Union, including small ones such as Georgia and Moldova. These unilateral declarations of changes in formal status were, of course, unconstitutional and were unrecognized by the centre.

51. For an account of the CIS in its first few years, see Martha Brill Olcott, Anders Åslund and Sherman W. Garnett, *Getting it Wrong: Regional Cooperation and the Commonwealth of Independent States* (Washington, DC: Carnegie Endowment for International Peace, 1999).

52. For example, Engels referred to national groups 'without a history', and 'small relics of peoples', supposedly no longer capable of sustaining an independent national existence, which ought to be incorporated into larger nations; quoted in Pipes, *Formation*, p.21. The point was amplified in M. Guboglo, 'Natsional'nye gruppy v SSSR', *Kommunist*, 1989, No. 10, pp.53–8. For an account of the September 1989 plenum see Ann Sheehy, 'Gorbachev Addresses Central Committee Plenum on Nationalities Question', *Radio Liberty Report*, Vol. 1, No. 39 (29 Sept. 1989), pp.1–4; also Roman Solchanyk, '"A Strong Center and Strong Republics": The CPSU's Draft "Platform" on Nationality Policy', *Radio Liberty Report*, Vol. 1, No. 35 (1 Sept. 1989), pp.1–4.

53. *Pravda*, 24 November 1990; for commentary see Ann Sheehy, 'The Draft Union Treaty: A Preliminary Assessment', *Radio Liberty Report*, Vol. 2, No. 51 (21 Dec. 1990), pp.1–6: this article contains a useful summary of the main provisions of the draft treaty.

54. Sheehy, 'Draft Union Treaty', p.4.

55. See I. Sh. Muksimov, 'Sovetskii federatizm i kompleksnoe eknomicheskoe i sotsial'noe razvitie soyuznoi respubliki', *Sovetskoe gosudarstvo i pravo*, 1989, No. 10, pp.3–13 (p.10).
56. *Pravda*, 9 March 1991. For commentary, see Ann Sheehy, 'Revised Draft of the Union Treaty', *Radio Liberty Report*, Vol. 3, No. 12 (22 March 1991), pp.1–4. Not all republics participated in the formal negotiations over the new treaty.
57. For a fuller list see Ann Sheehy, 'Fact Sheet on Questions in the Referendum of March 17 and Later Referendums', *Radio Liberty Report*, Vol. 3, No. 12 (22 March 1991), pp.4–6.
58. For assessments of the results in different republics and regions, see the issue of *Radio Liberty Report*, Vol. 3, No. 13 (29 March 1991); also, for assessments of the republican polls in Latvia and Estonia, see *Radio Liberty Report*, Vol. 3, No. 11 (15 March 1991), pp.22–8.
59. See *Pravda*, 24 April 1991; for commentary, see Roman Solchanyk, 'The Gorbachev–El'tsin Pact and the New Union Treaty', *Radio Liberty Report*, Vol. 3, No. 19 (10 May 1991), pp.1–3.
60. For an excellent summary of the events leading up to the collapse of the USSR and the emergence of the new Commonwealth, see the articles in *RFE/RL Research Report*, Vol. 1, No.1 (3 Jan. 1992).
61. See Olcott et al., *Getting it Wrong*.
62. For the text of the original agreement, see *RFE/RL Research Report*, Vol. 1, No.2 (10 Jan. 1992), pp.4–5.
63. Tuomas Forsberg (ed.), *Contested Territory: Border Disputes at the Edge of the Former Soviet Empire* (Aldershot: Edward Elgar, 1995).
64. I am indebted for ideas in this paragraph to a paper presented by Alexander Shnirkov, of the University of Kiev, at a conference in the Autonomous Region of Trento, Italy, in January 1991. A more recent study, which makes similar points, is George O. Lieber, 'Imagining Ukraine: Regional Differences and the Emergence of an Integrated State Identity, 1926–1994', *Nations and Nationalities*, Vol. 4, No. 2 (1998), pp.187–206.
65. The status of the Crimea, to which deported Tatars began returning in 1990, was determined in a referendum of doubtful legality held on 20 January 1991, when the population voted overwhelmingly to restore its status as an autonomous republic, a decision formally accepted by the Ukrainian authorities, even though both Tatars and the Ukrainian nationalist movement Rukh had urged a boycott of the poll; see Kathleen Mikhalisko, 'The Other Side of Separatism: Crimea Votes for Autonomy', *Radio Liberty Report*, Vol. 3, No. 5 (1 Feb. 1991), pp.36–8. Subsequent inter-republic agreements appear to have ruled out some of the mooted options. On the issue of the status of the Crimea, see Roman Solchanyk, 'Ukrainian–Russian Confrontation over the Crimea', *RFE/RL Research Report*, Vol. 1, No. 8 (21 Feb. 1992), pp.26–30.
66. According to polls cited in Lieber, 'Imagining Ukraine', p.204; Lieber notes, however, that there was a significant proportion of inhabitants of the Crimea (13%) who believed that the peninsula 'should be part of Russia'.
67. The question of the identity of Russia is raised in Solzhenitsyn, *Rebuilding Russia*, pp.11–13.
68. In January 1991, six Urals provinces established a 'Urals Parliament', based on Sverdlovsk, to coordinate their activities in support of the establishment of a market economy; see *Radio Liberty Report*, Vol. 3, No. 6 (8 Feb. 1991), p.44.
69. But a dominant Uzbekistan may be feared by non-Uzbeks; see James Critchlow, 'Will Soviet Central Asia Become a Greater Uzbekistan?', *Radio Liberty Report*, Vol. 2, No. 37 (14 Sept. 1990), pp.17–19.
70. See 'Mass Exodus Hits Central Asia', *Moscow News*, 1990, No. 40 (21–8 October), p.7.
71. See Lev Gudkov, 'Russians Outside Russia', *Moscow News*, 1990, No. 40 (21–8 October), p.7; Viktor Perevedentsev, 'Russians Outside Russia: Potential Refugees?', *Moscow News*, 1993, Nos 2–3 (15 January), p.11. For a fuller investigation of the position of ethnic Russians in the 'near abroad', see Neil Melvin, *Russians Beyond Russia: The Politics of National Identity* (London: Pinter, 1995).
72. Figure from Goskomstat Rossii, *Rossiya v tsifrakh: kratkii statisticheskii sbornik* (Moscow: Goskomstat Rossii, 2000), p.74, Table 5.10.
73. Gudkov, 'Russians Outside Russia'.
74. Solzhenitsyn, *Rebuilding Russia*, p.1.
75. On the broader issue of 'diaspora nationalities', see Graham Smith (ed.), *The Nationalities Question in the Soviet Union* (London: Longman, 1990), Part VI.

76. On 'matrioshka nationalism' see Ray Taras, 'Conclusion: Making Sense of Matrioshka Nationalism', in Ian Bremmer and Ray Taras (eds.), *Nations and Politics in the Soviet Successor States* (Cambridge: Cambridge University Press, 1993), pp.513–38; and Ray Taras, 'Conclusion: From Matrioshka Nationalism to National Interests', in Ian Bremmer and Ray Taras (eds.), *New States, New Politics: Building the Post-Soviet Nations* (Cambridge: Cambridge University Press, 1997), pp.683–705.
77. This was, in fact, implemented in the early years of the Soviet system. According to Bromlei, in the year 1933 there were some 250 national disticts and 5,300 national village soviets, with responsibility for justice and administration, education and cultural activity in local languages: see Bromlei, 'Natsional'nye problemy', p.25.
78. For example, the article by I.Sh. Muksimov, 'Sovetskii federatizm', discusses the possibility of different kinds of federal relationships; this article is discussed in Paul Goble, 'Towards a New Kind of Soviet Federalism?', *Radio Liberty Report*, Vol. 1, No. 49 (8 Dec. 1989), p.5.
79. The notion of a complex unitary state (in Russian, *slozhnoe unitarnoe gosudarstvo*) was put forward as a concept for possibly resolving Moldova's secessionist problems by the academic lawyer V. Lebedev at a conference in the Moldovan capital in May 1988, attended by the present author; he had developed the idea in a paper entitled 'Ideya natsional'noi gosudarstvennosti Respubliki Moldovy', prepared in November 1987. An example of such a state is the United Kingdom, where various legal relationships exist between England and Wales, Scotland, Northern Ireland, the Isle of Man, and the Channel Islands, with a further dimension of relations with the independent Republic of Ireland catered for in bodies that link Dublin and Belfast, and the recently established British–Irish Council serving as a forum for consultations among all political entities in the geographical 'British Isles' – something that is more than 'Britain and Ireland'.
80. On this issue see, for example, Anthony D. Smith, *Nations and Nationalism in a Global Era* (Cambridge: Polity, 1995), ch. 4.
81. See, for example, Kenichi Ohmae, *The End of the Nation State: The Rise of Regional Economies* (London: HarperCollins, 1996).

10

The Dissolution of Czechoslovakia

A Case of Failed State Building?

STANISLAV J. KIRSCHBAUM

The Czechoslovak state, although multinational in composition when it was created in 1918, was often considered an example of the successful application of the principle of self-determination that was invoked in re-organizing Central Europe from the ashes of the Habsburg, Romanov and Ottoman empires on the morrow of the Great War. This perception has survived, despite the fact that in a little more than seven decades it faced three major challenges to its existence from a minority nation.[1] Within 20 years, in 1938–39, Czechoslovakia was modified and then dismembered for six years as a result of external as well as internal factors; half a century after its creation, in 1968, the country underwent a major constitutional change; and again, in 1990–92, the former socialist federal republic, which had become the Czech and Slovak Federative Republic, faced a constitutional challenge which it failed to resolve. On 1 January 1993, Czechoslovakia disappeared and was replaced by the Czech Republic and Slovakia. It is now clear that it was a state that knew more conflict than stability in the relations between its constituent nations and national minorities.

There are two ways to approach the study of this state, which was once described as 'the island of democracy' in Central Europe. One is the minority management approach, brilliantly used by Carol Skalnik Leff in her study of national conflict in Czechoslovakia over the period 1918–87.[2] However, as we indicate below, this approach does not explain satisfactorily the direction and options of Slovak politics which brought about these challenges to the common state. The other approach, which is used here, is to focus on Slovak strategy and goals and their consequences for the stability and survival of the state.

From the moment of its creation, Czechoslovakia faced the necessity of having to deal with nationality relations and to offer solutions if nationality conflict were to be avoided or at least minimized. Two nations, the Czechs and Slovaks, and a number of national minorities – Germans (who outnumbered the Slovaks in 1918), Magyars, Ruthenians, Poles and others – were brought into the new state, whose boundaries were determined by geographical and strategic rather than nationality considerations.[3] The first challenge to its existence came almost simultaneously from the Germans and the Slovaks. The German challenge was to the Czechoslovak state, in particular the First Czechoslovak Republic (1920–38), and was, for all intents and purposes, settled at the end of the Second World War when most of the German population, some 2,921,000 people, were expelled from Czechoslovakia. A more enduring challenge was posed by the Slovaks.[4] Following an overview of the transformations of the Czechoslovak state and a presentation of the current balance, we examine its political culture, the principal source of tensions, and the state-building policies with which the Czechoslovak government sought to respond to the Slovak challenges. We include an evaluation of the consequences of these challenges for the organization and integrity of the state as well as for the validity of the theory of minority management and conclude with an overview of the political development of Czechoslovakia's successor states, the Czech Republic and the second Slovak Republic.

THE NATIONAL QUESTION IN CZECHOSLOVAKIA

In exploring the factors that lay behind the break-up of Czechoslovakia, it is useful to consider two sets of historical circumstance that in important respects contributed to this dissolution: those surrounding the very creation of the state itself, and those associated with the manner in which this state evolved politically. Their significance lay in the fact that relations between the two parts of the state were fundamentally influenced by the political culture the new republic sought to acquire, as we discuss below.

The Creation of the State

It is generally accepted that Czecho-Slovakia was created as a result of the decision of the Allied powers to reorganize Central Europe at the end of the First World War by applying the principle of self-determination to the nations of the region.[5] There were geopolitical reasons that motivated the great powers to opt for such a solution;[6] yet at the same time the creation of a common state for the Czechs and Slovaks coincided with the ambitions of exiled representatives of the two nations – among them Tomáš G. Masaryk and Edvard Beneš for the Czechs and Milan R. Štefánik and Štefan Osuský for the Slovaks – to break with Habsburg rule and to opt for common statehood. What was not at all clear when they set out was the nature of the ethos and organizational form of this state.

Theoretically, each nation could have considered the creation of its own state. Certainly where the Czechs were concerned, they had historical rights in the Lands of the Crown of St Wenceslas which entitled them to 'the resurrection of a state', as Masaryk would later entitle the French version of his memoirs.[7] For the Slovaks, the question was more theoretical as their historical rights were not as strong, the Empire of Great Moravia of the ninth century not having existed long enough to establish these.[8]

There was, however, another important factor that inhibited the creation of an independent state for the Slovaks. On the eve of the First World War, this Central European nation, whose educated and middle classes were undergoing the unrelenting pressure of Magyarization in the Hungarian part of the Habsburg Empire, did not possess a political and administrative infrastructure sufficiently developed to enable them to run their own affairs. For this reason, their leaders decided that a political union with the Czechs offered at that time the best option to enable the Slovak people to develop socially, economically and politically; at some later date, the possibility of having their own state might be taken up.[9]

The Slovak domestic leaders were unable, however, to voice such an option publicly until 1918; it was left to Slovaks abroad, especially in the United States, to prepare the documents that reflected this decision. In 1915, American Slovaks drew up the Cleveland Agreement, which stipulated a loose confederal arrangement with the Czechs. Under Czech pressure, Slovak representatives three years later signed the Pittsburgh Pact of 1918 along with Masaryk and other Czech representatives.[10] This proposed to give the Slovaks autonomy in handling their own affairs.[11]

As far as the Czechs were concerned, independence was an immediately viable option. Their major concerns centred around the size and composition of the state. Although within the borders of the Czech Lands they did constitute an absolute majority – 66.6% in Bohemia, 78.3% in Moravia, but only 47.4% in Silesia – they had to face the fact that within the borders of the new state they had a numerical plurality, with Germans making up the second major nationality.[12] A union with the Slovaks, a Slavic nation without recognized historical rights, and who made up 64.7% of the population in Slovakia, therefore looked like the solution that would give these two Slavic groups combined a numerical majority.[13]

This was also a time when states were being created according to the principle of national self-determination; a single nation therefore had to form the new state. To persuade the Allied Powers that such a nation existed, Czech leaders began to declare that the Slovaks were a branch of the Czech nation. For example, in his memorandum of 1915 to British Foreign Secretary Sir Edward Grey, Masaryk wrote: 'The Slovaks are

Bohemians in spite of their using their dialect as their literary language. The Slovaks strive also for independence and accept the programme of union with Bohemia'.[14] A new nation was being planned, as we shall see below.

The creation of Czecho-Slovakia came about as a result of activities in a number of countries.[15] But it is a meeting of a small group of people in Prague and the declaration that they issued on 28 October 1918 which is recognized as having given birth to the new state. How this came about was a harbinger of further developments. First of all, only one Slovak was present: Vavro Šrobár, a politically active physician who had studied in Prague and was well known to Masaryk and other Czech leaders. A leading member of a group called *Hlasists* (from *Hlas*, a Slovak periodical which advocated a political union of Czechs and Slovaks), he was, however, not a leading political personality in Slovakia at the time. He happened to be in the Czech capital and was thus able to attend the meeting of the Prague National Committee which issued the declaration; in fact, no thought had been given to the issue of an official invitation to Slovaks. As a member of Masaryk's circle, Šrobár was acceptable to the Czechs as a Slovak representative. Secondly, two days later, on 30 October, in Turčiansky Svätý Martin in Slovakia, unaware of the earlier Prague declaration, Slovak leaders met to declare themselves in favour of a political union with the Czechs; here, similarly, there was no official Czech representation. At neither meeting was there any substantive discussion of the definition and organization of the new state. This was left to the Czecho-Slovak National Committee whose headquarters were in Paris.

The timing and circumstances surrounding these declarations of independence and political union could not have been more inauspicious for the creation of a state in which Czechs and Slovaks were to be the constituent founding nations. Myths were created around them which sustained the political culture that the new state began to develop soon after the peace treaties were signed, as we discuss below.

In her study of Czech–Slovak relations since 1918, Leff argues that the events surrounding the creation of the new state were unfolding with such rapidity that there was no opportunity for a thorough and balanced approach.[16] This is correct as far as the details of the organization of the state are concerned. But in the light of the declarations made by the Czech leaders in exile during the war, and of subsequent developments, such an explanation is not conclusive about the type of state they had in mind. The fact is that the Czech leaders had decided and were determined to create a nation state, as Václav Klofáč, a Czech representative, declared at the Paris Peace Conference: 'We received an international mandate to create a Czechoslovak political nation with the entry of the Slovaks in the Czech political nation.'[17]

Although not altogether clear at the time, the Slovaks had been relegated to the role of a branch of the new Czechoslovak nation and were not recognized as a nation *per se*. Also, the agreements signed with the Slovaks in the United States and elsewhere were ignored. As a result, the Slovaks were not deemed to have a claim either in creating a state of their own or in the organization of a Czechoslovak state in the eyes of the Allied powers or of the Czechs.[18] In fact, the central government treated them as the weaker branch of the Czechoslovak nation, and Slovakia as the weaker part of the new state.

The Evolution of the State

Czechs and Slovaks had lived in two different administrations in the Austro-Hungarian Empire and had had different administrative and political experiences. The new state faced the difficult task of reconciling this legacy. Instead, the Prague leadership embarked on a process of integrating the Slovaks into the Czech administration. Šrobár, as Minister for Slovakia, was given virtual dictatorial powers in Slovakia by the central government and he proceeded to rule with an iron fist.[19] As we have shown elsewhere, this was one of the many blunders committed by Prague towards the Slovaks.[20] It was, however, consistent with the government's policy of (single) nation building, which was pursued with unrelenting vigour throughout the 20 years of the existence of the First Czechoslovak Republic (1920–38). When the constitution was adopted in 1920, Slovakia disappeared as an administrative unit and to underline the unitary nature of the state, the spelling was also changed from Czecho-Slovakia to Czechoslovakia.[21]

Unfortunately for the Czechs and the state, this policy backfired. Slovak nationalism was the outcome,[22] and this crystallized when the existence of the state was threatened in 1938–39 from the combined challenge of the Sudeten Germans and the Third Reich: the Slovaks opted for separation in order to save their nation and their territory from occupation by Germany, Hungary and Poland.[23] This decision was not without a certain price: the creation of the first Slovak Republic at a time when Germany was the predominant power in Central Europe, bent on imposing its ideological programme, resulted in severe constraints on Slovak domestic and external policies. Nevertheless, for six years (1939–45) the Slovaks lived in their own state; while the Czechs, who lived in what was left of the Czech Lands after the Munich Agreement, were brought into the Third Reich and their territory became the Protectorate of Bohemia-Moravia. In 1945, however, Czechoslovakia found itself back on the map of Europe.

Leff argues that the uncertainty and speed of the events around the re-creation of the Czechoslovak state during and after the Second World War were also responsible for the constitutional arrangement that was put in place at the end of the hostilities.[24] The evidence shows once more that this argument is unconvincing. Throughout the war, the Slovaks governed themselves in the first Slovak Republic and demonstrated in that short period that they were capable of doing so successfully, even under Berlin's overwhelming pressure;[25] at the same time, there were Slovaks who, primarily for political reasons, fought against the Slovak state, favouring instead a return to the Czechoslovak Republic. The latter either joined a resistance movement organized in the Slovak National Council which would seek to take power in Slovakia, or gave their allegiance to the provisional Czechoslovak government-in-exile that Beneš had created in London after the outbreak of hostilities. Some Slovak Communists were also in the leadership of the Communist Party of Czechoslovakia, then based in Moscow. Nevertheless, all groups worked together to launch a political and military action in Slovakia. A military uprising broke out in August 1944 and lasted until the German forces put an end to it two months later.[26] The fact that this action took place quite late in the war and was of very short duration testifies more to the frailty of the resistance movement, whose only convincing argument was that it was identified with those who were winning the war, than to the weakness of Slovak independence. However, the power of that argument was such that it enabled its leaders to negotiate the status of Slovakia in the recreated common state and to take power at the end of hostilities.

Beneš and the leaders of the Slovak resistance movement, in particular Slovak Communists, did not have the same priorities regarding post-war constitutional arrangements. Beneš wanted a return to the Republic of 1920,[27] whereas the Slovaks were pushing for a federal state.[28] They discussed these options in Moscow in March 1945. The ideological differences among the Slovak resistance leaders were such, however, as to allow the Czechs to overrule their weaker Slovak partners, and the federal solution failed to gain acceptance. On the other hand, the Slovak resistance movement succeeded in getting the Czech leadership to recognize not just a territorial and political jurisdiction called Slovakia, but also the existence of a Slovak nation;[29] the constitutional arrangement that arose out of this recognition was called 'the asymmetrical solution'. The Slovak National Council and the Board of Commissioners, which replaced respectively the parliament and government of the first Slovak Republic, were given some powers to handle Slovak affairs, while Prague continued to rule the country as if it were a centralized nation-state.

The Communist coup of February 1948 introduced a political system that was entirely different from anything that had existed up until then. Among other things, it also ensured that the country would continue to be ruled centrally. This fact, and the condemnation by the Communist regime of those Slovak Communists who had fought for a federal solution in the 1944 uprising, fuelled Slovak discontent. In addition, in 1960, the regime introduced a socialist constitution in which the limited executive powers that the Slovak National Council still possessed were further diminished to the point that they were more formal than real.

When the Communist regime began to liberalize in the 1960s, the federal solution reappeared. It became the object of public discussion in Slovak and in some Czech journals and reviews.[30] In January 1968 the dismissal of Antonín Novotný and his replacement by the Slovak Alexander Dubček as First Secretary of the Communist Party of Czechoslovakia allowed the federalization of the state to be one of the main reforms in the liberalization process of the spring and summer of that year.[31] Although the Soviet Union and other Warsaw Pact countries did not approve of the liberalization process and nipped it in the bud with an armed invasion in August, the Czechoslovak parliament nevertheless passed the federalization law on the eve of the 50th anniversary of the creation of Czecho-Slovakia, and the next day it was signed by President Ludvík Svoboda in the capital of Slovakia, Bratislava.

The federalization of the Czechoslovak state was influenced by the policy of 'normalization' that followed the invasion of the country. Formally, Czechoslovakia was a federal state; in actual fact, it continued to be centrally run through the Communist Party of Czechoslovakia. Although Dubček's successor, Gustáv Husák, also a Slovak, author of the policy of 'normalization' and ironically also considered by some to be the father of the federal state, made every effort to assuage Slovak discontent by ensuring Slovak economic development,[32] the policies of the regime and its tolerance of executive but not legislative federalism kept alive the discontent that Slovaks felt about the Czechoslovak state.

The Distribution of the Nationalities

The state that was re-created after the Second World War acquired a different national composition from the Czecho-Slovak Republic of 1918 (see Map 10.1). Most of the Germans had been deported, especially those in the Sudetenland which Britain, France and Italy had ceded to Germany in the Munich Agreement of 1 October 1938. In addition, in 1945, Ruthenia was incorporated into the Soviet Union. The Slovaks had become the second largest national group; more so than in 1918, the state could accurately be called Czecho-Slovakia. Actually, the spelling of Czechoslovakia was retained *despite* the fact that in each part of the country the constituent nation acquired a dominant position, as Table 10.1 indicates (see also Map 10.2).

Nevertheless, important national minorities also remained in the state, especially in Slovakia, where a policy to transfer the Magyars to Hungary after the war was proposed and partially put into effect.[33] However, in contrast to the First Republic where there was a steady influx of Czechs, the number of Czechs living in Slovakia actually decreased.[34] In the Czech Lands, on the other hand, there took place over the years a transfer of Slovaks to the former Sudetenland; accusations were made that they had been subjected to a policy of deliberate Czechization. The federalization of

TABLE 10.1
CZECHOSLOVAKIA: NATIONAL COMPOSITION BY REPUBLIC, 1988

Nationality	Czech Lands		Slovakia		Czechoslovakia	
	000s	*%*	*000s*	*%*	*000s*	*%*
Czech	9,745	94.1	63	1.2	9,808	62.8
Slovak	419	4.0	4,565	86.7	4,984	31.9
Ukrainian	10	0.1	38	0.7	48	0.3
Russian	5	0.0	2	0.0	7	0.1
Polish	70	0.7	3	0.1	73	0.5
Magyar	23	0.2	576	10.9	599	3.8
German	50	0.5	3	0.1	53	0.3
Others	38	0.4	14	0.3	52	0.3
Total	10,360	100.0	5,264	100.0	15,624	100.0

Source: *Statistická ročenka ČSSR 1990* (Praha: Státní nakladatelství technické literatury, 1990), p.100.

the state also meant the presence of Slovaks in federal ministries, most of which were in Prague. If the question of national minorities was not as acute as it was when the state was created, the Hungarian question in Slovakia and the situation of Slovaks in the Czech Lands nevertheless remained questions on the political agenda and were used by those who sought to prevent the dissolution of the state.

THE SOURCES OF CZECH–SLOVAK TENSION

The changes that the Second World War and its aftermath brought to Czechoslovakia made it a binational state. When one looks back at all the attempts at transforming the state in order to solve national conflict, it is clear that they were influenced by the political culture that had been introduced at the time of its creation; and this remained to the end the principal source of tension between the two nations. Indeed, the debate and constitutional discussion that took place in 1990–92 cannot be fully appreciated without an understanding of the initial political culture and the modifications that it underwent since the creation of the state.[35] A second factor that needs to be considered lies at the level of institutions rather than culture: the state-building policies pursued by the political elite.

Political Culture

During the Paris Peace Conference, Beneš, Czecho-Slovakia's Foreign Minister, declared before the New States Commission that the new state

MAP 10.1
CZECHOSLOVAKIA: CZECHS AND SLOVAKS, 1930

MAP 10.2
CZECHOSLOVAKIA: NATIONALITIES BY REPUBLIC, 1988

Percentage

0% to 20%
20% to 50%
50% to 80%
80% to 100%

Prague

SILESIA
45.0%

BOHEMIA
63.0%

MORAVIA
Brno 65.0%

SLOVAKIA
71.3%

TRANSCARPATHIAN
RUTHENIA 4.8%

Bratislava

Prague

CZECH REPUBLIC
94.1%

Brno

SLOVAK REPUBLIC
1.2%

Bratislava

(a) Czechs

Prague

CZECH REPUBLIC
4.0%

Brno

SLOVAK REPUBLIC
86.7%

Bratislava

(b) Slovaks

would have 'a liberal regime which would resemble very much that of Switzerland'.[36] This referred in fact primarily to the Germans and the treatment that they could expect in a state where they had become a minority. Even so, had the Swiss model been seriously considered by the Czech elite, and had it indeed been introduced, the political culture of Czechoslovakia would not only have reflected the multinational composition of the state, but the central government might also have averted the challenges that the Germans and also the Slovaks made to the existence of the First Republic. As it turned out, the creators of the state had decided to embark on an altogether different path.

It was Czech political values that were imposed on the state from the outset. This is explained in part by the political thinking of the time. France, as a result of the influence of certain French political circles, had played an important role in the creation of Czechoslovakia.[37] The French Republic was a unitary and centralized state, and was seen as a model to be emulated. Given the importance of the principle of nationality in the creation of the Central European states, it is not surprising that a unitary rather than a federal state was introduced in Czecho-Slovakia. This very fact enabled it to adopt the political programme of the nation that was in effect given the responsibility of governing the state: the Czechs. In addition, having successfully persuaded the Allied powers that the Slovaks were not a nation *per se*, the Prague elite felt that they had a free hand in extending their political values to the Slovaks.[38] They relentlessly pursued this policy, referred to in the literature as Czechoslovakism, throughout the entire period of the First Republic.

Some western students of Czechoslovakia argue that pluralism is one of the predominant features of Czech political culture, especially in the First Republic, which was Central Europe's only democracy in the interwar period.[39] This view has recently been challenged by Eva Schmidt-Hartmann, who has detected anti-democratic features in Czech political life and political parties long before the Communists came to power.[40] H. Gordon Skilling also argues that there are 'certain defects or weaknesses in the pluralist tradition, and the presence of a contradictory tendency towards authoritarianism'.[41] Still, to the extent that the First Republic was a democracy, it can be argued that it was also pluralist. The question is: how pluralist was it?

Diffusion and dispersion of political power are the major characteristics of pluralism; Czech political culture did not fully meet these criteria in the First Republic.[42] Above all, diffusion and dispersion of power to other national groups such as the Slovaks or the Germans was not on the agenda. Thus, when transposed to the Czechoslovak state, Czech political culture was pluralist for the Czech nation but rather less so for the others.

This was particularly clear where the Slovaks are concerned. What the imposition of Czech political culture in the First Republic meant for them was the abandonment of their national values and identity. There was no question of the dispersion and diffusion of power, as agreed to, for example, in the Pittsburgh Pact of 1918. Masaryk, who had signed it, dismissed it in his memoirs as 'a local understanding between American Czechs and Slovaks upon the policy they were prepared to advocate'.[43] No effort was made to create a binational 'Czecho-Slovak' political culture; rather, what became Czechoslovak political culture was nothing more than Czech political culture writ large. As Manfred Alexander indicates, this ultimately had serious consequences because 'the structure of the Czechoslovak Republic as a *Czech* national state proved to be the greatest danger to democracy'.[44]

As far as the Slovaks are concerned, many became unwilling to identify with the state's political culture because they perceived it as assimilatory, restrictive and manipulative even if it contained pluralist features and allowed for the expression of alternative views. They did not see it as accepting any input from the Slovaks except that which strengthened Czech aims and justified government policies. To most Slovaks, the Czechoslovak state was basically a Czech state not only because of the numerical balance between the two groups, but also because the union of the Czechs and Slovaks into a Czechoslovak nation meant, given the numerical strength of the Czechs, the eventual assimilation of the Slovaks into the Czech nation. This was acknowledged by Beneš, who told the Slovaks in 1933:

> One may possibly object that this [political unification] is and will be a means to assimilate progressively the Slovaks and that the Czech element, materially and culturally stronger, would slowly overcome the Slovak element. I would not be completely honest if I did not say openly that I wish for a progressive unification, along evolutionary lines, of the two branches of our nation in all respects.

He then went on to explain why the Slovaks could never be granted autonomy in a passage that outlines an extraordinary vision of Czechoslovak and Central European politics:

> I am not for separatism, nor for political autonomy because it would very simply be a new major *artificial* political obstacle to the normal and inevitable biological and sociological evolution of our nation, a measure that would not have the consequences we expect and would only complicate our regular evolution, an evolution that is being achieved on the basis of the guidelines of general national progress in Europe, set by the biological and sociological laws of our present social and national entity which also correspond to the general, cultural and national state of our nation and to the evolution of all of Central Europe.[45]

It is not surprising that the Slovaks, whose support of the Slovak People's Party made it the main party in Slovakia, found themselves mostly in opposition.[46] They consequently developed their own political culture which contained many of the same features as its Czech counterpart, although not as a result of the attempt to impose it on them. But Slovak political priorities were also modified and modulated by the need to fight for national survival, as had been the case in a restrictive political system like the Hungarian one before 1918 or as was the case in a more or less pluralist one as in Czechoslovakia. This fight for survival galvanized political activity in Slovakia and produced a more collective approach to politics, which encouraged the main parties to seek above all to achieve the objectives they were fighting for. In the First Republic, this meant not only the attainment of autonomy as defined in the Pittsburgh Pact, but also giving Czechoslovak pluralism a binational character and eliminating the assimilatory aspects of the ideology of Czechoslovakism. The failure to achieve both of these goals before the state was destroyed after the Munich Conference of September 1938 did not mean the success of the First Republic in imposing Czech political values on the Slovaks. The process had simply run out of time; the Slovaks were now on their own.

Skilling argues that German interference in the late 1930s in Czechoslovakia brought about 'the destruction of the pluralist society and government which had been developed during the two decades of independence and the forced imposition of a Nazi political culture'.[47] This may explain the appeal of Communism in the Czech Lands after the war, but recent research suggests that such a conclusion is not applicable where the Slovaks are concerned.[48] The political system in the first Slovak Republic had been pluralist although in a somewhat limited fashion, and had also adopted some authoritarian features, primarily, although not uniquely, out of political necessity in order to minimize German interference in Slovak affairs.[49] The six years of statehood also contradicted a claim often made in Prague during the interwar years that the Slovaks were politically immature, in need of tutelage, and incapable of governing themselves.

However, the experience of the first Slovak Republic served the Slovaks in a paradoxical way in the re-created Czechoslovak Republic. Their state had been allied with Germany during the war and its disappearance was the price the Allies forced them to pay for this alliance. This decision gave the Czechoslovak government the opportunity not only to exact retribution but also, by condemning and executing its leaders for treason to the Czechoslovak Republic, to ensure, through these trials – especially that of Jozef Tiso, President of the first Slovak Republic – that 'Slovak separatism' would never threaten the existence of the common state again.[50] On the other hand, the experience of 1939–45 confirmed the existence of a Slovak nation quite capable of handling its own affairs. As of 1945, the Czechoslovak political system, whether semi-pluralist (during the three years preceding the Communist takeover) or authoritarian (1948–89) was formally binational. In its structure, however, the state became initially asymmetrical, as no Czech equivalent of the Slovak National Council and Board of Commissioners was created and the Czechoslovak government was dominated by Czechs. It was not clear, therefore, whether the political values were Czecho-Slovak rather than Czechoslovak.

When they came to power in 1948, the Communists preferred not to foster the binational character of the state in their attempt to create a socialist society. In addition to substituting authoritarianism for pluralism, they refused to federalize the state as they had promised they would do when they came to power, ensured that Slovak participation was kept at a minimum and involved only those who were disposed to accept Prague's guidance, especially in Slovakia. It is interesting to note, for example, that until the 1960s the two leading Communist personalities in Slovakia were Viliam Široký, a Hungarian, and Karel Bacílek, a Czech. With the promulgation of a socialist constitution in 1960, the central government subordinated Slovakia even further by reducing the powers of the Slovak National Council and the Board of Commissioners; this subordination was underlined symbolically by changing Slovakia's historical national coat of arms (the two-armed cross on three peaks, with a flame on top of Slovakia's highest peak).

During the liberalization process of 1968, the leadership of the Communist Party of Czechoslovakia was accused of having sought since 1948 to re-introduce the assimilationist policies of the First Republic.[51] The fact is that Czechoslovak political culture had been maintained in the first 20 years of Communist rule and it had not only become authoritarian, but had also tended to be even more assimilatory, restrictive and manipulative towards the Slovaks than it had been in the First Republic. This flew in the face of Marxist-Leninist ideology, whose perspective on the national question implied institutional recognition of national minorities but which otherwise underpinned the authoritarian features of the regime. The asymmetrical model was attacked by Communist theorists in the 1960s.[52] Their arguments helped to bring about federalization in 1968 and thereby anchor constitutionally the binational organization of the state.

The liberalization process of 1968 seemed to promise the reintroduction of pluralism to Czechoslovak political life. However, once again, the international context, whose importance Skilling recognizes when defining Czechoslovakia's political culture, intervened and re-imposed authoritarianism when the armies of the Warsaw Pact invaded in August 1968.[53] During the period of 'normalization', the tension that had existed hitherto between the centralizing tendencies of the regime and the centrifugal force of Slovak nationalism was minimized through policies of economic investment in Slovakia. However, the single party system did not allow for the full implementation of federalism. All decisions were still taken in Prague; Slovak input remained minimal, usually restricted to matters of purely Slovak interest. The repressive character of the regime further enhanced the asymmetrical character of political rule in the country as well as the perception that the political culture, despite federalism, was still very much Czechoslovak rather than Czecho-Slovak. This was openly acknowledged after the fall of the Communist regime, as Vladimír Repka writes:

> Even from the point of view of an historically very short period as that of the last forty-six years, the consequences of the latest developments are very evident. There is in Slovak society a moral decline and a national schizophrenia that shows itself in a split into two implacable camps. This catastrophic situation is the result of the 'normalization' attempts of the Czech-Marxist regime which supplanted Beneš' aggressive anti-Slovak chauvinism even more effectively, transplanting with all available means the idea of a united Czechoslovak state, in other words, state Czechoslovakism. In short, with the Communist hammer, they succeeded there where they had failed in the inter-war years, namely to change our national essence. The Czechoslovakization of two Slovak generations, thanks to Communist jails, eliminated to some degree not only national, but also human dignity in Slovak society.[54]

The fall of Communism in November 1989 reintroduced pluralism. With it the question of the binational character of the state was also brought to the fore. The Slovaks lost no time in finding out whether the Czechs considered them equal partners. It was clear that even after close to seven decades in the same state (the years of the first Slovak Republic excluded) there were doubts in the minds of many Slovaks about their place in Czechoslovakia's political value hierarchy. This uncertainty was best voiced by the Slovak writer Vladimír Mináč who, in answer to an article by the Czech writer Ludvík Vaculík that was very critical of the Slovaks, stated:

> Vaculík writes that 'it is an honest duty to be a Czechoslovak'. However, what you find behind a Czechoslovak is a badly covered pure Czech who, in a curious fashion, has made his the land of the Slovaks and if he has not yet done so, then he wants to do so. But a Slovak does not want to be a Czechoslovak, he does not want to be shoved behind a foreign facade, he wants to be himself, independent and equal. Is that so difficult to understand?[55]

The debate in the Czechoslovak parliament in March 1990 around the hyphenation of the name of the country and the adoption of the new name of Czech and Slovak Federative Republic clearly indicated that Czechoslovak political culture still reflected Czech political values and that this had failed to take root among the Slovaks. Nevertheless, attempts were made during 1990–92 to accommodate the two sets of political values, but these failed. This failure to reach a constitutional agreement and the results of the June 1992 elections paved the way for the dissolution of the state. Yet in the months preceding the dissolution, which took effect on 31 December 1992, public opinion polls in Slovakia (as in the Czech Lands) suggested that if a referendum had been held on the break-up of the common state, it would not have passed. In the absence of further information to explain these results, it may be suggested that they reflected the perceived cost of separation as well as some degree of nostalgia. For the Slovak political elite, however, there was no retreating from its desire to see Slovak political values develop in Slovakia. This was a further indication that Czechoslovak political culture had not succeeded in taking hold in Slovakia. This failure was also the result of the state-building policies of the Czechoslovak government, policies that represented their response to the Slovak challenges.

State-Building Policies

In the wake of a major change such as the destruction of the Habsburg Empire, it is not surprising that the states that arose out of it lost no time in seeking to achieve consolidation and stability. As we have indicated above, Czecho-Slovakia, which faced the additional challenge of reconciling the dual administrative legacy of the Austro-Hungarian Empire, opted for the *Gleichschaltung* of the Slovaks into the Czech administrative system. This set the tone for Prague's state-building policies, which did not include territorial-management solutions. In fact, the Czechoslovak parliament refused on three occasions – in 1922, 1930 and 1938 – to consider bills dealing with the autonomy of Slovakia, which had been promised in the Pittsburgh Pact.

A variety of measures were used by the central government to establish a strong central administration. What must be noted for the First Czechoslovak Republic is the fact that the public service was composed overwhelmingly of Czechs. Thousands were sent to Slovakia to occupy positions not only in state but also in local administration, as well as in education and even industry. Prague had excluded from the Czechoslovak public service most Slovaks who had worked in the Hungarian administration on the grounds that they were most likely Magyarones and thereby constituted a threat to the new state; Hungarian irredentism was deemed by the central government to be one of the greatest threats to the existence of the state. On the other hand, there is no indication that Czechs who had worked in the Austrian or Imperial administration were excluded, and many ended up being sent to work in Slovakia.

In the beginning, most Slovak political leaders welcomed Czech help, recognizing that Slovakia was in need of assistance. However, it became clear in a very short time that the Czech personnel set in motion the assimilation of the Slovaks. Karol Sidor, who observed this influx of Czechs into Slovakia, reported: 'After barely ten months of life in common, it was already clear that it would not be possible to find a settlement and maintain peace between the Czechs and Slovaks without interested external intervention both in the formation and consolidation of the Czecho-Slovak Republic.'[56]

In addition to the establishment of state control in Slovakia, Prague employed a variety of measures to pursue its policies, from rewarding compliant Slovaks with positions in the state administration to isolating those who openly favoured the granting of autonomy to Slovakia. The electoral process helped to bring home the advantages of voting for Czechoslovak parties, particularly those that formed the government, rather than Slovak parties, especially the Slovak People's Party. Leaders of Slovak branches of Czechoslovak parties, such as Šrobár of the Social Democrats and Milan Hodža and Ivan Dérer of the Agrarians, were rewarded with cabinet positions; Hodža even became Prime Minister of Czechoslovakia from 1935 to 1938. Another favourite measure was press censorship, especially of *Slovák*, the daily of the Slovak People's Party. Joseph A. Mikuš chronicles some of these measures; he also shows that Prague's record in awarding state positions to Slovaks was quite dismal.[57] In the light of this evidence one may well question the degree of pluralism in Czechoslovak political culture in the interwar years.

Economic policies towards Slovakia were also meant to serve primarily Czech interests, while attempts were made to give Slovakia some measure of economic development.[58] But the emigration of Slovaks to Western Europe, Australia and the North American continent, especially in the 1930s, which was a solution to chronic unemployment, indicates that Slovakia occupied a secondary position in the economy of Czechoslovakia.[59]

Prague's state-building policies in the interwar years succeeded in creating a relatively modern state, but one which served the Czech population much better than the Slovak one. This accounts to a great extent for the strength of Slovak nationalism.[60] When the Slovaks declared their independence in March 1939, there were not many who regretted the Czechoslovak state, as Wolfgang Venohr points out:

> It is now admitted that the Tiso-state [the first Slovak Republic] did not have to fear a plebiscite, that it was accepted by the majority of the Slovak nation, and that the liquidation of the Czechoslovak Republic was not considered in Slovakia as a national disaster, but

rather it was greeted as the liberation from twenty years of Czech domination and generally as a national success.[61]

Despite all the changes the Slovaks experienced during their six years of statehood and despite the promises made to the leaders of the 1944 uprising if they ended Slovak independence, when Slovakia was re-incorporated into the Czechoslovak state in 1945, Prague returned with only minor variations to its pre-war state-building policies. These dictated that the state structure of the Slovak Republic be dismantled as rapidly as possible, that Czechoslovak institutions be re-established in Slovakia and that the powers given to the Slovak National Council and the Board of Commissioners not only be limited but above all that they be subordinated to central ministries. In the political atmosphere of 1945–48, the power struggle between Communists and non-Communists helped the central government to force the Slovak National Council to accept three agreements which in effect achieved the virtual subordination of Slovakia to Prague.[62]

The Communist takeover of 1948 and the imposition of single-party rule merely strengthened Prague's hold over Slovakia. To ensure that there would be no challenge from the Slovaks, those Communists who had fought in the 1944 uprising and favoured a federal system were accused and found guilty of Slovak bourgeois nationalism and removed from the scene. The Communist Party of Slovakia became a regional party, totally subordinated to the Communist Party of Czechoslovakia; it could do very little either to oppose Prague or pursue autonomous policies. The socialist constitution of 1960 merely re-affirmed the centralizing tendencies of the regime.

It is only in the liberalizing atmosphere of the 1960s, when destalinization was on the agenda of Communist politics in the Soviet Union and Eastern Europe, that the Communist Party of Slovakia, in the press and through some of the Slovak national organs, began to question the policies of the central government and the evolution of the state since 1948. Indirectly, the Slovaks were challenging state-building policies and by evoking the aims of the 1944 uprising, namely the establishment of a federal state, they were demanding radical political and constitutional change. Once again, Prague's state-building policies had backfired.

It might be interesting to speculate what would have happened to Czech–Slovak relations if the 1968 liberalization process had not been interrupted by the Warsaw Pact invasion of August. There were interesting debates in the Slovak press about which came first for the Slovaks: federalization or democratization. In the Czech Lands, only the latter was of real interest. A different type of federal structure might have been put in place than the one that was adopted in October 1968. It was, nevertheless, a territorial management solution. It survived the August invasion, but it also succumbed to the 'normalization' process; centralism came once again to the fore. For another two decades, although with a greater number of institutions in Slovakia to carry out social and economic policies, the Slovaks were ruled from Prague. One could say that there was institutional 'democratic centralism'. On the other hand, there is sufficient evidence to suggest that the central government paid greater attention to Slovakia, especially in its economic policies.[63] Even so, the regime was pursuing a form of socialist Czechoslovakism, as a Marxist historian noted in 1983:

> It is evidently only a question of time for the prerequisites to develop, under new and most favourable conditions, based on the recent history of mutual relations, which will lead to the acceleration of the total development and rapprochement of the Czechs and Slovaks and the nationalities living in the republic, and to the attainment of such a synthesis that the notion of a 'Czechoslovak people' will be the symbol of a new qualitative unity of all the citizens of the ČSSR.[64]

As it is clear that all policies were decided in Prague, one can conclude that there had really been little change with federalization. If anything, state-building policies had continued to be negative reactions rather than solutions to Slovak challenges.

THE PATH TO DISSOLUTION

When Communism collapsed in Central Europe in the autumn of 1989, the issue of the definition of the common state and the relations between the Czechs and Slovaks reappeared. It became the object of public discussion, heated at times, in parliament and in the press. On 29 March 1990, Slovak deputies proposed to the Czechoslovak parliament that the name of the country revert to the 1918 spelling, namely Czecho-Slovakia. The Czech majority offered a compromise that was regarded as nothing less than an insult by the Slovaks: abroad and in the Czech Lands, the spelling would be without a hyphen, whereas in Slovakia a hyphen could be used. The result was a mass demonstration in Bratislava on the following day in favour of the independence of Slovakia. Then, on 11 April the Czechoslovak parliament adopted a new name for the common state: the Czech and Slovak Federative Republic. Discussions began almost immediately between representatives of the Czech and Slovak Republics on the division of powers and the organization of the state. Six main series of discussions on constitutional reform took place involving representatives of the Czech National Council, the Slovak National Council and the federal government: in Trenčianské Teplice in August 1990, in Lány on 10 May 1991, in Budmerice on 31 May 1991, in Kroměřiž on 17 June 1991, in Častá-Papiernička on 12 November 1991 and in Milovy on 4 February 1992. Before the Lány conference there were meetings in Vykary with Czechoslovak President Václav Havel on 4 and 12 February and 4 March 1991. In addition, Havel himself sought on two occasions to give the process a push, in a speech to the federal parliament on 24 September 1991 and by proposing a law on a referendum on 21 January 1992; the latter, however, failed to secure adoption by the federal parliament.

The Trenčianské Teplice conference tackled the question of the respective powers of the federal government, the Czech National Council and the Slovak National Council. The agreement that was signed also stipulated that the Czech and Slovak Republics would seek to be incorporated into European institutions as separate entities. The ratification by the Czech and Slovak National Councils of the outcome of the meeting meant that both republics became responsible for their own economies as of 1 January 1991. Slovakia was also given the right to establish a ministry of international relations. In Lány, the discussion centred on the federal constitution, with the Slovaks accepting the proposal that an agreement would be signed by the Czech and Slovak National Councils on the principles of the new constitutional arrangement instead of a state treaty. In Budmerice, there was discussion of the different types of constitutional arrangement but no agreement; in addition, Havel expressed the wish that the constitution should be ready before the elections, whereas some politicians suggested that the elections be postponed. In Kroměřiž, it was agreed that a federal commission would draft a legal treaty between the two republics which could be revised but would also be approved by the two National Councils and then passed back to the federal parliament for approval. The treaty would formulate the broad division of powers and the basis for a new constitution. The constitution would be prepared for ratification by the national councils. Finally, a Federal Council would be created to oversee all federal laws. Both the Czech and the Slovak National Councils were expected to bring the process to a close by the end of 1991 with their respective constitutional projects.

At the Častá-Papiernička meeting, where further issues were discussed, the first signs that the process could end in failure appeared. It became evident that, despite the agreement reached in Kroměřiž, there were serious differences in the two approaches: the Slovaks were leaning more and more in the direction of a confederal state which acknowledged the sovereignty of Slovakia, whereas the Czechs argued for a strong, centralized federation. No agreement was reached at that meeting, but the Slovak National Council carried on as agreed in Kroměřiž and published the Slovak constitutional project on 27–28 December 1991. No Czech project was proposed. A last-ditch effort to find a compromise was made in Milovy, but the text, which was known as the 'Milovy Constitutional Propositions', failed to gain approval in the Slovak National Council. There were no further meetings between the two National Councils.

These negotiations took place against the backdrop of a public debate in Slovakia that made it clear that the federal system of 1968 was not an adequate constitutional arrangement, primarily because it still gave too many powers to the federal government. It was perceived as being dominated by the Czechs. It is worth noting that while the Slovaks were examining various options, no similar attempt was made in the Czech Republic. By the time of the June 1992 elections, the need to move rapidly away from a command economy to a market one was seen in the Czech Republic as requiring a strong central government, and it is with this platform that Václav Klaus fought the elections. Czech policy had come full circle. But the Slovaks, and especially Vladimír Mečiar, could not accept, for economic as well as constitutional reasons, what was tantamount to a return to old centralizing state-building policies.

The election of Mečiar – who had campaigned on a platform of slower economic change and a confederal solution – as prime minister of Slovakia, and of Klaus – whose platform stressed above all the need to move rapidly towards a market economy rather than constitutional reform – as prime minister of the Czech Republic, brought the question of relations between the two nations to a head. The Slovak National Council voted to declare the sovereignty of Slovakia on 17 July 1992. Mečiar then made an attempt to come to a solution with Klaus, but the latter, arguing that a market economy could only accommodate a centralized form of government, forced the only remaining alternative: the creation of two separate states. At their meeting on 22–23 July 1992, the two leaders agreed that the federation would be dissolved on 31 December, and the federal parliament approved this on 25 November. In the last five months of 1992, the two sides negotiated the division of federal assets, and the divorce took place in an orderly fashion.

There is a double thread running through the events that preceded the two transformations and finally the dissolution of the common state of the Czechs and Slovaks: first, the clear enunciation by the Slovaks of their perception of their position and role, and their determination to change the state in order to achieve their objectives; and, secondly, the resistance of the Czech elite to acknowledging the Slovaks as equal partners with a say in its definition and organization. The challenge to the political elites of both nations was to find a process and a solution that took both factors into account without at the same time allowing either to be the sole determinant. The history of Czechoslovakia, and especially its dissolution, which took place without any external pressure, indicates more than just the failure to meet that challenge.

THE NATIONAL QUESTION AND TERRITORIALITY

As an example of the territorial management of national conflict, Czechoslovakia is not a state that found a solution. This is not because territorial management was not attempted; as we saw, from 1945 on, Slovakia existed as a political and administrative entity. It was a failure because the central government sought at each opportunity to diminish or deny the value and validity of territorial management. This approach was dictated by the political culture that existed in the state from the moment of its creation.

Explaining the Break-up of Czechoslovakia

The importance of political culture cannot be underestimated; it influences all policies, including territorial management solutions. The problem with Czechoslovakia's political culture is that it remained Czech and never became Czecho-Slovak. This was at the root of the state's national conflicts. In each of the three challenges, territorial management was only a partial solution; the political system was also expected to reflect the new reality. This it failed to do. As a result, national conflict did not abate, and in the end the common state was dissolved. Leaders of multinational states who refuse to acknowledge the need to adapt their state's political structure in response to challenges from minority nations imperil the very existence of the state, as the example of Czechoslovakia clearly indicates.

Such a conclusion obliges us to look at the approaches taken in the literature on the challenges by minority nations, in particular the case of the Slovaks. There are two ways to approach the study of the Slovak question in Czechoslovakia. The preferred one in Western and Marxist literature is to see it in terms of minority management; this includes territorial management solutions. Leff's study is in this respect one of the best. Writing before Communism fell in Central Europe, she nonetheless concludes:

> The internal balance of power within the state, therefore, has been precisely wrong for successful accommodation of national tensions. Slovakia is too small and closely related a nation not to provoke Czech efforts to bring it into line. It is, however, too large and distinct a nation to suffer such attentions gladly or docilely. A weaker Slovak grouping might have had to settle, perforce, for some form of cultural autonomy. A stronger one would have had greater bargaining power within the state in times of normalcy.[65]

The minority management approach does enable one to examine the various tools used to manage the national minority. For example, Leff examines political structure, political culture and leadership interaction.

In this approach, the weight of the analysis is on the state, and the minority's reaction is measured in terms of its effects or consequences for the integrity of the state. The analysis contains a normative premise about the permanence of the given state.

When minorities make a national challenge to a state, they do so because they feel that it is responding inadequately to their needs, and because they are convinced that they would be better off in their own state. This means in effect that the challenge is not to the notion of statehood, but rather to the fact that the state in which they find themselves is not *their* state. The minority management approach fails to recognize this dimension and is therefore unable to propose solutions that could in the end protect the integrity of the state under study. Leff's conclusion brings out this conundrum:

> The current regime [Communist, pre-1989] still faces the same two choices with which earlier leaders have wrestled. The acceptance of political arrangements that honour the assumptions of bipolar politics will only serve to institutionalize and reinforce the national distinctiveness of each region still further, perhaps irreversibly. Integrationist policies, on the other hand, given the current social structure and national sensitivities, are out of step with the character of the binational society and will thus breed conflict.[66]

The other approach is to accept the minority nation as one with the right to determine whether the state does in fact seek to accommodate its needs and whether it gives it the opportunities for development, and to judge the state's performance according to these criteria. This has been our approach.[67] Our examination of Slovak challenges in the Czechoslovak state has been along these lines and it leads to the conclusion that the cohabitation experiment by the two nations has been a failure. From it, we also draw two conclusions concerning the relationship between the minority nation and the state:

1. In the first place, the political system of the state must reflect the political culture of both the minority and the majority nations. Whereas the word *Czechoslovak* itself might have been perceived by those who coined it as representing both nations, in its intent it represented the Czech policy of assimilation of the Slovak nation. The Slovaks also noticed that abroad the word was too cumbersome and would often be reduced to 'Czech', with which Slovaks would be labelled. Clearly, the state's political culture was not sending the right message to and about the Slovaks and they reacted accordingly, in 1938, in 1968 and in 1992.

2. Secondly, state-building policies must find a balance between the needs of the minority nation and the imperatives of protecting and

maintaining the integrity of the state. There is always the danger that the majority nation considers the state its own; the Czechs certainly did. The result is that the minority nation withdraws into its own territorial limits from which it then assails the state itself. This was clearly the case in Czechoslovakia. In 1918, the Slovaks gladly left Hungary to form a common state with the Czechs. They only asked that Prague grant Slovakia autonomy as had been agreed in the Pittsburgh Pact, and give Slovaks the chance to serve in the public service. But Prague failed on both counts. In the postwar era, autonomy was granted, but only formally, and the opportunity given to the Slovaks to join the public service was only marginally improved. The state was assailed again because the central government was unable to find the right balance between both nations in its state-building strategy and in its political culture. During the post-Communist era, when open discussion and debate was possible, it was the history of state-building policies as much as the unwillingness of the Czech political elite to accommodate Slovak demands that brought about the dissolution of the common state.

The National Question in the New Republics

Czecho-Slovakia broke up on 31 December 1992, one second before its successors states, the Czech Republic and the Slovak Republic, came into existence at the stroke of midnight on New Year's day, 1993. The creation of the Slovak Republic gave the geographical name of Slovakia a final and definite legitimacy.[68] However, the break-up of the common state was not greeted with universal acceptance, especially in scientific scholarship.[69] There are two explanations for this reaction. The first is normative and bases itself on a specific historical perception of the common state. The fall of communism in 1989 was seen as offering Czechoslovakia (as it was spelled at the time) an opportunity to re-establish a link with a past based on the legacy of its founder, Tomáš G. Masaryk, and on the state's reputation as the only democracy in Central Europe in the interwar years.[70] In addition, its abandonment to German expansionism by the Western powers in 1938[71] and to Soviet communism a decade later weighed heavily on the conscience of the West. Much of what we present in this chapter about Czech–Slovak relations in the interwar period was either unknown or subsumed under the democratic reputation of the common state. The second reason has to do with the direction that post-Communist development has taken in both the Czech Republic and Slovakia, the topic to which we now turn.[72]

The Czech Republic. Divested of the economic and constitutional burden that Slovakia would have presented to the Czech leadership had Czecho-Slovakia not dissolved, politics and economic life in the Czech Republic

under the leadership of Klaus embraced fully both democratic development and a rapid transformation to a market economy. The economic
structure of the common state had favoured the Czech Lands far more
than Slovakia. Most businesses that could readily be privatized and light
industries, as well as the production of durable consumer goods, were
located in the Czech Republic, while resource extraction and heavy armaments industries were in Slovakia. The privatization of state-owned assets
was therefore very attractive to domestic as well as foreign investors,
making the transfer to a market economy much simpler. The Czech
economy quickly became one of the best performing in Central Europe,
but it did not escape all the problems connected with the transformation
process that other Central European economies were experiencing. The
Klaus government resigned in November 1997 as a result of bankruptcies,
especially in the banking sector, and financial scandals.[73] The elections of
June 1998 brought to power Miloš Zeman of the Social Democrats, who
has been unable to emulate the success of his predecessor. As one observer
remarked at the end of the decade: 'The once-celebrated star of Central
Europe is now plagued by economic recession and political paralysis.'[74]

Czech politics also benefited greatly from the political legacy of
Czecho-Slovakia. The First Republic provided a model when the time
came to replace the Communist system with a democratic one; post-
Communist leaders emulated its positive aspects while seeking to avoid
its negative ones.[75] The sudden and almost total collapse of the
Communist Party had resulted in an 'extensive debate about how
democracy should be shaped in the immediate aftermath of the collapse
of communism.'[76] This had two consequences for the development of
Czech democracy. In the first place, according to a study of popular attitudes, 'Czech discourse's enthusiasm for democracy and participation
knows few bounds, in both its approval of the emerging post-communist
political system and in its hopes for a fuller and deeper democracy in
future.'[77] Secondly, the Czech model of democracy underwent a change
from participatory to majoritarian democracy after the dissolution of the
federation. The Czech government's decision to move rapidly towards a
market economy had encouraged the formation of 'a well-organized and
well-balanced party able to meet the requirements of a classic parliamentary democracy'.[78]

The latter conception, first proposed by Klaus and brought about by
his government, is at the heart not only of a political debate since the 1998
elections, but also of the question of the Czech Republic's membership in
European institutions. In 1999, along with Poland and Hungary, the
Czech Republic was admitted to full membership in the North Atlantic
Treaty Organization (NATO). Although initially promised, there was no
referendum on the government's decision to accept membership because
of a low level of public support for NATO. As far as the European Union
(EU) is concerned, the situation has been only marginally different;

opinion polls have indicated and continue to indicate lukewarm public acceptance. Nevertheless, the Czech government lost no time over the years in completing most of the 30 chapters outlined in accession talks and, as a result, the Czech Republic is listed in an October 2002 EU report among the candidates for EU accession in 2004.

Another issue that has an impact in democratic development in the Czech Republic is the question of minorities, in particular the Roma. There are also questions concerning the Germans. As Leff writes, 'there are *Czech* minority problems, even if not all of them are visible in the census data.'[79] While some of the issues are historical, for example the Beneš Decrees where the German minority is concerned, there are economic, citizenship, and educational issues where the Roma are concerned; none presents any sort of representational or constitutional challenge to the state. Ultimately, they are issues of public policy.

The economic slowdown that the country experienced after 1997, divergent conceptions in the ongoing debate on democratic development, as well as a low level of public support for the government's European policies have been some of the challenges the Czech Republic has been facing. Matthew Rhodes writes: 'The future direction of the Czech Republic (and indirectly of its neighbors) hinges on difficult choices to be made in the near-term future. An escape from the current impasse will require political leaders to articulate the link between Western institutions and Czech national interests more consistently and persuasively, though recent experience suggests that this alone will not suffice.'[80]

Slovakia. The dissolution of the common state brought out a major difference between Slovakia and the Czech Republic that has not been without consequences for Slovak political development: the presence of the national minorities, in particular the Magyars (this may be seen in Table 10.1). However, initially the challenges were of another kind because Czecho-Slovakia had left Slovakia a different legacy from that left to the Czech Republic. Slovakia's experience of anything approaching self-administration (which fell well short of self-government) was confined to the two decades of Communist federalism (1969–89). From 1989 on, as we saw above, the issue centred around the question of Slovak self-government in a common state with the Czechs or in an independent state.

By opting for independence, in addition to solving the economic and social challenges of post-Communist transformation, the Slovak government had to consolidate the new state and give it the necessary tools to ensure its proper functioning. The government had to introduce legislation that would facilitate the transition from the previous regime, ensure the process of decommunization, strengthen civil society, and inculcate in the population a sense of responsibility in all aspects of social, economic and political life. This was a monumental task, made all the more difficult by the absence of a state tradition in Slovakia; until 1993, Slovak politics as well as the administration of Slovakia went first though Prague. Mečiar was thus not only the creator of the second Slovak Republic, but also the political leader who gave democracy its start and ensured its development. The opposition, composed of many politicians described as 'Czechoslovak' – a definition that is meant to put in doubt their loyalty to the Slovak nation (they had voted against the dissolution of the federal state) – criticized above all the ways and means by which the Mečiar government handled the post-Communist transformation process. Only on occasion did they abandon their partisan approach to work with the government to ensure the consolidation of the new state.

Even before it was over, the Mečiar era was described as a period when Slovakia was experiencing a 'struggle for democracy'.[81] This is not a totally fair assessment, especially if Slovakia's record is compared with that of other Central European states. Part of the reason for such a conclusion comes from the government's social, economic and foreign policy programme, in particular Slovakia's relations with Russia, and part from the fact that Mečiar was categorized among Central Europe's post-Communist leaders as a demagogue.[82] His forceful personal qualities were, for some, reminiscent of the style and methods of the previous regime. His charismatic style was certainly not that of an understated, phlegmatic, rational, non-emotional and patient western politician, but then neither was that of the opposition politicians. As a result, politics and political discourse in Slovakia were often anything but edifying, as Mečiar himself acknowledged: 'The level of political dialogue is low.' He also pointed out in the same interview on Slovak Radio that Slovakia had many advantages, but that it 'also has the huge disadvantage of questioning itself'.[83] As the focus was on him as prime minister, Western commentators often used the demagogue description and his government's programme as the basis for their scepticism about the development of democracy in Slovakia.[84] However, Mečiar's policies also contributed to a sense of unease among the Slovak electorate.

On 25–26 September 1998, in Slovakia's fourth elections since the fall of communism, the Mečiar era came to an end. His party, the Movement for a Democratic Slovakia, won the greatest number of seats, 43 out of a total of 150 in the National Council of the Slovak Republic, but was unable this time to form a government. Apart from the Slovak National Party with 14 seats, no other party was willing to accept the invitation to join in a coalition government. Instead, ten opposition parties[85] found enough common ground to form one, and Mikuláš Dzurinda of the Christian Democratic Movement and leader of the Slovak Democratic Coalition became the country's third prime minister. The new government embarked on a policy of ensuring Slovakia's integration in Western institutions. The next round of elections, held four years later, on 21–22 September 2002, confirmed the public's acceptance of the course taken since 1998; Dzurinda was reelected prime minister, even though his party, now called the Slovak Democratic and Christian Union, came second to Mečiar's party, which, once again, was unable to find coalition partners to form a government. A little over a month after the elections, Slovakia was named in an EU report among the 10 countries to be included in the 2004 enlargement. Likewise, at the NATO Prague Summit on 22 November 2002, Slovakia was one of seven former Communist states in Central Europe invited to join the Atlantic Alliance in 2004. Although listed in 1994 and 1995 by the United States Congress among the Central European countries to join NATO in the first enlargement, Slovakia was dropped from the list in 1996 as a result of American uncertainty about Mečiar's commitment to democratic development in Slovakia. Similarly, Western European governments and EU institutions were equally uncertain about Slovak democratic development under Mečiar, indicating quite openly that Slovakia's chances of being invited to participate in the first EU enlargement were in jeopardy as long as he was prime minister.[86]

During the Mečiar era, one of the issues that distinguished Slovak political life from that of the Czech Republic was the question of minorities, in particular Slovak–Magyar relations. Since independence, the main issue has centred around the rights claimed by the Magyar minority who make up 10.8% of the population of Slovakia and live in areas along the Slovak–Hungarian border. For many Slovaks, the treatment of the Magyar minority has been more than just a question of minority rights, in particular language rights; also at stake are the integrity of the Slovak Republic, the treatment of the Slovak minority in Hungary and Slovak–Hungarian relations. Relations with the Magyar minority are, therefore, governed not only by Bratislava's policy towards it, but also by Budapest's reactions and the European conventions that govern the treatment of national minorities. There is also another issue that is central to Slovak–Hungarian relations, the Gabčíkovo-Nagymaros dam. This dam involves more than just bilateral relations between two states. At stake are environmental and economic issues. Given the powerful Hungarian lobby in the West, the Slovak government was the object not only of heavy criticism in the western press, but also of strong pressure to accede to Hungarian demands on both issues (the dam and Magyar minority rights). This pressure, in turn, had an often contradictory impact on both the government and the population.

The Magyar minority has been asking Bratislava to grant it 'collective rights' that include autonomy in cultural affairs, the use of Hungarian in public places and the control of the schools where Magyars are in a majority. Given the equivocal behaviour of Slovakia's Magyar politicians prior to independence, the Mečiar government decided to be seen to strengthen the Slovak character of the second Slovak Republic by forbidding bilingual signs on local roads and the signature of names in

Hungarian in birth registers. The symbolic value of these measures for both Slovaks and Magyars was far greater than their actual impact. Slovakia also underwent an administrative reorganization that divided the country in March 1996 into eight regions and 80 districts that cut right across Magyar districts. Magyar politicians saw this as a blatant case of gerrymandering. But it is the Language Law, passed in November 1995, that drew the greatest reaction, not only from the Magyar minority, but also from Budapest and abroad. It required that all public employees speak Slovak and that all public ceremonies, except weddings, also be held in Slovak.

Despite the debate that raged domestically over the Magyar minority and the pressure exerted by the EU and the Organization for Security and Cooperation in Europe (OSCE) for a law to protect minority languages, the Slovak government did not modify its position throughout Mečiar's tenure as prime minister.[87] The Slovak government argued that with this law the Magyars had all the rights that their Slovak counterparts enjoy; in addition, as foreign Minister Pavol Hamžík declared, 'the Hungarian minority in Slovakia enjoys a higher standard of rights compared with minorities in Europe – and significantly better than the Slovak minority's position in Hungary.'[88]

In its handling of Slovak–Hungarian relations, the Mečiar government reacted to a variety of pressures, ranging from nationalist demands at home not to concede anything to the Magyars, provocative signals from Hungary – in particular during the Hungarian minority summit held on 3–6 July 1996 in Budapest to which Magyar politicians from Slovakia were invited and in which they participated[89] – and demarches from the OSCE, the Council of Europe, and the EU. Nevertheless, despite the language law and the differences over the Gabčíkovo-Nagymaros dam, and perhaps as a testimony of the importance and need for good relations, Slovakia and Hungary signed a state treaty in the spring of 1995. Only at the end of March 1996 did the Slovak government ratify it, while Hungary had done so in June 1995.

After the September 1998 elections the Dzurinda government prepared a new minority language law that the Slovak parliament approved on 10 July 1999. While the bill included recommendations made by the OSCE, it did not meet demands of the Hungarian Coalition Party, which proposed that mother tongue usage for official purposes be authorized in localities where minorities make up 10% (and not 20%, as the bill proposed) of the population, and that minority linguistic rights be extended to education and culture. Although Budapest's reaction was unfavourable, complaining that the law was passed without the consent of the Hungarian Coalition Party which voted against it, the EU, on the other hand, welcomed it.[90] On 20 July, President Rudolf Schuster promulgated the law.

Slovak–Magyar relations have also been affected by the 'Status Law' that was adopted by the Hungarian parliament on 19 June 2001. The law, which took effect on 1 January 2002, gives Hungarians living outside Hungary the right to work in Hungary for three months each year, as well as social, health, transportation and education benefits after they have applied for a certificate proving their Hungarian origin. This certificate is to be issued by a Hungarian authority on the recommendation of Magyar organizations in the countries in question. From the moment it was passed, the law drew criticism from Slovakia because it was seen as infringing on Slovak sovereignty and failed to respect basic norms of international relations and the provisions of the Slovak–Hungarian treaty. On 18 December 2001, Slovak Foreign Minister Eduard Kukan told journalists that Bratislava would not allow Budapest to apply its controversial Status Law on Slovak territory: 'Some things [in the law] are unacceptable for us and therefore it will not be valid on our territory.'[91] On 20 February 2002, the Slovak government approved measures designed to safeguard Slovakia's interests in the face of the Hungarian Status Law; at the same time it indicated that it was conducting further talks with Budapest in order to reach an agreement on this issue.[92] On 11 September 2002, after months of negotiations, representatives of both the Hungarian and Slovak governments agreed on the need to amend the law so as to reflect the recommendations of the European Commission for Democracy and Law, known as the Venice Commission.[93]

CONCLUSION

The failure to maintain the common state of the Czechs and Slovaks is a lesson in how a state ought not to deal with a minority nation. This, at least, is what the history of Czechoslovakia tells us; the history of a state called Czecho-Slovakia might well have been quite different. The common state nevertheless left a legacy to its successor states that has been of value in their post-Communist development. It would not be unfair to suggest that the Czech Republic considers itself its direct successor and inheritor of its democratic tradition. This is best exemplified by the fact that despite an agreement not to retain any Czechoslovak symbols after dissolution, the Czech Republic kept Czechoslovakia's flag as well as the initials of ČSA (Československé Aerolinie) for Czech Airlines. For Slovakia, the legacy was an ambiguous one; on the one hand, the common state had had a democratic tradition that belonged as much to the Slovaks as it did to the Czechs. However, the Slovaks had also acquired a political experience that was reactive and oppositional, focusing on Slovak national issues, rather than one that stressed the need to develop democratic and open society values. This is the challenge that the government and inhabitants of the second Slovak Republic have been facing and continue to face. In this respect, and for other reasons as well, namely those having to do with Slovak national development, the dissolution of Czechoslovakia was anything but unnecessary.[94]

NOTES

1. Vocabulary is not the least problem when studying Czechoslovakia. The one term that we avoid in this article is 'ethnic'. As far as Czechoslovakia is concerned, the term is hardly ever encountered in the literature, whether official or scholarly. The terms that are used are *nation, nationality* and *national minority*, regardless of the fact that they may be difficult to define exactly. The term 'minority nation' is used here to contrast it with a majority nation; the meaning is numerical. Also, for a Canadian, the term 'ethnic' has a definite connotation, backed by a great deal of scholarship in such journals as *Canadian Ethnic Studies*; it refers to those Canadians of other than native, French and Anglo-Celtic origins.
2. Carol Skalnik Leff, *National Conflict in Czechoslovakia: The Making and Remaking of a State, 1918–1987* (Princeton: Princeton University Press, 1988).
3. According to the 1921 census, Czechs numbered 6,818,995; Germans 3,123,568; Slovaks 1,941,942; Magyars 745,431; Ruthenes (registered as Ukrainians and Russians), 461,849; Jews 180,855; Poles 75,853; and others 206,726 – out of a total population of 13,374,364 citizens and 238,808 aliens (for a total of 13,613,172 inhabitants). The statistics on the Czechs are arrived at by subtracting those obtained on the Slovaks from those classified as 'Czechoslovaks' in the 1921 census. They are therefore not completely accurate as the census did not distinguish between Czechs and Slovaks. See Václav L. Beneš, 'Democracy and its Problems, 1918–1920' in Victor S. Mamatey and Radomír Luža (eds.), *A History of the Czechoslovak Republic 1918–1948* (Princeton: Princeton University Press, 1973), p.40, and Owen V. Johnson, *Slovakia 1918–1938: Education and the Making of a Nation* (Boulder, CO: East European Monographs, 1985), p.79, for the statistics on the Slovaks.
4. For a history of Slovakia and the Slovaks, see Stanislav J. Kirschbaum, *A History of Slovakia: The Struggle for Survival* (New York: St. Martin's Press, 1995); chapters 8–12 present the period under analysis.
5. This is the spelling that was used in the Treaty of St. Germain of 1919 which created the new state. Later, when the constitution was adopted in 1920, the spelling was modified to signify that this was the state of a single nation, the Czechoslovaks, rather than the state of the Czechs and Slovaks.
6. For an examination of United States policy towards Central Europe see Victor S. Mamatey, *The United States and East Central Europe* (Princeton: Princeton University Press, 1958); French policy is examined in François Fejtö, *Requiem pour un empire défunt* (Paris: Lieu Commun, 1988).
7. See Thomas G. Masaryk, *La résurrection d'un Etat* (Paris: Plon, 1930).
8. The Empire of Great Moravia has always played an important role in the historical consciousness of the Slovaks even if it did not acquire the status of a historic right. For more on Great Moravia, see Kirschbaum, *History of Slovakia*, chapter 2.
9. A controversy was to arise a decade after the creation of the state around an alleged secret clause in the Turčiansky Sväty Martin Declaration (known as the Martin Declaration) of 30 October 1918. According to Vojtech Tuka, member of parliament for the Hlinka Slovak People's Party, in an article published in *Slovák* (Bratislava) on 2 January 1928, there had been a secret clause in the Martin Declaration which allowed the Slovaks to review their status in Czechoslovakia ten years after the creation of the state, with the option of leaving and creating their own state. The clause was never produced and Tuka was tried for treason on the basis of evidence that he had been receiving funds from Hungarian sources.
10. For more on these documents, see Stanislav J. Kirschbaum, 'The Cleveland and Pittsburgh Documents', *Slovakia*, Vol.36, Nos. 66–67 (1990), pp.81–97. See also Marian Mark Stolarik, 'The Role of American Slovaks in the Creation of Czecho-Slovakia, 1914–1918', *Slovak Studies*, Vol.7 (1968), pp.7–82.
11. An English translation of the Pittsburgh Pact is found in Joseph M. Kirschbaum, *Slovakia: Nation at the Crossroads of Central Europe* (New York: Robert Speller & Sons, 1960), p.236.

12. According to the 1921 census, the Germans constituted 33.0% of the population in Bohemia, 20.9% in Moravia and 40.5% in Silesia; in the territory of Czechoslovakia, the Czechs represented 50.8%, the Germans 23.4% and the Slovaks 14.5%. The statistics on the Czechs and Slovaks cannot be considered as accurate, as pointed out in note 3.

13. In the 1921 census, where the Czechs and Slovaks were counted together as Czechoslovaks, they totalled 8,760,937 or 65.3% of the population of Czechoslovakia; Beneš, 'Democracy', p.40.

14. R.W. Seton-Watson, *Masaryk in England* (Cambridge: Cambridge University Press, 1943), p.125.

15. See Josef Kalvoda, *The Genesis of Czechoslovakia* (Boulder, CO: East European Monographs, 1986).

16. Leff, *National Conflict*, p.274.

17. Quoted in Ferdinand Peroutka, *Budování státu* (Praha: F. Borovy, 1936), Vol.1, p.213. Regarding Štefánik and Osuský, the Slovak leaders involved in the creation of Czecho-Slovakia, both were initially in agreement with their Czech colleagues. There are indications, however, that Štefánik soon disagreed with them. He was killed on his way to Slovakia to see the situation for himself. His aircraft was shot down by a Czech anti-aircraft battery – it was never established whether this had been accidental or deliberate (he was flying in an aircraft with Italian colours which looked too much like Hungarian ones) – and he became a hero in the eyes of the Slovaks. Osuský, on the other hand, became Czechoslovakia's ambassador to France for the entire period of the First Republic.

18. A.J.P. Taylor writes: 'Masaryk revived the radical idea of 1848 and proposed to create a single "Czechoslovak" nation by will-power. Masaryk knew little of the Slovaks; the others knew even less. That was his strength in dealing with the allied leaders'; A.J.P. Taylor, *The Habsburg Monarchy 1809–1918* (Harmondsworth: Penguin Books, 1967), p.258. An astute observer of the creation of Czechoslovakia, commenting on Klofač's declaration, observed: 'This [the declaration] was true, but otherwise nothing else was true. If you read carefully the quotation, it is clear that there did not exist a Czechoslovak nation. The astonishment towards Slovak events that took place later resulted from the fact that this had been forgotten'; see Peroutka, *Budování státu*, Vol.1, p.213.

19. For more on how Šrobár ruled in Slovakia see Stanislav J. Kirschbaum, 'The Slovak People's Party: The Politics of Opposition, 1918–1938', in Stanislav J. Kirschbaum (ed.), *Slovak Politics* (Cleveland, OH: Slovak Institute, 1983), pp.158–63.

20. Stanislav J. Kirschbaum, 'Nationalism in the First Czechoslovak Republic 1918–1938', *Canadian Review of Studies in Nationalism*, Vol.16, Nos.1–2 (1989), p.174.

21. In 1927, a law was passed in the Czechoslovak parliament which defined Slovakia as a *krajina* (province) with an assembly and a president. This new province was not, however, given either legislative or executive powers. The state administration and legislation remained centralized.

22. For more on this see Kirschbaum, 'Nationalism', pp.169–87.

23. The events around the Slovak declaration of independence are examined in František Vnuk, 'Slovakia's Six Eventful Months October 1938–March 1939)', *Slovak Studies*, Vol.4 (1964), pp.7–164. The threat of dismemberment was not a hollow one: in the Vienna Award which was imposed on Slovakia by Germany and Italy as a result of Hungarian territorial demands made after the Munich Agreement, Slovakia lost 10,390 sq. km with 854,217 inhabitants. For more on the Vienna Award and on German attempts to destabilize post-Munich Czecho-Slovakia (the spelling of 1918 had been restored), see Theodore Prochazka, Sr., *The Second Republic: The Disintegration of Post-Munich Czechoslovakia (October 1938 – March 1939)* (Boulder, CO: East European Monographs, 1981).

24. Leff, *National Conflict*, p.86.

25. On the first Slovak Republic, see Stanislav J. Kirschbaum, 'The Slovak Republic and the Slovaks', *Slovakia*, Vol.29, Nos.53–4 (1980–81), pp.11–38. See also Kirschbaum, *History of Slovakia*, chapter 9. For a different, rather critical view of the first Slovak Republic see Yeshayahu A. Jelinek, *The Parish Republic: Hlinka Slovak People's Party 1939–1945* (Boulder, CO: East European Monographs, 1976).

26. On the events of August 1944, see Kirschbaum, *History of Slovakia*, chapter 10. The uprising of 1944 is one event that Slovak Marxist historiography examined almost down to the smallest detail. It contrasts with the cursory examination they gave the first Slovak Republic; such is also the case with western scholarship. For more on the issue of the first Slovak Republic in Slovak and western scholarship, see Stanislav J.

Kirschbaum, 'The First Slovak Republic (1939–1945): Some Thoughts on its Meaning in Slovak History', *Österreichische Osthefte*, Vol.41, Nos.3–4 (1999), pp.405–25.

27. Kirschbaum, *History of Slovakia*, pp.207–10. Beneš also tried unsuccessfully to control the resistance movement in Slovakia by relying on his only Slovak ally, Šrobár.

28. See Stanislav J. Kirschbaum, 'Federalism in Slovak Communist Politics', *Canadian Slavonic Papers*, Vol.19 (December 1977), pp.446–51.

29. Beneš did so only reluctantly, and then by also stating that he recognized a Slovak, a Czech and a Czechoslovak nation. See Gustáv Husák, *Svedectvo o Slovenskom národnom povstaní* (Bratislava: Vydavateľtvo politickej literatúry, 1964), p.462. With regard to the recognition of Slovakia as a territorial and political unit, it can be argued that Slovakia had already been recognized as such on 22 November 1938, when the Czechoslovak parliament passed a law granting Slovakia autonomy and renaming the country Czecho-Slovakia. However, Beneš's approach during the war was that everything that had happened during and after the Munich Agreement was invalid and the re-created state of Czechoslovakia was returning to the Constitution of 1920. See Kirschbaum, *History of Slovakia*, p.210.

30. For an analysis of the debate around the federal solution, see H. Gordon Skilling, *Czechoslovakia's Interrupted Revolution* (Princeton: Princeton University Press, 1976), pp.451–89.

31. For an examination of the liberalization process of 1968, see Galia Golan, *Reform Rule in Czechoslovakia 1968–1969* (Cambridge: Cambridge University Press, 1973).

32. Husák was very much in line with the policies that the Slovak Communists had adopted towards Slovakia as early as 1937. See V. Široký, *Industrializácia Slovenska – pevný základ večného bratstva českého a slovenského národa* (Bratislava: Pravda, 1949).

33. It is estimated that 90,000 Hungarians from Slovakia and 80,000 Slovaks from Hungary were 'exchanged' in 1946. See Vasyl Markus, 'National Minorities in East-Central Europe after 1945: Concepts, Models and Reassessments', in Manuel J. Pelaez (ed.), *Public Law and Comparative Politics: Trabajos en homenaje a Ferran Valls i Taberner,* XVII (Barcelona: Promociones y Publicaciones Universitarias, S.A., 1991), p.4875. See also Kalman Janics, *Czechoslovak Policy and the Hungarian Minority, 1945–1948*, adapted from the Hungarian by Stephen Borsody (New York: Social Science Monographs Distributed by Columbia University Press, 1982).

34. In 1921, there were 71,733 Czechs in Slovakia; by 1938, their number had increased to 120,926. See Joseph A. Mikuš, *Slovakia: A Political History: 1918–1950* (Milwaukee: Marquette University Press, 1963), pp.35 and 37.

35. For an examination of the debate in Slovakia, see Kirschbaum, *History of Slovakia*, pp.259–63. See also Stanislav J. Kirschbaum, 'Les Slovaques et le droit des peuples à disposer d'eux-mêmes: à la recherche d'une solution', in André Liebich and André Reszler (eds.), *L'Europe centrale et ses minorités: vers une solution européenne?* [Publications de l'Institut Universitaire de Hautes Etudes Internationales] (Genève, Paris: Presses Universitaires de France, 1993), pp.89–100.

36. See Documentation internationale, *La Paix de Versailles* (Paris: Les éditions internationales, 1929), Vol.10, p.54.

37. For the role of the French in the creation of Czecho-Slovakia, see Fejtö, *Requiem,* pp.305–65.

38. The extent to which the Czechs were successful in persuading the Allied powers in the case of the Slovaks can be seen in their ability to prevent Andrej Hlinka, the leader of the Slovak People's Party, from addressing the Peace Conference in 1919. As he had travelled on a Polish passport, they had him arrested by the French police and then, upon his return to Czecho-Slovakia, had him detained in Moravia until after the 1920 elections. Despite his detention, he still managed to get elected in a Slovak constituency.

39. See H. Gordon Skilling, 'Czechoslovak Political Culture: Pluralism in an International Context', in Archie Brown (ed.), *Political Culture and Communist Studies* (Armonk, NY: M.E. Sharpe, 1984), p.115.

40. See Eva Schmidt-Hartmann, 'People's Democracy: The Emergence of a Czech Political Concept in the Late Nineteenth Century', in Stanislav J. Kirschbaum (ed.), *East European History* (Columbus, OH: Slavica Publishers, Inc., 1988), pp.125–40.

41. Skilling, 'Czechoslovak Political Culture', p.115. He also attributes these characteristics to the Slovaks.

42. According to one definition, pluralism is 'the diffusion and dispersion of power in a political system from central authorities to more or less autonomous groups, organizations and individuals'; Stephen White, 'Communist Systems and the "Iron Law of

Pluralism"', *British Journal of Political Science*, Vol.8, No.1 (1978), p.101 quoted in Skilling, 'Czechoslovak Political Culture', p.116. Skilling expands this definition to one that characterizes a parliamentary democratic system.

43. Thomas G. Masaryk, *The Making of a State* (New York: Frederick A. Stokes, 1927), p.220.
44. Manfred Alexander, 'Leistungen, Belastungen und Gefährdungen der Demokratie in der Ersten Tschechoslowakischen Republik', *Bohemia*, Vol.27, No.1 (1986), p.85. Italics in the original.
45. Edouard Bénès, 'Discours aux Slovaques sur le présent et l'avenir de notre nation', *Le monde slave*, (février 1934), pp.42–5. Italics in the original.
46. In 1925, to honour its founder and leader, Andrej Hlinka, the Slovak People's Party was renamed the Hlinka Slovak People's Party. For a critical view of the activities of the Hlinka Slovak People's Party, especially in the second decade of the First Republic, see James Ramon Felak, *'At the Price of the Republic': Hlinka Slovak People's Party, 1929–1938* (Pittsburgh: University of Pittsburgh Press, 1994).
47. Skilling, 'Czechoslovak Political Culture', p.126.
48. In the 1946 elections, the Communists obtained 40.2% of the vote in the Czech Lands with the rest divided among non-Communist parties, whereas in Slovakia they obtained only 30.4% while the Democratic Party scored 60.4%. This result is attributed to a great extent to the Slovak experience during 1939–45. This greatly influenced the tenor of Slovak political life until 1948. For an examination of this period see Robert Letz, *Slovensko v rokoch 1945–1948* (Bratislava: Ústredie slovenskej kresťanskej inteligencie, 1994) and Michal Barnovský, *Na ceste k monopolu moci. Mocenskopolitické zápasy na Slovensku v rokoch 1945–1948* (Bratislava: Archa, 1993).
49. If a constitution is an indicator of political culture, according to Karin Schmid, the constitution of the Slovak Republic 'can best be described as an authoritarian system with rather surprising democratic features'; Karin Schmid, 'The Constitution of the Slovak Republic', in Kirschbaum, *Slovak Politics*, p.214. See also Stanislav J. Kirschbaum, 'The Meaning of Statehood in the First Slovak Republic, 1939–1945', paper read at the Sixth World Congress for Central and East European Studies, Tampere, Finland, 31 July 2000, to be published in a congress volume.
50. On the Tiso trial, see Bradley Abrams, 'The Politics of Retribution: The Trial of Jozef Tiso in the Czechoslovak Environment', in István Deák, Jan T. Gross and Tony Judt (eds.), *The Politics of Retribution in Europe* (Princeton: Princeton University Press, 2000), pp.252–89. It is interesting to note that the Czechoslovak state was very punitive towards those Slovak politicians whom it saw as placing the interests of the Slovak nation ahead of those of the state. The most flagrant cases are those of Andrej Hlinka (see note 38), Vojtech Tuka (see note 9), Jozef Tiso, and the leaders of the 1944 uprising who were condemned for Slovak bourgeois nationalism during the Communist regime. Slovak émigrés who worked on behalf of the independence of the Slovak nation were also the object of attacks by the Czechoslovak government.
51. On 29 March 1968, the Bratislava Communist daily *Pravda* published a document that had been prepared by the National Socialist Party of Czechoslovakia (Beneš's party) in 1946 on how to proceed with the assimilation of the Slovaks. In a comment accompanying the publication of the document, the editors indicated that 'The memorandum of the National Socialists was dangerous for Comrade A. Novotný and his collaborators because, at first glance, it resembled their own political practice'.
52. The first challenge was made in 1963 when Miloš Gosiorovský presented the leadership of the Communist Party of Czechoslovakia with a memorandum arguing against the asymmetrical system and for a federal solution, using the Soviet Union and Yugoslavia as examples of how Marxists properly dealt with the 'national question'. He drew the ire of First Secretary Antonín Novotný, and the First Secretary of the Communist Party of Slovakia, Alexander Dubček, had to protect him. His memorandum was not published until 1968 in the Slovak journal *Historický časopis*. See Miloš Gosiorovský, 'K niektorým otázkam vzťahu Čechov a Slovákov v politike Komunistickej Strany Československa', *Historický časopis*, Vol.16, No.3 (1968), pp.354–406.
53. Skilling, 'Czechoslovak Political Culture', pp.124–7.
54. Vladimír Repka, 'Čo ma teší, trápi, zlostí', *Nový Slovák*, 36/1991, 2 September 1991.
55. Vladimír Mináč, 'Naša česko-slovenská otázka', *Nové slovo*, 21/1990, 24 May 1990.
56. Karol Sidor, *Slovenská politika na pôde pražského snemu (1913–1938)* (Bratislava: Andreja, 1943), Vol.1, p.71.
57. See Mikuš, pp.35–8.
58. See Victor S. Mamatey, 'The Development of Czechoslovak Democracy 1920–1928', in

Mamatey and Luža, *History of the Czechoslovak Republic*, pp.114–20.

59. According to available statistics, out of 400,193 persons who left Czechoslovakia in the years 1920–38,213,185 or 54% were from Slovakia; see Mikuš, p.38.

60. Kirschbaum 'Slovak Nationalism', pp.179–81.

61. Wolfgang Venohr, *Aufstand für die Tschechoslowakei. Der slowakische Freiheitskampf von 1944* (Hamburg: Christian Wegner Verlag, 1969), p.26.

62. These agreements, known as the Prague Agreements, are examined by H. Gordon Skilling, 'Revolution and Continuity in Czechoslovakia, 1945–1946', *Journal of Central European Affairs*, Vol.20, No.4 (1961), pp.357–77 and František Vnuk, 'Slovak–Czech Relations in Post-War Czechoslovakia, 1945–1948' in Kirschbaum, *Slovak Politics*, pp.323–34.

63. The economic development of Slovakia was nevertheless directly tied to the Czechoslovak economy; see Jaroslav Chovanec, *The Czechoslovak Socialist Federation* (Bratislava: Pravda, 1976), p.84.

64. Viliam Plevza, *Socialistické premeny Československa* (Bratislava: Pravda, 1983), p.420.

65. Leff, *National Conflict*, pp.276–7.

66. Ibid., p.297.

67. See Kirschbaum, *History of Slovakia*.

68. The term *Slovakia*, as a geographical and political concept, is relatively recent; it appeared for the first time in the nineteenth century, in a petition to the Habsburg emperor in 1849. It is in the First Republic that the term first defined the territory of 'Upper Hungary', which is how Slovakia was referred to in Austria-Hungary. It acquired a political definition in the First Republic, initially in the Peace Treaties which spelled Czecho-Slovakia with a hyphen. See note 5.

69. This is particularly the case in the following analyses: Eric Stein, *Czecho/Slovakia: Ethnic Conflict, Constitutional Fissure, Negotiated Breakup* (Ann Arbor: The University of Michigan Press, 1997), John F.N. Bradley, *Czechoslovakia's Velvet Revolution* (Boulder, CO: East European Monographs, 1992), and Jiří Musil (ed.), *The End of Czechoslovakia* (Budapest: Central European Univesity Press, 1995). A more detached presentation is found in Frédéric Wherlé, *Le divorce tchéco-slovaque. Vie et mort de la Tchécoslovaquie 1918–1992* (Paris: L'Harmattan, 1994). For more on this question see Michael Kraus and Allison Stanger, 'Contending Views of Czechoslovakia's Demise' in Michael Kraus and Allison Stanger (eds.), *Irreconcilable Differences? Explaining Czechoslovakia's Dissolution* (Lanham, MD: Rowan & Littlefield, 2000), pp.7–25.

70. For some, Czechoslovakia's first and only post-Communist president, Václav Havel, embodied the legacy of Masaryk. See Rob McRae, *Resistance and Revolution: Václav Havel's Czechoslovakia* (Ottawa: Carleton University Press, 1997). According to John S. Dryzek and Leslie Holmes, Havel did 'see himself as heir to the "politics of truth" of T.G. Masaryk; his presidential web site equates their political philosophies'. See John S. Dryzek and Leslie Holmes, 'The Real World of Civic Republicanism: Making Democracy Work in Poland and the Czech Republic', *Europe-Asia Studies*, Vol.52, No.6 (2000), p.1060.

71. According to Vera Olivova, in 1938 Czechoslovakia was 'brought to her knees, not by [Adolf] Hitler but by her own allies'. See Vera Olivova, *The Doomed Democracy: Czechoslovakia in a Disrupted Europe 1914–1938*, translated by George Theiner (Montreal: McGill-Queen's University Press, 1972), p.250

72. This is the approach taken by Robin H.E. Shepherd, *Czechoslovakia: The Velvet Revolution and Beyond* (London: Macmillan, 2000).

73. For a detailed analysis of the problems that the Czech Republic has been experiencing see Jeffrey M. Jordan, 'Patronage and Corruption in the Czech Republic', RFE/RL *East European Perspectives*, Vol.4, No.4 (20 February 2002), and Vol.4, No.5 (6 March 2002). See also Shepherd, *Czechoslovakia*, pp.39–127.

74. See Matthew Rhodes, 'Czech Malaise and Europe', *Problems of Post- Communism*, Vol.47, No.2 (2000), p.57.

75. As Magdalena Hadjiisky writes: 'The "founding fathers" of post-1989 democracy were also aware of what appeared to many as the main failure of the First Republic. The institution of the "petka" (pet in Czech means five) had then helped to provide the leadership of the five parties of the governing coalition with a degree of political influence that outweighed their respective electoral support levels. It also instituted a regime where political change had become very difficult, whatever the electoral results might be.' See Magdalena Hadjiisky, 'The Failure of the Participatory Democracy in the Czech Republic', *West European Politics*, Vol.24, No.3 (2001), p.47.

76. Ibid., p.45.

77. Dryzek and Holmes, 'Real World', p.1058.
78. Hadiijsky, 'Failure', p.50.
79. Carol Skalnik Leff, *The Czech and Slovak Republics: Nation Versus State* (Boulder, CO: Westview Press, 1997), p.169.
80. Rhodes, 'Czech Malaise', p.65.
81. See Minton F. Goldman, *Slovakia Since Independence: A Struggle for Democracy* (Westport, CT: Praeger, 1999). See also Soňa Szomolányi and John A. Gould (eds.), *Slovakia: Problems of Democratic Consolidation* (Bratislava: Slovak Political Science Association/Friedrich Ebert Foundation, 1997).
82. See J.F. Brown, *Hopes and Shadows: Eastern Europe After Communism* (Durham, NC: Duke University Press, 1994), p.34. According to a recent analysis, Slovak political life was subjected to a new 'ism' during the Meciar era. See Kieran Williams, 'Introduction: What was Meciarism?' in Kieran Williams (ed.), *Slovakia after Communism and Meciarism* (London: School of Slavonic and East European Studies, University College, SSEES Occasional Papers No.47, 2000), pp.1–16.
83. 'Slovak Prime Minister on NATO, EU', *OMRI Daily Digest*, Part 2, 15 October 1996.
84. See for example Sharon Fisher, 'Slovakia: Backtracking on the Road to Democratic Reform,' in Open Media Research Institute, *Building Democracy: The OMRI Annual Survey of Eastern Europe and the Former Soviet Union 1995* (Armonk, NY: M.E. Sharpe, 1996), pp.25–31.
85. The coalition had a 93-seat majority and comprises the Slovak Democratic Coalition with 42 seats (composed of the Christian Democratic Movement, the Democratic Union, the Democratic Party, the Social Democratic Party of Slovakia, and the Green Party of Slovakia), the Party of the Democratic Left with 23 seats, the Party of Civic Understanding with 13 seats, and the Hungarian Coalition with 15 seats (composed of the Hungarian Christian Democratic Movement, the Hungarian People's Party, and Hungarian Coexistence). In opposition were the Movement for a Democratic Slovakia and the Slovak National Party with 57 seats.
86. Prior to the 2002 elections, Western officials made it abundantly clear that Slovakia's integration in NATO and the EU would be in doubt if Mečiar were reelected. For more on the Mečiar era and on the 2002 elections, see Stanislav J. Kirschbaum, 'The Slovak Elections of 2002 and the "Mečiar Factor"', *Transitions*, 2002, in press.
87. For more details on Slovak–Hungarian relations, see Goldman, *Slovakia*, pp.123–36.
88. Quoted in ibid., p.136.
89. For more details on this meeting, see Sharon Fisher and Zsofia Szilagyi, 'Hungarian Minority Summit Causes Uproar in Slovakia', in Open Media Research Institute, *Forging Ahead, Falling Behind: The OMRI Annual Survey of Eastern Europe and the Former Soviet Union 1996* (Armonk, NY: M.E. Sharpe, 1996), pp.36–9.
90. 'European Commission Welcomes Slovak Minority Language Law', *RFE/RL Newsline*, Part 2, 13 July 1999.
91. 'Slovakia to Prevent Hungary from Implementing Status Law', *RFE/RL Newsline* Vol.5, No.239, Part 2, 19 December 2001.
92. 'Slovak Cabinet Approves Anti-Status Law Measures', *RFE/RL Newsline*, Vol.6, No.34, Part 2, 21 February 2002.
93. 'Slovakia, Hungary Agree on Need to Amend Status Law', *RFE/RL Newsline*, Vol. 6, No. 172, Part II, 12 September 2002.
94. See Kirschbaum, *History of Slovakia*. For an approach that claims that post-Communist politics in Slovakia is devoid of historical content see Shari J. Cohen, *Politics Without a Past: The Absence of History in Postcommunist Nationalism* (Durham, NC: Duke University Press, 1999).

11

The Dissolution of Yugoslavia

Secession by the Centre?

DANIELE CONVERSI

The dissolution of three multinational states in central and eastern Europe in the early 1990s posed a major challenge not only to the international community but also to the world of the social sciences. The break-up of a state is not just traumatic for its inhabitants (though many of them may welcome this development); it may also threaten the stability of neighbouring states and it is an event that requires explanation both as an important theoretical question and because of its public policy implications.

This chapter explores the circumstances behind the break-up of Yugoslavia. It begins with a discussion of general theories relating to secession. It then proceeds to examine the Yugoslav case in the light of these, providing an outline of the evolution of the national question in Yugoslavia, assessing the role of the various forces that contributed ultimately to the collapse of the state and looking at the mechanics of this process itself. In particular, this chapter considers the argument that, in addition to the most obvious factors that contribute to the fragmentation of a state (secessionist tendencies in its peripheries clashing with an initial unwillingness on the part of the international community to accept the break-up of a political system), Yugoslavia's fate was also conditioned by a disposition on the part of its 'core' Serbian nationality to follow its own path of secession in purely ethnic terms.[1]

SECESSION: GENERAL PERSPECTIVES

Why are theories of secession relevant to an understanding of developments in Yugoslavia? Misunderstanding about political phenomena rooted in inadequate concepts may have repercussions in real political life: international misconceptions about the origins of a crisis are likely to promote unsound foreign policy decisions. In other words, ideas and concepts are crucial in framing action. The study of secession has been seriously impeded by an obvious dearth of theoretical tools. In the case of Yugoslavia, this vacuum has been filled by impromptu interpretations, such as the 'ancient-hatred' theory, the 'clash of civilizations' paradigm, various 'civil war' explanations and competing conspiracy theories.[2]

Theories of Secession

The idea of secession is an unattractive one in international politics. The term has acquired a distinctly negative connotation in American political thought, parlance and practice, based on the memory of the American civil war, when 11 Southern states attempted to secede by forming the 'Confederate States of America' (1861–65).[3] The USA has had a generally adverse stand towards secession internationally. This was the perspective that informed American support of the Pakistani regime against Bangladesh's struggle for independence and of the Indonesian army's invasion of East Timor.[4] It also led to the initial refusal to recognize Slovenia and Croatia before 1992. The attitude was simultaneously confirmed during George Bush's trip to Kiev, Ukraine (29 July–1 August 1991), when the US President publicly condemned the country's secessionist drive, warning the Ukrainians against 'hasty' moves towards independence. However, less than a month later (24 August 1991), Ukraine indeed declared its independence – in the immediate aftermath of the failed Communist Party *putsch* (19–21 August).

For geopolitical and demographic reasons of power and prestige, secession is seen as illegitimate and hazardous in diplomatic circles and is sternly resisted by states and governments world-wide. According to Ralph Premdas, 'no state dismembers itself willingly; no separatist movement has been proffered victory on a platter'.[5] There is therefore a pro-state bias in all, or almost all, international relations accounts of internal conflicts. This bias is shared by politicians, who often instinctively support central states against secessionist trends, a position that has been criticized as 'catastrophic short-termism'.[6]

In recent years secession has received belated, though abundant, scholarly attention – an attention which has obviously increased in the 1990s. Even though some scholars had dealt before with related phenomena, the first low-key attempt to formulate coherent theories of secession appeared in the 1970s from several disciplinary angles.[7] Anthony D. Smith in sociology and Walker Connor in political science approached the issue from the standpoint of 'separatism' and 'self-determination', while Colin Williams collected a series of contributions on 'national separatism'.[8] Crawford Young attempted the first systematic comparisons in former colonial areas, notably in Africa and Asia, while Donald Horowitz was possibly the first to conduct a wide-ranging comparative investigation of ethnic conflict, in which secession was analysed in detail as one of the possible outcomes.[9] The moral implications of secession also began to be questioned in political philosophy.[10] In general, these early works were conceived in the framework of wider scholarly endeavours, and hence were often less than systematic. On the other hand, the literature on 'self-determination' was more extensive, but it concentrated primarily on former colonial countries.[11]

Finally, the 'discovery' of nationalism (and, hence, secession) in international relations just about preceded the collapse of communism. Most international relations theorists, such as James Mayall, took the view that the international system had placed permanent restraints on the possibility of secession, failing to contemplate that until 1989 such a world order was a by-product of the Cold War and hence was far from being a long-term solution.[12] This may suggest that, given the intrinsic conservatism and state-centred bias of the discipline, international relations is inescapably a late-comer to the socio-political developments of its times. However, the study of secession began really to take off after the break-up of ex-Communist multinational states, generating a veritable industry. The post-Cold War literature included contributions from several theoretical and disciplinary angles, ranging from rational choice theory to peace studies and moral philosophy.[13] In the last of these areas, the focus on the 'legitimacy' of secession also dealt with its causes and *raison d'etre*, thus containing both a prescriptive and an analytical dimension. A typology of possible ways of 'regulating' ethnic conflict has also been delineated for us. This brackets secession with 'partition', and presents both in the framework of self-determination as a political principle.[14]

What is the relationship between secessionism and irredentism?[15] Donald Horowitz has identified a 'convertibility of claims' between the two, a coinage that, as we shall see, well fits our description of Serbian secessionism-cum-irredentism.[16] However, in principle, the two dimensions should be kept clearly distinct. Irredentism is often considered one of the most dangerous forms of nationalism precisely because it unremittingly identifies nation and state. Minorities which are supposed to be 'stranded' abroad or to have drifted apart from their homeland are expected to be redeemed by association with a sole unitary state, a single government, culture, language, power hierarchy and set of laws. Irredentism articulates itself as a series of mega-projects (Greater Germany, Greater Serbia, Greater Croatia, Greater Hungary, Greater Romania, Russia's 'near abroad' and so on) which have in common their underlying reciprocal intolerance and, hence, their mutual incompatibility. It conceives the nation as an organic, homogeneous whole, all members of which are supposed to dwell under a common political roof and to bow to a single authority.

In the twentieth century, irredentism played a central role in the explosion of two world wars and endless conflicts, including the first two Gulf wars and the disintegration of Yugoslavia. Moreover, one can find a mirror-like (and relatively unexplored) relationship between irredentism and ethnic cleansing, which runs as follows: if the existence of 'external' minorities is considered an unbearable injustice and the presence of ethnic kin outside one's state borders is assailed, then 'internal' minorities are also perfunctorily repudiated, finding themselves under severe threat. The generalized rallying cry becomes homogenization. When 'stranded' minorities are seen as victims, internal minorities are simultaneously seen as an enemy fifth column and as a menace to the country's integrity. The designated 'victims' can only be redeemed with the help of the fatherland. In brief, ethnic cleansing can be seen as irredentism's logical finale. Finally, irredentism creates immense international instability by attempting to aggrandize existing states, hence propagating alarm and panic amongst both neighbours and the international community at large.

Secession by the Centre

Despite the burgeoning literature in this area, the possibility of secession occurring from within the centre has been largely ignored. The prevalent assumption is that secession can only take place in the periphery. The possibility that central authorities, or even dominant ethnic groups, may be willing to secede is not even contemplated. A partial exception is represented by Allen Buchanan, who makes two interesting distinctions: central versus peripheral secession, and majority versus minority secession.[17] In the first case, the area wishing to secede occupies a peculiar (central) geographical position within the country, forming its very core. Buchanan aptly describes this pattern as 'hole-of-a-donut' secession – it will not merely create a landlocked polity, but one entirely encircled by its erstwhile host state. For this reason, the secessionists could in principle free-ride on the public goods of the state even after secession has taken place. If, for instance, Tatarstan were to secede from Russia or some Indian reservations from the USA, they would have to rely entirely on the host state for some basic functions, such as national defence. Therefore, this type of secession rarely occurs, as geopolitical conditions discourage it; neither is it likely to be accepted by the host state.[18] As a rule, that is why secession occurs almost always in the geographical periphery of the host state.

As for the distinction between majority and minority secession, Buchanan does not perhaps sufficiently clarify whether 'minority' is merely a demographic concept or also entails a sociological dimension (related to such characteristics as relative social status or practices of discrimination). Indeed, as he recognizes, majority secession is usually referred to in the literature as 'exclusion' of the majority by the minority (as in South Africa in the heyday of the apartheid system, or in Serbian-occupied Kosovo before 1999). In short, the first criterion is entirely territorial or geographic, while the second is mostly demographic or sociological. But neither is suitable as an explanation of the wish of a dominant group to carve out an irredentist project from a territory which was at least in part under its direct political control (albeit such control did not remain uncontested in the Serbian case, given the counter-balancing power of other groups).

Although this chapter focuses on Yugoslavia as the quintessential example of central secession, other candidates should not be ruled out. For instance, Czechoslovakia's division can arguably be analysed as an example of peaceful secession by the centre (the Czech Republic), rather than by the periphery (Slovakia). As is well known, the democratizing government in Prague opted to solve its financial and political disputes with Bratislava by getting rid of the burden at once – by allowing Slovakia to secede, rather than conceding it more autonomy. However, the reality was that the main nationalist movement operated in Slovakia, while the Czech side was relatively free of nationalist mobilization. The centre never developed a fully-fledged secessionist movement, but simply allowed the federation to dissolve.[19] Similarly, the case of Russia can probably be better described as one of 'laissez-faire' pragmatism rather than as secession by the centre in a strict sense.

In some cases, particular parties or movements appear to advocate secession by the centre, or at least 'majority secession' from the minority. One example is the Reform Party in Canada, which claims to represent English-speakers from the 'oppressed' majority and favours a centralized, mono-cultural Canada, even if this means 'seceding' from Quebec. English mother-tongue speakers are a clear majority of Canada's population (about 60%; see chapter 2), so the demographic imbalance is conspicuous here. However, the Reform Party is electorally stronger in Canada's western periphery (extending to British Columbia), rather than in the centre of the country per se (Ontario and the capital Ottawa), so 'secessionism by the centre' would be a misnomer. The picture is further complicated by the existence of a competing 'secessionist' movement, claiming a separate identity for each western province as well as for Western Canada as a whole, and overlapping with Native American land rights claims.[20]

Neither can the Eritrea–Ethiopia relationship be considered a case of secession by the centre. Eritrea was able to secede from Ethiopia in 1993 only after its allies, the troops of the Ethiopian liberation movement, had captured the capital, Addis Ababa, ushering in a new regional order. Since the movement developed in the periphery, this is again not a case of secessionism by the centre. Moreover, the Amhara minority (32%, if counted with the Tigreans) had consistently tried to dominate the country with a mixture of pure coercion (during Col. Menghistu Haile Mariam's Marxist-Leninist dictatorship, 1977–91) and consensus (during Emperor Haile Sellassie's rule to 1975, through the use of more neutral imperial symbols, the co-optation of local elites and networks, and the emphasis on a common Coptic Christian heritage). In any event, the

Amharas never did attempt to secede from the rest of the country, or at least they did not openly and successfully do so.[21] After 1993, resistance against Eritrean 'invasion' was pitiless and fierce due to Amhara fear of losing their centuries-old privileged status.[22]

Finally, the Malaysia–Singapore relationship can be included as a possible contender. Singapore's independence in 1965 was warmly encouraged, or even pushed, by the Malaysian Federation, since its Chinese majority exerted an all-too-powerful influence on the mainland's own ethnic Chinese minority. By contrast with Yugoslavia, the international community did not contest this particular type of secession; hence, the move occurred peacefully and in mutual agreement. This may be defined as a case of secession by the centre, but not in an unqualified way. In fact, Singapore better matches the process defined by Alexis Heraclides as 'ejection', as it was in practice 'booted out' by the Malaysian federation.[23]

Thus, secessionism by the centre is a rare phenomenon. Even in the case of the former Soviet Union and Czechoslovakia, political fragmentation can be seen as part of a larger historical pattern of state dissolution and decolonization. The Yugoslav case was different: in Serbia, a powerful nationalist movement emerged before the break-up of the state, and indeed actually encouraged this outcome. From a distant, foreign, international perspective, secession seemed to occur first in the periphery (Slovenia and Croatia). Yet, these republics had been pressed into developing their reactive forms of secessionism as the state's continuing legitimacy was called into question. Nationalist movements were already at work in Slovenia and especially Croatia, but, given their recent (indeed persisting) experience of lack of democratic freedoms, they had to wait for strong signals from the centre before setting their own secessionist agenda and openly declaring their statements of purpose. Once the central state was delegitimized, both central and peripheral nationalism took advantage of the legitimacy vacuum to press their claims in the direction of independence.

THE NATIONAL QUESTION IN YUGOSLAVIA

As in the analysis of nationalist tensions in other societies, two principal issues are relevant to our understanding of the circumstances in which political conflict in the former Yugoslavia came to a head in the early 1990s. The first is the political and constitutional context, viewed historically: the process of state building, and the shape that the Yugoslav state finally took in the years before its collapse. The second is the ethnonational balance, and the dynamics of competition between the various nationalities. We now look at these issues in turn.

The Evolution of the State

The *first Yugoslavia* was established on 1 December 1918 as the Kingdom of Serbs, Croats and Slovenes by bringing together a number of existing entities carved out of the former Ottoman Empire (before the First World War) and the former Habsburg Empire (as a consequence of the war). The most important of these was the Kingdom of Serbia. The core of what is now central Serbia had achieved the status of an autonomous principality within the Ottoman Empire already by 1815 and, more substantially, in 1830–33. It became formally independent in 1878, and extended its borders southwards to include what are now roughly Kosovo and Macedonia (1913). The second component was the Kingdom of Montenegro, which had long maintained its status as an independent principality ruled by Orthodox prince-bishops. Its independence was recognized internationally in 1878, and in 1910 it proclaimed itself a monarchy. Third, two Hungarian possessions were absorbed: Croatia-Slavonia (an autonomous region of Hungary, formerly the old Kingdom of Croatia), and Vojvodina (a southern Hungarian district then inhabited by several ethnic groups, mostly Germans, Hungarians and Serbs). Fourth, two major zones of Austria were incorporated: Carniola, a predominantly Slovene-speaking autonomous crownland with other areas inhabited by Slovenes, and Dalmatia, a predominantly Croatian autonomous Austrian possession on the Adriatic coast with important Italian minorities. Finally, the new state also included Bosnia-Herzegovina, a distinctive territory that had long been part of the Ottoman empire, but which had been occupied by Austria-Hungary in 1878 and formally annexed in 1908 as a territory under joint Austrian-Hungarian tutelage.

The new state was a mainstay of the Anglo-American international order resulting from the re-drawing of the world map after the First World War. The name 'Yugoslavia' was officially adopted on 3 October 1929 by a decree of King Alexander I (1888–1934). This replacement of the earlier multi-national name symbolized the strongly centralist tendencies of the interwar state, and resulted in nationalist unrest spreading throughout the country, culminating in the assassination of the king in 1934. Yugoslavia's constituent parts had entered the union with different objectives and for different reasons. Some envisaged it on a federal basis of mutual respect and appreciation, but the actual outcome was a centralized structure.

The reality was that, as the former Kingdom of Serbia lay at the core of the new arrangement, its ruling dynasty had indeed assumed power in the new state. A sizeable portion of Belgrade's elites saw the new state as an arena for nationalist expansion and consolidation – and as 'war booty' from the victorious superpowers. With the rise of centralist nationalism and fascism all over Europe, state elites saw a chance to establish complete supremacy for the Serbian element. The fact that the capital was located in Belgrade, seat of the old Serbian kingdom, meant that, already at its inception, Yugoslavia was tempted to identify with the foregoing polity and, following the prevailing *Zeitgeist*, to centralize itself on the general model of the surrounding European nation-states. As Slovenian, Croatian and Macedonian elites were to discover, the international conditions of the time were propitious for extreme centralization. Under the impact of expanding fascism even a multinational state such as Yugoslavia was able to recentralize itself in the name of 'national unity'.

This first Yugoslavia survived until 1941, when the country was occupied by Nazi Germany and Fascist Italy, which dismembered it, turning Croatia into a puppet state, the so-called 'Independent State of Croatia' (1941–45). This came under the rule of Ante Pavelic's *Ustasha* movement, whose principal aim was an ethnically pure Croatia. Other areas were annexed by Italy and Hungary.

The *second Yugoslavia*, known as the Federal People's Republic of Yugoslavia, came into being following the partisan victory at the end of the Second World War, and lasted until its disintegration in 1991. The reconstitution of the state and its success until the late 1980s – notwithstanding economic difficulties, including falling real incomes and rising unemployment in its later years – owed much to the leadership and vision of the charismatic partisan leader Marshall Josip Broz Tito (1892–1980), himself of mixed Croat-Slovene parentage. Tito's efforts to smooth interethnic conflict by restraining Serbian centralism and chauvinism and drawing all Yugoslavs into a common front against Fascism were successful, and laid the basis for new federal arrangements, which were also, of course, a reaction to the centralism of the interwar period. Tito was himself fond of repeating what was later to become a cliched summary of the country's new structure: Yugoslavia had six republics, five nations, four languages, three religions, two alphabets and one party.[24] Overworked though it may be, the first and last points in this summary provide a useful framework for analysis of Yugoslavia's polity, and the remaining points (to which we turn in the next section) draw attention to the central characteristics of Yugoslav society.

Under Tito, several constitutions (1946, 1953, 1963 and 1974) were approved: each defined clearly the relationship between centre and periphery and each deepened the decentralization implicit at the outset, when the federal character of Yugoslavia was still conceived in imitation of Lenin's federal restructuring of the USSR. The new state was made up of six autonomous republics (Bosnia-Herzegovina, Croatia, Macedonia, Montenegro, Serbia and Slovenia), a gesture designed to recognize both its multinational character and the long-established borders that had been wiped out in the centralizing state established in 1918. In addition, two regions of Serbia (Kosovo-Metojija – later known simply as Kosovo – and Vojvodina) were given autonomy, and this was greatly extended in

1974. The areas and populations of the republics and provinces are indicated in Table 11.1.

The 1963 constitution introduced the practice of 'self-management', inaugurating a phase of economic liberalization and 'market socialism' which become a powerful myth for the West's liberal left. Economic liberalization called for greater transparency in decision making and for new forms of power sharing. But, although liberalization began far ahead of other communist states, political parties remained illegal until the late 1980s. Democratic reform followed, rather than preceded, the example of other East European countries.

The 1974 constitution marked a decisive step towards confederation, paving the way for an institutionalized political balance and a power-sharing 'government by consensus'. Tito himself attempted to prepare the country for post-Titoism by emphasizing decentralization and equality between the republics, which now obtained a veto over federal legislation: decision making required consensus among the republics, thus encouraging participation while preserving national unity. The constitution was thus a *tour de force* of balanced interethnic engineering to check the impending growth of Croatian and especially Serbian nationalism. It also set the basis for a rotating presidency in the post-Tito era: one representative of each of the six republics and of Serbia's two autonomous provinces would form a collective presidium, and the post of Federal President would rotate between them annually.[25] These provisions initially succeeded in their aim of preventing the return of Serbia's domination, but at the cost of weakening the Federal President's role.

TABLE 11.1
YUGOSLAVIA: AREA AND POPULATION BY REPUBLIC, 1981–91

Republic	Area	Population (000s)	
	km²	1981	1991
Serbia	88,361	9,314	9,779
Central Serbia	*55,968*	*5,705*	*5,809*
Kosovo	*21,506*	*1,574*	*1,956*
Voivodina	*10,887*	*2,035*	*2,014*
Montenegro	13,812	584	615
Croatia	56,538	4,601	4,784
Bosnia and Herzegovina	51,129	4,124	4,365
Slovenia	20,251	1,892	1,966
Macedonia	25,713	1,909	2,034
Total	255,804	22,425	23,543

Source: *Eastern Europe and the Commonwealth of Independent States 1992*. 1st edn. (London: Europa, 1992); 3rd edn. [for 1997] (London: Europa, 1996).

The constant rotation of leaders contributed to a sense of generalized inefficiency and excessive bureaucracy, a shortcoming that was later to be skilfully exploited by Milošević with his populist 'anti-bureaucratic' campaign, which was in reality an attack on the constitution.

Thus, even before Tito's death in 1980, the constitutional and political links holding Yugoslavia together had become looser. By 1974, the autonomy framework had created a situation in which each republic had become a semi- or quasi-sovereign entity. By now, the entire country was held together not merely by the Titoist *nomenklatura's* tight centralized control, but also by continuous negotiations and accommodation, resulting in an internal system of 'balance of power'.[26]

A potentially important counterbalance to the centrifugal tendencies of the constitution was the centralizing force of a unitary communist party (renamed the League of Communists of Yugoslavia in 1952). Although the party became organized along federal lines, and the various republican sections were able to achieve considerable autonomy in time, the dominance of the party's central committee long remained unchallenged. The party retained control over government appointments, notwithstanding the implications of this practice for economic reform and inter-republican cooperation. Unlike other communist parties, it was rather independent of Moscow, especially after 1948, when Tito unexpectedly broke with Stalin, pulling Yugoslavia out of the Cominform, the international communist organization (this also led to Yugoslavia's leading role in an international 'third force', the non-aligned movement, after 1956).

As the party became increasingly stratified between federal and regional organizations, however, its capacity to provide the cement to hold Yugoslavia's loose constitutional building blocks together became increasingly undermined. The Serbian party was the first to adopt a strong nationalist line, but in general all parties were able to incorporate demands emerging from grassroots movements, the most important of which was towards self-determination. In republics other than Serbia and Montenegro, the local communist parties reacted to the rise of Milošević by refusing to accept his policy. This led them to align themselves with powerful emerging mass movements in favour of democracy and self-determination. But, notwithstanding efforts to redefine themselves, the renamed communist parties were replaced in most republics by nationalist coalitions.

Nations and Minorities

The very idea that Yugoslavia had 'five nations, four languages, three religions and two alphabets' raises serious issues about Yugoslav statecraft. The challenge of listing the nations and the languages lies at the core of this difficulty. Identifying the three religions and the two alphabets is much easier. Originally, the five nations were the three mentioned in the original name of the state after 1918 (Serbs, Croats and Slovenes) plus the Macedonians and the Montenegrins. Recognizing the existence of a separate Macedonian nation (and language) was not unproblematic, but it seems to have been a genuinely positive gesture that was effective in reconciling the population of this contested region to the post-1945 state. The existence of a Montenegrin identity separate from a Serbian one depends largely on adherence to historical symbolism rather than to contemporary divisions in the domains of language, religion and culture. Census data show that most Montenegrins feel themselves not to be Serb.

On the other hand, what of the 'nations' not included in this list? Five of the Yugoslav Republics corresponded to one or other of the five nations just listed; but in the sixth, Bosnia-Herzegovina, the Serbo-Croatian speaking Muslim group (which constituted a plurality but not a majority of the population) was reluctant to accept the designation 'Serb' or 'Croat'; the recognition of a separate ethnic 'Muslim' nation (*narod*) followed. Furthermore, one of the largest minority groups, the Albanians, was not formally classified as a 'nation' at all; it was a 'national minority', and thus not entitled to its own republic. The Hungarians, too, were classified as a 'national minority'; like the Albanians, they had their 'own' state elsewhere, outside Yugoslavia's frontiers, and were entitled only to autonomy within Serbia.

Neither is the listing of Yugoslavia's languages easy. Adding Macedonian to Serbo-Croat and Slovene gives us a list of three Slavic languages. But most students of linguistics have seen Serbian and Croatian as no more than dialectal variants of the same language, Serbo-Croatian, differentiated most obviously by the fact that the latter, like Slovene, uses the Roman alphabet while the former typically uses a variant of the Cyrillic alphabet. Yet, even this distinction was sometimes blurred, as until 1991 the Montenegrins used mostly Cyrillic, and the Serbs used both alphabets.[27] The Bosnian Muslims preferred the Roman alphabet. Macedonian, a new language that has been developed most intensively in the twentieth century, also uses Cyrillic script. Once again, however, we need to note the numerical significance of speakers of certain non-Slavic languages, including Hungarian and especially Albanian.

This pen-picture of the national question in Yugoslavia may be completed by considering the importance of religion. In some cases, religious and linguistic frontiers reinforce each other strikingly: Slovenes tend to be of Catholic origin, for instance, Albanians are typically Muslim and Macedonians are Orthodox. But the Serbo-Croatian speaking population is divided by putative 'religion', which in these cases presents national boundaries more robust than those of language. We thus get a strong linkage between Croats and Catholicism and between Serbs and

Montenegrins and Orthodoxy, while Serbo-Croatian speaking Muslims tend to opt for a separate identity. However, religion was not a perfectly differentiating factor, since there were Catholic Serbs and Orthodox Croats, albeit in small numbers.[28] More important still, the official doctrine of atheism had affected religious beliefs in all three religions, though to different extents.

An indication of the national composition of Yugoslavia and its component parts on the very eve of its dissolution is given in Table 11.2 and the geographical distribution of the major nationalities is illustrated in Map 11.1. This shows the ethnic breakdown in each republic in 1991, though the census taken in this year is particularly problematic, as it was conducted during a state of war. It will be seen that only one republic, Slovenia, was substantially mono-ethnic (while only a negligible number

TABLE 11.2
YUGOSLAVIA: NATIONAL COMPOSITION BY REPUBLIC, 1991

Republic	Serb	Monte-negrin	Croat	Muslim	Slovene	Mace-donian	Yugo-slav	Other
Serbia	65.9	1.4	1.1	2.5	0.0	0.5	3.3	25.3(a)
Central Serbia	87.9	1.3	0.4	3.0	0.0	0.5	2.5	4.4
Kosovo	9.9	1.0	0.4	3.4	0.0	0.0	0.2	85.1(b)
Voivodina	56.8	2.2	3.7	0.3	0.0	0.9	8.7	27.4(c)
Montenegro	9.3	69.1	1.0	14.6	0.0	0.2	4.3	1.5
Croatia	12.2	0.2	78.1	0.9	0.5	0.1	2.2	5.8
Bosnia and Herzegovina	31.2	.	17.2	43.4	.	.	5.5	2.7
Slovenia	2.4	0.2	2.8	1.4	87.8	0.2	0.6	4.6
Macedonia	2.1	0.0	0.0	1.5	0.0	65.3	0.8	30.3(d)
All republics, 1991 (%)	36.3	2.3	19.8	9.9	7.4	5.9	3.1	15.3 (e)
All republics, 1981 (%)	36.3	2.6	19.7	8.9	7.8	6.0	5.4	13.3 (f)

Note: Due to widespread non-cooperation with the census by Albanians in Kosovo in 1991, the data reported here are not the 'official' census data. In the 'other' column, the figures include the following groups in the case of the respective notes: (a) Albanians 17.1%; (b) Albanians 81.6%; (c) Hungarians 16.9%; (d) Albanians 21.7%; (e) Albanians 9.2% and Hungarians 1.6%; (f) Albanians 7.7% and Hungarians 1.9%.

Sources: Federal Republic of Yugoslavia, *Statistical Yearbook of Yugoslavia, 1999* (Belgrade: Federal Statistical Office, 1999), and, for Albanians, Milovan Zivkovic and Milutin Prokic, 'Official Statistics on National Minorities', paper presented at the IAOS Conference on Statistics, Development and Human Rights, 4-8 September 2000, Montreux, Switzerland; available www.statistik.admin.ch/about/international/ zivkovic_final_paper.doc [2002-03-06]; Republic of Croatia, *Census of Population, Households, Dwellings and Farms 31st March, 1991: Population according to Ethnic Group by Settlement.* Documentation 881 (Zagreb: Central Bureau of Statistics, 1992); *Statistical Yearbook of the Republic of Slovenia 2001* (Ljubljana: Statistical Office of the Republic of Slovenia, 2001), available www.gov.si/zrs/eng/index.html [2002-03-05]; *Eastern Europe and the Commonwealth of Independent States 1997*, 3rd edn. (London: Europa, 1996).

of Slovenes lived outside their own republic). All the other Republics had sizeable minorities, and in one (Bosnia-Herzegovina) none of the three groups (Serbs, Muslims, Croats) actually had a majority.[29]

ETHNONATIONAL TENSIONS AND THE STATE

We have already referred to the relatively loose nature of the Yugoslav federation. Before exploring the separatist trends that broke the surface in a range of different contexts it should be stressed that there were also powerful forces working to hold the state together. One of these, the Communist Party, has already been discussed; indeed, it was precisely the weakening authority of the party, arising not only from ethnonational considerations but also from the collapsing prestige of communist ideals in the late 1980s, that facilitated the break-up of the state.

The second centralizing institution was the Yugoslav People's Army. In many countries, the military establishment is the sector most prone to use force as an answer to ethnic tensions. By definition, the military see themselves as defenders of the sacred unity of their 'fatherland', and the Yugoslav army was no exception. In this, the ethnic structure of the senior ranks of the army was both a strength and a weakness. Already in 1986, well before the break-up, 60% of the higher cadres and officer corps were ethnic Serbs.[30] Despite Tito's overall efforts to decentralize the country, the army stood as a lone exception and was one of the few institutions to remain heavily dominated by Serbs but committed to defend the territorial integrity of Yugoslavia.[31] The army was a unitary structure imbued by communist ideology; yet, notwithstanding its centralizing influence, there were powerful factors working in an opposite direction, and it is to these that we now turn.

Serbian Nationalism

Apart from the small principality of Montenegro (independent de facto since 1718 and de jure since 1878), Serbia was the first nation in the Balkans after Greece (1822) to fully enfranchise itself from the Ottoman 'yoke' (1878). It was thus also the least likely to renounce independence in the name of Yugoslav principles. As Seton-Watson put it, Serbia would not allow its 'strong wine to be dissolved in the weak water of Yugoslavia'.[32] The irredentist ambitions of the Serbs became manifest under the dictatorship of King Alexander, and Ivo Banac observed that during the first Yugoslavia the monarchy was seen as 'the visible symbol of Serbia's state continuity'.[33] Since the first Yugoslavia was centred on the Serbian monarchy in Belgrade, most Serbs considered the new state

MAP 11.1
YUGOSLAVIA: MAJOR NATIONALITIES BY REPUBLIC, 1991

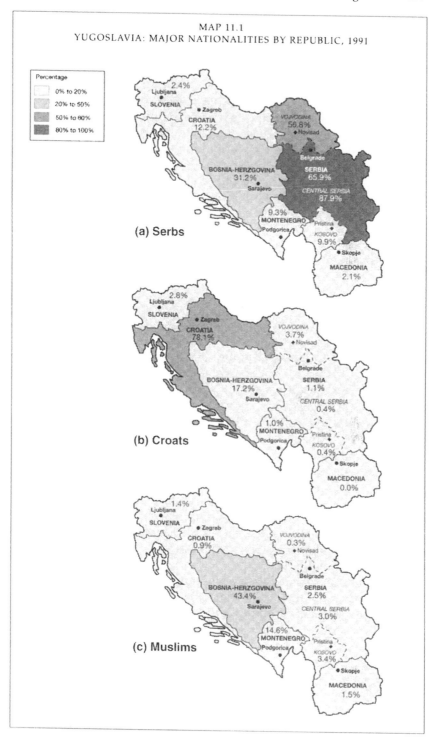

as a 'natural' successor and continuation of the old Kingdom of Serbia.

This attitude alienated non-Serbs, who took every available opportunity to rebel. Following German occupation during the Second World War, two major forces emerged in Serbia: the Yugoslav Communists led by Tito's partisans, and the Serbian nationalists, guided by Draza Mihailovich (1893–1946) and his *Chetnik* movement. The Serbian *Chetniks* were initially seen by the Allies as potential partners in the fight against the Germans, but, because of a degree of Serbian–Nazi collaboration, and the Chetniks' obvious incapacity to hold the country together, the Allies decided finally to support the Communist-led partisans.[34] The *volte-face* of Britain, a traditionally pro-monarchical country, created a sense of betrayal among Serbs everywhere, including the important Serbian diaspora in the UK, which remained nationalist and anti-communist to the backbone. This 'high treason' was particularly resented by the *Chetnik* sympathizers converging around the figure of the exiled king in London.

Croatian Nationalism

The roots of Croatian nationalism date back to the eighteenth century, when Croatia belonged to the Austro-Hungarian empire. Unlike nationalism elsewhere in Eastern Europe, Croatian nationhood was initially less founded on cultural or linguistic grounds than on historical memories of statehood. Insofar as one was a Croatian nationalist, linguistic identity was downplayed in favour of historical, ethnic and even religious elements. Serbo-Croatian had been early identified as a common language. In 1850, a literary agreement was signed accepting the *stokavian* dialect for a standard orthography for both Serbian and Croatian, while incorporating spelling reforms to draw them as close together as possible.[35] The Croatian elites, though accepting this compromise, were concerned more about historical continuity than language. Their emphasis was on 'historical rights' and on continuity with a suitable medieval state embodied in the *Triune* (three in one) Kingdom of Croatia, Slavonia and Dalmatia. Ethnic origin was initially less important than institutional continuity.[36]

In addition to the distinguishing features of religion and alphabet already discussed, different conceptions of what it meant to be a Croatian have been competing over the years. The 'Great Croatia idea' espoused by Ante Starčević (1823–96) was a re-interpretation of the nineteenth century 'Illyrian' (proto-Yugoslav) ideal in Croatian ultra-nationalist terms.[37] Differences between Serbs and Croats were alleged to be inherently biological. Paradoxically, however, as soon as a Serb accepted Croat national consciousness, such differences would no longer matter. Starčević and other authors simultaneously included Serbs in the Croat nation and branded them as an inferior race, but this ambiguity reflected the authors' implicit admission of the fundamental similarity between the two peoples.[38]

This theme was taken up by other Croat nationalists, who emphasized the allegedly huge biological differences between Serbs and Croats. As elsewhere, such an emphasis on race (which in the Balkans is coupled with a tendency towards politically motivated historical revisionism) served to compensate for the absence of clearly defined cultural markers between the two groups. As a consequence, nationhood was to be both inclusive and exclusive. The view was taken that 'the Croatian nation should include those who, in the course of time, had become Orthodox or Muslims ... It was possible to speak of those who lived in the region known as Serbia as "Serbs", but it was wrong to speak of Serbs as a nation'.[39]

Croats and Serbs cooperated in their struggles against Hungarian domination (in 1848 and in 1867–68). Liberal Catholics inspired by pro-Illyrian Bishop Strossmayer (1815–1905) and his People's Party were particularly open to collaboration with Serb leaders. In truly pre-ecumenical spirit, Strossmayer's goals were even more ambitious, as he strove to unite both churches, Roman Catholic and Serbian Orthodox, around a common Serbo-Croat language and a shared Yugoslav idea – despite Serbian nationalist accusations that this was a prelude to conversion to Catholicism and other fears of potential Croatian domination.

Following a period in which Croatian nationalism took a relatively moderate form through the Peasant Party in the first Yugoslavia, Croatia was conferred a form of 'statehood' as an Axis puppet state under the *Ustasha* regime of the dictator Ante Pavelić (1889–1959). In reality the country was divided into two spheres of influence, respectively German/Nazi and Italian/Fascist. In the German-controlled area some of the worst crimes against humanity occurred; as is widely known, the *Ustasha* regime was responsible for the murder of tens of thousand of Jews, Gypsies, Serbs and Croat opponents.

With the advent of Titoism, Croatian national sentiments did not die out. The economic prosperity of the 1960s eventually triggered demands for political freedom. The 'Croatian Spring' (1969–71) was a broadly based movement led by local Communists who demanded reform in the areas of politics (further decentralization and autonomy), culture (the recognition of Croatian language) and the economy (a call for transparency of economic transactions between republics). The movement was soon banned, resulting in the arrest of its main leaders – but it was to remain a catalyst for subsequent developments, especially after Tito's death. It ended in late 1971 with the arrest of large sections of the Croatian leadership (including the former partisan General Franjo Tudjman). In December 1971 a purge of the Croatian party began, followed by similar purges in Serbia, Slovenia and Macedonia and continuing well into 1972. From that moment until early 1991, Croatian nationalism was apparently mastered. But the party and the state skilfully incorporated some of the Croatian requests, as well as the concerns of other republics, culminating in the adoption of the 1974 constitution.

Slovene Nationalism

Though lacking a memory of past statehood, Slovenia was clearly identified as a nation on the basis of its language. Fearful of Germanization while still part of the Austro-Hungarian Empire, Slovenian elites emphasized linguistic and cultural distinctiveness, rather than history and ethnicity. This provided a shared 'core value' around which they could easily build a solid national identity; Slovene borders were clearly identifiable on quasi-objective criteria and hence became less disputable.[40] Slovene nationalism was thus under less pressure than nationalism elsewhere in the Balkans to stress interethnic boundaries. As a result, it manifested itself in a more peaceful character. This self-confidence was reinforced by the fact that Slovene remained an official language throughout Yugoslav history.

Within Socialist Yugoslavia, the Republic of Slovenia was one of the driving forces towards increasing decentralization. The second most prominent member of the old regime after Tito, Edvard Kardelj (1910–79), a Slovene deeply committed to federalist principles, was the main theoretician of the self-management doctrine. As the former head of Slovenia's partisans he enjoyed unparalleled respect, and following his role as Yugoslavia's first Vice-President (1945–53), he played a leading part in drafting all of the federal constitutions – in particular, that of 1974, whose main goal was to curb Serbian hegemonism.[41] Given its success in this respect, and due to its wealthier status, Slovenia was a crucial force in keeping the federation together. Secessionist aspirations were muted and toned down before the rise of Milošević. In other words, Slovenian elites had vested interests in the continuation of Yugoslavia as a unified country and as a single economic market, notwithstanding their complaints about what were in effect financial subsidies by Slovenia to poorer republics and the potential economic attractions of Slovene independence.

The Question of Bosnia-Herzegovina

Although Bosnia had experienced its own interethnic tensions over the centuries and these had survived in certain districts, a rich tradition of diversity, pluralism and tolerance developed there over many centuries and flourished until quite recently, only to be shattered at the close of the millennium.[42] A Bosnian state was created in the twelfth century and reached its apogee under King Tvrtko I (second half of the fourteenth century). The medieval neo-Manichaean religion of the Bogomils had its centre in Bosnia. Bosnia's pluralist heritage in terms of syncretic movements and 'religious bridge building' dated back at least to the late Middle Ages.[43] In the contemporary period, everyday practices and traditions of consensus were echoed in the political sphere by coalition building and a custom of pragmatic compromise.[44] Being one of the most ethnically diverse republics, Bosnia-Herzegovina was seen as the crucible of ethno-national accommodation in Yugoslavia and the litmus test of supranational multiethnicity.

In 1971, the Muslims of Bosnia-Herzegovina were elevated to full national status, from national minority to constituent nation (*narod*), although the new status was constitutionally enshrined only in 1974. By the early 1990s, local dynamics appeared to be contributing to the emergence of a new Bosnian identity, a blending of people from Muslim, Serbian and Croatian backgrounds, in a highly secularized society where intermarriage was increasingly the norm. The older bridge-building tradition was reinforced under Tito: each group was treated equally, while official persecution against all three religions faded after 1950. Although state-sanctioned atheism persisted and had a lasting effect in undermining the religious basis of society, religiously-derived identities re-emerged in the 1990s as a consequence of ethnic essentialism. Religion played a largely symbolic role, since official atheism had left a strong secular mark on society: 40 years of atheist propaganda succeeded in substantially erasing religious beliefs, but this only resulted in reinforcing formerly 'religious' boundaries that were now devoid of theological or normative content. The conflict that subsequently developed can hence be described as a war between Catholic atheists, Orthodox atheists and Muslim atheists. A secularized form of 'religious belonging', referring mainly to ethnicity and descent, had become the only widely-shared and binding element used to differentiate Serbs from Croats and others.[45]

Other Forms of Nationalism

While in the early 1990s world attention was focused on the war between Belgrade and its three northern republics, other tensions appeared not far below the surface. As Yugoslavia was disintegrating, the Macedonians were faced with an unwelcome dilemma: whether to remain within what would now be an overwhelmingly Serb-dominated Yugoslavia or face the risks (both external, given long-standing Greek claims, and domestic, in view of the size of the Albanian minority) of pursuing independence. For Montenegrins, too, the relationship with Serbia would in future be fundamentally different. But even within Serbia itself storm clouds were gathering, as tensions with the Albanian population of Kosovo grew.

Macedonian nationalism has been visible since at least 1894 (with the establishment of the Internal Macedonian Revolutionary Organization), and a separate Macedonian language was envisaged around that period amongst the Macedonian diaspora, notably in St. Petersburg (1902). True to its Leninist principles, already by 1924 the Communist Party of Yugoslavia had promised Macedonians the right of self-determination, and in 1934 a Communist Party conference voted for the establishment of a separate Macedonian Party. Following the partisan victory, a Macedonian state was proclaimed on 2 August 1944. The government of the People's Republic of Macedonia was set up in 1945 and soon, as part of Yugoslavia, adopted a constitution (1946) with Macedonian as the official language. In 1967 a Macedonian Academy of Arts and Sciences and an autocephalous Macedonian Orthodox Church were created, marking substantial recognition of the distinct character of the republic.

The position in Montenegro was rather different. Ethnically, Montenegrins are not distinguishable from Serbs, but memory of past statehood is strong. Under Austro-Hungarian tutelage, Montenegro remained an independent principality and achieved full independence in 1878. However, it was occupied by Austria during the First World War, and King Nikola I fled to Italy. The power vacuum was immediately filled by Belgrade's monarchy, which annexed the country despite widespread popular resistance culminating in the so-called Christmas Uprising (7 January 1919) – a rebellion that persisted until at least 1926.

With its predominantly Albanian population but deep roots in the historical consciousness of the Serbs as a core part of the original Serbian monarchy, Kosovo was also in a special position. Recognition of the area's special status within Serbia, first as an autonomous region, then as an autonomous province, failed to resolve the problem. The 1974 constitution granted Kosovo more autonomy, weakening Serbia's capacity to intervene. Tension along the Serbia–Kosovo line spilled over into violence in 1981, however, and the relationship with Belgrade remained tense. In an important sense, one of the first battles in the war that resulted in the break-up of Yugoslavia took place there, when, in 1989, Serbian President Milošević in effect abolished Kosovo's autonomy. This was written into the Serbian constitution of 1990 – which also ended the autonomy of Vojvodina – notwithstanding resistance from the local Albanian population and protests from the other republics.

THE PATH TO DISSOLUTION

The circumstances that finally led to the collapse of the old Yugoslavia shared some similarities with parallel processes elsewhere. On the one hand, the collapse of communism took place at an uneven pace in the various regions, providing additional ideological fuel to an escalating ethnonational conflict. On the other hand, the international community belatedly began to show a disposition to offer recognition to fragments of former multinational states, an attitude that had traditionally been resisted because of fear of a 'domino effect'.[46] The distinctive feature of the Yugoslav case, however, was the new nationalist drive within the Serbian core of the state and the reaction that this evoked within the peripheral regions, topics to which we now turn.

Discontent in the Centre

A key date in the process of Yugoslavia's break-up was September 1986, when the first draft of a Serbian nationalist *Memorandum* appeared, with signatures by the major Serbian intellectuals. This had originated in an earlier decision of the Serbian Academy of Arts and Science and was part of a plan backed by the army, police, state security services and the church. The document's secessionist content hid behind a veil of unitarist rhetoric, but was nevertheless palpable. The Serbs were portrayed as victims of 'genocidal terror' by the Albanians, of 'economic exploitation' by the Slovenes, of cultural assimilation by the Croats, of religious conversion by the Muslims, and of systematic historical impairment by the Titoist regime – including an alleged attempt to replace the Cyrillic alphabet with Latin script and the supposed stealing of Serbian writers by 'others'.[47] The undertone was also strongly irredentist; as Noel Malcolm states, 'the fundamental argument of the Memorandum was that the "Serb people" throughout Yugoslavia was a kind of primary entity, possessing a unitary set of claims and rights which transcended any mere political or geographical division. It was the pursuit of that "integrity" which would eventually destroy Yugoslavia'.[48]

Slobodan Milošević's ascent to power as President of the Central Committee of the League of Communists of Serbia (and, thus, as de facto leader of the republic) in 1987 marked a significant political advance for this perspective. A turning point in the translation of Serbian nationalism into political reality took place in 1989, when Milošević abolished Kosovo's and Vojvodina's autonomy, engendering intense protest in all other republics. Finally, Serbian secessionism culminated with the approval in 1990 of the Republic of Serbia's constitution, in which the word 'Yugoslavia' is not mentioned once.[49]

The Albanian demographic explosion, that is the high fertility of Albanians in comparison to Serbs (their birth rate being many times higher), exerted a crucial emotional impact on the emergence of present-day Serbian nationalism. In Tito's years, remarkable economic aid had been channelled into Kosovo, making it the most heavily subsidized Yugoslav region, but this development strategy did not result in a change of basic demographic patterns. This fear of demographic decline was mostly derived from rapid urbanization and de-ruralization.

Although it was also experienced in Croatia and by other ethnic groups, it was only in Serbia that it was systematically and unremittingly utilized to stir up the flames of radical nationalism.

Another ingredient encouraging the Serbian campaign was the fact that the Serbs were indigenous to seven of the eight federal units; as in the case of the Croats, Albanians and Bosnians, their alleged territorial contiguity was broken by what nationalists perceived as Tito's 'imposed' boundaries. If the Serbs had made up an absolute majority of the population, perhaps Serbian secessionism would have been undermined, as other roads, such as assimilation, hegemonic control and religious conversion would have been seen as feasible or practicable in order to secure their dominant position.

Dissent in the Peripheries

The rise of Milošević and his assault on provincial autonomy caused great concern amongst all other republics. With control of Kosovo and Vojvodina now in Serbian hands and Montenegro generally sympathetic, Milošević could normally count on the support of four of the eight members of the Yugoslav collective presidency. But it was in the most economically advantaged and wealthy republic, Slovenia (the most vociferous defender of Kosovo's autonomy and an active campaigner for Albanian rights) that these concerns began to translate into concrete political propositions. The first stirrings of a more overtly independence-minded attitude took place in the capital, Ljubljana. An amendment to the constitution adopted in 1989 by the Slovene Assembly transformed the republic into a quasi-sovereign state, whose parliamentary laws were given precedence over those of Belgrade in several areas. The first postwar multiparty parliamentary elections (April 1990) were won by *Demos*, a coalition of democratic anti-regime forces, campaigning on a self-determination ticket. In a gesture of symbolic continuity, Milan Kučan, candidate of the former Communist Party, was elected President of the Republic (while the Christian Democrat Lojze Peterle became head of the government).

In response to Belgrade's threats, Slovenia adopted a declaration of sovereignty, with its new constitution implying the transformation of Yugoslavia into a confederation. In retaliation, Belgrade introduced customs duties on Slovene products. This was followed by a referendum (23 December 1990), in which 88.2% of Slovene voters opted for independence (voter turnout was 93.2%). The results were officially declared on 26 December 1990 – now annually celebrated as Independence Day. The Slovene Assembly began transferring powers from federal to republican institutions in March 1991 and unilaterally declared its independence on 25 June 1991 (along with Croatia, as discussed below). The outcome was a short, sharp war with a decisive outcome. On 27 June 1991, the

Yugoslav army set out across Slovenia to seize border posts. But this advance was halted by Slovenian territorial defence units, which also blockaded Yugoslav army barracks. The war lasted ten days and resulted in nearly 100 casualties. On 7 July, the Yugoslav army desisted from further military attacks. At the encouragement of the European Community, Slovenia accepted a moratorium on independence, and international bodies continued for some time to treat Yugoslavia as a single entity (it was only three months later that Ljubljana took over control of its own borders and introduced its own currency). The Yugoslav army withdrew its last soldier from Slovenian soil on 25 October 1991.[50]

While military resistance to Slovenia's secession was ultimately limited, the case of Croatia suggests a quite different strategy on the part of Belgrade: the seizing of as much land as possible before external forces would agree on a new international order. The initial goal of the Yugoslav army was to destroy all forms of resistance in Croatia and to bring it to heel. Under the nationalist leadership of Franjo Tudjman, Croatia soon mobilized on the pattern of Slovenia. A two-round election (April–May 1990) was won by the Croatian Democratic Union (HDZ), a Christian Democrat and nationalist coalition campaigning for the republic's self-determination within its current boundaries. The HDZ achieved an absolute majority in the Parliament after Tudjman was elected President (8 April 1990). Belgrade's response to the nationalist advance in Croatia was to mobilize Serbian minorities living in Croatia along ethnic lines (particularly in Knin, Krajina and Eastern Slavonia). The war thus took an irreversible ethnic turn. On 17 August 1990 a Belgrade-inspired revolt by Croatian Serbs in Knin started the armed conflict and by 17 March 1991 a Serbian Republic of Krajina declared its independence. This resulted in the first attempts to establish ethnically pure areas. Serbian *ethnic* secession preceded Croatia's declaration of independence on 'non-ethnic' *territorial* grounds (25 June 1991).

In a nutshell, Belgrade's position was that Slovenia could opt, if it so chose, to exit immediately from the federation, whereas Croatia could only exit after radically changing its boundaries along ethnic lines. It is important here to stress the *'could'* factor: the possibility of accepting external secession *faute de mieux* as a masquerade for promoting central secession. When the Yugoslav army attacked Slovenia, it did so on the grounds that it had to protect the frontiers of Yugoslavia, rather than to protect a Serbian ethnic minority there. The legitimizing principle was entirely different in the two cases. In Slovenia, it could be presented as a last-ditch attempt to hold Yugoslavia together. In contrast, the attack on Croatia could be more easily identified as a Serbian separatist assault to destroy what remained of the federation from within. Its results were the first cases of ethnic cleansing carried out by Yugoslav army-supported militia groups against non-Serbs, mostly Croats.

The position in Bosnia-Herzegovina was yet more complex. Unlike other Yugoslav republics, it was never allowed to develop an ethnically exclusive identity. Balkan nationalism is typically predicated on an ethnic basis; but as Bosnia was a multiethnic republic, it encountered serious problems of legitimacy from the outset. Only a civic form of nationalism could have held the republic together. However, at the beginning of post-communist transitions civic institutions were by definition fragile; and since ethnonationalism is almost everywhere a more powerful force than civic nationalism, Bosnia suffered from a major drawback.

Largely in response to developments in Slovenia and Croatia, Bosnia declared its independence on 1 April 1992. Immediately, a Belgrade-inspired rebellion of ethnic Serbs led by Radovan Karadjić was sparked off. Shortly before this, all Bosnian Serbs in the Yugoslav army had been transferred to units stationed in Bosnia. In this way, Belgrade 'handed over to Karadjić an army of 80,000 soldiers fully equipped with sophisticated weapons which they used to target civilians while Milošević contrived to pay and supply this army by stealth so that he could deny having any connection with it'.[51] Boundary building became an extremely ferocious process, since many of those defined *post-facto* as 'Muslims' were formerly identified as either Serbs or Croats, or as some combination of the two. Years of regional mobility between the republics had fostered many mixed marriages, where the partners and often their offspring did not consider themselves as either Serbs or Croats, but simply as Serbo-Croats, Bosnians, or even 'Yugoslavs'.

By the early 1990s a Croatian project to partition Bosnia-Herzegovina had already begun on the pattern of its Serbian 'role model'.[52] This resulted in atrocious acts of ethnic cleansing and in the destruction of symbols of interethnic understanding by Croatian ultra-nationalists, most notoriously the bridge of Mostar. With the further eruption of the conflict, couples of mixed nationality and individuals of heterogeneous identity were compelled to make ethnic choices; in a pattern common in such war situations, national belonging was forced upon average citizens by violence. Mixed marriages and their offspring, however reluctant to accept ethnic categorization, were forced to opt for just this. Ethnic 'cleansing' followed, amounting to precisely what the words imply.

The final outcome in Bosnia was largely dictated by the international community. Already on 29–30 June 1991, following the Yugoslav army's intervention in Slovenia, German chancellor Helmut Kohl and other leaders had proposed the recognition of the seceding republics at a European summit. However, this was strongly opposed by the USA, Britain and France.[53] The latter countries supported the preservation of a Serbian-dominated Yugoslavia, while allegedly keeping an eye on the possibility of new federal arrangements.[54] The delayed process of recognition is often identified as a key factor in the war escalation. Slovenia and Croatia finally became members of the United Nations on 22 May 1992, along with Bosnia-Herzegovina.[55]

With the structure of the old state substantially destroyed, the last stages in its disintegration proceeded. Following a referendum, Macedonians voted for independence on 8 September 1991. The Republic adopted a new constitution on 17 November 1991, but it was recognized internationally only in 1993, its name posing a particular difficulty in the eyes of Greece. Its official name is now the 'Former Yugoslav Republic of Macedonia' (FYROM), a label designed to sidestep the difficulty that Macedonia is also the name of a Greek province. As the century drew to a close, relations between the Macedonian authorities and the large Albanian minority deteriorated dangerously, though the arrival of NATO forces in 2001 helped to contain tensions.

This left Montenegro as the only other republic, apart from Serbia, in what was now a two-member Yugoslav federation. Constitutionally, Montenegro is on a par with Serbia, but the political and demographic imbalance is huge (the population of Serbia outnumbers that of Montenegro by about 15 to 1). Notwithstanding close cultural and historical links between Montenegro and Serbia, Montenegro, too, began to edge towards independence, but this was opposed by the West. Under encouragement from the European Union, Serbia and Montenegro began to negotiate a new federal relationship, one that would replace the structures of the 'third' Yugoslavia.

But, as is well known, there were problems not only between the republics and Belgrade, but also within the Republic of Serbia itself. Here the central problem was that of Kosovo, whose autonomy had been brought to an end in 1989–90. Efforts by the Kosovo assembly to establish the province's independence failed, and in the mid-1990s confrontation with the Milošević regime escalated. Ethnic Albanian militants were able to mobilize and arm fairly effectively, engaging in a guerrilla war in response to Serbian attempts to control the situation by means of forced population transfers. This culminated in NATO involvement in the conflict and a decisive defeat for Belgrade in 1999, with Kosovo being placed under UN administration and becoming virtually a UN protectorate.

CONCLUSION

Two major sets of factors led to the break-up of Yugoslavia: internal factors and international ones. These can in turn be subdivided into secondary sub-factors. This chapter has mostly focused on the internal dimension of the break-up – the international dimension has been addressed in separate studies.[56]

The key internal factor was the advent of a new form of power at the centre – the rise of Milošević and Serbian nationalism. The movement personified by Milošević proposed a radical form of ethnic irredentism whose effect would be to destroy the constitution from within. With the undermining of the constitution and its delicate system of balance of power, there had in effect been a Serbian *coup d'état*. Given the high level of national consciousness in other republics, notably Croatia and Slovenia, this development was highly subversive of existing Yugoslav institutions.

This is not the place to review in detail the international factors that formed the backdrop to the collapse of Yugoslavia. Initial western support for the preservation of Yugoslavia under Milošević changed very slowly. Initially it was unanimous, but a few countries soon began to break ranks and to distance themselves from Belgrade. In a process that I have documented elsewhere, this resulted in tensions between western governments as some began to abandon the principle of maintaining the integrity of Yugoslavia as a member of the international community.[57] As is well known, Milošević survived the break-up, until the US-led NATO intervention. It could indeed be argued that the American century, inaugurated by Woodrow Wilson' s massive propaganda to win Europe's hearts and minds, concluded with the defeat of the Serbs in Kosovo and the end of Milošević in 1999.

ACKNOWLEDGEMENTS

I wish to express my warmest thanks to Crawford Young and Branka Magas for comments on earlier drafts, and to John Coakley for his editorship.

NOTES

1. The theory of 'secession by the centre' as applied to former Yugoslavia has been thoroughly discussed in Daniele Conversi, 'Central Secession: Towards a New Analytical Concept? The Case of Former Yugoslavia', *Journal of Ethnic and Migration Studies*, Vol.26, No.2 (2000), pp.333–56. The internal and international dimensions of the break-up have been explored in Daniele Conversi, *La desintegració de Iugoslàvia* (Barcelona/Catarroja: Editorial Afers-El Contemporani, 2000).
2. For a critique of the 'clash of civilizations' paradigm and the 'ancient-hatred' theory, see Daniele Conversi, 'Resisting Primordialism and other *-isms*', in Daniele Conversi (ed.), *Ethnonationalism in the Contemporary World: Walker Connor and the Theory of Nationalism* (London: Routledge, 2002).
3. See Philip Abbott, 'The Lincoln Propositions and the Spirit of Secession', in Percy B. Lehning (ed.), *Theories of Secession* (London: Routledge, 1998).
4. See Christopher Hitchins, *The Trial of Henry Kissinger* (London: Verso, 2001).
5. Ralph R. Premdas, 'Secessionist Movements in Comparative Perspective', in Ralph R. Premdas, S.W.R. de Samarasinghe and Alan B. Anderson (eds.), *Secessionist Movements* (London: Pinter, 1990), p.13.

6. John Roper, cited by Milan Popovic, 'Before the Storm', *Montenegrin Mirror*, September 2000, accessed at www.ndc.cg.yu/eng/DOCUMENTS/Mnmirror.pdf [2002-03-18].

7. Following decolonization, many studies dealing with the topic appeared. Sir Ivor Jennings wrote about the difficulty of universally applying the principle of self-determination – quoted in John McGarry and Brendan O'Leary (eds.), *The Politics of Ethnic Conflict Regulation: Case Studies in Protracted Ethnic Conflict* (London: Routledge, 1993), p.12. Perhaps the best known is Rupert Emerson's analysis of the break-up of empires and secession; see *From Empire to Nation: The Rise to Self-Assertion of Asian and African Peoples* (Cambridge, MA: Harvard University Press, 1960).

8. Walker Connor, 'Self-Determination: the New Phase', *World Politics*, Vol.20 (1967), pp.20–53, reprinted in Walker Connor, *Ethnonationalism: The Quest for Understanding* (Princeton: Princeton University Press, 1994). See also Anthony D. Smith, ' Separatism and Multi-Nationalism', in *National Identity* (Harmondsworth: Penguin, 1991), Ch.6, pp.123–42; and Colin Williams (ed.), *National Separatism* (Vancouver: University of British Columbia Press; Cardiff: University of Wales Press, 1982).

9. Crawford Young, 'Biafra, Bangladesh and Southern Sudan: the Politics of Secession', Ch.12 of *The Politics of Cultural Pluralism* (Madison: University of Wisconsin Press, 1976); Donald L. Horowitz, 'The Logic of Secessions and Irredentas', in Donald L. Horowitz, *Ethnic Groups in Conflict* (Berkeley: University of California Press, 1985). For a more recent development of Horowitz's approach, see Donald L. Horowitz, 'Self-Determination: Politics, Philosophy, and Law', in Ian Shapiro and Will Kymlicka (eds.), *Ethnicity and Group Rights* (New York: New York University Press, 1997).

10. Harry Beran, 'A Liberal Theory of Secession', *Political Studies*, Vol.32 (1984), pp.21–31. For a recent re-statement of this early approach, see Harry Beran 'A Democratic Theory of Political Self-Determination for a New World Order', in Lehning, *Theories of Secession*.

11. Ioann Lewis, 'Introduction', in Ioann Lewis (ed.), *Nationalism and Self-Determination in the Horn of Africa* (London: Ithaca Press, 1982); Benjamin Neuberger, *National Self-Determination in Post-colonial Africa* (Boulder, CO: Lynne Rienner, 1986); Alexis Heraclides, *The Self-Determination of Minorities in International Politics* (London: Frank Cass, 1992), pp.21–32.

12. James Mayall, *Nationalism and International Society* (Cambridge: Cambridge University Press, 1990).

13. On the respective areas, see Michael Hechter. 'The Dynamics of Secession', *Acta Sociologica*, Vol.35 (1992), pp.267–83; Robert A. Young, 'How do Peaceful Secessions Happen?', *Canadian Journal of Political Science*, Vol.27, No.4 (1994), pp.773–92; and Will Kymlicka, 'Is Federalism a Viable Alternative to Secession?', in Lehning, *Theories of Secession*.

14. McGarry and O'Leary, *Politics of Ethnic Conflict Regulation*, p.14.

15. Donald L. Horowitz, '*Irredentas* and Secessions: Adjacent Phenomena, Neglected Connections', *International Journal of Comparative Sociology*, Vol.33, Nos.1/2 (1992), p.118–30; Naomi Chazan (ed.), *Irredentism and International Politics* (Boulder, CO: Lynn Rienner; London: Adamantine Press, 1991).

16. Horowitz, '*Irredentas* and Secessions'.

17. Allen Buchanan, *Secession: The Morality of Political Divorce from Fort Sumter to Lithuania and Quebec* (Boulder, CO: Westview Press, 1991), pp.51, 151–62; see also Allen Buchanan 'The International Institutional Dimension of Secession', in Lehning, *Theories of Secession*.

18. Similarly, Beran argues that 'enclaves are anathema in contemporary politics', even though a few remnants (Monaco, San Marino, Vatican City) persist in present-day Europe; Harry Beran, 'A Democratic Theory of Political Self-Determination for a New World Order', in Lehning, *Theories of Secession*, p.51.

19. On the break-up of Czechoslovakia, see Jiri Musil (ed.), *The End of Czechoslovakia* (Prague, Budapest: Central European University Press, 1995).

20. See Don Ray and Ralph R. Premdas, 'The Canadian West: A Case of Regional Separatism', and Alan B. Anderson, 'Ethno-nationalism and Regional Autonomy in Canada and Western Europe', in Premdas, Samarasinghe and Anderson, *Secessionist Movements*.

21. On the contrary, the Amhara have developed over the centuries a certain assimilationist tradition; see Christopher Clapham, *Transformation and Continuity in Revolutionary Ethiopia* (Cambridge: Cambridge University Press, 1988), pp.1–30.

22. See Ruth Iyob, *The Eritrean Struggle For Independence: Domination, Resistance, Nationalism, 1941–1993* (Cambridge: Cambridge University Press, 1995); Dan Connell, *Against All Odds: A Chronicle of the Eritrean Revolution* (Lawrenceville, NJ: Red Sea Press, 1997); Roy Pateman, *Eritrea: Even the Stones Are Burning* (Lawrenceville, NJ: Red Sea Press, 1997).

23. Heraclides, *Self-Determination*, p.25

24. Some variants added that Yugoslavia had 'seven neighbours' (or, sometimes, 'seven frontiers'); others replaced 'one party' by 'one country' or 'one goal'.

25. Branka Magas, *The Destruction of Yugoslavia: Tracking the Break-Up 1980–92* (London: Verso, 1993), p.291.

26. Valerie Bunce, *Subversive Institutions* (Cambridge: Cambridge University Press, 1999); Sabrina P. Ramet, *Balkan Babel: The Disintegration of Yugoslavia from the Death of Tito to the Insurrection in Kosovo* (Boulder, CO: Westview Press, 1999).

27. Thomas F. Magner, 'Yugoslavia in Sociolinguistic Perspective: Introduction', *International Journal of the Sociology of Language*, No.52 (1985), pp.5–8.

28. For instance, Seton-Watson mentions a small community of Catholics in Southern Dalmatia who considered themselves to be Serbs; Hugh Seton-Watson, *Nations and State: An Enquiry into the Origins of Nations and the Politics of Nationalism* (London: Methuen, 1977), p.134.

29. The first constitution of the Federative People's Republic of Yugoslavia (1946) already recognized Bosnia and Herzegovina as a state of equal citizens – Serbs, Muslims and Croats.

30. According to James Gow, *Legitimacy and the Military: The Yugoslav Crisis* (London: Pinter; New York: St. Martin's Press, 1992), pp.139–52. See also Robin Alison Remington, 'State Cohesion and the Military', in Melissa K. Bokovoy, Jill A. Irvine and Carol S. Lilly (eds.), *State–Society Relations in Yugoslavia, 1945–1992* (New York: St. Martin's Press, 1997), pp.61–78.

31. See Tom Cushman, *Critical Theory and the War in Croatia and Bosnia* [Donald W. Treadgold Papers in Russian, East European and Central Asian Studies, No.13, 1998] (Seattle: University of Washington Press/Henry M. Jackson School of International Studies); and Conversi, 'Central Secession'.

32. Quoted in Branimir Anzulovic, *Heavenly Serbia: From Myth to Genocide* (London: Hurst; New York: New York University Press, 1999).

33. Ivo Banac, *The National Question in Yugoslavia: Origins, History, Politics* (Ithaca, NY: Cornell University Press, 1984), p.145.

34. On Serbian–Nazi collaboration, see Philip J. Cohen, *Serbia at War with History* (College Station, TX: Texas A&M University Press, 1996) and Walter R. Roberts, *Tito, Mihailovic, and the Allies, 1941–1945*, new edn. (Durham, NC: Duke University Press, 1987).

35. Damir Kalogjera, 'Attitudes towards Serbo-Croatian Language Varieties', *International Journal of the Sociology of Language*, No.52 (1985), pp.93–110. Thus, the other two Croatian dialects, *kajkavski* (spoken in an area of Northern Croatia contiguous to Slovenia) and *ćakavski* (spoken in Istria and the islands of the Dalmatian coast), which were less similar to Serbian, were marginalized; Banac, *National Question*, pp.77–81; Elinor Murray Despalatovic, *Ljudevit Gaj and the Illyrian Movement* (Boulder, CO: East European Quarterly; New York: Columbia University Press, 1975).

36. On the language issue, see Walker Connor, *The National Question in Marxist-Leninist Theory and Strategy* (Princeton: Princeton University Press, 1984); Frits W. Hondius, *The Yugoslav Community of Nations* (The Hague: Mouton, 1968); James W. Tollefson, 'The Language Planning Process and Language Rights in Yugoslavia', *Language Problems and Language Planning*, Vol.4, No.2 (1980), pp.141–56; James W. Tollefson, 'Language Policy and Power: Yugoslavia, the Philippines, and Southeast Asian Refugees in the United States', *International Journal of the Sociology of Language*, No.103 (1993), pp.73–95. Even by early 2002, the federal constitution of the third 'Yugoslavia' (in effect, of Serbia-Montenegro) mentioned Serbian as the official language, while the Serbian constitution paradoxically speaks of Serbo-Croatian.

37. The Illyrian movement proposed a union of all Southern Slavs (Yugo-Slavs); among its inspirers were the Croatian writer Ljudevit Gaj (1809–72), a precursor of Yugoslavism and collaborator with the Bosnian Serb language scholar Vuk Karadjic (1787–1864). It is significant that a square in Zagreb was named after Ante Starcevic in 1990 as part of a wider revisionist plan; see Srdjan Trifkovic, 'The First Yugoslavia and the Origins of Croatian Separatism', *East European Quarterly*, Vol.26, No.3 (1992), pp.345–70; Slavenka Drakulic, 'The Smothering Pull of Nationhood', *Yugofax*, No.6 (1991), p.3. According to some, this was one of a host of semiconscious choices implemented by Franjo Tudjman's nationalist government in order to 'invite' Serbian repression; see also Tom Gallagher, *Outcast Europe: The Balkans, 1789–1989: From the Ottomans to Milošević* (London, New York: Routledge, 2001).
38. Trifkovic, 'First Yugoslavia', pp.365–6.
39. Seton-Watson, *Nations and States*, p.134. The role played by opposition has been crucial in the construction of both Serb and Croat national identities. As Trifkovic ('First Yugoslavia', p.366) points out, even to an Ustasha (supporter of the Nazi-puppet state created during the Second World War) 'the Serb' was 'an integral part of his Croatness. Without him, Croatdom could not be defined, let alone practiced'.
40. Joseph Paternost, 'A Sociolinguistic Tug of War between Language Value and Language Reality in Contemporary Slovenian', *International Journal of the Sociology of Language*, No.52 (1985), pp.9–30; Tollefson, 'Language Policy'.
41. Carole Rogel, 'Edvard Kardelj's Nationality Theory and Yugoslavian Socialism', *Canadian Review of Studies in Nationalism*, Vol.12, No.2 (1985), pp.343–57
42. Noel Malcolm, *Bosnia: A Short History* (New York: New York University Press, 1994).
43. H.T. Norris, *Islam in the Balkans: Religion and Society Between Europe and the Arab World* (London: Hurst, 1994), pp.263–8.
44. Robert J. Donia and John V.A. Fine, *Bosnia and Hercegovina: A Tradition Betrayed* (New York: Columbia University Press; London: Hurst, 1994).
45. Daniele Conversi, 'Nationalism, Boundaries and Violence', *Millennium: Journal of International Studies*, Vol.28, No.3 (1999), pp.553–84.
46. For a challenge to the international security assumption that secessionist movements are likely to spawn a generalized 'domino effect', see Daniele Conversi, 'Domino Effect or Internal Developments? The influences of international events and political ideologies on Catalan and Basque nationalism', *West European Politics*, Vol.16, No.3 (1993), pp.245–70.
47. See also Nenad Dimitrijevic, 'Words and Death: Serbian Nationalist Intellectuals 1986–1991', in Andras Bozoki (ed.), *Intellectuals and Politics in Central Europe* (Budapest, New York: Central European University Press, 1998), pp.119–48.
48. Noel Malcolm, *Bosnia: A Short History*, p.207.
49. This should be distinguished from the constitution of Serbia and Montenegro, adopted on 27 April 1992, and paradoxically known as 'constitution of the Federal Republic of Yugoslavia'.
50. Slovenia's new constitution (adopted on 23 December 1991) established a democratic republic with conventional political institutions. Two autonomous national communities, the Italian and the Hungarian (less than 1% of the population) are represented in the National Assembly and have been granted recognition in other areas, including the right to form their own organizations and institutions (in the media, economic, cultural and scientific research fields, education in their own language, and the right to develop relations with the respective 'motherlands').
51. Laura Silber and Allan Little, *The Death of Yugoslavia* (London: Penguin Books/BBC Books, 1995), pp.245–50.
52. Attila Hoare, 'The Croatian Project to Partition Bosnia-Hercegovina, 1990–1994', *East European Quarterly*, Vol.31, No.1 (1997), pp.121–34.
53. Daniele Conversi, *German-Bashing and the Breakup of Yugoslavia*, Donald W. Treadgold Papers in Russian, East European and Central Asian Studies, No.16 (Seattle: University of Washington Press/Henry M. Jackson School of International Studies, 1998); Wolfgang Deckers, 'Two Souls, Twin Realities: German Foreign Policy from Slovenia to Kosovo', *Central Europe Review*, Vol.2, No.26 (2000), [online version: www.ce-review.org/00/26/deckers26.html]; Ramet, *Balkan Babel*; Brendan Simms, *Unfinest Hour:*

How Britain Helped to Destroy Bosnia (London: Allen Lane/Penguin Press, 2002); Karl Cordell, 'Germany's European Policy Challenges', *Regional and Federal Studies*, Vol.10, No.2 (2000), pp.141–5.

54. Gallagher, *Outcast Europe*; Sabrina P. Ramet and Letty Coffin, 'German Foreign Policy toward the Yugoslav Successor States, 1991–1999', *Problems of Post-Communism*, Vol.40, No.1 (2001), pp.48–64.

55. The attitude of the international community to Bosnian independence was ambiguous, and recognition was half-hearted; on the consequences, see Mark Thompson, *A Paper House: The Ending of Yugoslavia* (New York: Vintage Books, 1993); Branka Magas, *The Destruction of Yugoslavia: Tracking the Break-Up 1980–92* (London: Verso, 1993); Simms, *Unfinest Hour*; David Rohde, *Endgame: The Betrayal and Fall of Srebrenica, Europe's Worst Massacre since World War II* (New York: Farrar, Straus and Giroux, 1997).

56. Conversi, *German-Bashing*; Daniele Conversi, 'Moral Relativism and Equidistance: British Attitudes to the War in Former Yugoslavia', in Tom Cushman and Stipe Mestrovic (eds.) *This Time We Knew: Western responses to the War in Bosnia* (New York: New York University Press, 1996).

57. Conversi, *German-Bashing*; Simms, *Unfinest Hour*.

12

Conclusion

Towards a Solution?

JOHN COAKLEY

The contributions that constitute the core of this volume provide sufficient material for us to seek to generalize, in conclusion, about the character of the state's response in the territorial domain to the issues raised by ethnic conflict. An obvious approach is to begin with the issue raised in the introduction: the menu of options open to the state. Following an elaboration of this point, the discussion turns to the theme of this book, as developed in the chapters that have undertaken case studies of the territorial management of ethnic conflict. Looked at from the perspective of the state elites, the question is this: what patterns are there in approaches to the management of ethnic problems, and how may the selection of one of these rather than another be accounted for? Finally, a short concluding section seeks to highlight some common themes that emerge from the book.

STATE AND TERRITORY: THE OPTIONS

In the context of persistent and powerful ethnic demands, the state has a number of options open to it.[1] Some of these are essentially or entirely non-territorial. Those which do have a territorial component may all be classified in terms of the pattern of division of power between a political centre and sub-state units. One of the more systematic explorations of these relationships is Duchacek's 11-point scale, useful as a framework for describing this pattern. At one extreme lies totalitarian centralism, the ultimate stage in unrestricted elite control; following this, we have a less thoroughgoing variant, authoritarian centralism. The next three stages correspond with different types of unitary state: those which are pluralistic but centralized, those which are moderately decentralized, and those which are highly decentralized. At the mid-point in the scale lies federalism. This is followed by formal confederation, and then by permanent regional organizations or common markets. The last three

FIGURE 12.1
DUCHACEK'S TERRITORIAL ORGANIZATION SCALE

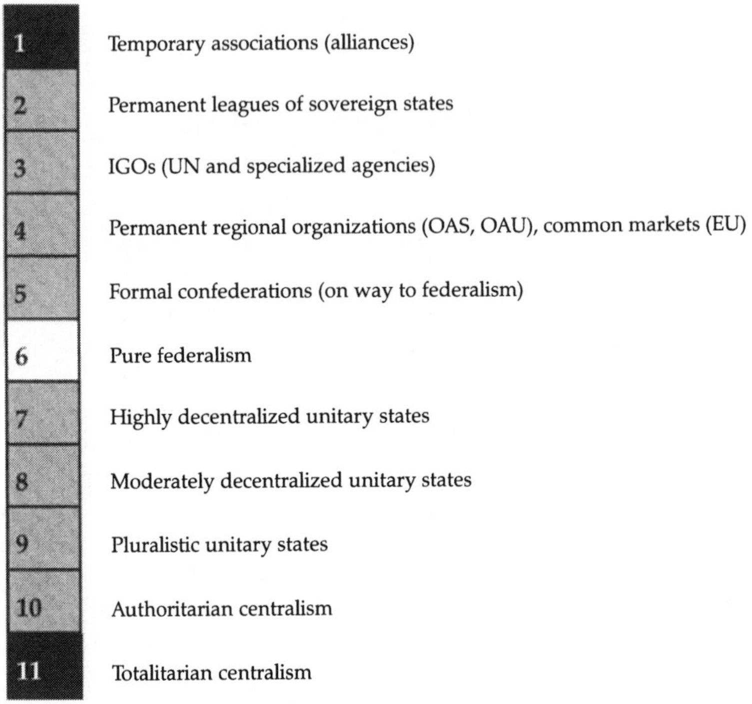

1	Temporary associations (alliances)
2	Permanent leagues of sovereign states
3	IGOs (UN and specialized agencies)
4	Permanent regional organizations (OAS, OAU), common markets (EU)
5	Formal confederations (on way to federalism)
6	Pure federalism
7	Highly decentralized unitary states
8	Moderately decentralized unitary states
9	Pluralistic unitary states
10	Authoritarian centralism
11	Totalitarian centralism

points on the scale are made up of different kinds of relationships between sovereign states: inter-governmental organizations such as the United Nations and its specialized agencies; permanent leagues of states; and temporary associations of states.[2]

For present purposes, this scale is unnecessarily refined. In examining the relationship between the political centre and its territories, we may therefore group some of these positions (specifically, the first three, the second two, and the last four) to produce a five-class typology; some of the resulting categories are renamed. The first category is that which ignores territory and seeks alternative solutions to problems of ethnic conflict, solutions that rest on an assumption of territorial *centralism*. Second, the state may in varying degrees acknowledge the existence of alternative territorial power centres within the state itself. In such cases, the relationships between the state and sub-state territories may for convenience be placed in three categories: *regionalism*, where the state has devolved power to subordinate units, *federalism*, where a balance is maintained between jurisdictions at the two levels, and *confederalism*, where the central state exists only because of powers devolved on it by its component members.[3] These categories shade into each other, and particular states may well have evolved in one or other direction between regionalism and confederalism, but the distinction in principle remains clear: whether ultimate authority remains at the central level (regionalism) or at the level of the component units (confederalism), or is shared between the two (federalism). We also need to consider the end of the road as far as devolution from the centre is concerned: political *disintegration*. Finally, it should be noted that not all relationships between the centre and the component units are symmetrical; we need to consider also the special case of *asymmetrical* relationships between a centre and adjacent territories.

It should not be assumed, however, that elites are unconstrained in determining the shape of ethnic policy. The geography of ethnic settlement patterns plays a crucial role in ruling out certain types of approach and in facilitating others. Effective territorial approaches imply a minimum degree of spatial segregation, but in concrete cases this is commonly absent. Indeed, we may identify three models of the spatial distribution of ethnic groups (let us assume for simplicity that there are only two groups, and that they are of equal size).

The first model is one of complete intermingling: the two communities are distributed randomly in the same geographical space, and no area, large or small, is inhabited entirely by members of one community. There is, of course, no perfect example of this, but contemporary Northern Ireland comes close to illustrating this pattern (see Map 8.1), as did Bosnia in the former Yugoslavia. Although the population is far from being randomly distributed, both communities are spread throughout the entire territory. Thus, the 1991 census showed that none of the

FIGURE 12.2
THREE MODELS OF ETHNIC CONTACT

(a) Intermingling	(b) Ghettoization	(c) Separation

Note: Each model is based on the assumption that there are two ethnic groups of equal size, represented respectively by the colours black and white.

province's 556 electoral wards was entirely monoethnic (though in one ward in Belfast's suburbs there were only three Catholics, while in another ward in the centre of Derry there was only a single Protestant).[4] At a higher level of aggregation, only two of Northern Ireland's 26 districts had a minority of less than 10%; and most districts (17) had a minority greater than 25%.

Next is the intermediate position: neither group has a coherent territory, but there is no intermingling at local level. Instead, the two communities are entirely ghettoized, with points of contact at a minimum. Pre-partition Cyprus comes close to illustrating this model. According to the 1960 census, a clear majority of the island's 635 villages (463) were entirely monoethnic, and many of the remainder were almost entirely so. If we move to a higher level of territorial organization, however, we find that none of the island's six districts had a Turkish majority. Indeed, the Turkish minority was represented in all districts, its share of the population ranging from 12.6% to 24.4%.[5]

In the third model there is complete, large-scale territorial segregation, with the two communities occupying entirely separate territories. Belgium comes close to illustrating this pattern. According to the 1947 census (the most recent official statistical source in this area), most communes were overwhelmingly dominated by one language group; eight of the nine provinces had very small minorities (the proportion of French speakers in the four Flemish provinces ranged from 3.1% to 8.6%, and the proportion of Dutch speakers in the four Walloon provinces ranged from 0.3% to 2.7%); and even the mixed province of Brabant was divided between a French-speaking south (3.9% Dutch) and a Dutch-speaking north (5.7% French, if we ignore the capital territory of Brussels).[6] Overall, as Liesbet Hooghe shows in chapter 4 of this volume, French speakers accounted for only 4.9% of the population in Flanders and Dutch speakers for only 2.0% in Wallonia (see also Map 4.1; for similar patterns in Canada and former Czechoslovakia see Map 2.1 and Map 10.2). In Cyprus, following the massive re-settlement of Greeks in the south and Turks in the north that accompanied partition in 1974, spatial polarization became even starker than in Belgium. By 2002, the proportion of Turks in the (southern) Republic of Cyprus was 0.1%, and of Greeks in the north 0.2%.[7]

Centralism

The refusal to concede territorial recognition of ethnic diversity may, then, arise from a pattern of ethnic intermingling that makes spatial devolution of power impossible. But it may also reflect a type of 'melting pot' assimilationist strategy. This 'Jacobin' solution has been characteristic of certain European states (with France since the Revolution as the prototype), and it was the general model followed with great success in the English-, French-, Spanish- and Portuguese-dominated colonies and former colonies of the western hemisphere, and with lesser success in the African and Asian colonies of European powers. The notion of assimilation to the dominant culture appears to be by far the most common strategy of all for dealing with problems of ethnic diversity. In the contemporary western world, it is more obvious in cases where it is still resisted (such as Turkey) than where it has substantially succeeded (such as several states of western Europe); but there are other parts of the world (such as central and eastern Europe) where policies of overt assimilation have been discontinued decades ago.[8]

In other cases, perhaps because subordinate minorities are seen as unthreatening or as too threatening, or perhaps for some other reason, the state may decide to concede certain collective rights of a non-territorial kind. There are several ways in which it can do this, none of them precluding additional measures of territorial devolution. Essentially, these approaches may be either politico-administrative or linguistic-cultural, and, in each of these cases, they may apply to all of the state (including its centre) or to particular domains only. The following strategies may, then, be identified:

1. A sharing of central resources takes place within the context of politico-administrative centralization of power. This may be implemented as some kind of informal ethnic incorporation by the introduction of ethnic quotas, as in Sri Lanka and Pakistan, or it may take the form of fully-fledged *consociationalism*, with elaborate post-sharing and compromise arrangements, as in Belgium and Switzerland.[9]

2. Politico-administrative power is decentralized along non-territorial lines. Since the exercise of real political power normally requires the fixing of territorial frontiers, the extent of power that may be devolved to authorities whose jurisdiction is non-territorial is limited. This mechanism is often referred to as *cultural autonomy*, and it was applied in inter-war Estonia after 1925 and in contemporary Belgium (though in the latter case it has been overshadowed by the parallel state reform along territorial lines).[10]

3. The same linguistic-cultural provisions apply to the whole state, but these permit the use of more than one language in interactions with the public authorities. The provisions themselves may vary from case to case, with such countries as Finland and Canada in the most liberal position, where there is, at least in theory, *state-wide bilingualism* and all citizens are entitled to use their own language with the central administration. The existence of *state-wide diglossia* is rather different: here a single language is recognized as valid for interaction with the

central state (whether an external language, such as English and French in many African states, or an internal one, such as Russian in the former Soviet Union), even if a majority of the population uses a different language for domestic and other local purposes.

4. Separate linguistic regimes operate in different parts of the state. Certain regions may be granted the right to use a local language for official purposes in a system of *inter-regional bilingualism,* as in Italy, Spain and the United Kingdom. Additional examples are Finland and Belgium, which illustrate the fact that the language regimes in operation at state and sub-state levels may be independent of each other.

In some circumstances, the depth of the division between ethnic groups may be so profound that no accommodation of the type described above is possible. Instead, a variety of ingenious devices is used by the dominant group to liaise with the estranged minority in areas where, for practical reasons, some kind of contact is essential. The 'shadow games' played by Palestinian representatives in Jerusalem with city officials from 1967 to the late 1980s are one such example (see Alex Weingrod's account in chapter 6 of this volume). The 'incident centres' operated by Sinn Féin with British government approval in Northern Ireland during 1975 are a second. In each case, minority grievances on practical matters could be referred to the state by a mechanism that did not commit the minority to recognizing the legitimacy of the regime.

A final ethnic-management instrument that has proved valuable to the central state is the party. In single-party states, the official party may seek to reflect ethno-territorial differences (as in the former Soviet Union) or to paper them over (as in Kenya and Tanzania), but in each case the party has played a powerful role in ethnic integration. Thus, the Communist Party of the Soviet Union, the Kenya African National Union and the Revolutionary Party (CCM) in Tanzania played significant roles in ethnic conflict management.

Regionalism

The regionalist strategy is based at least in part on the premise that ethnic protest can be undercut by the concession of at least a symbolic degree of regional autonomy. Arguments relating to economic planning and administrative rationality are also normally present, however, and regionalization is typically embarked on as a measure designed to resolve a number of problems.[11] Its essential principle is the devolution of authority from the centre to regional authorities; its essential weakness lies in the fact that the centre can limit or withdraw this autonomy, subject only to the political feasibility of this course of action.

Regional devolution varies both in the extent to which it recognizes sub-state ethnic boundaries and in the degree of power devolved. Three large western European states, France, Italy and Spain, began to follow their own distinctive paths in this direction in the 1970s, but with rather different outcomes.[12] In Italy and in Spain a great deal of power was devolved, and early recognition was given to units where there were elements of ethnic distinctness – in Italy, to Sicily and Sardinia already in the 1940s, and in Spain to Catalonia and the Basque Country in 1980.[13] In fact, Spain ultimately became in effect a federal-type state, with the powers of the regions (called autonomous communities) being constitu- tionally copper-fastened (see below). In France, by contrast, fewer powers were devolved, though there was significant recognition of ethnic factors if the regional reforms there are viewed against the back- drop of the Jacobin tradition of the French state.[14] Examples of two types of sleight of hand by central governments in their regionalization exper- iments are afforded by these cases, both calculated to undercut regional ethnic distinctiveness. On the one hand, in Italy the concession of autonomy to the region of Trentino-Alto Adige in 1948 represented the creation of a new region, in which overwhelmingly Italian-speaking territory was added to the German-speaking province of South Tyrol to dilute the German character of the new entity. In Spain, in a rather different approach, Valencia was not included in the new region of Catalonia, while Navarre was excluded from the Basque Country; and in France the *département* of Nantes, historically part of Brittany, was excluded from the new region of Brittany.[15]

Federalism

While federalism bears some similarity to regionalism, there is an essen- tial difference: powers are not merely devolved by the centre, but a divi- sion of powers between the two levels (together with a definition of concurrent powers) is formally written into the constitution.[16] Federalism is not necessarily a response to ethnic diversity, and, indeed, many of the best-known examples of federal government are in states whose popu- lations are mono-ethnic, or almost so. To take them in descending order of population size, the examples of the United States, Brazil, Mexico, Germany, Argentina, Venezuela and Australia illustrate this. In other cases, such as Austria, the state is now virtually mono-ethnic, even though the multinational nature of pre-1918 Austria was one of the reasons for the institutionalization of this form of government.

In other cases, a federal arrangement was either adopted initially or was retained to deal with problems of ethnic diversity.[17] We may detect three patterns of relationship between ethnic territories and federal units of area. In the first, the ethnic divisions cut across the boundaries of the federal units; there is little correspondence between ethnic and political boundaries. Malaysia is an example: the principal ethnic groups (Malays,

Chinese and Indians) are dispersed over the 12 states. India and Pakistan might at one time have been additional examples, but both have been moving in the direction of the third category described below.

In the second type, minority ethnic groups are given autonomy but they may be divided among several federal units, and the dominant ethnic group is also so divided. Spain, to the degree that it may legitimately be described as 'federal', is one example: it has 17 regions (12 Castilian, two Catalan and one Galician, with two other areas: Valencia with a 49% Catalan-speaking population, and the Basque Country, approximately 25% Basque speaking). Canada is another example: its 13 provinces and territories are mainly English-speaking but one, Quebec, is French-speaking (another, New Brunswick, has a large French-speaking minority and is officially bilingual) and the new territory of Nunavut, created in 1999, has an Inuit majority. Similarly, Switzerland, though formally a confederation, is in reality a federation of 26 cantons and half-cantons; of these, 19 are German-speaking, six French-speaking and one predominantly Italian-speaking.

Third, in a few cases the boundaries of the ethnic groups correspond with those of the federal units. The former Soviet Union, with its 15 union republics, offers such an example. The former Yugoslavia is a more ambiguous case: five of the six republics (Slovenia, Croatia, Montenegro, Serbia and Macedonia – that is, all except Bosnia and Herzegovina) corresponded with varying degrees of accuracy to the territories of ethnic nationalities (though the distinction between Montenegrins and Serbs is not clear-cut, and the ethnic Muslims were a minority of 40% in their 'own' republic, Bosnia and Herzegovina). The former Czechoslovakia, with a clearly defined federal division between Slovakia and the Czech lands, is a better example; and, apart from the issue of control of the capital territory of Brussels, the partition of Belgium between Flanders and Wallonia is yet another case. These last examples draw attention to the exceptional difficulties that arise in dyadic federations, where there are only two territorial units, often of similar size and power, and therefore more likely to be engaged in a polarized struggle than in the case of federations made up of larger numbers of units.[18]

Confederalism

Although confederalism may be defined relatively easily in principle, it appears in practice to be an intermediate stage between federalism and decomposition into independent states. The fact that 'pure' examples are so difficult to find points to the essential instability of this strategy of dealing with ethnic tensions: confederations appear to be half-way houses from federation to independence, or, in the opposite direction, from international organization to federation.

There are three recent examples of the first of these types of confederation, each of them discussed elsewhere in this volume: the former Soviet Union, the former Yugoslavia and the former Czechoslovakia. In each case, efforts were made to halt a slide from federation to disintegration by devising a looser form of association. The Commonwealth of Independent States, linking most of the former Soviet republics, initially appeared to be the most successful of these initiatives, but has receded into relative insignificance.

There are several obvious examples of movement in the opposite direction. The Swiss 'Confederation' may, indeed, once have lived up to its name, but in recent years (and, perhaps, since 1848) it has in effect been a federation. German unity in 1871 was preceded by several confederal experiments, with the German Confederation (1815–66) as the longest-lasting of these. In the western hemisphere, the Confederacy of the United States of America (1781–89) was an important predecessor of the United States as we know that entity today, but even after the latter had come into existence in 1789 the real source of power – whether this lay in Washington, DC, or in state capitals – continued to be a matter of dispute. It was only after the civil war of 1861–65, as significant for the definition of the character of the political system as the Swiss *Sonderbund* war of 1847, that it became clear that ultimate power lay in the centre, and that the political system was a federal rather than a confederal one.[19] Confederalism may also have been a stage in the rapid evolution of the European Economic Community into the European Community and then into the European Union.

Disintegration

It is hardly possible to go further in yielding to ethnic minority demands than the actual concession of the minority's right to sovereign statehood. Historically, of course, the route to statehood has depended on organic territorial evolution over a long time-span, with military conquest by an emerging centre and dynastic union of existing hereditary possessions as very common paths, and free association of adjacent territories in pursuit of common interests as an occasional factor. But once this process had largely absorbed all territories likely to acquire statehood by this means – essentially, by the nineteenth century – other routes became more prominent.[20] The disintegration of empires and secession from other multi-national states became increasingly common phenomena. The process of European withdrawal from colonial territories overseas was one aspect of this, especially in the middle of the twentieth century; rather more traumatic was the disintegration of empires made up of adjacent territories and built up over a long time-frame, as in the case of the dissolution of the Habsburg monarchy in 1918, of the Ottoman Empire even earlier than this, and in 1991, of the Soviet Union (whose ancestor, the Russian Empire, had survived remarkably well in a territorial sense after 1917–18).[21]

Fragments of disintegrating empires are frequently anxious to establish their complete sovereignty with respect to their former ruling powers, but looser associations of states sometimes take the place of former empires. Thus, the British Empire became transformed into the Commonwealth of Nations (1931), though some countries, such as Ireland and Burma, eventually preferred to remain aloof. Efforts on the part of France to emulate this model through the creation of a French Union (later, French Community) that would include the territories of the former colonial empire were rather less successful. The Soviet Union's space on the map was occupied by the Commonwealth of Independent States (1991), though, again, some countries – notably, the Baltic republics – chose an entirely separate path.

Asymmetrical Relationships

The discussions above have by default rested on an assumption of symmetry: that the centre relates to all of its regions in essentially the same way. Even classical federalism is, however, not normally strictly symmetrical; certain regions may be given more powers than others,[22] the capital territory may fall outside the ambit of the federal arrangement, and there may be special territories, such as virgin lands, which are administered directly by the federal authorities.[23] Indeed, an early analysis of types of federalism identified an asymmetrical model as an alternative to the more typical symmetrical model, recognizing the fact that different territories might relate to the centre in different ways.[24]

Asymmetrical approaches to the territorial management of ethnic conflict are common, and rest on the assumption that, while it may be possible to treat the regions of the 'core' territory of the state in a uniform way (for example, by subjecting them directly to central government), peripheral ethnic dissent can be undermined by the concession of some kind of special status to peripheral areas, normally by the introduction there of an extra layer of government. In principle, the division of powers between such areas can follow the same pattern as in regional, federal and confederal arrangements.

The most obvious examples of asymmetrical autonomy fall into the first of these categories: the central authorities have conceded autonomy to certain regions, but the survival of this autonomy rests on the continued willingness of the central authorities to tolerate it. The special position of Northern Ireland within the United Kingdom from 1921 to 1972 is one example; in the same category fall the five regions of Italy to which certain powers were devolved before state-wide regionalism was implemented in 1970, and Catalonia and the Basque Country in Spain before a general federal-type structure was introduced. The relationship of Slovakia to Czechoslovakia before 1968 and of Kosovo and Vojvodina to the Yugoslav republic of Serbia were similar, and particularly elaborate schemes of asymmetrical devolution were implemented in the former Soviet Union. In addition to symmetrical federalism at union level, certain union republics devolved power to autonomous republics, autonomous regions and autonomous areas. Thus, there were 16 autonomous republics within the Russian federation, two in Georgia and one each in Azerbaidzhan and Uzbekistan; there were five autonomous regions in the Russian federation and one each in Georgia, Azerbaidzhan and Tadzhikstan; and there were 10 autonomous areas, all in Russia. Similarly, India has introduced elements of asymmetrical autonomy in its contentious relationship with the state of Jammu and Kashmir.

Examples of asymmetrical territorial distributions of power in which the centre permanently cedes power to the sub-state level are more difficult to find. In principle, Russia's autonomous republics and Serbia's autonomous areas fall into a category corresponding with federalism, but in practice in such arrangements the relative power of the centre tends to be so great that the autonomy of the units to which power has been devolved cannot be guaranteed. The manner in which Serbia managed to undermine the autonomy of Kosovo and Vojvodina illustrates this. One of the few examples of a territory where there is a firm, constitutionally guaranteed form of asymmetrical federalism is the Åland Islands, which have had autonomous status within Finland since 1920, though this arrangement rests not merely on the Finnish constitution but on international guarantees. It is even more difficult to find examples of asymmetrical relationships that correspond to confederalism. These examples tend to be micro-states, ranging from the Isle of Man's relationship with the United Kingdom (with formal sovereignty vested in the British crown) to Monaco's association with France (where the principality remains formally independent).

GENERAL PATTERNS

Having provided a framework for analysis of the territorial options open to states in dealing with their ethnic minorities, we may go on to try to generalize about the experience in the case studies undertaken in this volume. Broadly speaking, we may detect three general approaches (entailing a further grouping of the territorial options discussed in the previous section): attempts to preserve as much as possible of the power and authority of the central state (though perhaps arranging for some forms of non-territorial devolution, or power sharing), attempts to reconcile minority demands with the integrity of the state by embarking on a policy of territorial restructuring, and attempts to buy peace (or attain other objectives) by allowing the state to disintegrate. It may be difficult to place a particular case unambiguously in one of these categories. The priorities of elites may change radically over time, different sections of the elite may advocate different approaches, and there may be cases that fall into more than one category, or perhaps outside all of them.

Defending the State

A very characteristic reaction by dominant elites to challenges from minorities is to seek to incorporate their elites in the state structure, especially if the minorities possess such political and other resources that they can be neither ignored nor repressed. The long-running, violent conflicts in Israel, Northern Ireland, South Africa and Sri Lanka indeed suggest that certain subordinate groups possess or possessed sufficient military capacity to threaten the stability of the state. In two of these cases, Northern Ireland and South Africa, a peace process of relatively long duration created negotiating space within which the outlines of a settlement could be hammered out; in the other two, it is too early to assess the prospects for a political settlement.

In South Africa, as Anthony Egan and Rupert Taylor show, the initial response of the minority white regime under apartheid was to follow a twin track: on the one hand, to hive off the African population into 'homelands' or 'bantustans' where they would be encouraged to accept autonomy or 'independence'; on the other, to incorporate the Coloured and Indian populations by offering each of them its own house of parliament, alongside that of the Whites, which would continue to be the dominant one. This reflected the reality that, like pre-1974 Cyprus, South Africa was characterized by a form of ghettoization; but the government was sufficiently powerful to contemplate changing the realities of geography by encouraging the 'resettlement' of the African population in the bantustans, thus producing a pattern more akin to that of large-scale spatial separation, at least between Africans and the rest of the population. Not surprisingly, with the dismantling of apartheid, the new system reacted strongly to both prongs of this approach. On the one hand, the new constitution of 1996 provided for a system that fell well short of federalism, though the new provinces were given considerable powers; and the redrawn provincial boundaries gave priority to physical and administrative criteria over ethnic ones. Second, the new constitution also reacted to the consociational tendencies of the old regime (consociationalism, indeed, had acquired a negative reputation given its use as a prop for apartheid); individual equality before the law and majority rule were the guiding principles of the new order. Constitutionally, then, the central state was strengthened; White minority rule sustained through policies of ethnic devolution (territorial and non-territorial) was replaced by the force of universal, equal suffrage that brought the African population into a position of political dominance.

Although the Northern Ireland peace process was strongly influenced by the South African model, there were important respects in which its thrust was quite different. If we look first at Northern Ireland as a self-contained entity, majority rule had been the preferred formula of the Unionist (Protestant) ruling group from the establishment of the regime in 1921 down to its collapse in 1972. This formula guaranteed political power over the 35% Catholic minority. The key strand in the 1998 agreement represented a reversal of this approach: the new Northern Ireland administration was essentially consociational, with parliamentary strength being translated into seats in the government in accordance with the d'Hondt principle. But, as Joseph Ruane and Jennifer Todd point out, Northern Ireland cannot simply be seen as a self-contained entity: its majority feels British and wishes to remain within the United Kingdom, while its minority stresses its Irish links. The spatial intermingling of the two populations (though modified by a degree of ghettoization in larger urban areas) militates against any kind of internal territorial solution; but the external associations of the two communities have encouraged another, very imaginative, territorial approach. In a second strand, the 1998 agreement provided for the creation of a set of all-Irish bodies that would promote cooperation between Northern Ireland and the Republic of Ireland and provide an outlet for the Irish identity of the community. In a third strand, it also provided for a British-Irish Council linking the two islands, a development of particular interest to the unionist majority. It should also be pointed out that reference to 'majority' and 'minority' is hazardous: Catholics are now close to 50% of the population, and another provision of the 1998 agreement allows Northern Ireland to leave the United Kingdom and join the Republic, if a majority so wishes – an unusual indication by a state of willingness to allow a portion of its territory to secede freely.

Given the profound differences between Northern Ireland and South Africa, and the further distinctiveness of a third case, Israel, the tendency for inter-continental links between these cases to be perceived and articulated strongly is striking. In the summer of 2002, many Israeli flags were to be seen in the Protestant districts of Belfast, while Palestinian flags were flown on the Catholic side. These same Catholic districts had earlier supported the ANC in South Africa, just as many Protestants had supported the National Party regime there. Indeed, the dilemma for Israeli Jews shows some similarities to that of Northern Ireland Protestants. In both cases, the dominant community is of immigrant origin (though long-established in Northern Ireland, and much more recent in the case of Israel).[25] In Israel, too, the demographic lead of the Israeli Jewish population is insecure. As Alex

Weingrod shows, Jews account for about 55% of the population within the borders of the territories under the control of the government. Within Israel proper, the Israeli Palestinian minority is sufficiently small (19%) not to pose a threat, and is politically marginalized. In the West Bank, where the bulk of the Palestinian population is concentrated, Jewish settlements have contributed to a steady change in the spatial relationship between the two populations, and have made more feasible the prospects of a bantustan-type approach, by which Palestinians would be allowed 'independence' in a set of separate, mainly land-locked entities. Securing agreement on the shape of a territorial carve-up is likely to prove formidably difficult; but even that would leave other questions unanswered, with the issues of control over Jerusalem and the right of Palestinian refugees to return as further major stumbling blocks. Asher Arian summarized the relationship between Israeli Jews and the Palestinian territories eloquently, in a way that also epitomized the historical choice facing Whites in South Africa and Protestants in Northern Ireland:

> The dilemma is stark – if the territories are annexed, what is to become of the inhabitants? It is inconceivable that they not be granted full citizenship rights, a fact that would sharply tip the demographic trends and endanger the Jewish state in the sense of having a Jewish majority. Tampering with voting rights would be unacceptable, and depleting the population would be unconscionable. Continuing the military rule is also inappropriate; as the issue festers, it becomes more difficult to solve.[26]

In Sri Lanka, too, the prospects for an ultimate settlement remain uncertain. Here, consociational elements, fitfully present since independence in 1948 and surviving until the early 1980s, helped to accommodate the Tamil minority, as Jeyaratnam Wilson shows. The degree of spatial polarization of the two main communities has been sufficient to allow the Tamils to demand autonomy for their own area in the North, but population movement and state-sponsored colonization policies have undermined the ethnic cohesiveness of this area. As in the three other areas discussed above, relationships between the communities have been aggravated by historical disparities in the socio-economic status of the various groups, with one group – not necessarily the majority – being seen as associated with traditional privileges (South African Whites, Northern Ireland Protestants, Israelis, Tamils). Although the groups are in varying degrees spatially concentrated, the pursuit of a territorial settlement in these cases has been aggravated by the fact that the contending groups typically wished to control much more land than they actually inhabited – normally, the whole of the territory that they shared with the other group or groups.

Restructuring the State

In a second group of cases, the state structure lends itself to the accommodation of ethnic dissent, or it can at least be overhauled with a view to doing so. Of all such structures, it is perhaps the federal one that is best equipped to cope with ethnic problems. Many instances could be cited, but Switzerland offers an apposite example. There, the 'Jura problem' was substantially resolved by allowing the Jurassiens to establish their independence – from the canton of Bern! The Jura was then duly welcomed into the Swiss Confederation in 1979 as a new canton.

In Belgium, as Liesbet Hooghe shows, the state was fundamentally restructured, explicitly to take account of the ethnic (or communal) problem. Although its ancient liberal democratic constitution endorsed the principle of majority rule, this in effect copperfastened the position of dominance of Belgium's French-speaking elites (themselves linked to a linguistic community that was smaller than Belgium's Flemish-speaking majority). The position changed only slowly in the middle of the twentieth century and several strands of reform took off in 1970. One of these was an increasingly explicit consociationalism; the second was a form of communal or non-territorial autonomy, with the creation of separate cultural councils for the two communities; and the third was regional reform. While consociationalism has continued since then at the level of the central state, the most dramatic developments have been at the other two levels. Given the relatively clear-cut spatial polarization of the two communities (if we ignore the issue of Brussels), it is not surprising that community-based devolution on non-territorial lines has been difficult to achieve: the Flemish-speaking community and the region of Flanders, for instance, are virtually identical in territorial extent, and it made sense for the Flemish cultural council and the regional council of Flanders to merge in 1980. Indeed, territorial reorganization of the Belgian state went well beyond mere regionalization; in a series of further constitutional reforms, it had been transformed into fully-fledged federalism by 1993.

If the federalization of Belgium followed an intensification of the ethnic problem, the relationship in Canada was the reverse of this. The federation came first; the Quebec issue, at least in its current intense form, followed. Of course, the roots of the conflict in Canada lie in part in the very different histories of the country's various parts, and in particular in the distinctive legacies of British and French rule. Unlike the United States, where former Dutch, French and Spanish territories fell victim to the cultural hegemony of the British presence, Francophone culture managed to thrive in Canada, partly because of a departure from British cultural policy elsewhere that permitted this outcome. The federal system acted as a sympathetic framework within which the Francophone population of one province, at least, could protect and cultivate its heritage. Later pressure for a higher degree of autonomy from Canada, or for complete independence, raised a number of issues, as is clear from Jean Laponce's discussion: for minorities within Quebec, for Quebec's relationships with the broader Francophone community in Canada, for this community's relationship with the Canadian federation and its bilingual status, and for the character of Canadian federalism. It also raised the issue of symmetry within federations: may certain component units be more independent than others, or should concessions to one unit be accompanied by concessions to all? This difficulty remains unresolved, and Quebec's right to independence continues to be much more vigorously contested than the right to secession in other cases discussed in this book (especially in central and eastern Europe).

The case of Pakistan raises yet further questions. Here the formal federal structure dated from independence, but it was the very creation of the state itself (rather than its internal structure) that was designed to respond to a particularly intense problem: the relationship between Hindus and Muslims on the Indian subcontinent. This problem remains unresolved, as the continuing conflict over Kashmir shows. Charles Kennedy focuses on another set of fascinating relationships: between the various ethnic groups within Pakistan, the provinces within which they are concentrated, and the state itself. Although there have been numerous central government plans to decentralize authority in the state, and intense, if episodic, demands for greater provincial autonomy, Pakistan has thus far remained in reality a highly centralized state. The current military government's attempt to devolve authority to Pakistan's 104 largely mono-ethnic districts, the 'Local Government Plan', remains highly contested, as do the decentralization provisions embedded in the proposed constitutional reforms promulgated in mid-2002. The unfortunate reality is that two of Pakistan's other problems overshadow the question of ethnic devolution (though each of them has implications for this): the conflict with India over Kashmir, and the spillover effects of the war in Afghanistan in a context where ethnic groups straddle the border with Pakistan.

Dissolving the State

Finally, in three chapters in this book authors examine cases of state dissolution. The three cases have a number of obvious features in common. First, all three parent states were multinational entities in which ethnic boundaries were extremely clearly drawn at the social level. We can measure precisely and reliably the relative size of the different ethnic communities, in a way that would be impossible in western Europe and that is difficult outside Europe.[27] These differences were also reflected in the territorial structure of the state, whose federal system sought, in varying degrees, to give political expression to the interests of the major national groups. Second, and perhaps related to this, all three entities were located in the continent of Europe, a circumstance that may have facilitated acceptance of the process of disintegration by the international community, which, as Daniele Conversi points out in chapter 11, has traditionally been supportive of the geopolitical status quo. It is likely – though not certain – that the international community would have fought harder to maintain the integrity of those multinational states in Asia where ethnic tensions are present; and international opposition to the disintegration of African states would probably be even more intense, given the Pandora's box that secession by even one ethnic group there would open up. International opposition to the secession of Katanga from the Congo and of Biafra from Nigeria in the 1960s illustrated this, and it was Eritrean determination rather than international sympathy that permitted Eritrea's secession from Ethiopia in 1991. Fears of this kind are more muted in Europe, where the political integration of western Europe – to be followed by the steady incorporation of much of central and eastern Europe – has been the dominant theme of recent decades. Third, and most obviously of all, the disintegration of the three entities coincided in each case with the collapse in the authority of a powerful and relatively centralized ruling party, the Communist Party. An essential ingredient in the disintegration of the state was a concomitant disruption of the authority of the party: on the one hand, the party itself came under pressure from its ethnonational components; on the other it lost state power to alternative political forces.

These processes were to be seen most clearly in the former Soviet Union, as Ronald Hill shows. There, national minorities made up approximately half of the population, and the larger of these possessed formidable political, cultural and economic resources. Indeed, 14 of them already had their own state structure, with some of the trappings (if not the reality) of sovereignty. Two, Ukraine and Belorussia, were even members of the United Nations. Furthermore, the international community had never fully recognized the territorial integrity of the post-war Soviet state: the incorporation of the three Baltic republics was deemed illegal, and a number of western states continued to recognize diplomats appointed by regimes that had gone out of existence in 1940. Given the character of the ethnic mosaic that was the Soviet Union, the Communist Party played a critical role in maintaining political cohesion. The collapse in the authority and popularity of the party under the presidency of Gorbachev was therefore catastrophic, and left space for the emergence of a powerful alternative focus of power in Russia proper.

The pattern of disintegration in Yugoslavia resembled this. The historically dominant nationality, the Serbs, were in an even weaker position than their Russian counterparts, accounting for only 36% of the population. The smaller nationalities were thus relatively more powerful than in the Soviet Union: the Croats and Slovenes were not only large as a share of the population, they also occupied the most economically developed part of the state. With the exception of the ethnic Muslims, a minority even in Bosnia-Herzegovina, the major nationalities each had a republic of its own, even if it also had to contend, typically, with local minorities, as Daniele Conversi points out. The partition of Yugoslavia may also have been assisted by geopolitical history. Croatia and Slovenia had belonged, for centuries, to the Austro-Hungarian monarchy; Serbia, Macedonia and Montenegro had been part of, or claimed by, the Ottoman Empire, while Bosnia-Herzegovina was a frontier zone, part of the Ottoman Empire that was occupied by Austria-Hungary in 1878 and formally annexed in 1908. It is unlikely that even six decades of co-existence in a common state would have eliminated perceptions of these differences from the subconscious mind of Yugoslavs or, indeed, of the international community; the evidence suggests that, in a pattern not dissimilar to the Soviet Union, a sufficiently strong shared Yugoslav identity had simply failed to develop. The Communist Party, similarly, had begun to fragment into its separate national groups even before it lost power to other political forces in most of the republics. Since the only remaining traditional agency of cohesion, the army, also found itself neutralized, as in the Soviet Union, there was nothing to prevent the collapse of the state.

In many respects, the dissolution of Czechoslovakia was the most surprising of all. It is true that the two major nationalities, Czechs and Slovaks, were relatively clearly defined in terms of geographical origin and political history (having belonged respectively to the increasingly separate Austrian and Hungarian parts of the Habsburg monarchy). But culturally they were close, and, although the Slovak language was developed in a way that highlighted its differentiation from Czech, this was by no means an inevitable development. The state had become a symmetric dyadic federation in 1968, as Stanislav Kirschbaum shows, after a long period during which the de facto domination of the Czechs was reflected also in constitutional law. Precisely because of the relatively powerful position of the Czechs (who not only amounted to 63% of the population but also enjoyed a higher level of economic development), the prospects for maintaining the integrity of the state seemed reasonable. As in the case of Yugoslavia, it is likely that a long period of political co-existence since 1918 had failed to replace entirely older territorial loyalties by a new shared spatial image. In any case, the collapse of the Communist Party need not have led as painlessly as it did to the separation of the two parts of the state. It is possible that in this case, again, the international stakes were lower because of the existence of an expanding European Union.

CONCLUSION

As pointed out in the introduction to this book, the cases analysed in detail here are not – and could not be – perfectly representative of the global position. Before seeking to draw more definite conclusions, it is appropriate to make some general remarks about the overall pattern. It would be refreshing to be able to base these on quantitative analysis; but ethnic conflict is hard enough to define, and even harder to measure, while 'territorial restructuring' presents similar challenges. But it would probably be safe to say that most states do not react to ethnic conflict by conceding territorial autonomy. Of the world's 191 states in 2001, approximately 23 were classed as federal, and a few others recognized distinctive regions with varying degrees of autonomy. But the number of states experiencing ethnic conflicts or with politicized communal minorities at this time was very much greater: depending on the instrument of measurement, this ranged from 41 to 116 (see Introduction). There may, of course, have been good reasons for this: the minority may live in dispersed areas, or its demands may be directed at goals other than territorial autonomy. But even if we look at the most systematic approach to sub-state autonomy, federalism, it becomes clear that its relationship to efforts to resolve ethnic conflicts is imperfect, as we have seen already. It is true that in some cases – Belgium, Bosnia-Herzegovina, Cyprus (in a formal sense), Ethiopia and Russia – the federal system is indeed a response to ethnic diversity. In a larger number of cases, however, it is not: Argentina, Australia, Brazil, Germany, Mexico, the United States and Venezuela are obvious examples. So too are the smaller federations of Comoros, the Federated States of Micronesia, Saint Christopher and Nevis, and the United Arab Emirates, where, however, there are strongly defined territorial identities (indeed, the Emirates is arguably the best example of a confederation). Austria now belongs to this category too, even if it was once deeply divided ethnically (though that was before 1918). This leaves us with a few cases where the federal system was introduced for other reasons but was in time found to constitute a useful contribution to the resolution of ethnic problems: Canada, India, Pakistan (though the constitution is currently undergoing a wholesale revision), Switzerland and the new Yugoslavia, and in Malaysia where the federal system cuts across existing lines of ethnic division rather than coinciding with them.

The discussion of ethno-territorial relations in this chapter has of necessity over-simplified a very complex phenomenon. It is appropriate therefore to qualify this discussion by drawing attention to four caveats. First, 'ethnicity' has been discussed here as a relatively simple, objective phenomenon and, by implication, it has been assumed that populations can be partitioned into neatly-defined, discrete categories. Ethnic affiliation is in reality much more complex. On the one hand, people vary in the intensity of their attachment to the ethnic group to which they are attributed; on the other, 'membership' of an ethnic group need not be exclusive. There may be an overlapping set of communities with which people feel a sense of affiliation (for instance, Antwerp–Flanders–Belgium–Europe) and it may be quite misleading to attempt to attribute a person's basic identification to a single level. While census takers in central and eastern Europe may thus force individuals into a restricted set of ethnic categories, survey evidence from western Europe illustrates a much more complex set of overlapping loyalties.[28] Furthermore, ethnic identity is far from being an immutable independent variable; it may itself be influenced by the process of ethnic mobilization (rather than simply constituting a contributory force for this).

Second, ethnic conflicts are not always simply about symbolic matters (indeed, perhaps they are *never* confined to these). Competition over resources and economic arguments frequently underlie political arguments in favour of territorial restructuring, and in some cases such considerations outweigh ethnic ones. The process of disintegration of Yugoslavia and the Soviet Union was similarly assisted by sharply diverging ideological preferences between the centre and the peripheries, with Communists lingering in power at the centre while pro-capitalist forces took control in certain republics. The fact that political forces associated with sharply different ideological positions came to power in the Czech Lands and in Slovakia was a contributory factor to the break-up of Czechoslovakia, as noted by Kirschbaum (chapter 10, this volume). The struggle of Russia for independence of the Soviet Union similarly makes little sense if viewed as an ethnic conflict between an entrapped nationality and the centre; ideological conflict and a struggle for power within the political elite go further in explaining what was on the surface an essentially counter-intuitive process. By 'counter-intuitive' here is meant failure to conform to the logic of ethnoterritorial power: dominant ethnic groups typically seek to maximize their territorial control (for example, it is unlikely that England will try to secede from the United Kingdom). On the other hand, Conversi argues (this volume, chapter 11) that the Serbian role in the break-up of Yugoslavia was calculated, and one can indeed see advantages from the Serbs' perspective: a territory with which they had identified since 1918 might have disintegrated and they might have lost more of its territory than they had expected, but they are now a decisive majority rather than being simply a large minority. The Flemish relationship with Belgium also raises interesting questions: though constituting a majority of the population, Dutch speakers had historically been characterized by relatively low social status and political marginalization, and their political resurgence in recent decades was associated with the goal of autonomy in relation to Belgium rather than with the object of capturing the institutions of the state.

Third, the capacity of territorial restructuring to resolve ethnic tensions should not be overestimated. It has already been pointed out that ethnic boundary lines are rarely clearly drawn. Certain tensions in a polyethnic state may be resolved by dissolution into units corresponding to the component ethnic groups, but there tend to be problems in principle and in practice. The problem of principle is that the new units are typically also polyethnic, and conflicts have been simply moved to a different level and multiplied, with the original conflict possibly being reproduced in microcosm. The problem of practice is that in many cases the successor states are much less tolerant of ethnic minorities than the original parent state, as may be seen in certain former Soviet and Yugoslav republics. Indeed, the discussion of the Soviet Union by Ronald Hill (this volume, chapter 9) draws attention to the possibility that some sets of ethnic relations are so complex that they simply cannot be disentangled by any form of territorial restructuring.

Fourth, and most importantly, the whole definition of any ethnic conflict is a matter of political perspective. The detached observer may see obvious signs of ethnic conflict, often very violent ones; but identifying what the problem is may be much more difficult. Is the state simply doing its best to ensure that the greater material and symbolic good of the greatest number is satisfied? Or is an ethnic group simply giving legitimate expression to its right to cultural and political self-determination? This question has been side-stepped in this chapter, but by implication the issue has been addressed from the perspective of the state rather than from that of the subordinate ethnic group. This is not to deny the validity of the other perspective (which, indeed, finds expression elsewhere in this volume, most notably in the contributions of Laponce, Kirschbaum and Wilson); rather, it represents a necessarily arbitrary device to simplify a problem of rather exceptional complexity.

Nevertheless, the material considered in this book shows that ethnicity has a striking capacity to bring about the downfall of even the most powerful of states and to cause the territorial restructuring of others (though in many cases the disruptive capacity of ethnic tensions is reinforced by other factors). It is also paradoxical that as the Soviet Union, Yugoslavia and Czechoslovakia were breaking up and Belgium, Spain, the United Kingdom and Canada were looking for new ways to shift power to their regions, a countervailing process has also been at work. This is the political integration of Europe, an example that runs sharply contrary to the general trend of decentralization of power (though it must be acknowledged that the European integration movement has also had strands supportive of regional autonomy).

Indeed, the historical experience of the latter decades of the twentieth century suggests that these apparently very different forces have a momentum of their own. The process of European integration has advanced through a number of steady stages, and there is no evidence that it is yet close to its final point. The decentralization of power from the centre, similarly, seems to have an irreversible and progressive character. But it would be unsafe to assume that no change in direction is possible: autonomous regions have lost their autonomy in the past, and will do so in the future. But political autonomy that is congruent

with the geographical spread of an ethnic community tends to reinforce ethnic commitment, other things being equal. This feature of the
relationship between politics and society is likely to make it increasingly difficult for those states that have embarked on territorial reorganization projects designed to resolve ethnic tensions to undertake a
fundamental change in this broad approach to one of the political
world's more intractable issues.

ACKNOWLEDGEMENTS

I would like to thank Daniele Conversi, Ron Hill, Charles Kennedy, Stanislav Kirschbaum,
Jean Laponce, Rupert Taylor, Tobias Theiler and Alex Weingrod for comments on an earlier
draft.

NOTES

1. For reviews, see John Coakley, 'The Resolution of Ethnic Conflict: Towards a
   Typology', *International Political Science Review* Vol.13, No.4 (1992), pp.341–56; and John
   McGarry and Brendan O'Leary, 'Introduction: The Macro-Political Regulation of
   Ethnic Conflict', in John McGarry and Brendan O'Leary (eds.), *The Politics of Ethnic
   Conflict Regulation: Case Studies of Protracted Ethnic Conflicts* (London: Routledge, 1993),
   pp.1–47.
2. Ivo D. Duchacek, *The Territorial Dimension of Politics within, among and across Nations*
   (Boulder, CO: Westview, 1986), pp.112–18.
3. In this chapter, these three words are used to refer to forms of political organization;
   they are, of course, frequently used in other contexts to refer to political programmes
   or ideologies of specific kinds, or to refer to the movements that seek to advance these
   programmes or ideologies.
4. Calculated from data supplied by the Office of the Registrar General for Northern
   Ireland.
5. Calculated from *US Army Area Handbook for Cyprus* (Washington, DC: US Government
   Printing Office, 1964).
6. Calculated from *Annuaire statistique de la Belgique*, Vol.81 (1960), p.50, and Kenneth D.
   McRae, *Conflict and Compromise in Multilingual Societies: Belgium* (Waterloo, Ontario:
   Wilfrid Laurier University Press, 1986), p.40.
7. Calculated from data supplied by the United Nations Peacekeeping Force in Cyprus,
   April 2002.
8. See George Schöpflin, *Nations, Identity, Power: The New Politics of Europe* (London:
   Hurst, 2000); and Daniele Conversi, 'Post-Communist Societies between Ethnicity and
   Globalization', *Journal of Southern Europe and the Balkans*, Vol.3, No.2 (2001), pp.193–6.
9. Arend Lijphart, *Democracy in Plural Societies: A Comparative Exploration* (New Haven,
   CT: Yale University Press, 1977).
10. On this concept, see Kenneth McRae, 'The Principle of Territoriality and the Principle
    of Personality in Multilingual States', *Linguistics* Vol.158 (1975), pp.33–54.
11. For a review, see Michael Keating, *State and Regional Nationalism: Territorial Politics and
    the European State* (London: Harvester Wheatsheaf, 1988), esp. pp.167–244.
12. See Yves Mény, 'The Political Dynamics of Regionalism: Italy, France, Spain', in Roger
    Morgan (ed.), *Regionalism in European Politics* (London: PSI, 1987), pp.1–28; Siamak
    Khatami, 'Decentralization: A Comparative Study of France and Spain since the
    1970s', *Regional Politics and Policy*, Vol.1, No.2 (1991), pp.161–81.
13. See Robert Leonardi, 'The Regional Reform in Italy: From Centralized of Regionalized
    State', *Regional Politics and Policy*, Vol.2, Nos.1–2 (1992), pp.217–46; Cezar Diaz Lopez,
    'Centre–Periphery Structures in Spain: From Historical Conflict to Territorial-

Consociational Accommodation', in Yves Mény and Vincent Wright (eds.), *Centre–Periphery Relations in Western Europe* (London: George Allen & Unwin, 1985), pp.236–72; Daniele Conversi, 'Autonomous Communities and Ethnic Settlement in Spain', in Yash Ghai (ed.) *Autonomy and Ethnicity: Negotiating Competing Claims in Multi-Ethnic States* (Cambridge: Cambridge University Press, 2000); and Jean-Claude Douence, 'The Evolution of the 1982 Regional Reforms: An Overview', in John Loughlin and Sonia Mazey (eds.), *The End of the French Unitary State? Ten Years of Regionalism in France (1982–1992)* (London: Frank Cass, 1995), pp.10–24.

14. See John Loughlin, 'Regionalism and Ethnic Nationalism in France', in Mény and Wright, *Centre–Periphery Relations*, pp.207–35; and John Loughlin, 'A New Deal for France's Regions and Linguistic Minorities', *West European Politics*, Vol.8, No.3 (1985), pp.101–13.

15. In the Spanish cases, long-established historical traditions and public opinion played a role in determining the shape of these arrangements; in Navarre, for instance, there was substantial opposition to the province's incorporation in the Basque Country. In France, similarly, it was the relatively weak sense of Breton territorial identity that permitted the partition of Brittany between two regions.

16. For early general but still very useful descriptions of federalism, see K.C. Wheare, *Federal Government*, 4th edn. (London: Oxford University Press, 1963) [first published 1946]; and Carl J. Friedrich, *Trends of Ferderalism in Theory and Practice* (London: Pall Mall Press, 1968). Later general overviews include Ivo D. Duchacek, *Comparative Federalism: The Territorial Dimension of Politics* (New York: Holt, Rinehart & Winston, 1970); Preston King, *Federalism and Federation* (London: Croom Helm, 1982); Murray Forsyth (ed.), *Federalism and Nationalism* (London: Leicester University Press, 1989); Michael Burgess and Alain-G. Gagnon (eds.), *Comparative Federalism and Federation: Competing Traditions and Future Directions* (London: Harvester Wheatsheaf, 1993); and Bertus de Filliers (ed.), Evaluating Federal Systems (Cape Town: Juta, 1994).

17. On this issue, see Alain-G. Gagnon, 'The Political Uses of Federalism', in Burgess and Gagnon, *Comparative Federalism*, pp.15–44 (at pp.21–6). See also Graham Smith (ed.), *Federalism: The Multiethnic Challenge* (London: Longman, 1995), and Brendan O'Leary, 'Federations and the Management of Nations: Agreements and Arguments with Walker Connor', in Daniele Conversi (ed.), *Ethnonationalism in the Contemporary World: Walker Connor and the Theory of Nationalism* (London: Routledge, 2002).

18. See Ivo D. Duchacek, 'Dyadic Federations and Confederations', *Publius: The Journal of Federalism*, Vol.18, No.2 (1988), pp.5–31.

19. For a review of these and other cases, see Murray Forsyth, *Unions of States: The Theory and Practice of Confederation* (London: Leicester University Press, 1981).

20. For a general review of the state-building process, see Walter C. Opello, Jr., and Stephen J. Rosow, *The Nation-State and Global Order: A Historical Introduction to Contemporary Politics* (Boulder, CO: Lynne Rienner, 1999). The same process is extensively examined from the perspective of international law; see, for example, Hurst Hannum, *Autonomy, Sovereignty, and Self-Determination: The Accommodation of Conflicting Rights* (Philadelphia: University Pennsylvania Press, 1992), and Antonio Cassese, *Self-Determination of Peoples: A Legal Perspective* (Cambridge: Cambridge University Press, 1995).

21. The Soviet Union failed in the long term to hold onto the old tsarist territory of Poland and the autonomous grand duchy of Finland; it won back its losses in the Baltic states and in Bessarabia in 1940. For interpretative overviews of the dissolution of these empires, see Karen Barkey and Mark von Hagen (eds.), *After Empire: Multiethnic Societies and Nation-Building: The Soviet Union and the Russian, Ottoman and Habsburg Empires* (Boulder, CO: Westview, 1997); and for a systematic analysis of the withdrawal of European powers from their overseas possessions see Muriel E. Chamberlain, *The Longman Companion to European Decolonisation in the Twentieth Century* (London: Longman, 1998).

22. For example, in both Spain and Italy (discussed above in the context of symmetrical models) certain regions are given 'special' powers that are not exercised by others.

23. Ramesh Dutta Dikshit, *The Political Geography of Federalism: An Inquiry into its Origins and Stability* (New Delhi: Macmillan, 1975), pp.243–52.

24. Charles D. Tarlton, 'Symmetry and Asymmetry as Elements of Federalism: A Theoretical Speculation', *Journal of Politics*, Vol.27, No.4 (1965), pp.861–74. For a discus-

sion of this concept at a different level, see Michael Keating, 'Asymmetrical Government: Multinational States in an Integrating Europe', *Publius: The Journal of Federalism*, Vol.29, No.1 (1999), pp.71–86.

25. The proportion of Jews in the present territory of Israel or under Israeli occupation was 4.0% in 1882, rising, mainly as a consequence of immigration, to 63.8% in 1982; see Asher Arian, *Politics in Israel: The Second Generation* (Chatham, NJ: Chatham House Publishers, 1985), p.21.

26. Arian, *Politics in Israel*, pp.6–7.

27. In this, language assists: the English word 'nationality', for example, is translated into at least two quite different terms in Russian: *grazhdanstvo* (meaning political nationality, or citizenship) and *natsional'nost'* (meaning ethnic nationality); yet another term, *narodnost'*, is used to refer to smaller ethnic groups. This distinction is normal in other eastern European languages, but does not exist in the major languages of western Europe.

28. On the political implications of enforced choice in the census, see Paul Teleki and Andrew Rónai, *The Different Types of Ethnic Mixture of the Population* (Budapest: 'Athenaeum', 1937), esp. pp.28–30; on overlapping loyalties in western Europe see John Coakley, 'Conclusion: Nationalist Movements and Society in Contemporary Western Europe' in John Coakley (ed.), *The Social Origins of Nationalist Movements: The Contemporary West European Experience* (London: Sage, 1992), pp.212–30.

Index